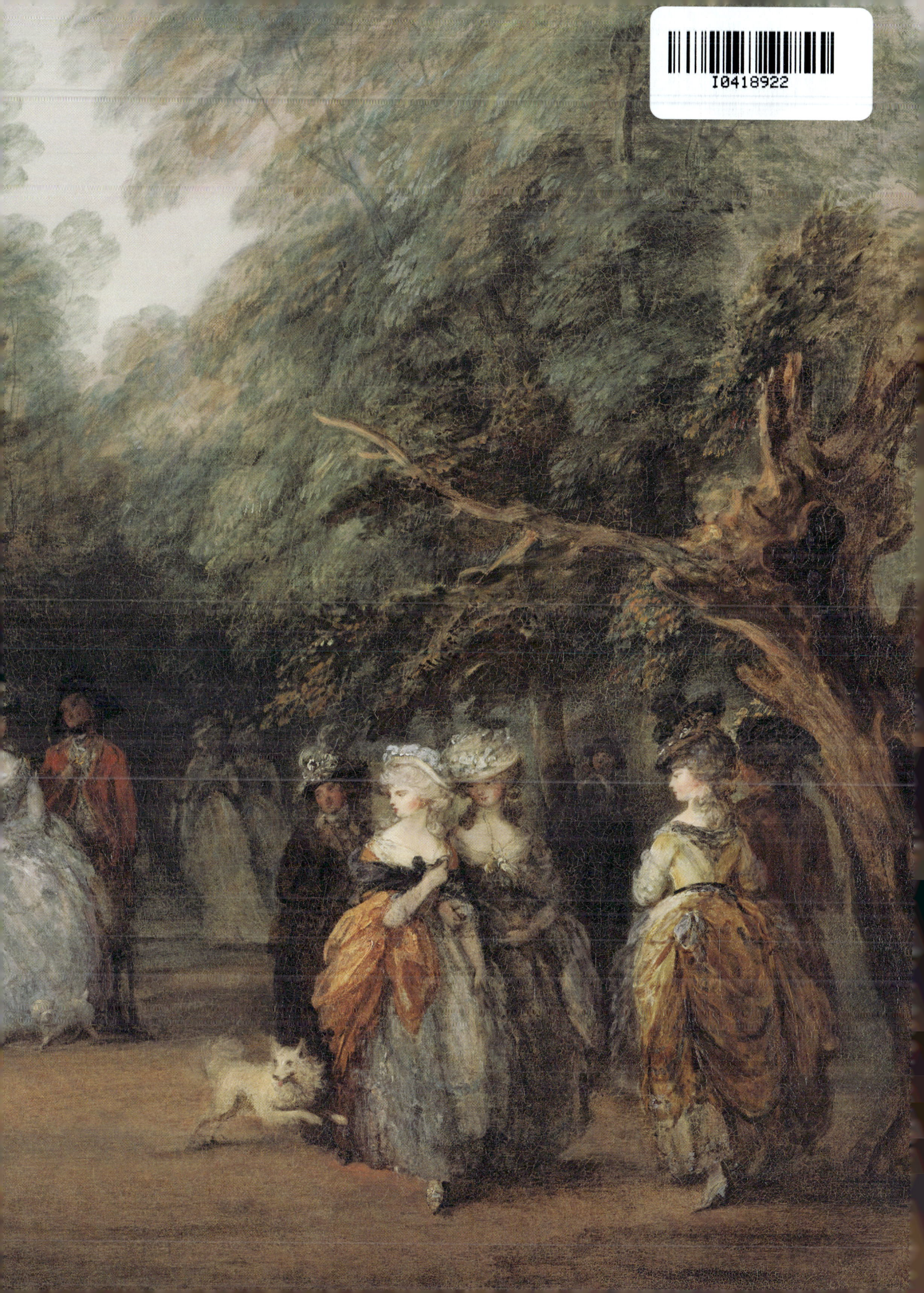

GAINSBOROUGH

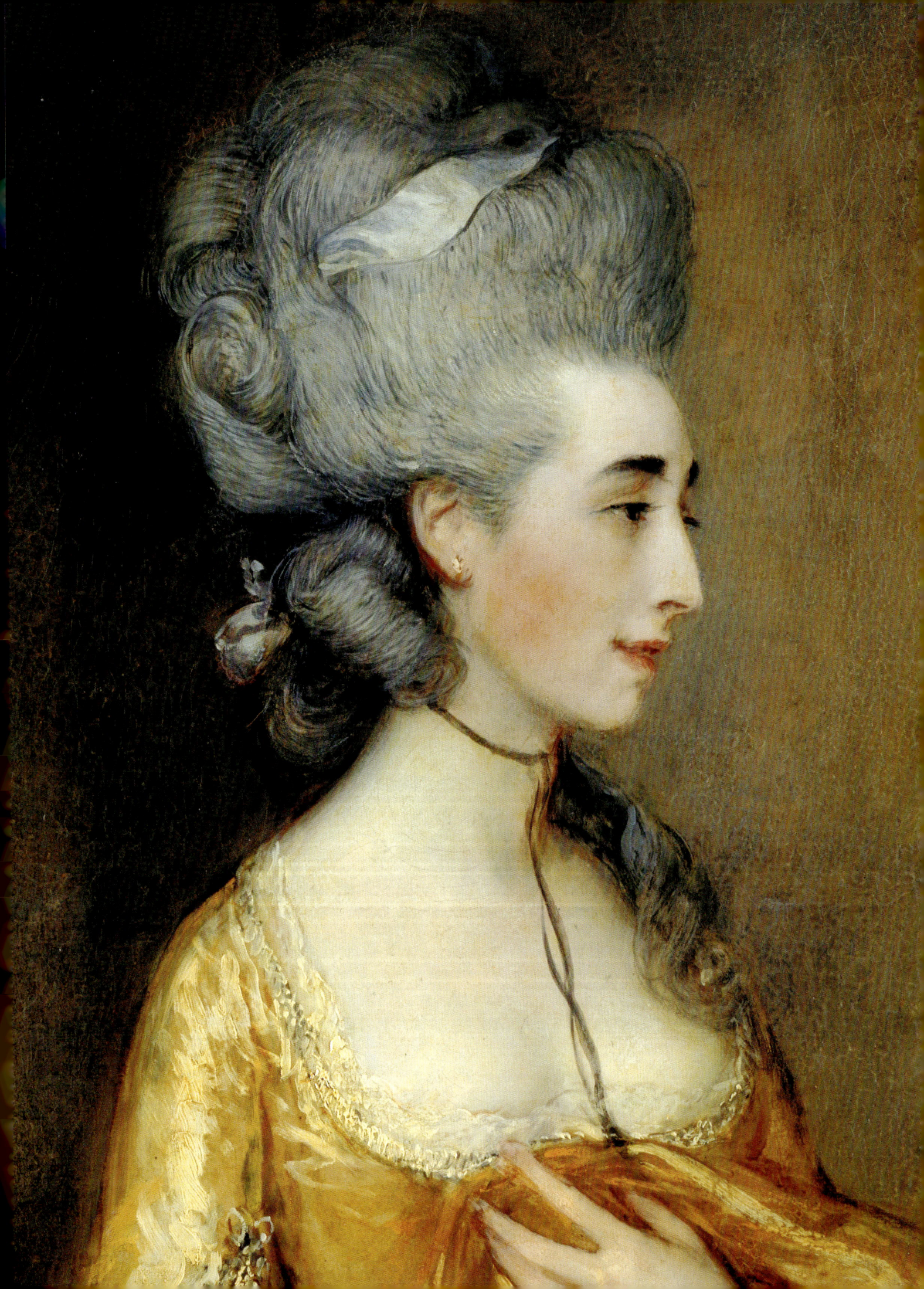

GAINSBOROUGH

The Fashion of Portraiture

AIMEE NG

with an essay by KARI RAYNER

RIZZOLI ELECTA *in association with* THE FRICK COLLECTION

CONTENTS

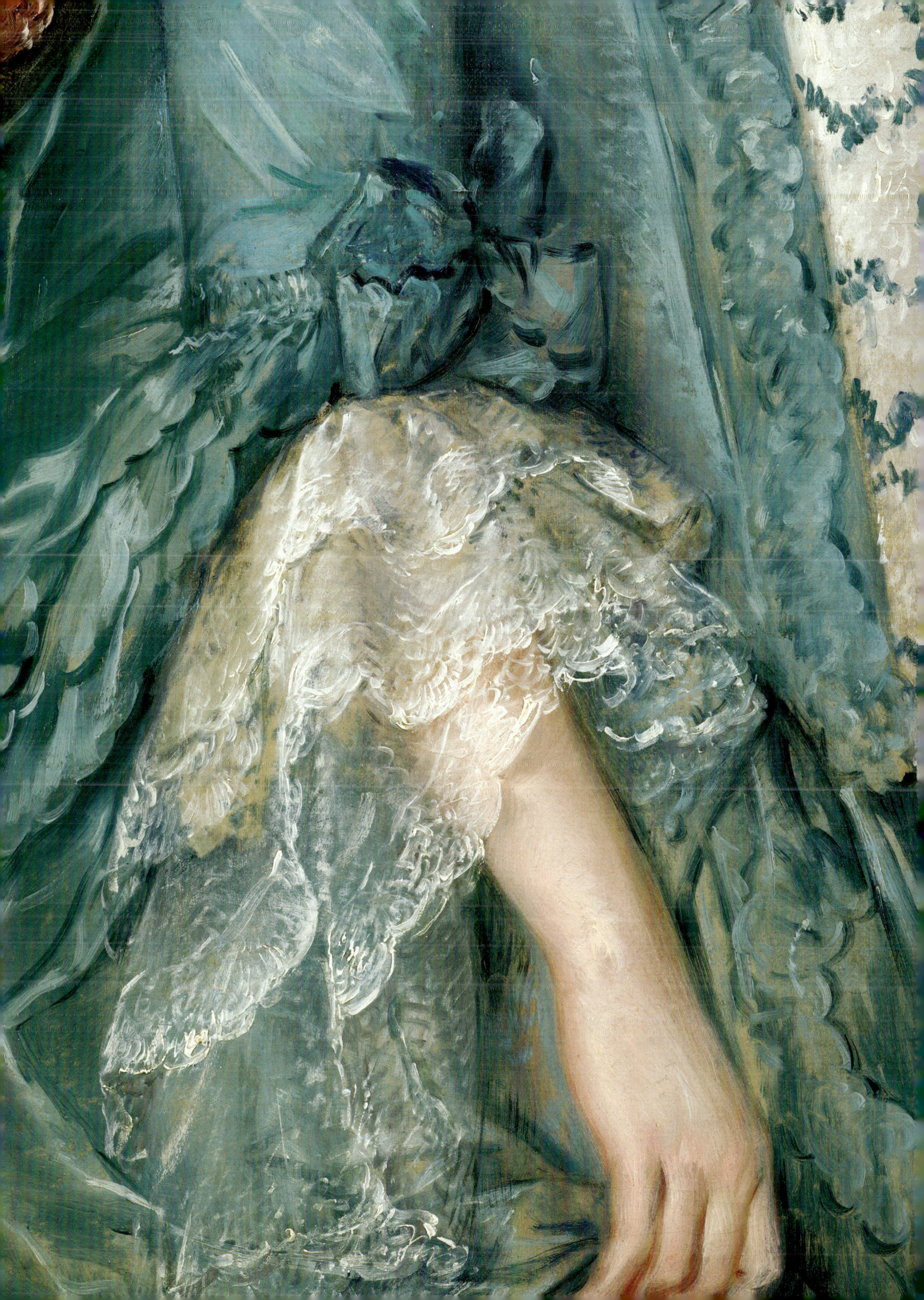

DIRECTOR'S FOREWORD

"FASHION IS GENTILITY running away from vulgarity, and afraid of being overtaken by it." With these words, the British painter and member of the Royal Academy of Arts James Northcote commented on the constant quest of his contemporaries to stay on top of fashion and thus escape the "vulgarity" of what might be considered outdated or insufficiently refined.

Thomas Gainsborough, among the founding members of the Royal Academy, was one of the leading portraitists of his time. In contrast to his great rival, Sir Joshua Reynolds, the founding president of the Royal Academy—whose portraiture frequently made reference to classical statues or grand historical events—Gainsborough captured the personalities of his sitters through the elegance, movement, and sensory qualities of the fashionable garments in which they presented themselves. As Aimee Ng eloquently demonstrates in this publication, fashion and apparel are the keys to understanding aspects of the lives, identities, and possibly places in history of the various sitters in Gainsborough's portraiture.

We are extremely grateful to Aimee, the Frick's John Updike Curator, both for her astute text examining the ways portraiture and fashion were interconnected in the eighteenth century and for her exemplary work on the exhibition it accompanies. We also acknowledge Kari Rayner, Associate Conservator of Paintings at the J. Paul Getty Museum, for her informative essay on the materials and techniques that shaped Gainsborough's signature style.

At the Frick, thanks also go to Xavier F. Salomon, former Deputy Director and Peter Jay Sharp Chief Curator, and to the Board of Trustees. We are very grateful to Editor in Chief Michaelyn Mitchell, who managed the production of the catalogue and, with Assistant Editor Gemma McElroy, expertly edited the texts. The hard work of the entire staff has made this project possible. In particular, we extend our thanks to Tyler Beard, Tia Chapman, Julia Day, Allison Galea, Lisa Goble, Caitlin Henningsen, Patrick King, George Koelle, Alexis Light, Sara Muskulus, Christopher Roberson, Heidi Rosenau, Justin Samson, April Kim Tonin, and Sean Troxell. We are indebted to exhibition designer Patrick Herron and lighting designer Anita Jorgensen and her team. At Rizzoli, Margaret Chace, Charles Miers, and, above all, Senior Editor Philip Reeser have been wonderful collaborators on the production of this catalogue. We thank them and the designer, William Loccisano.

Finally, we wish to acknowledge the lenders and funders, whose generosity made this project possible. The catalogue is funded by Dr. Tai-Heng Cheng, and the exhibition it accompanies is made possible with support from an anonymous donor in honor of Ian Wardropper. Additional funding is provided by Michael and Jane Horvitz, Dr. Arlene P. McKay, The Helen Clay Frick Foundation, James K. Kloppenburg, David and Kate Bradford, Katie von Strasser - InspiratumColligere, the Dr. Lee MacCormick Edwards Charitable Foundation, Edward Lee Cave, Mr. and Mrs. Hubert L. Goldschmidt, Jennifer Schnabl, the Malcolm Hewitt Wiener Foundation, Bradley Isham Collins and Amy Fine Collins, Siri and Bob Marshall, Bailey Foote, Alexander Mason Hankin, Brittany Beyer Harwin and Zachary Harwin, and Otto Naumann and Heidi D. Shafranek.

AXEL RÜGER
Anna-Maria and Stephen Kellen Director
The Frick Collection

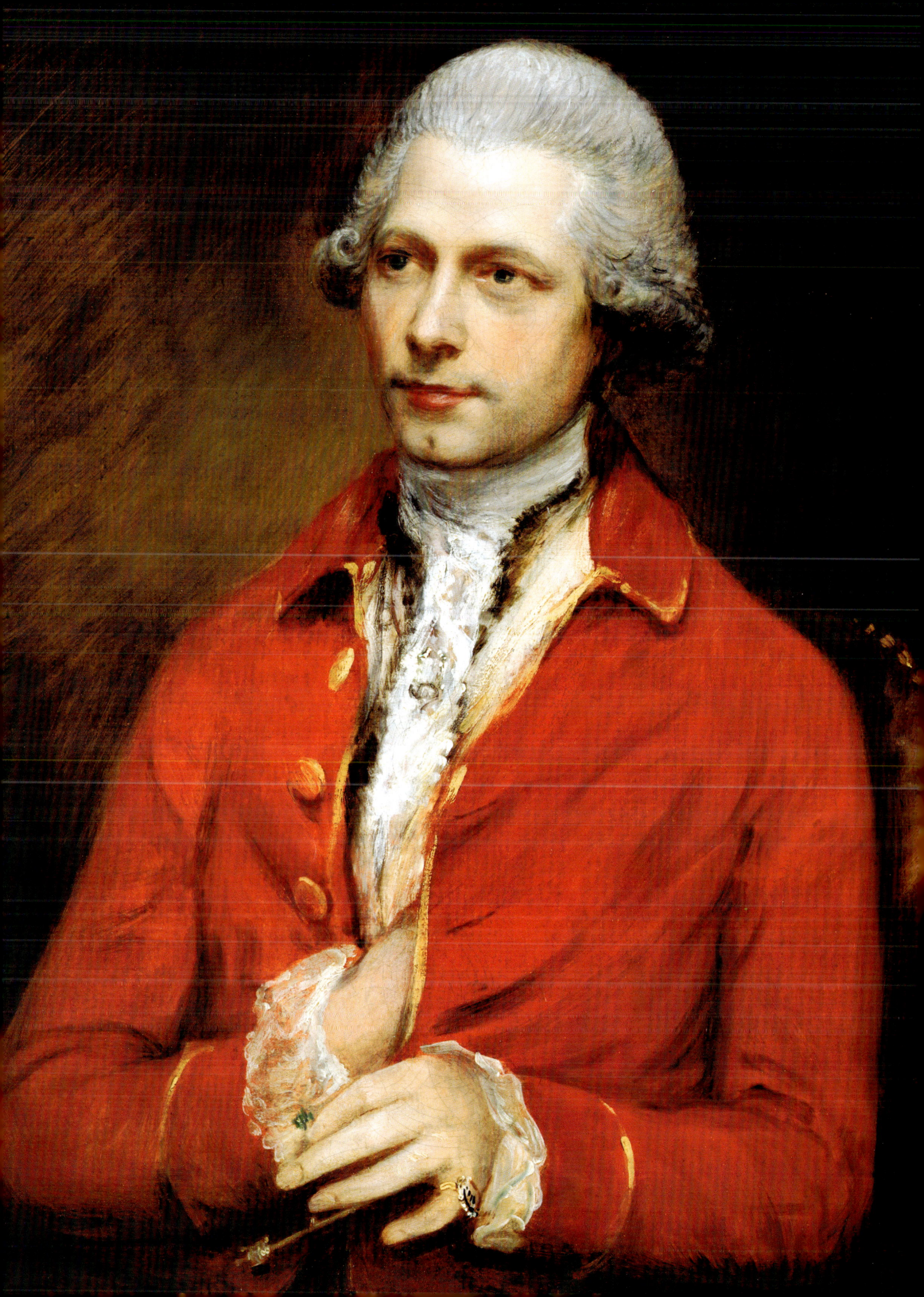

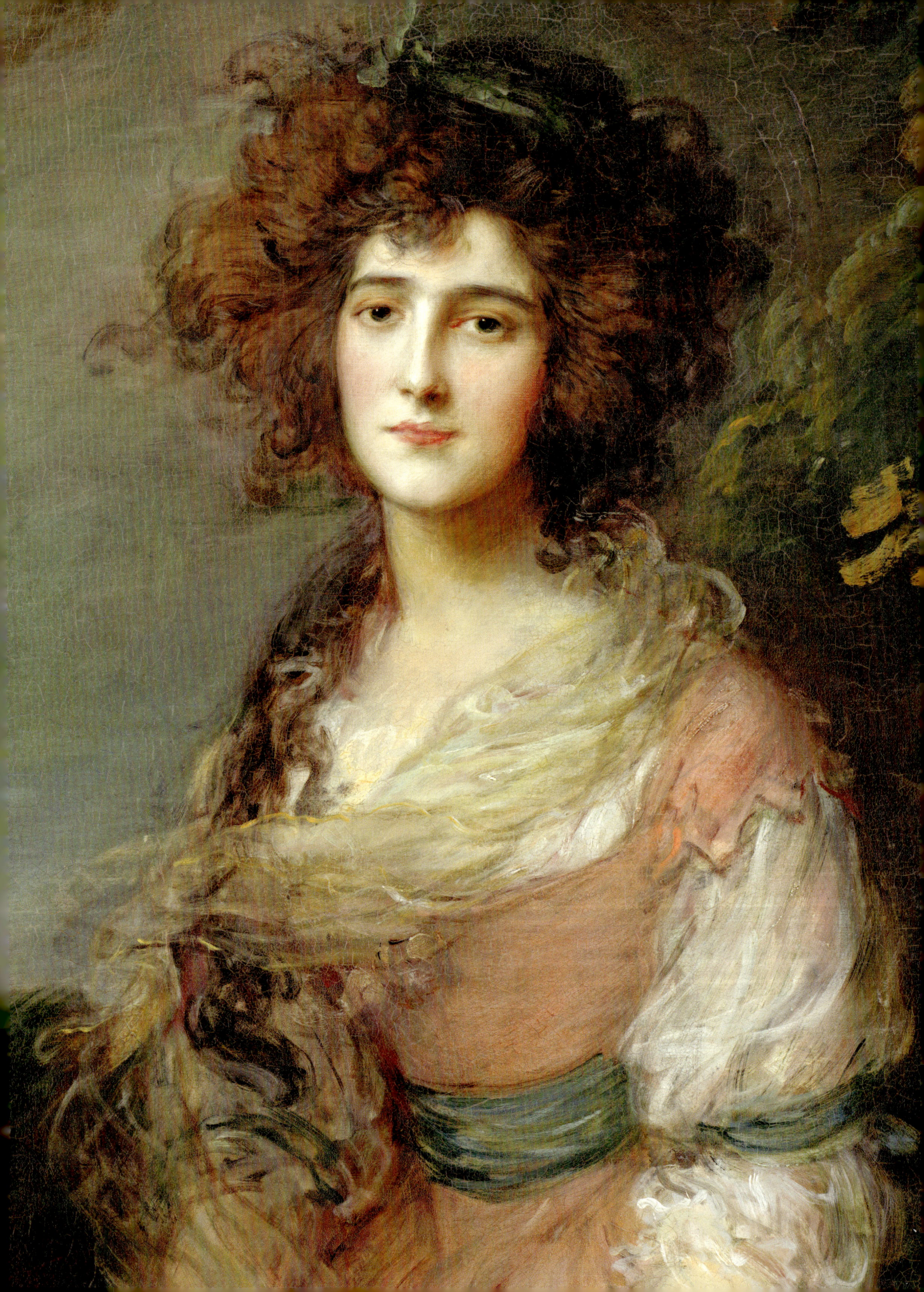

PREFACE

Posterity interprets the lives of notables in the long eighteenth century in many different and sometimes contentious ways, but everyone can agree that they wore fabulous clothes.

—Joseph Roach, 1930

THE SPECTACULAR AND, TO MODERN EYES, at times absurd fashions in portraits by Thomas Gainsborough and his contemporaries continue to fascinate viewers today. The appeal of these demonstrations of taste, status, and wealth persists in tension with increased attention, over the last few decades, to the injustices that often made such extravagance possible. A focus on the history of colonialization and enslavement as it relates to art has inspired exhibitions and publications, and led to revised museum labels and institutional reports, in the same way that contemporary art has "activated" Old Master galleries, and the fields of television and theater reimagine their own historical narratives. These efforts have not been without friction. People with diverse perspectives continue to debate important and thorny issues like which works of art should be relegated to museum storage and which stories should be supported with funding and resources. Crucially, these difficult discussions underscore the ways in which art was and is part of a complex social world. Museumgoers today are better equipped than ever to revel in the extraordinary attire depicted in an eighteenth-century portrait while recognizing its place in a complicated and at times uncomfortable human story.

Gainsborough: The Fashion of Portraiture necessarily deals with clothing and personal attire, exploring how fashion was understood in Gainsborough's time and how it touched every level of society. This catalogue and the exhibition it accompanies draw on excellent recent publications and exhibitions on Georgian fashion that analyze portraits as precious documents of dress. At the heart of this project, however, are the paintings themselves. Portraits are not simply records of what people looked like and wore—though some are. What the artist painted his sitters wearing at times had little to do with how they dressed in real life and, like portraiture itself, was a construction and invention in paint. This publication investigates the myriad functions of portraiture in eighteenth-century British life, its role in the expansive industry of fashion, and how portraits themselves were subject to forces of fashion. Styles and makers of portraits went in and out of fashion just as clothes did.

The resurgence of interest in eighteenth-century British portraits at the turn of the twentieth century attests to fashion's ups and downs. After decades of relative indifference, American collectors like the Vanderbilts, Huntingtons, Mellons, and Fricks eagerly paid astronomical sums to acquire from British collections portraits by Reynolds, Romney, and, above all, Gainsborough. Henry Clay Frick purchased eight works by Gainsborough and after his death, in 1919, the museum's trustees acquired two more. The Frick's exceptional holdings of the art of Gainsborough inspired this exhibition, the first in the history of the museum to be devoted to the artist and the first devoted to his portraiture in New York City.

ACKNOWLEDGMENTS

MY FIRST AND MOST LONG-STANDING THANKS go to Xavier F. Salomon, the Frick's former Deputy Director and Peter Jay Sharp Chief Curator, for his support of this project over the years it took to come to fruition. A mentor and friend, Xavier has been a guiding light all along the way. I am also grateful to Axel Rüger, Anna-Maria and Stephen Kellen Director, and Director Emeritus Ian Wardropper, as well as the Frick's trustees.

When this project began, I was a novice in the topic of British art but was fortunate to meet scholars willing to bring me into the fold. A 2015 conference organized by the Paul Mellon Centre and Gainsborough's House—led by Mark Hallett, Mark Bills, and the late Giles Waterfield—and a roundtable about upcoming Gainsborough projects, convened by Martin Postle, were crash courses on the richness and possibilities of the field. I am grateful to those who welcomed me at these events and others since. I am particularly thankful to Lowell Libson and to Jonny Yarker, whose expertise, passion, and introductions opened doors, hearts, and minds. Among the many people who have contributed to the shaping of this project, through help with research and loans and general support, I am especially grateful to Nancy Anderson, Tim Barringer, Emily Beeny, Candace and Frederick Beinecke, Caroline Campbell, Emma Capron, John Chu, Amy Concannon, Louise Cooling, Jessica David, Martina Droth, the Duke of Buccleuch and Queensberry, the Duke of Norfolk, Adam Eaker, the Earl of Radnor, Christopher Etheridge, Gabriele Finaldi, Nicola Hopkinson, Alice Insley, Franklin Kelly, Jongwoo Kim, Cory Korkow, Maximilian Kummer, Lucinda Lax, Charles Lister, Rebecca Lyons, Scott MacDonald, Judy Mann, Courtney J. Martin, Mary McMahon, Angus Methuen-Campbell, James Methuen-Campbell, Martin Myrone, Christina Nielsen, Alexandra Ormerod, Steven Parisien, Crispin Powell, Rory Powell, David Pullins, Anna Reynolds, Christine Riding, John Martin Robinson, Jennifer Scott, Hannah Segrave, Karen Serres, Susan Sloman, Sasha Suda, Chloe Woodrow, Carolyn Yerkes, and Oleg Zabava.

Kari Rayner, Associate Conservator of Paintings at the J. Paul Getty Museum, has been a gracious contributor to this catalogue and enriches it with her essay. I am thankful for her patience and collaboration during the long gestation. Special thanks are also due to colleagues at the Metropolitan Museum of Art who treated and examined the Frick's Gainsboroughs in the show: Silvia Centeno, Charlotte Hale, Derek Lintala, Dorothy Mahon, and, formerly of the department, Michael Gallagher. For their brilliant work, I am indebted to exhibition designer Patrick Herron, graphic designer Matthew Kafoury, and lighting designer Anita Jorgensen and her team. Philip Reeser and his colleagues at Rizzoli have, as always, been wonderful publishing partners.

Over the course of a major renovation, closure, reopening, and other dramatic changes, my colleagues at the Frick have been extraordinary, and the entire staff is due credit and thanks. Work on this project has spanned the (not insubstantial) tenures of three exceptional curatorial assistants: Eloise Owens and Gemma McElroy, who have gone on to great things, and, most recently,

Emma Mortensen, whose tenacity, reliability, and cleverness make her an asset far beyond this project. To all three, my thanks for contributing research and support and generally for keeping me from losing my mind. The museum is blessed with a team of talented and unflappable registrars, art handlers, preparators, and conservators led by Allison Galea, Chief Registrar and Exhibitions Manager, and Julia Day, Chief Conservator, along with Patrick King, Senior Preparator. They move mountains with precision and grace. So too does Jenna Nugent, Head of Curatorial and Exhibition Projects. I can never find the words to sufficiently thank Editor in Chief Michaelyn Mitchell, whose discernment and compassionate honesty improve everything I write. In editing and managing the book, she is supported by Assistant Editor Gemma McElroy and Editorial Assistant Serena Rattazzi, to whom I am grateful. At the Frick, I also acknowledge Tyler Beard, Marie-Laure Buku Pongo, Angie Calderwood, Tia Chapman, Blanca del Castillo, Lisa Goble, Caitlin Henningsen, Bailey Keiger, George Koelle, Alexis Light, Yifu Liu, Sara Muskulus, Jeremy Ney, Christopher Roberson, Heidi Rosenau, Alexis Sandler, Justin Samson, April Kim Tonin, and Sean Troxell. An unforgettable 1,500-mile drive around the English countryside, visiting Gainsboroughs and much else with Giulio Dalvit, the Frick's Associate Curator (who did all the driving), transformed this project and a friendship, and I am grateful to him for this.

We are very much indebted to the lenders, whose generosity made this project possible: the National Gallery of Canada; the J. Paul Getty Museum; the Royal Collection Trust; Dulwich Picture Gallery; the Saint Louis Art Museum; Kenwood House, English Heritage; the Metropolitan Museum of Art; the Fine Arts Museums of San Francisco; the Huntington Library, Art Museum, and Botanical Gardens; the Royal Academy of Arts, London; the National Gallery, London; the Wallace Collection; the Courtauld Gallery; Tate Britain; Gainsborough's House; Ickworth House, National Trust; the Yale Center for British Art; Boughton House, His Grace the Duke of Buccleuch and Queensberry; the National Gallery of Art, Washington; and Arundel Castle, His Grace the Duke of Norfolk.

The privilege of getting to work on projects such as this means a lot of time away from home. I am fortunate to have a village of friends and trusted caregivers, parents who will drop everything to fly to New York, and a spouse who—besides being a font of knowledge on British culture, a gentle critic, and much else—always makes coming home feel so good.

AIMEE NG
John Updike Curator
The Frick Collection

INTRODUCTION

GAINSBOROUGH, PORTRAITS, AND FASHION

PORTRAITURE AND FASHION were inextricable from each other in eighteenth-century Britain. What to wear in a portrait was a chief concern for patrons, who were paying good money to look their best for posterity. It was also a problem for artists. Thomas Gainsborough contended that clothes could make or break a portrait, writing to a plaintive Lord Dartmouth in 1771 that his wife's "picture will look more like [her] and not so large when dressed properly," meaning if she were wearing contemporary clothing—as he depicts the actor Sarah Siddons (facing page) in the latest fashion—and not "fancy" (as in fantastical) dress.[1] In another letter to Lord Dartmouth, he stated plainly the challenge that fashion posed to portrait painters: "I am very well aware of the Objection to modern dresses in Pictures, that they are soon out of fashion and look awkward; but as that misfortune cannot be helped we must set it against the unluckiness of fancied dresses taking away Likenesses, the principal beauty and intention of a portrait."[2] It comes as no surprise that Gainsborough found himself having to repaint portraits to update styles that had gone out of fashion. Gainsborough seems to have considered himself, as a portraitist, a key player in modern British fashion. Discussing the subject of women's fashion in Britain, he reportedly remarked: "I once, in conversing with his Majesty [George III] on the subject of modern fashions, took the liberty to say, your painters should be employed to design the costumes."[3]

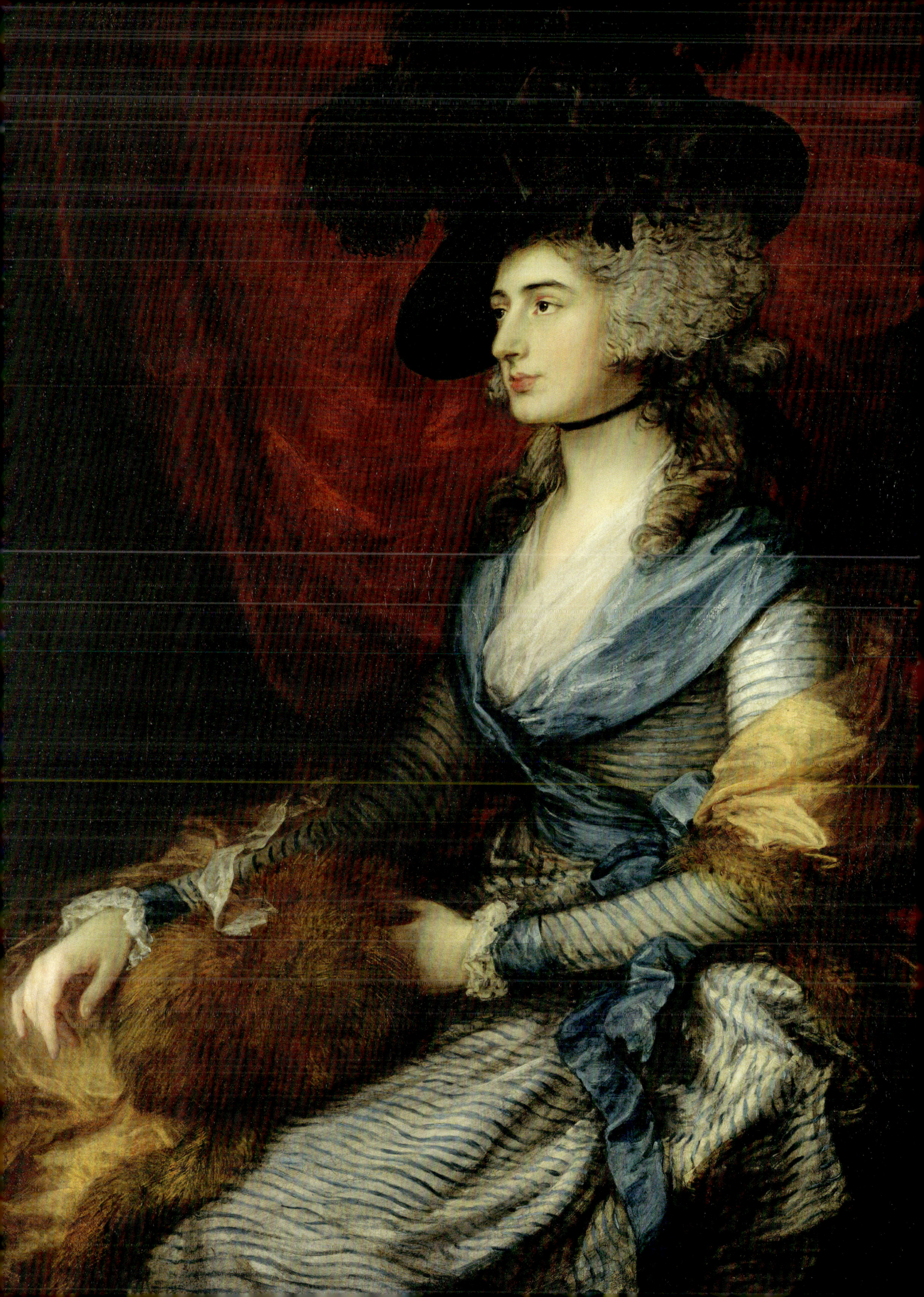

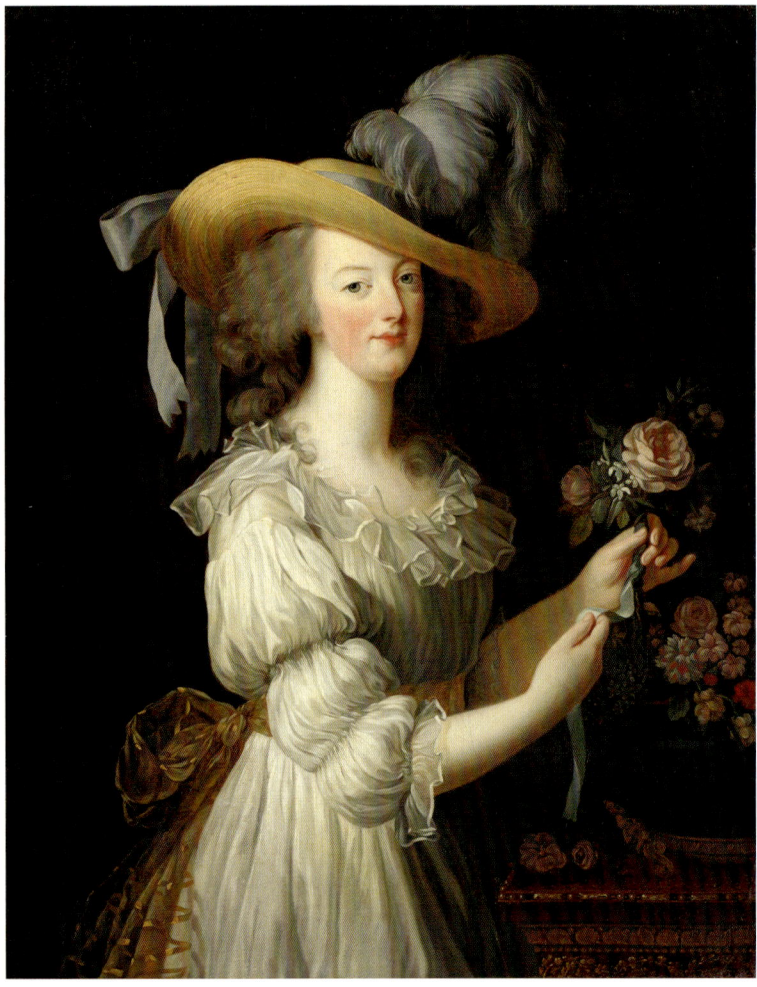

FIG. 1
Élisabeth Louise Vigée Le Brun
Marie-Antoinette in a Chemise Dress, 1783
Oil on canvas
35⅜ x 28⅜ in. (89.8 x 72 cm)
Hessische Hausstiftung, Kronberg
(WO B 8250)

FIG. 2
Glove Maker, 1765
From *Encyclopédie*, edited by Denis Diderot
and Jean le Rond d'Alembert (Paris, 1765)

The subject of what to wear in portraits reached the highest levels of the Royal Academy of Arts, whose president, Joshua Reynolds, insisted in his *Discourses* that Gainsborough was wrong and prescribed instead clothing in the style of ancient Greece and Rome. Clothing in portraits represented rank, wealth, political and familial alliances, formality and intimacy, even the time of day. It could provoke uproar and censorship, as did Élisabeth Louise Vigée Le Brun's portrait of Queen Marie-Antoinette in a chemise gown (fig. 1), which was removed from the Paris Salon of 1783 because it was insufficiently formal, showing her in a state of undress. By the time the style made it over to Britain, worn by the Duchess of Devonshire the following year, it had become the latest fashion.[4] The momentary outrageousness of an eighteenth-century outfit may not be obvious to viewers today, a reminder that fashion is a language understood only by those "in the know."

Contemporary sources detail the labor, time, and resources required to achieve the extraordinary apparel and effects depicted in Gainsborough's portraits, such as the towering hairstyles worn in the 1770s, which could take hours to build and required an extensive list of ingredients.[5] Staggering sums of money traded hands to outfit the fashionable class.

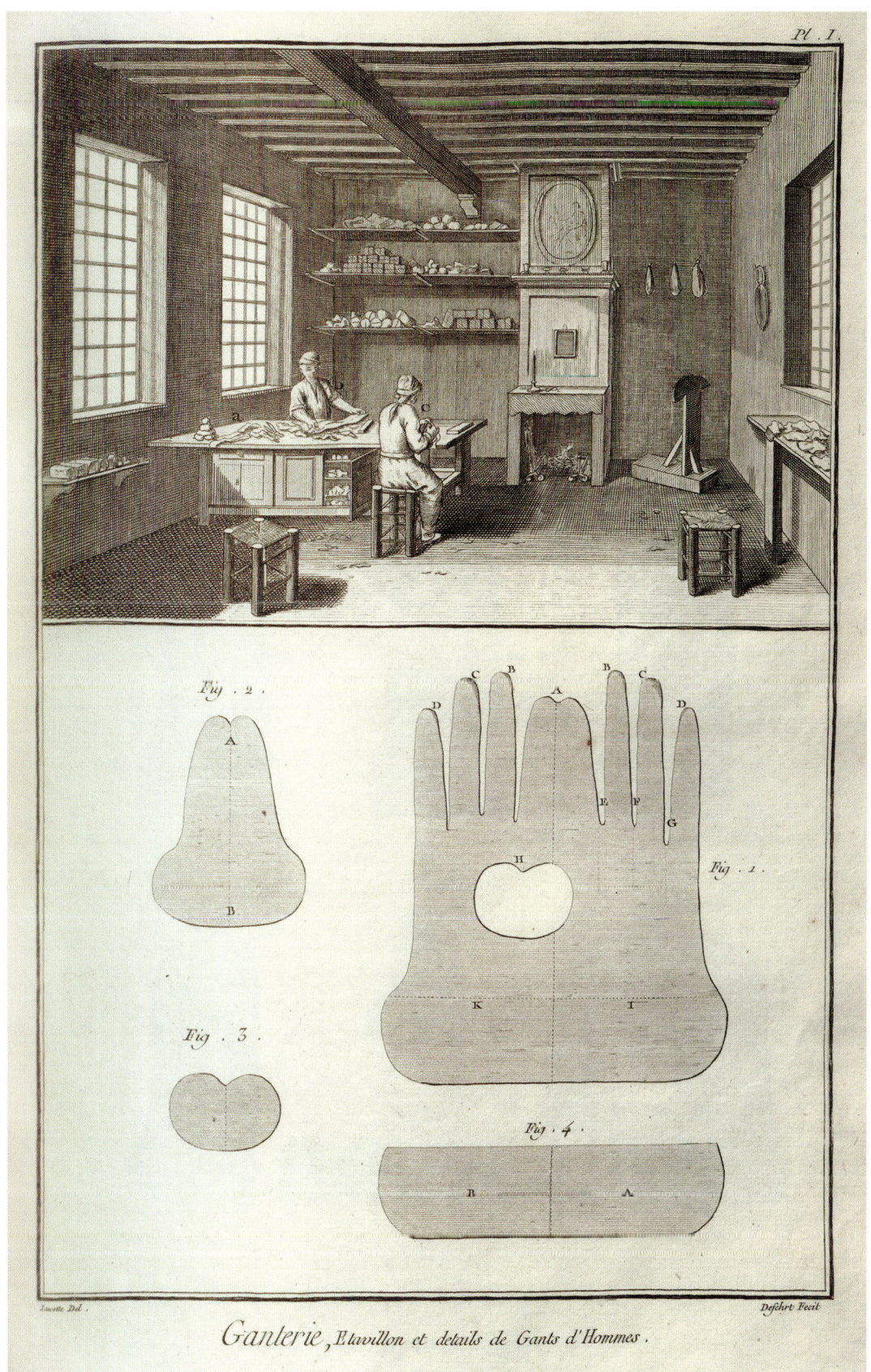

Fig. 2

Fig. 1

Fig. 3

Fig. 4

Ganterie, Etavillon et details de Gants d'Hommes.

15

Even imitation jewels were costly when a particular style was in fashion.[6] When periods of mourning restricted what could be worn in public, the industries suffered—from dressmakers and lacemakers to jewelers and silk merchants. The creativity and expertise essential to fashion come into view in diagrammatic images about trade, for example in Denis Diderot's *Encyclopédie* (fig. 2), which presents trades like glove making as orderly, pleasant activities. The toil of these industries instead emerges in reports of workers' protests, such as the mob of Coventry ribbon makers who revolted in 1776 over reduced wages, and the violent attack in 1753 on an inventor who made weaving processes more efficient and thus less dependent on human workers (see p. 32).[7] The makers behind fashion become even harder to see in the hands of artists such as Gainsborough, who edited, embellished, and invented attire and appearances. Though he seems to have precisely documented Lady Howe's lace apron (cat. 5), necklaces of pearls, and every other element of her attire from Leghorn hat to buckled shoe, there is no way of knowing if, for example, the Hon. Frances Duncombe owned the blue satin dress dripping in pearls in which Gainsborough painted her (cat. 14) or if anything like it actually existed. As eminent fashion historian Aileen Ribeiro observed, "Compared to what women actually owned, what is depicted in portraits is a selection of garments and fabrics that appealed to the artist's eye."[8]

Nonetheless, society portraits were extensions of their sitters. The painted images were subject to the same forces of fashion as the people they depict. Like the cut and cloth of a jacket, the shape, size, and facture of a painted portrait could be avant-garde or passé. The name and reputation of the portraitist mattered just as much as that of the designer or fashion house. Poses, settings, and conceits—like the pastoral theme that dressed men and women as shepherds and shepherdesses (see cat. 23)—positioned sitters in relation to prevailing fashions, whether they are shown idling among a group in a conversation piece, standing regally in a full-length portrait, or engaged in their profession or hobby. Newspapers recognized the latest clothing trends depicted in Gainsborough's portraits, while the artist himself acknowledged the evolution of his practice by referring to his own most recent style.

One aim of this catalogue and the exhibition it accompanies is to illuminate how eighteenth-century viewers understood fashion in ways that may be lost or less obvious to modern audiences. Semantic mapping of the term is of limited use here. Fashion was, and remains, interchangeable with *mode* and *vogue*. Some of the ten definitions for *fashion* (and six related terms, such as *to fashion* and *fashionist*) in Samuel Johnson's *Dictionary of the English Language* (first published in 1755) cohere with modern usage. Others carry less familiar inflections, such as fashion as a social rank ("condition above the vulgar") and as a function of time and sequence ("Manner imitated from another, way established by precedent").[9] The four essays in this publication explore aspects of fashion as it was understood in Gainsborough's time and as it had to do with the art of portraiture. Woven through these pages are human stories, of work and skill and of aspiration and loss. Though the portraits by Gainsborough that survive today represent a tiny fraction of British society, the lives of countless laborers, makers, merchants, and models are bound to these paintings and their histories.

With little exception, Gainsborough attended to every swath of satin and knot of lace himself, eschewing the convention of employing specialist drapery painters. Even if his primary assistant, his nephew Gainsborough Dupont (cat. 10), contributed to painting clothing, Gainsborough built a reputation for handling it primarily on his own.[10] Cloth and clothing were part of his life from an early age. One account describes him as a child working in his father's shop decorating shrouds and other items.[11] His cousin Thomas had a tailoring business in London; his sister Susanna, a millinery shop in Sudbury.[12] In Bath, Gainsborough's picture room, or showroom, was adjacent to his sister Mary's millinery shop, with his painting room, or studio, upstairs.[13] This arrangement offered to clients perusing her wares the prospect of his portraiture and vice versa, surely inspiring ideas for adornment in life and in paint.[14] In London, where he lived in Schomberg House at 87 Pall Mall, his neighbors at 89 Pall Mall were a succession of drapers and milliners.[15] In Gainsborough's world, the trappings, trade, and power of fashion were everywhere, from magazines to tailors, on display at the opera and on promenades, and his portraits were at the heart of it. The nineteenth- and early-twentieth-century fashion designer Lucy, Lady Duff-Gordon, celebrated the power of a dress to create a new identity for its wearer: "Put even the plainest woman into a beautiful dress and unconsciously she will try to live up to it. It is as if for her the designer has created a new personality; her every movement reflects increased self-confidence, a new joy of living."[16] For Gainsborough, the power of the portraitist to shape his subject may have been even greater.

NOTES

1   Gainsborough to the Earl of Dartmouth, April 18, 1771; Hayes 2001, 91.

2   Gainsborough to the Earl of Dartmouth, April 13, 1771; Hayes 2001, 90. For the portraits of Lady Dartmouth, see Belsey 2019, 1: no. 238 and no. 239.

3   Angelo 1904, 1: 274.

4   Ribeiro 1995, 71.

5   *A Treatise on the Art of Managing, Improving, and Dressing the Hair on the most improved Principles of that Art* was published as an addition to *The New London Toilet* (1778), which described itself as a "compleat [*sic*] collection of the most simple and useful receipts for preserving and improving beauty, either by outward Applications or internal Use."

6   Clifford 2004, 199.

7   Porter 1990, 336.

8   Ribeiro 1995, 78.

9   Only the tenth definition of fashion as "the horses leprosy," is no longer in use. From Johnson's *Dictionary* (1755):
    Fashion (*façon*, French)
        1. Form, make, state of anything with regard to appearance
        2. Make or cut of cloaths [*sic*]
        3. Manner, sort, way
        4. Custom operating upon dress, or any domestic ornaments
        5. Custom, general practice
        6. Manner imitated from another; way established by precedent
        7. General approbation; mode
        8. Rank; condition above the vulgar
        9. Anything worn
        10. The farcy; a distemper in horses; the horses leprosy

10   Thicknesse 1770, 96–97: He "not only paints the face; but finishes, with his own hands; every part of the drapery, this, however trifling a matter it may appear to some, is of as great importance, to the picture; as it is fatigue and labour to the artist – The other eminent Painters, either cannot; or will not be at that trouble." On Gainsborough's assistance from Gainsborough Dupont and others, see Sloman 2002, 70, and Belsey 2019, 1: 6. On Gainsborough's payment of 20 guineas to drapery painter Peter Toms on August 21, 1776, see Hayes 1982, 188, 234n.13.

11   Bills 2018, 33.

12   H. Belsey in Sudbury 1988, 20; Bills 2018, 25.

13   On nomenclature around artists' rooms, see Sloman 1996.

14   Bryant (2003, 187) suggests that Gainsborough may have encouraged clients like Lady Howe (cat. 5) to appear in fashionable dress in their portraits in part because of his studio's proximity to his sister's shop.

15   Sloman 2021, 19–20. regarding Gainsborough's *Mrs. Sarah Siddons* (page 13), that it is "tempting to see it as a showpiece that worked not only for Gainsborough and the sitter, but for Mrs. Dyde [one of the milliners] as well."

16   Duff-Gordon 1932, 71.

MANNER

MORE THAN WHAT THEY WORE

Society portraiture had become so popular in Britain by the mid-eighteenth century that, according to Swiss artist Jean André Rouquet (1701–1758), it was a farce. Of the throngs of portraiture patrons, Rouquet wrote, "It is the fashion that carries them to a painter of whom they have no great opinion, to engage him out of vanity to draw their picture, which they have no occasion for, and which they will not like when finished."[1] Expressed with the contempt of an artist who was not in fashion, Rouquet's remark was published in 1755, when Gainsborough was cultivating his career in Ipswich, a port city in Suffolk removed from London's cosmopolitan crowds. At the time, Gainsborough was still years from being in the privileged position to decry the "curs'd face business" that would keep him too busy to paint his beloved landscapes.[2] Over the course of his nearly five-decade-long career, he would make hundreds of portraits. These served numerous functions in British life: commemorating and anticipating events such as marriage, celebrating achievements, affirming alliances, memorializing loved ones, and much more beyond the essential purpose of constructing images of identity. He made them in various formats, styles, and types according to functions and fashions that dictated both what his sitters wore in their pictures and the appearance of the portraits themselves.

Gainsborough addressed the inherent conflict between portraiture and fashion in his oft-quoted 1771 admission to Lord Dartmouth that modern outfits in portraits quickly go out of

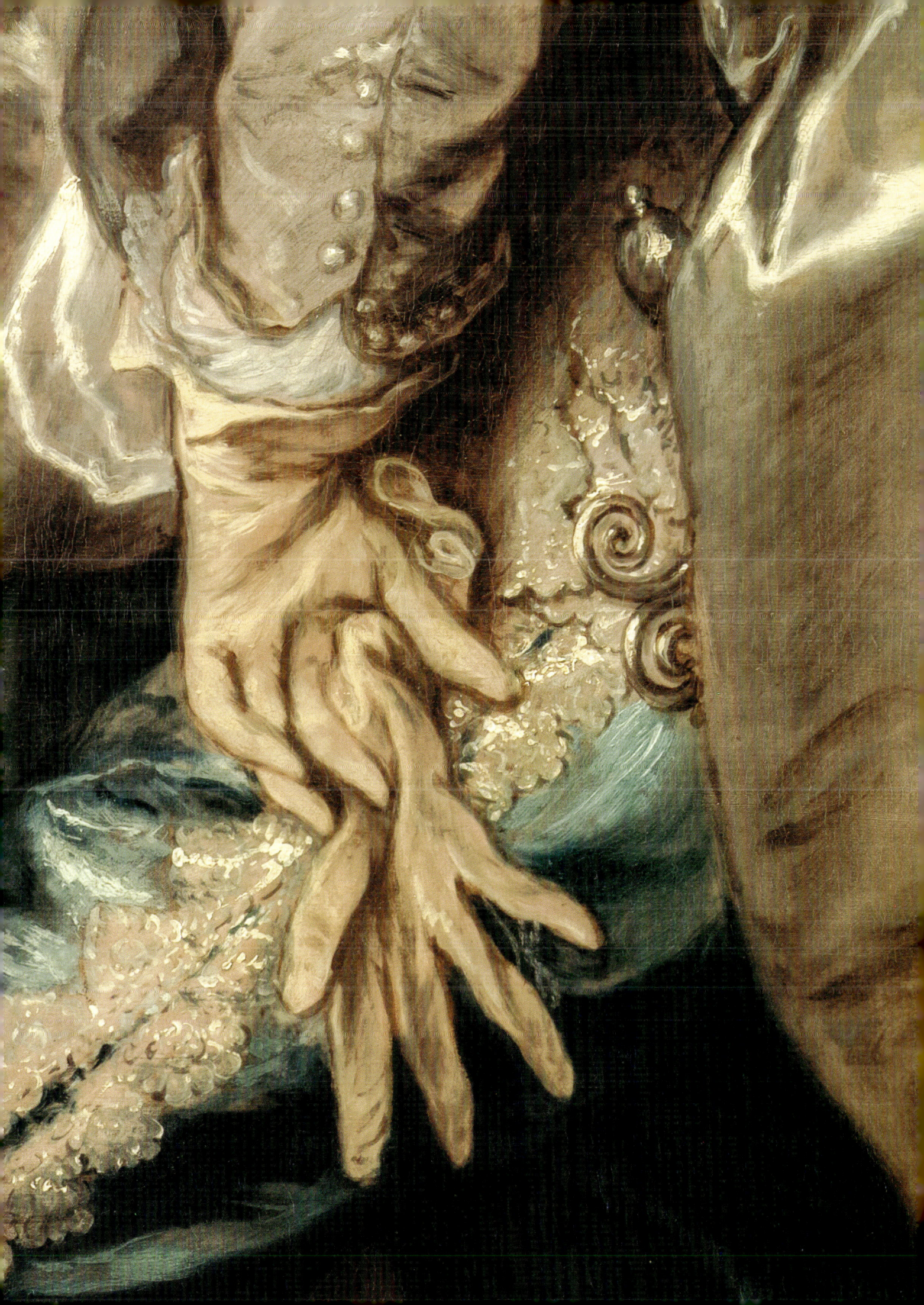

fashion and "look awkward."[3] In his resistance to "fancy" or non-modern dress in portraits, he was willing to repaint portraits for anyone who later regretted their initial choices of contemporary clothing. Many took him up on it.[4] While Joshua Reynolds asserted that modern clothing destroyed a portrait's "dignity,"[5] Gainsborough believed in the transformative power of contemporary fashion—in his words, "the amazing Effect of dress"—in achieving likeness.[6] Over the course of his mature career, Gainsborough explored the possibilities of "Van Dyck dress," with its historical and modern associations, as a solution to portraiture's problem with fashion. Otherwise, with little exception, he clothed his sitters in contemporary wear.[7]

In general, men had more recourse to avoiding fashion's traps than women did, since men had the option to wear uniforms and professional attire.[8] Some fifteen reverends sat for Gainsborough, and they are nearly indistinguishable from each other in their cassocks, tabs, and bob wigs. Captain Augustus Hervey, later 3rd Earl of Bristol, signals his belonging to an institution greater than himself by wearing naval uniform in his portrait (cat. 7). Samuel Linley (cat. 16) may appear to modern viewers dressed as a gentleman in a black neckcloth and waistcoat, blue coat, and white shirt, but his contemporaries would have recognized him as a midshipman in the Royal Navy by the white tab and gold button at his collar. At the time, subjects of portraits shown at London's annual art exhibitions were rarely identified in the titles (resulting in unhelpful catalogue lists of *Portrait of a Gentleman* and *Portrait of a Lady*, etc.). Portraits of male sitters sometimes were titled by professions, such as Hervey's picture, which appeared at the 1768 Society of Artists exhibition as *A Sea Officer*. Women lacked equivalent sartorial options, an exception being ladies of the peerage, who, like male peers, could wear the official red and fur-lined robes of their class (or, as in the case of the Duchess of Cumberland, stand next to them; fig. 3). Otherwise, Gainsborough's female sitters were left to shape their identity from the many categories, permutations, and styles of contemporary women's dress.

Pendant portraits of Captain Lord Richard Howe and Lady Howe (see fig. 41 and cat. 5) exemplify the difference. From head to toe, she displays the absolute latest trends in dress and accessories, while her husband wears his uniform.[9] Incidentally, Captain Howe's uniform is nearly identical to that of Captain Hervey, revealing their parallel ranks. Options for contemporary female fashion were so numerous that some considered the entire industry impossible for men to understand.[10] It makes sense that the majority of the portraits Gainsborough reworked (or offered to rework) were of female subjects, while he typically altered men's portraits to update symbols of status, such as uniforms and attributes of rank (see fig. 63).[11] Hair was an arena for extravagant styles for women, and showing their natural hair—even if supplemented by pads and powder—was a respectable convention, while for men, "it was universally recognized that masculine authority was vested in the wig."[12]

One valuable anecdote about sitting for portraits in the eighteenth century is the Duchess of Rutland's exasperated account of being told to bring a selection of dresses to Reynolds's studio, only to have him select a white "bedgown" for her portrait.[13] No such insight into Gainsborough's sittings is known; his surviving correspondence does not describe his sitters' clothes, and there is no evidence that they actually wore the clothing in their portraits or that

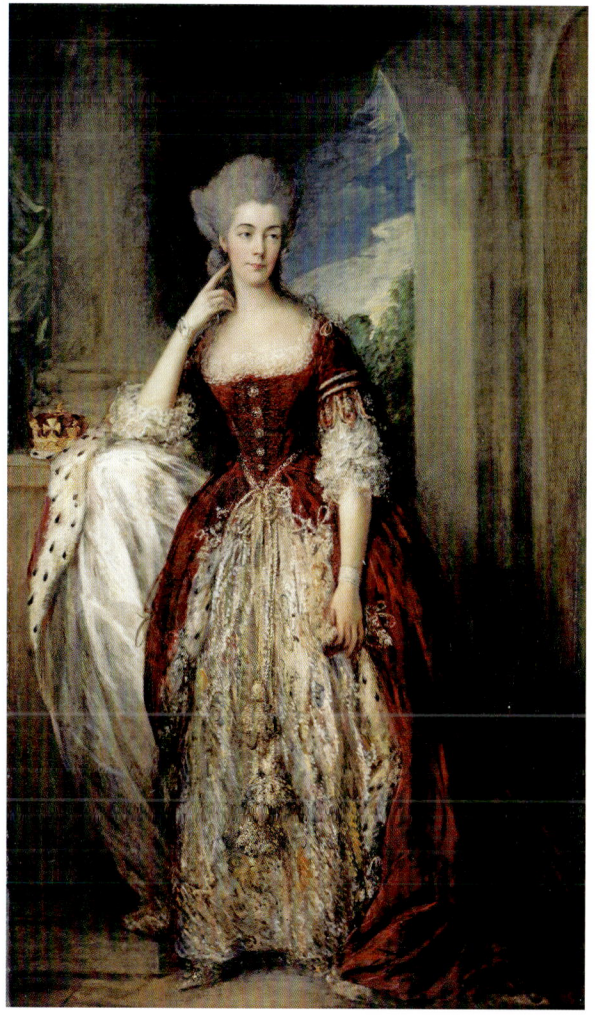

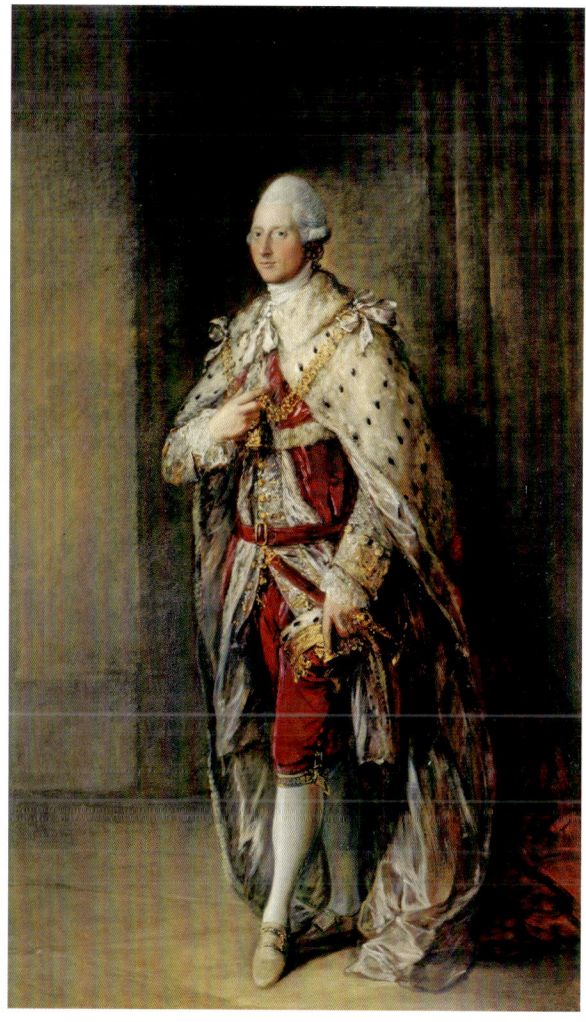

FIG. 3

Thomas Gainsborough

Anne, Duchess of Cumberland, 1773–84

Oil on canvas, 95³/₁₆ x 56⅛ in. (241.7 x 142.6 cm)

Royal Collection Trust, London (RCIN 405937)

FIG. 4

Thomas Gainsborough

Henry Frederick, Duke of Cumberland, ca. 1773–77

Oil on canvas, 94⅝ x 56⁵/₁₆ in. (240.3 x 143 cm)

Royal Collection Trust, London (RCIN 405936)

it existed as such at all.[14] It has been suggested that the doll-like figures in his early, small-scale conversation pieces (in the words of one scholar, "marionettes rather than people")[15] result from his painting from dressed lay figures (posable wood models; see p. 37). Given his family associations with the clothing and fashion industries—especially his sister's millinery shop adjacent to his Bath studio—he probably had access to Pandoras, dolls dressed in miniature versions of the latest, primarily Parisian, clothing styles (fig. 5). These fashion dolls were sent to milliners in Europe, Britain, and their colonies before the proliferation of fashion magazines circulated clothing trends more efficiently.[16]

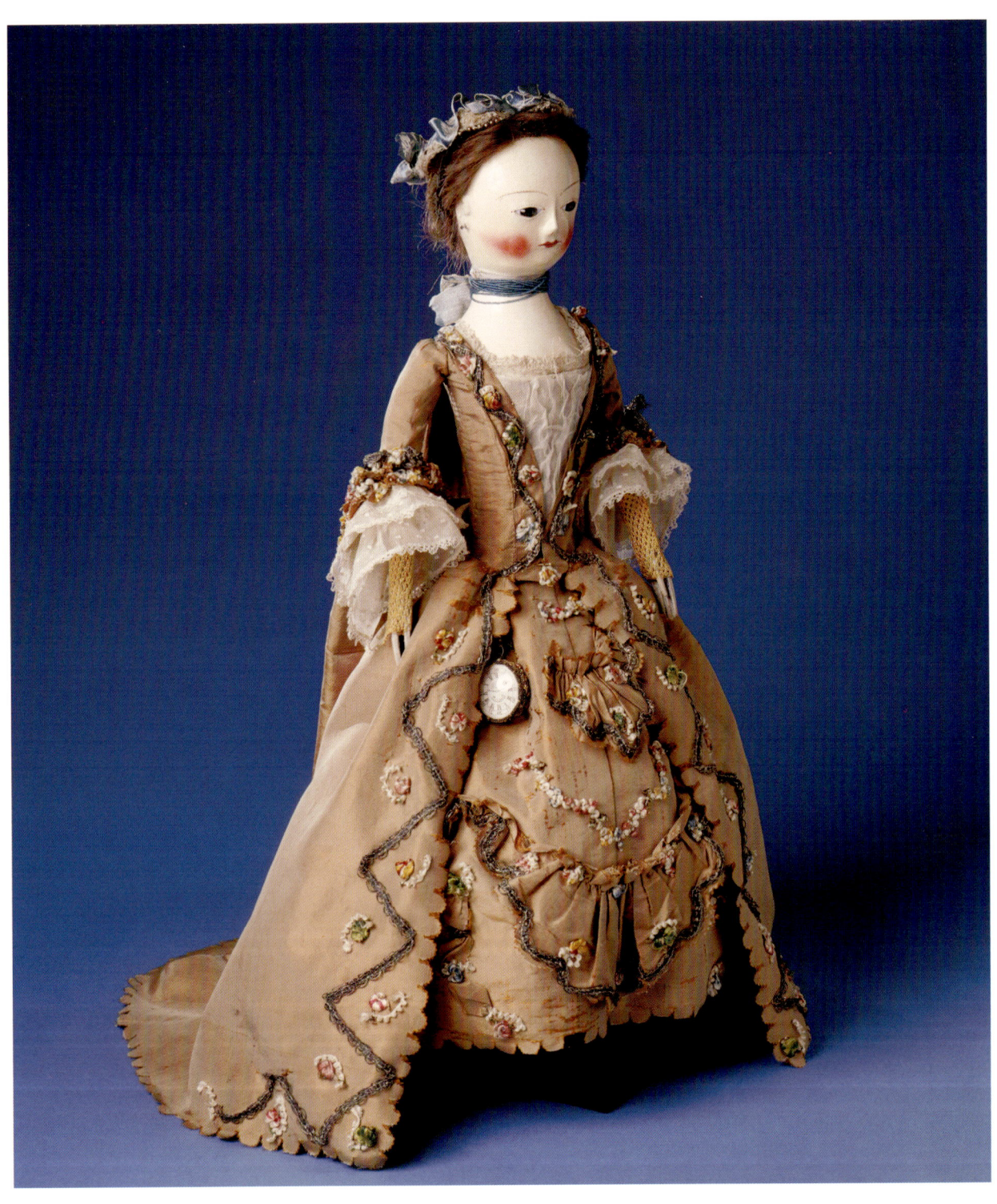

FIG. 5
Unidentified maker
Fashion Doll, 1755–60
Wood, silk, and other materials
h. 23⅝ in. (60 cm)
Victoria and Albert Museum, London (T.90-1980)

Countless rules of decorum relating to the time of day, with whom one was meeting, and the nature of activities and events governed what Gainsborough's sitters wore in their daily lives. One chose to be "dressed" (the fullest expression of a type of clothing, the most formal) or "undressed" (denoting less-formal attire rather than lack of clothing), with morning dress, evening dress, nightgowns (referring to an informal gown rather than sleepwear; see cat. 5),[17] riding costume, and fancy dress (what might today be worn to a costume party), each having their time and place. Thus, in addition to the risk of wearing a style that goes out of fashion, one challenge of choosing what to wear in a portrait was the specificity of clothing. It is no wonder that Gainsborough and his clients experimented with transcending the mores of contemporary fashion with Van Dyck–style inventions. While clients grappled with what to bring from real life into their portraits, some contemporaries were concerned with the influence portraits could have on trends in real life.[18] The fluidity between painted images and contemporary personas underscores the role of portraits as both records of and players in the forces and cycles of fashion.

Rouquet's comments on the farcical state of society portraiture emphasize that fashion's grip on portraits extended to the image's style and form, as well as to the persona of the artist. Though head and bust portraits remained ubiquitous, beginning in the 1720s, a type of small-scale group portraiture called conversation pieces, or "family pieces," became the vogue in England.[19] These were inspired by Dutch paintings of the previous century, popularized especially through the work of William Hogarth and informed by the recent *fêtes galantes* of Jean-Antoine Watteau. When Gainsborough first established himself as an independent artist in the 1740s, long before he developed what would become his signature style, he followed this trend. At that point, however, conversation pieces were already beginning to go out of fashion and were increasingly associated with a provincial style.[20] Gainsborough's forays into the genre show him closely emulating the format and style of his teacher, Francis Hayman (cat. 3 and fig. 39), with whom he had collaborated by painting the landscape portions of some of his conversation pieces.[21] As Hayman abided by conventions of the trend, however, Gainsborough found ways to innovate and individualize.

Conversation pieces typically showcase the fashionable interiors of family homes as extensions of their owners' identities, with domestic furnishings presented as attributes that reinforce an image of status and wealth.[22] Gainsborough set his conversation pieces exclusively out of doors, which allowed him to indulge his interest in, and talent for, landscape painting and lent the portraits a sense of informality. In a practical sense, outdoor settings freed him from having to reproduce a recognizable interior associated with the sitters, making it possible for sittings to take place in his studio rather than at their homes.[23] The woodland setting in *Peter Darnell Muilman, Charles Crokatt, and William Keable* (cat. 1) is whimsical, suited to the trio's music making, and offers a neutral ground for the disparate social ranks of the sitters. In *The Gravenor Family* (cat. 3), the discordance between the earthy, agrarian setting and the silky, structured dresses in which the daughters gingerly recline (alluding to wealth and purity in their satiny pinks and whites) points to the symbolic nature of the landscape: The brook and wheat field that flank the sitters imply their fecundity in both resources and breeding.

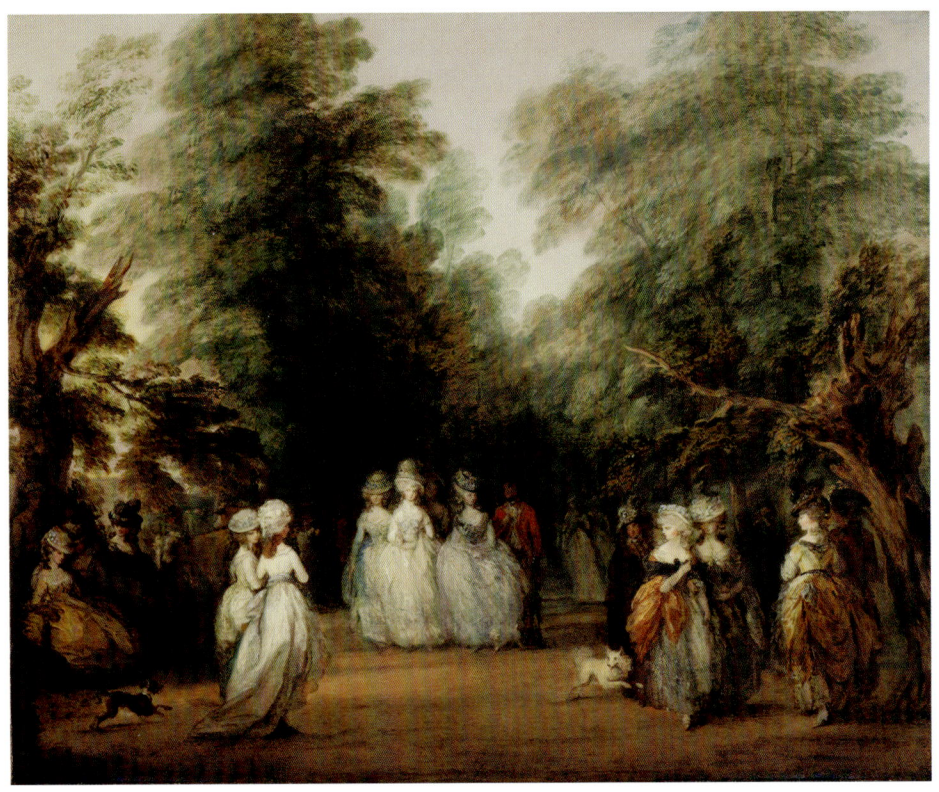

Modern scholars have called Gainsborough's iconic *Mr. and Mrs. Andrews* (cat. 2) "radical," an "eccentric masterpiece" that, while operating within the bounds of a trend also "represented a dead end in the conversation piece tradition."[24] It does not appear to have been the last of his conversation pieces, however (see cat. 3), suggesting that the individual needs of patrons could compel him to revert to convention. In *Mr. and Mrs. Andrews*, the artist activates the landscape as a "third portrait" along with the couple who owns the land, rendering it so precisely that modern scholars claim to be able to identify the very oak tree under which the pair sits. The author Philip Thicknesse (1719–1792) takes credit for being among those who encouraged Gainsborough to leave his provincial practice and "try his talents at portrait painting" in "that fluctuating city" of Bath, the fashionable spa town frequented by Britain's elite society and those who wanted to be part of it.[25] There Gainsborough transferred with his family in 1759 and abandoned conversation pieces for the grand life-size portraiture that would earn him fame. Toward the end of his life, Gainsborough seems to have revived the conversation piece in his signature style. Contemporary rumor implied that *The Mall at St. James's Park* (fig. 6) included portraits, and his group painting of the Duke and Duchess of Cumberland with Elizabeth Luttrell (fig. 7) suggests that he may have been reflecting on the conversation pieces of his early days, perhaps wondering if the cycles of fashion would bring such works back into vogue.[26] Like his independent portraits of dogs (cat. 13), which were not particularly in vogue or lucrative in Gainsborough's time, he pursued genres of painting even when they were not fashionable.[27]

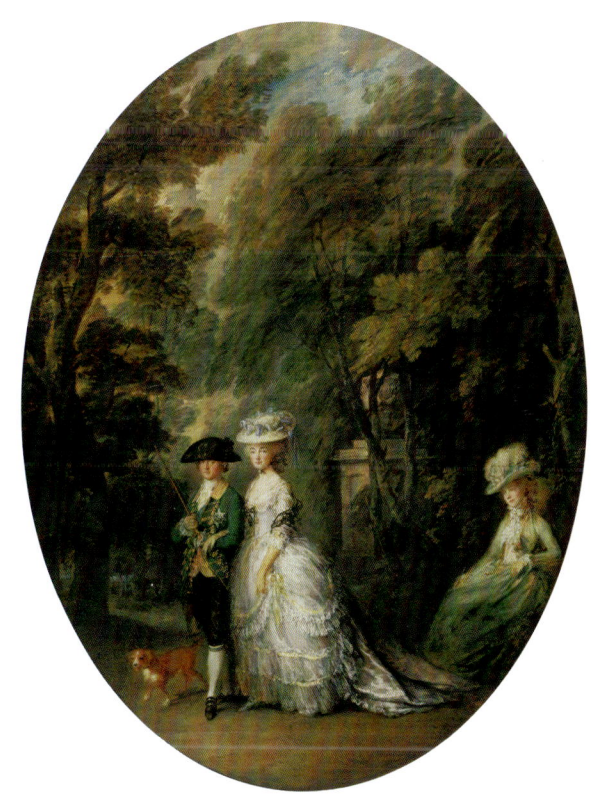

FIG. 6
Thomas Gainsborough
The Mall at St. James's Park, ca. 1783
Oil on canvas
47½ x 5 ⅞ in. (120.7 x 147 cm)
The Frick Collection, New York (1916.1.62)

FIG. 7
Thomas Gainsborough
Henry, Duke of Cumberland
with Anne, Duchess of Cumberland,
and Lady Elizabeth Luttrell, ca. 1785–88
Oil on canvas
64⅜ x 49 in. (163.5 x 124.5 cm)
Royal Collection Trust, London (RCIN 400675)

Without oversimplifying the situation with a present-day comparison, in this system the portraitist's name and style became something like a brand with which clients sought to associate themselves. During his fourteen years in Bath, punctuated by visits to London and its annual public exhibitions, Gainsborough began to build the signature styles that make his paintings recognizable as "Gainsboroughs," depicting the fashionable people of the region and those who traveled there for the Bath season.[28] As one contemporary observed, he developed a "manner of pencilling"—a style—that "was so peculiar to himself, that his works needed no signature."[29] His interest in painting sitters in contemporary dress became as much of a signature as his painting style.[30] It was not always a smooth process. Letters record him assuaging dissatisfied clients and offering to modify portraits or even repaint them entirely.[31] In one case, he had to explain why the surfaces of his paintings looked as rough as they did ("in order to show them as made with paint").[32] By 1774, he had conquered the Bath market and had shaped his reputation in London through sending paintings to annual exhibitions held in the capital, with reviews more and more often commenting on his characteristic style. One reviewer gushed: "But what shall I say of the Pencilling? I really do not know; it is so new, so very original, that I cannot find Words to convey an idea of it. I do not know that any Artists, living or dead, have managed their Pencil in that Manner, and I am afraid that any Attempt to imitate it will be attended with ill-success."[33] In 1774, Gainsborough moved his practice to London, where he found both success and greater competition. Here he would develop a mature style that has been described as a "gossamer web of sheer paint."[34]

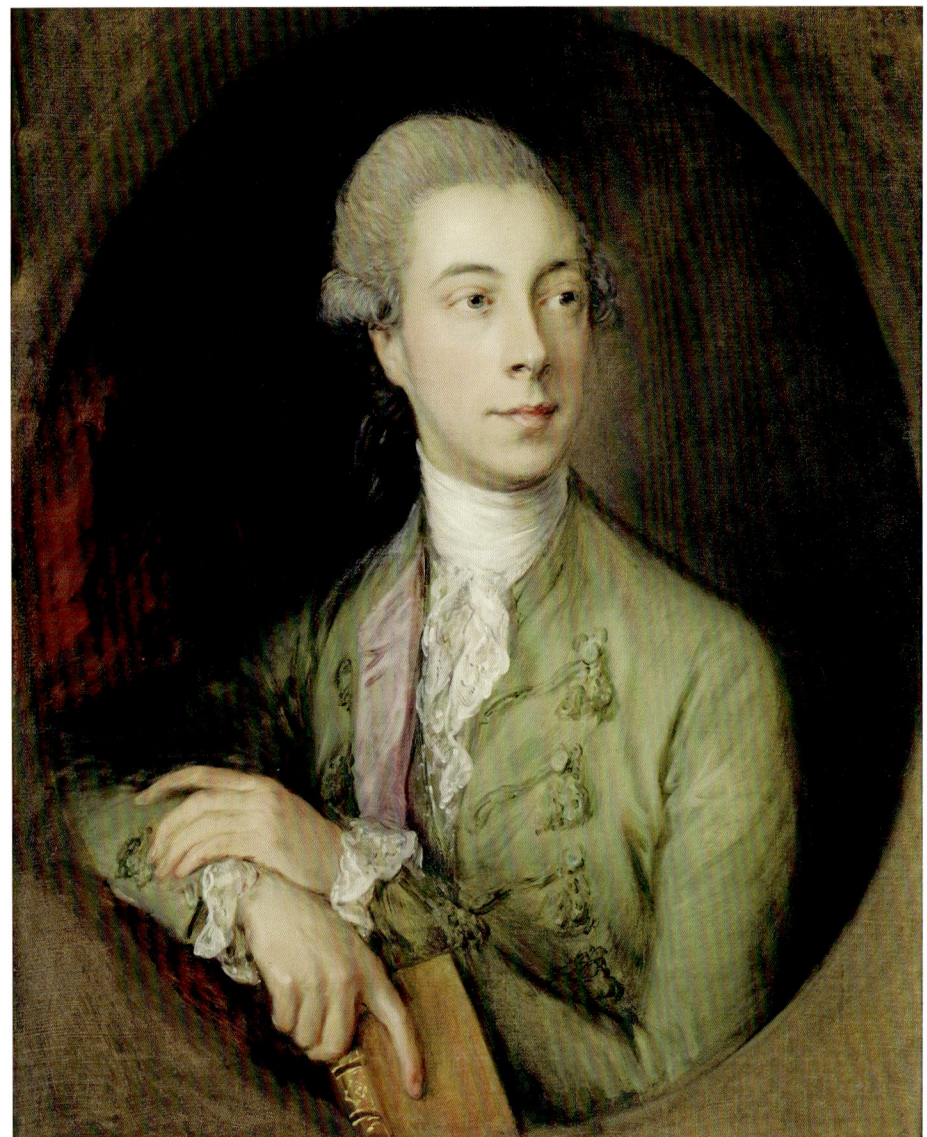

FIG. 8
Thomas Gainsborough
Richard Paul Jodrell,
ca. 1774
Oil on canvas
30¼ x 25⅛ in.
(76.8 x 63.8 cm)
The Frick Collection,
New York (1946.1.154)

FIG. 9
Joshua Reynolds
Mrs. Richard Paul Jodrell,
1774–76
Oil on canvas
30½ x 25¼ in.
(77.5 x 64.1 cm)
Detroit Institute of Arts
(77.7)

Any number of factors prompted patrons to choose one portraitist over another, including cost, availability, and, perhaps above all, personal preference. The practice of opening an artist's private showroom to potential clients was part of a marketing strategy: depictions of famous, well-respected, or even highly attractive anonymous sitters were like endorsements for an artist, with examples of portraits offering options after which patrons could model their own.[35] It went the other way as well: The showroom of a fashionable painter could lift the profile of a sitter.[36] On occasion, a husband and wife chose different portraitists for their paintings, reflecting their individual tastes and interests. Gainsborough's *Richard Paul Jodrell* (fig. 8), for instance, shows the subject dressed in modern wear, while, for the pendant portrait of the same size and format, his wife went instead to Reynolds, who pictured her in an "exotic" dress unimaginable in Gainsborough's hands (fig. 9).[37] Sitters also patronized more than one por-

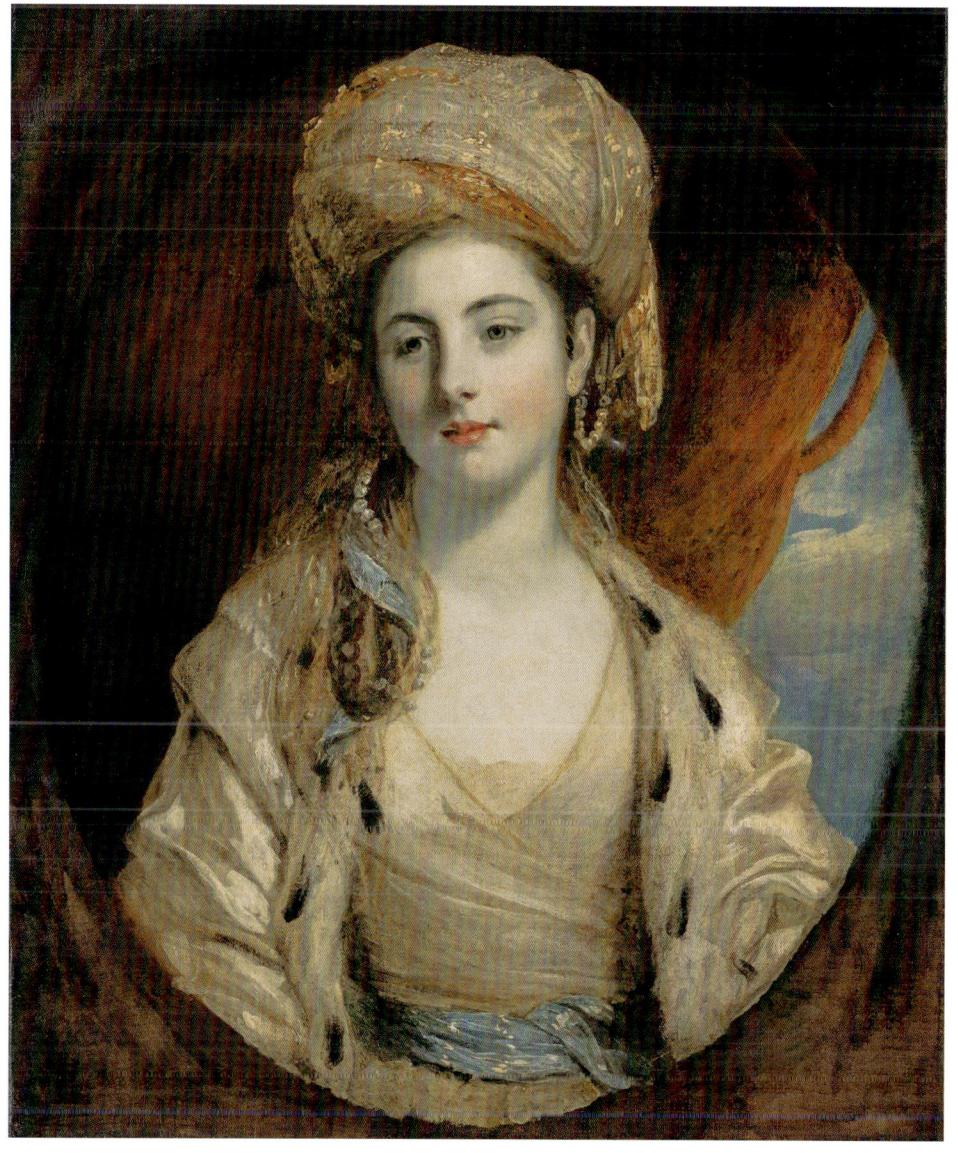

traitist for varied images of themselves, enjoying the translation of their likeness into distinct styles. The 3rd Earl of Darnley appears to have commissioned portraits of his niece Theodosia Magill around 1765 from both Reynolds and Gainsborough, resulting in different versions of the same sitter at the same time.[38] That the comparison may not have been entirely profitable for Gainsborough is implied by a letter to the earl alluding to modifications he would make to "Miss Magill's Picture."[39] The evaluation and categorization of artists' styles were helped along by critical reviews in daily newspapers, which often pitted Gainsborough against Reynolds. The second wife of Samuel Moody chose George Romney as her portraitist, distinguishing hers from Gainsborough's portrait of Moody's beloved, late first wife (cat. 19).[40]

By the time of his death at age sixty-one in 1788, Gainsborough had achieved royal patronage and, after a final break with the Royal Academy exhibition hanging committee in

1784, had been showing exclusively in his own showroom in Schomberg House, on Pall Mall, near the monarch's residence, then at St. James's Palace, and the salesroom of art auctioneer James Christie (cat. 17). He left his remaining works to be disposed of by his widow and his nephew Gainsborough Dupont. The auction took place in Gainsborough's own rooms, reportedly to assure buyers that the works were untouched by other hands and were authentic Gainsboroughs—suggesting that attempts to counterfeit Gainsborough's style were a valid concern.[41] Christie did the same when he auctioned the remainder of Gainsborough's studio contents in 1792 despite his own salesroom being nearby. Dupont's success in emulating so closely his uncle's style was also his demise, for it seems to have inhibited his personal style. Although he showed his work at the Royal Academy after his uncle's death, he did not achieve independent fame and never became a fashionable society painter in his own right.

It has been suggested that part of Gainsborough's success in the 1770s and 1780s was that British fashion evolved to optimally suit his painting style.[42] Tumultuous changes in France beginning with the events of 1789 had a profound effect on Parisian fashion—long the origin of many trends in British style—and it is tempting to wonder how changes in the fashion of clothing would have affected Gainsborough's portraits.[43] Four years after his death, his main rival, Reynolds, died, and the young Thomas Lawrence took up the reins as the most fashionable portraitist in Britain, remaining so beyond the long rule of George III (r. 1760–1820).

1 Rouquet 1755, 40.

2 Postle (2002, 20) points out that by the mid-1750s, Gainsborough in Ipswich was painting about seven or eight portraits a year compared to Reynolds, who in 1755 "entertained well over a hundred sitters in his London studio." In a 1770 letter to James Unwin, Gainsborough wrote: "I have been just going to write to your Brother many times for your direction but have been always prevented by the curs'd Face Business"; Hayes 2001, 78.

3 Hayes 2001, 90.

4 On alterations in Gainsborough's portraits, see Belsey 2019, 1: 5.

5 Reynolds 1959, 140: The painter who "wishes to dignify his subject . . . will not paint her in the modern dress, the familiarity of which is sufficient to destroy all dignity."

6 Letter from Gainsborough to Lord Dartmouth, April 13, 1771; Hayes 2001, 89.

7 One exception is *Penelope, Viscountess Ligonier*, which Gainsborough exhibited at the Royal Academy with the title *A Portrait of a Lady in a Fancied Dress; Whole Length*, along with its pendant; see p. 69.

8 This includes servants, for only male servants (who were visible to an employer's guests) wore livery, while female servants did not. On blurred boundaries of class and status associated with servants' uniforms, see Buck 1979, 109. Pointon (1993, 107–10) discusses the greater range of options for men versus women in the dressing of hair and use of wigs.

9 Modern commentators (e.g., Bryant 2003, 184) refer to Lady Howe as "just having gone shopping."

10 Vickery (2009, 120) points to the following passage on millinery: "The milliner is concerned in making and providing the Ladies with Linnen [*sic*] of all sorts, fit for Wearing Apparel, from the Holland smock to the Tippet and Commode; but as we are got into the Lady's Articles, which are so very numerous, the Reader is not to expect that we are to give an exact List of everything belonging to them; let it suffice in general that the Milliner furnishes them with Holland, Cambrick [*sic*], Lawn, and Lace of all sorts, and makes these Materials into smocks, Aprons, Tippits, Handkerchiefs, Neckaties [*sic*], Ruffles, Mobs, Caps, Dressed-Heads, with as many *Etceteras* as would reach from *Charing-Cross* to the *Royal Exchange*"; "no Male trade," in Campbell 1969, 207.

11 S. Sloman (in Bath 2019, 71) emphasizes the rare case of Gainsborough updating a man's portrait (*Richard Tickell)* to keep up with fashion.

12 Pointon 1993, 110.

13 Leslie and Taylor 1865, 1: 248.

14 From a sitter's perspective, George Lucy describes sitting for two hours for his portrait with Gainsborough and that "the dress is to be entirely altered, a blue cloth coat with a little gold embroidery, which the painter thinks will give a little more life"; quoted in Sloman 1997, 327.

15 Vaughan 2002, 52.

16 Roche (1994, 475) notes that "In time of war, miniscule Pandoras dressed in déshabillés or négligés and life-sized Pandoras in full court dress enjoyed diplomatic immunity, and were even given cavalry escorts to ensure their safe arrival." On Gainsborough and lay figures, see p. 37.

17 Buck (1979, 41) describes the confusion around "nightgown": "Known to the French as *robe à l'anglaise*; an informal gown, particularly English in character and very generally worn. The name is confusing. Early in the century it may have meant a loose gown." What one wore to bed, meanwhile, may have been referred to as "bed nightgown" or "bedgown."

18 S. Sloman (in Bath 2019, 71) discusses fashions set by theatrical performers, such as Mary Robinson, and portraits playing a part in disseminating them. B. Leca (in Cincinnati and San Diego 2010–11, 91) points to Rouquet warning artists to avoid abetting the fashion for heavily rouged cheeks by not painting them in portraits.

19 On conversation pieces, see, especially, Shawe-Taylor 2009, Retford 2017.

20 Shawe-Taylor (1999, 128) points out that conversation pieces, though popular, "would never have been regarded as comparable with the life size portraits of Ramsay and Reynolds, by the 1760s, they would have seemed to be no more than a provincial, country-bumpkin means of self-advertisement." Postle (2002, 15) notes that they went out of style faster in London than in rural areas like Suffolk. They did not disappear entirely after the 1750s. Johann Zoffany, for example, produced them for Queen Charlotte well after the 1760s.

21 London, Washington, and Boston 2002–3, 42. In 1746–47, Gainsborough painted the landscape background for Hayman's portrait of the children of Grosvenor Bedford (Private collection).

22 Vickery 2009, 107: "Possessions were crucial props in self-fashioning, the skillful creation of an assemblage that came close to a self-portrait—a picture that could be shown off, rearranged or hidden as circumstances demanded."

23 Sloman 2002, 47: "Gainsborough himself said that he disliked visiting the homes of the nobility and felt he had been taken prisoner when he was tricked into painting Lord and Lady Ligonier at their country residence in the summer of 1770. The pattern of his studio practice, whereby sitters almost invariably came to him had been established in Ipswich and was continued in Bath with little change."

24 Retford 2017, 150. Waterhouse (1981, 135) calls it an "eccentric masterpiece."

25 Thicknesse 1788, 15.

26 Shawe-Taylor 2009, 148–50. See also Hayes 1975, 38.

27 D. Perkins (in Sudbury 2006, 13) on Gainsborough not being dissuaded by "the scant regard given to animal painting at this time."

28 On Gainsborough constructing a wholly independent strategy for his portraiture, see Postle 2002, 28–29. Kalinsky 1995, 16, on Gainsborough having "evolved a portrait style as well-mannered as his now more urbane clientele." On Gainsborough's developing a "unique style of his own," see Sloman 2002, 47, 62.

29 Edwards 1808, 142.

30 D. Solkin in London and Princeton 2018–19, 30, citing Rempel 1997.

31 For example, George Lucy declared that his second portrait "will scarcely deserve the carriage," unless the painter can alter it "much for the better"; letter from George Lucy to Gainsborough, April 5, 1759, cited in Sloman 1997, 327.

32 Hayes 2001, 10.

33 *St. James's Chronicle,* May 3–6 1777. On Gainsborough's originality and copyright law, see Martinez 2009.

34 A. French in London 1988b, 25.

35 Sloman 2002, 86: "His failure to send a truly representative selection of works to Spring Gardens [Society of Artists, 1761–68] underlines the importance he attached to his own exhibition rooms in Bath." Rouquet 1755, 42–43: "Every portrait painter in England has a room to shew [*sic*] his pictures, separate from that in which he works. People who have nothing to do, make it one of their morning amusements, to go and see these collections." On Reynolds's showrooms, see McPherson 2000, 409.

36 Women liked to have "their pictures exposed for some time in the house of that painter who is most in fashion"; Rouquet 1755, 40–41.

37 As another example, Gainsborough painted *Mrs. Peter William Baker* (see fig. 57) while her husband chose George Stubbs in 1782.

38 See Belsey 2019, 1: no. 182; Mannings 2000, 1: no. 244.

39 Belsey 2014, 305 (19A) and cat. 6, note 8.

40 Ingamells 2008, 206n.4.

41 "The newspapers of 1789 make it clear that Mrs Gainsborough's object in showing her husband's pictures in the rooms in which they were produced, and in refusing to part with any of them before the exhibition was opened, was to checkmate the forgers who were now more busy than ever. A writer who prophesies that the time is not far distant when a Gainsborough landscape will be sought for as eagerly as one from the brush of Claude or Rubens, says of the pictures then at Schomberg House: 'They are shown in the very rooms in which they were painted, and it is a pleasing reflection to a collector that he is able to select a picture with a confidence of its being a genuine work untouched and unimitated; so that no vile copy can in future strike him with surprise, and diminish from the value and scarcity of the work he possesses.' The same note is struck by the *Morning Post*, which agrees that 'it has been very properly observed on the pictures of Mr Gainsborough, that they should not be suffered to leave the rooms where his exquisite pencil gave them existence, till they are sold. A collector, thus convinced that no tampering brush has violated the touch of the great master, will select in security'"; Whitley [1915] 2016, 369.

42 Cherry and Harris 1982, 295.

43 Ribeiro 1995, 133–80; Higonnet 2024.

FASHION AND PAINTING INTERWOVEN IN GAINSBOROUGH'S PORTRAITS

KARI RAYNER

IN EIGHTEENTH-CENTURY BRITAIN, the intersections of the industries of fashion and painting—through common materials, manufacture, and trade—informed the evolution of Gainsborough's approach to and production of portraits. The meticulous rendering of fabrics and personal accoutrements was an essential element in the ever-growing demand for portraits, and the job of specialist drapery painters became increasingly profitable.[1] For Gainsborough, who typically painted drapery himself rather than relegate the task to apprentices or assistants, portraits were an opportunity to demonstrate his virtuosity in capturing the textures and sheens of different fabrics.[2] He developed a dynamic shorthand, exploiting the properties of his painting materials and simplifying forms in a way that enabled him to swiftly and economically capture the illusion of clothing's visual qualities. Exceptional even among his contemporaries, Gainsborough's nimbleness when it came to engaging with fashion contributed to his rise as one of the leading portraitists of the time.

The arts in Britain were an evolving concept, especially with the foundation of the Royal Academy of Arts in 1768 and the beginnings of a "British school" of artists. Painting and sculpture were regarded as industries of arguably equal status to textile production and other processes related to fashion.[3] The profession of "colormen"—specialist vendors of artists' materials—was well established by Gainsborough's lifetime; their precursors were grocers and apothecaries, reflecting the ubiquity and versatility of materials that could serve medicinal, cosmetic, and aesthetic purposes. The plant resin mastic, for example, could be used as a treatment for stomach ulcers and indigestion, as a binder for cosmetics, and as a varnish for paintings. By the mid- to late seventeenth century, artists' suppliers had largely assumed the time-intensive and laborious preparatory processes for

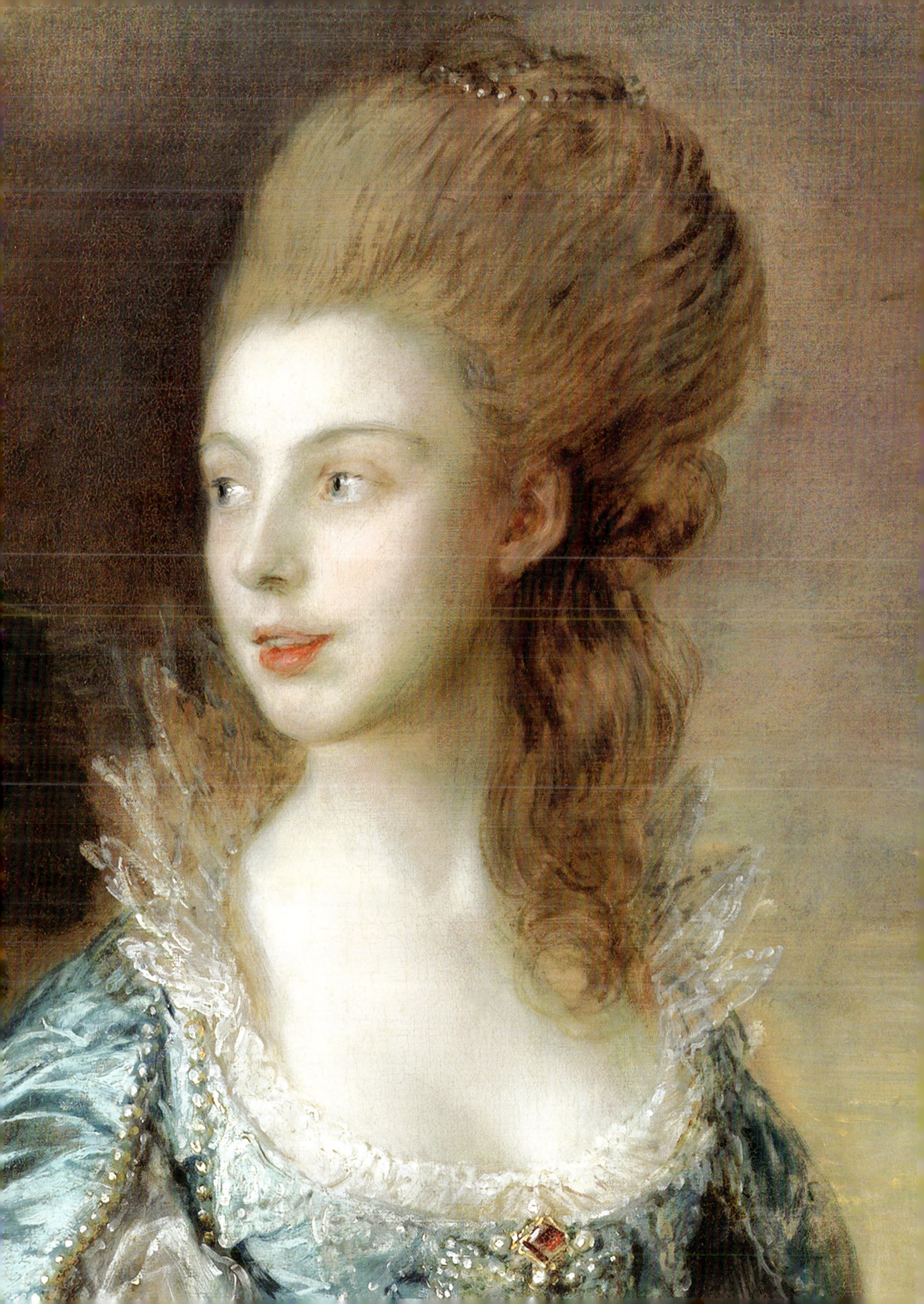

painting, including grinding pigments and priming canvases, effectively liberating artists from this labor; however, the permeability between industries remained.

Annual volumes of the journal *Transactions of the Society, Instituted at London, for the Encouragement of Arts, Manufactures, and Commerce* attest to the complex relationship between the industries of fashion and art.[4] *Transactions* celebrated achievements and offered "premiums" (medals or monetary rewards) for innovation in classes nominally under the jurisdiction of separate committees, including agriculture, chemistry, trade, manufacture, "Mechanicks," and the "Polite Arts" (associated with painting, sculpture, and drawing, as well as more niche types of production).[5] Although ostensibly separated into different categories, there were myriad connections. The inaugural issue of *Transactions* (1783) lauded advancements relating to colorants used for dyeing fabrics and for painting, primarily motivated by a nationalist agenda and the high cost of importing foreign materials. For instance, the agriculture section commended improvements in the national production of madder, used for dyeing fabrics and cosmetics and as a red pigment for the visual arts.[6] Meanwhile, premiums offered in the class of chemistry were said to have resulted in the identification of a substitute for verdigris and the discovery of a cobalt mine of benefit to the production of smalt.[7] Both verdigris and smalt were pigments for painting and had alternative uses, the former for dyeing fabric black and the latter for washing linen.[8] Distinctions in terminology relate to the different uses and properties of colorants: dyes are soluble in liquids such as water and capable of permeating materials like fabric, whereas pigments must be bound in a medium such as oil and applied to a substrate, such as a canvas.

Giving the "Polite Arts" equal footing as other, more "industrial" enterprises in the *Transactions* reflects the perceived national importance of the arts. In fact, considerable expense was devoted to the arts: The cumulative rewards given in this category in 1783 totaled approximately £8,595, a greater amount than was disbursed for any other category that year.[9] The agenda of promoting the arts is expounded upon in the section of the *Transactions* titled "Observations on the Effects of Rewards Bestowed in the Class of Polite Arts," which also associates advancements in the arts with those of fashion.[10]

Developments in linen production during the Industrial Revolution had implications for fashion and painting. In clothing, linen played a role in underclothes and as linings for outerwear, its stiff quality exploited to create stylish silhouettes.[11] Until the late eighteenth and early nineteenth centuries, linen was also the primary type of fiber used for canvas for easel painting. Domestic industries established in Ireland and Scotland during the eighteenth century increased availability and reduced the cost of linen fabrics in Britain; hitherto, raw flax had typically been imported from the Baltic region, whereas woven linens were primarily sourced from nations on the Continent, particularly France and Holland.[12] Innovations in textile production also impacted these industries: John Kay's 1733 patent of the flying shuttle, for example, sped up the weaving process (reducing the need for human labor to the extent that in 1753 Kay's home was attacked by protesting workers) and increased the maximum loom width.[13] The advent of new colorants was similarly impactful for both sectors, particularly the invention of Prussian blue, which seems to have been available in England by 1724, or even earlier.[14]

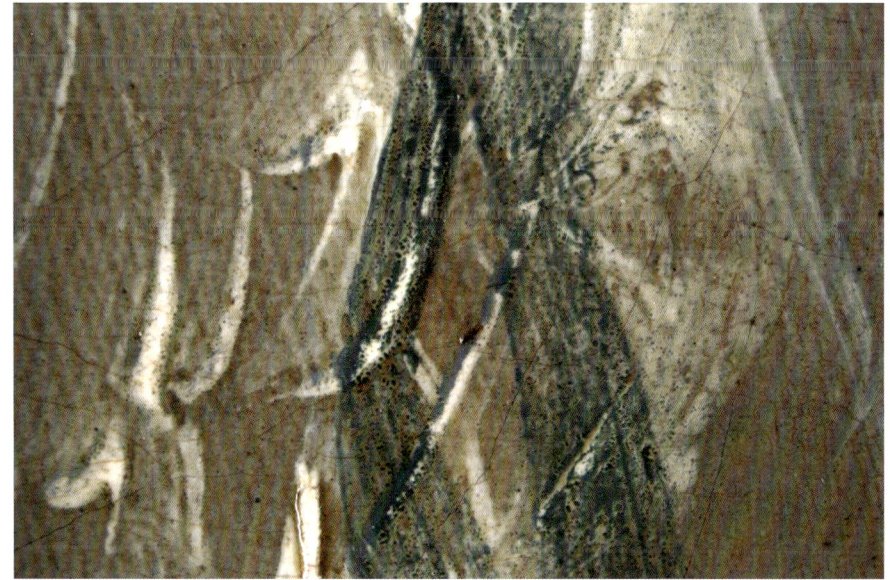

FIG. 10

Microscopic detail of suspected microcissing in the dark-blue paint film in *Sarah Hodges, Later Lady Innes* (cat. 4)

These developments in textiles and colorants permeated the niche market of materials available to artists, and artists' suppliers may have marketed new or improved materials as a business strategy. This is relevant for Gainsborough, who seems to have relied heavily on commercially available pre-prepared artists' materials. Surviving documentation links him with London-based colormen Charles Sandys, John Middleton, and "Scott in the Strand," among others.[15] Unlike many of his contemporaries, Gainsborough primarily had one apprentice but is not known to have employed a cadre of students and workshop assistants who could have stretched and primed canvases or prepared paints.[16] It thus would have been more expedient to purchase such materials ready-to-use.

Sourcing Canvas and Paints

A survey of Gainsborough's oeuvre shows that he often painted on standard-size canvases, most commonly three-quarters, half-lengths, and whole-lengths for portraits (30 x 25 in., 50 x 40 in., and 94 x 58 in., respectively).[17] Slight variations among his surviving paintings are likely due in part to his practice of painting with the canvas loose or to later interventions such as lining and re-stretching.[18] In other instances, he cut down canvases or added strips to achieve customized dimensions. The unusual proportions of *Sarah Hodges, Later Lady Innes*, for example, has led to the hypothesis that the portrait was painted for a specific location (cat. 4).[19] While many of his early works were painted on standard-size canvases, the non-standard dimensions of two early family portraits, *Mr. and Mrs. Andrews* (cat. 2) and *The Gravenor Family* (cat. 3), may have been related to the genre of conversation pieces or the works' landscape orientation.

Gainsborough's choice of canvas weight and weave seems to have been relatively consistent throughout his career. Twill, a fabric weave characterized visually by a diagonal pattern, resulting from the weft crossing two or more warp threads, became popular with some artists later in the eighteenth century, including Joshua Reynolds and George Romney. However, Gainsborough seems to have resisted this trend and often used fine- to medium-weight (10–18 threads/centimeter) plain-weave canvas.[20] The layer structure of the priming typically found on Gainsborough's canvases is likewise generally consistent with that found on many paintings by other artists from the period.[21]

Circumstantial evidence suggests that, even when he was operating from Sudbury and Ipswich, Gainsborough may have obtained paints pre-prepared by colormen. When viewed under a microscope, *Sarah Hodges, Later Lady Innes* exhibits a phenomenon called "microcissing" that was possibly linked to commercial preparation (fig. 10). At high magnification, much of the paint surface, particularly in the darker passages, appears as if it has not formed a cohesive film and instead separated into tiny islands. This drying defect is hypothesized to have formed as the result of an improperly high proportion of lead-based siccative (a substance that promotes drying) in the paint medium.[22] Since it is commonly found in paintings by a certain community of British artists during a narrow period in the early eighteenth century (so much so that the phenomenon has later been characterized as an "epidemic"), experts have posited that it may have been linked to a recipe prepared and sold by a London-based supplier.[23]

Colors Versus Colorants

Given the overlaps between textile dyes and artists' materials, it is tempting to think that a painter might choose to use the very material that would color the physical object. There would be a certain poetic parity if such were the case. However, the properties of some colorants make them better suited to oil painting than textile dyeing and vice versa. Therefore, as with most artists, Gainsborough's choice of pigments and colorants seems to have been driven largely by a combination of practical concerns and intended aesthetic effects (in contrast with Joshua Reynolds, who was seemingly less concerned with practicality and the longevity of his materials in his relentless pursuit of techniques of the "great masters").[24]

Consideration of Gainsborough's reds, yellows, and blues reveals ways in which his painting colors overlap with fashion's industries. Looking at Gainsborough's reds, anecdotal and analytical evidence suggests that he employed the traditional artists' pigments vermilion and red iron earths, as well as dye-based red lakes.[25] In order for dyes to be used as pigments, a material called a mordant must be added. This causes the dye to precipitate out of a liquid solution as a solid that can then be suspended in an oil medium for painting. Gainsborough used two colorants that were employed for both painting and dyeing fabric: cochineal, derived from insects, and madder, a plant-based dye.[26] The presence of red lakes has been blamed for a faded or washed-out look in some of his sitters' complexions. While in many cases this supposition is not backed by evidence, at least one painting is confirmed to have suffered from dramatic color shifts. The patchy appearance of the red coat in *Dr. Ralph Schomberg* was determined to be due to the uneven fading of a red lake made from imported cochineal (fig. 11).[27]

Of the range of yellow-hued pigments that Gainsborough used (including yellow lakes, yellow ochre, Naples yellow, orpiment, and raw sienna), yellow lakes are dye-based and have significant overlaps with the textile industry.[28] "Egg-yellow" was a popular shade for women's gowns that could be derived from several types of plants, including quercitron and turmeric.[29] Quercitron could similarly be used to manufacture a yellow lake pigment for painting. In at least one instance, Gainsborough is thought to have employed a pigment based on another dye manufactured from the plant buckthorn, also called "brown pink."[30] The usage of unspecified yellow lakes has been detected in several other paintings, all dated to the 1770s.[31] Alas, every one of these yellow, dye-based colorants is fugitive, fading upon light exposure in both textiles and paintings. Although Gainsborough's paint layering was generally economical, his

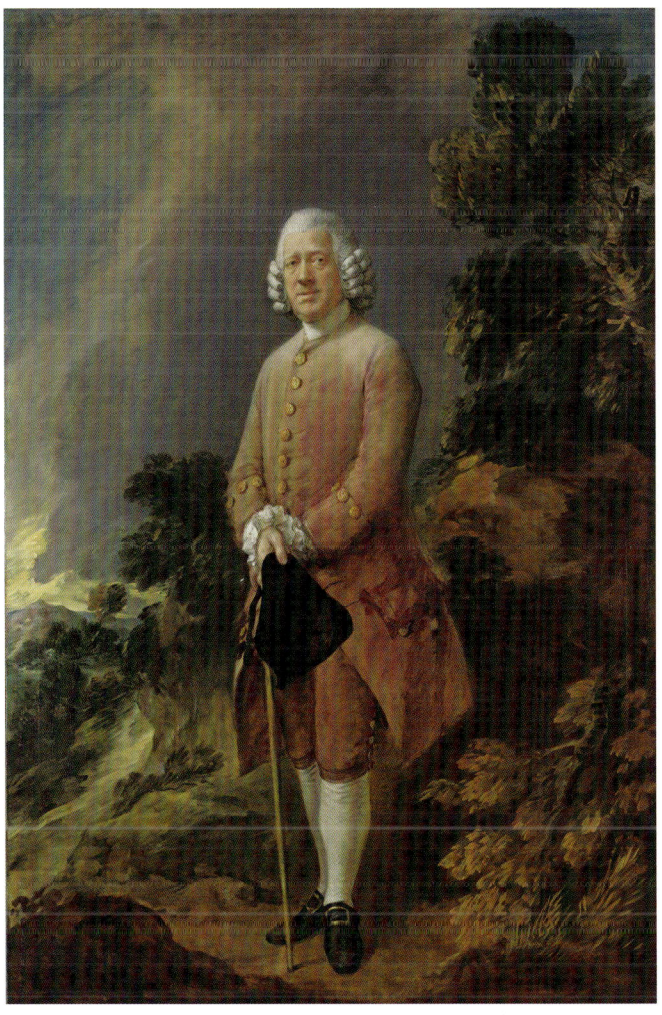

pigment mixtures could be quite complex. According to analytical results reported by Rica Jones and Martin Postle, a "shade of green in foliage, for example, may contain black, terre verte, Prussian blue, yellow, red, or brown ochres, Naples yellow, yellow lakes, and occasionally orpiment."[32] It is perhaps for this reason that the visual impact of faded yellow lakes is not obvious in Gainsborough's paintings, as it may typically have been a minor component or may have been added for subtle effect, now lost.

Due in part to the fame of *The Blue Boy* (fig. 43), Gainsborough is closely associated with blue. Of all the colors available at the time, blue was perhaps the most variable and versatile when it came to fashion: By 1765, there were twenty-four commercially identifiable shades of blue.[33] The two most prominent blue colorants used as dyes were indigo and Prussian blue.[34] However, while indigo is lightfast as a dye, in oil paintings it has a tendency to fade or discolor because of the chemical breakdown of the component indigotin. In two letters from about 1770, Gainsborough expressed appreciation for indigo he acquired from his friend William Jackson.[35] While these communications suggest that Gainsborough painted with this pigment, it is difficult to analytically confirm its presence in his works.[36] He may have used it primarily in watercolor form on a paper substrate, implied by his comment to Jackson: "To say the truth of your Indigo, 'tis delightful, so look sharp for some more (& I'll send you a drawing)."[37] It is somewhat more straightforward to confirm analytically the presence of Prussian blue; it seems that Gainsborough and his contemporaries used this pigment ubiquitously. Prussian blue is generally stable, but in the early years after its invention, it was apparently not always lightfast or could become greenish. Fading is said to have occurred in several of Gainsborough's paintings, including *Mr. and Mrs. Andrews*.[38] Other blue pigments traditionally used for painting have occasionally been identified in some of Gainsborough's works, including ultramarine and azurite, as well as azurite's synthetic equivalent, blue verditer.[39] Gainsborough also often used an optical blue, such as for skies, consisting of a mixture of charcoal and white that appears bluish in tonality without incorporating a truly blue colorant.[40]

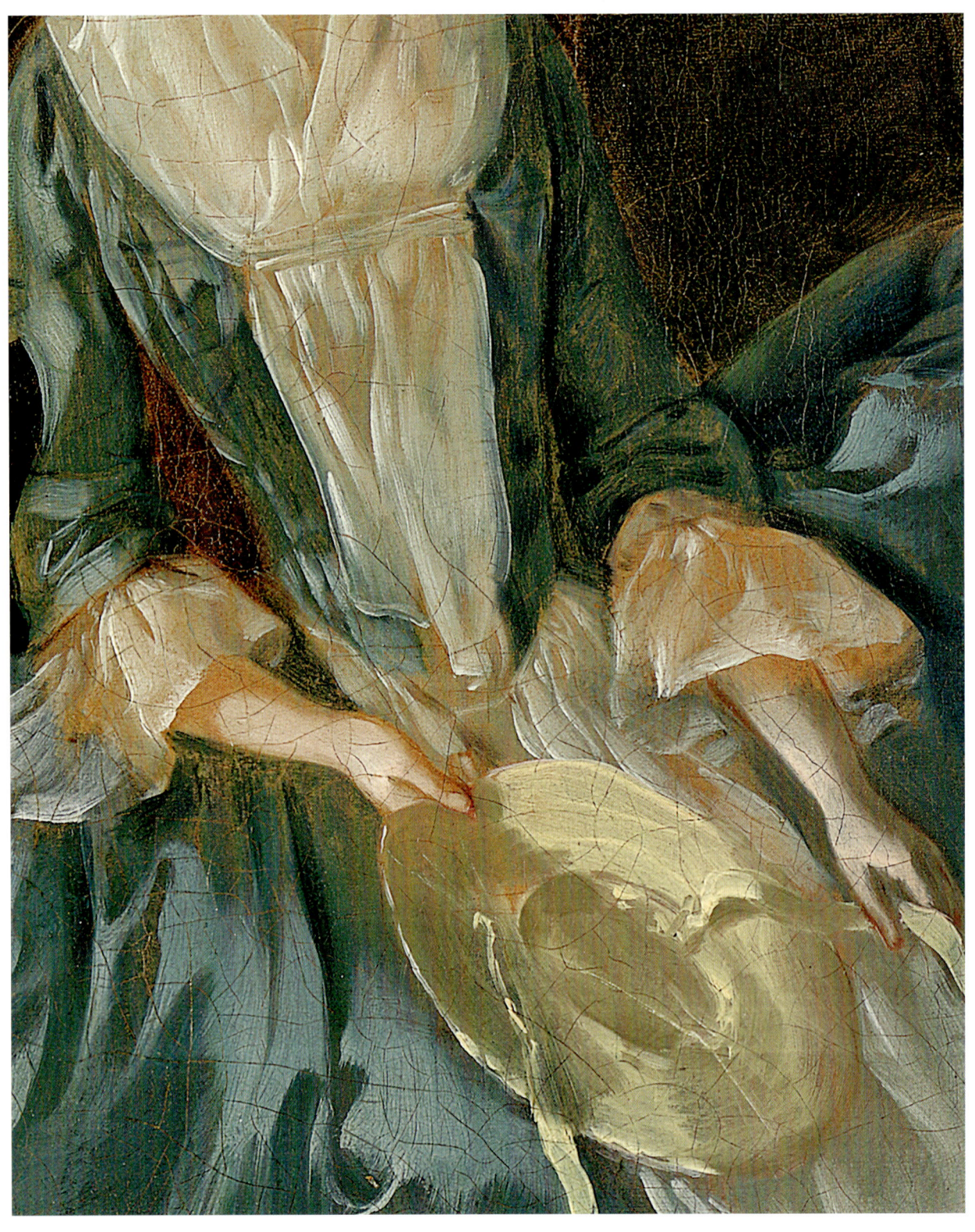

FIG. 12
Detail of *The Gravenor Family* (cat. 3)

Technical Evolution

The supports and pigments available to Gainsborough and his material choices impacted the appearance of his paintings, both when freshly completed and as they aged. However, while he seemed to prefer certain materials and use them regularly over the course of his career, his painting technique evolved substantially, particularly when it came to depicting his sitters and the materiality of fashion. By the time Gainsborough was established with a flourishing business in Bath, he had also learned to adapt his technique and level of finish, sensitively responding to situational cues and to his sitters' desires.

Gainsborough's early works show clear influences of his first masters, Hubert-François Gravelot and Francis Hayman. Specifically, the use of artists' mannequins had a significant impact on the visual qualities of his early conversation pieces. Also called "lay figures," these posable dolls of various sizes were precursors of the fashion or display mannequin.[41] Gainsborough owned at least two.[42] It has been suggested that he used lay figures as stand-ins for his 1750 painting *Heneage Lloyd and His Sister, Lucy* (Fitzwilliam Museum, Cambridge).[43] An overreliance on mannequins could, however, result in shortcomings that are regrettably conspicuous in this work. The figures are stiff and odd in scale compared to the landscape surrounding them. Contemporary discussion recognized these pitfalls: Joshua Reynolds cautioned that "any visible evidence of the mannequin would cause the painting to smack of the mere 'mechanic'" and warned that its use may result in "overly fussy handling of the drapery."[44]

Yet, even in Gainsborough's early conversation pieces, despite the stilted figures and the overt influence of his teachers, the emergence of his distinctive and innovative painting technique in the rendering of fabrics is apparent. Mrs. Gravenor's costume in *The Gravenor Family*, from about 1754, demonstrates this most clearly (fig. 12). The choice to prime the canvas with salmon pink—a relatively unusual color in British painting of this period but used by Gainsborough since at least 1748—is exploited to great advantage. The artist allowed this hue to show through in Mrs. Gravenor's bodice and lace cuffs, an efficient technique to effectively convey the translucency of the fabric by evoking the color of her skin. The sleeves themselves, like the rest of her dress, are similarly simple in terms of the paint layering and the limited range of values employed, with visible brushstrokes. This is particularly apparent in the sinuous, light-blue highlight that snakes along the hem of her skirt.

Gainsborough had a reputation for the swift execution of paintings. Later in his career, lay figures, in combination with a stock of costumes and props, provided a valuable means to reduce the time needed for patrons to sit for their portraits.[45] In most of his mature works, he avoided the telltale associations with mannequins; this may be due in large part to his increasingly virtuosic paint handling, both in his depiction of drapery and in his skill at capturing his sitters' likenesses. Although some critics derided Gainsborough's painting with terms such as "rough," "coarse," or "hatched," other contemporaries and modern scholars have appreciated its effect on the rendering of facial features.[46] Indeed, Gainsborough himself did not object to his paintings being characterized by "roughness of the surface."[47] The writer of Gainsborough's obituary in the *London Chronicle* celebrated the overall effect of this technique, noting "the extraordinary talent that had enabled the artist to give not merely the map of the face, but the character, the soul of the original . . . he shows the face in more points of view than one, and by that means it strikes every one [*sic*] who has once seen the original with being a resemblance."[48]

Painting Faces and Fabrics

The idealized face during this period was, as it is today, a construct as subject to the vagaries of fashion as clothing. Powdered wigs were ubiquitous, and cosmetics were heavily employed by the upper echelons of society. Contemporary treatises on beauty contain detailed recipes for cosmetics that reveal clear overlaps with painting materials, many of them toxic.[49] For instance, *The Art of Beauty, Or, A Companion for the Toilet*, published in 1760, includes lead white, mastic, and gum arabic among the ingredients of "a white face paint."[50] Lips and cheeks, meanwhile, were heightened with rouge made typically from cochineal or another type of dye, to achieve the blushing "English Rose" complexion.[51] Although the red mineral pigment cinnabar (and its synthetic counterpart, vermilion) was commonly employed in painting, its use as a rouge was cautioned for its association with symptoms of mercury poisoning.[52]

Portrait painters such as Gainsborough were tasked with depicting these cosmetic fashions in a way that was flattering but perhaps not always subtle. Heightened facial features were all the rage, and the strategic painter could use this to his advantage. As writer and critic George Cumberland noted, "having discovered that the highest coloured pictures are those which attract publick notice most . . . [the portrait painter] alters his style, or at least paints in that manner for the Exhibition," resulting in the "profusion of rosy cheeks, cherry lips, and black eye-brows, which thrust themselves on our notice the moment we enter a modern exhibition room."[53] With their crimson lips, subtly blushing cheeks, and prominent eyebrows, the sitters in Gainsborough's *Mrs. Sarah Siddons* (p. 13) and *Grace Dalrymple Elliot* (cat. 21) are notable exemplars of the perfectly made-up face.

Gainsborough's depiction of fabrics and other fashion elements could often be considered simplified and loosely rendered to the point of abstraction. His mature technique is characterized by economy, and he played with the viscosity of his paints to achieve different visual effects. His method of leaving underlying outlines partially visible to define forms and his efficient use of the ground color as a midtone are hallmarks of his drapery painting, exemplified in works like *Grace Dalrymple Elliott* (cat. 21 and fig. 13). Here, he left the torso in reserve and allowed much of the pinkish-beige ground to show through subsequent paint layers, serving as a midtone and suggesting the flesh beneath. The subtle pattern of the gauzy, blue-striped garment is convincingly conveyed with layers of translucent blues, browns, and yellows. Sparse, translucent strokes of red and pink paint suggest the form of the bow at the sitter's chest, with thin brown outlines indicating shadows. The rosette fasteners are equally minimal and abstract: They are composed of circles of light-gray and white defined by curling strokes of dark brown. The sitter's bodice is topped with a light edging of lace indicated solely by hasty squiggles of white and light gray paint. Faint, diagonal strokes of paint at the sitter's shoulders and neck, more apparent in the infrared reflectogram than to the naked eye, suggest that a thin veil covers her décolletage (fig. 14). Gainsborough varied the viscosity of his paint to achieve different effects: The fluidity of his application is particularly apparent in the sitter's earrings and in the yellow stripes down her sleeves, the paint pooling and dripping because of its liquidity.

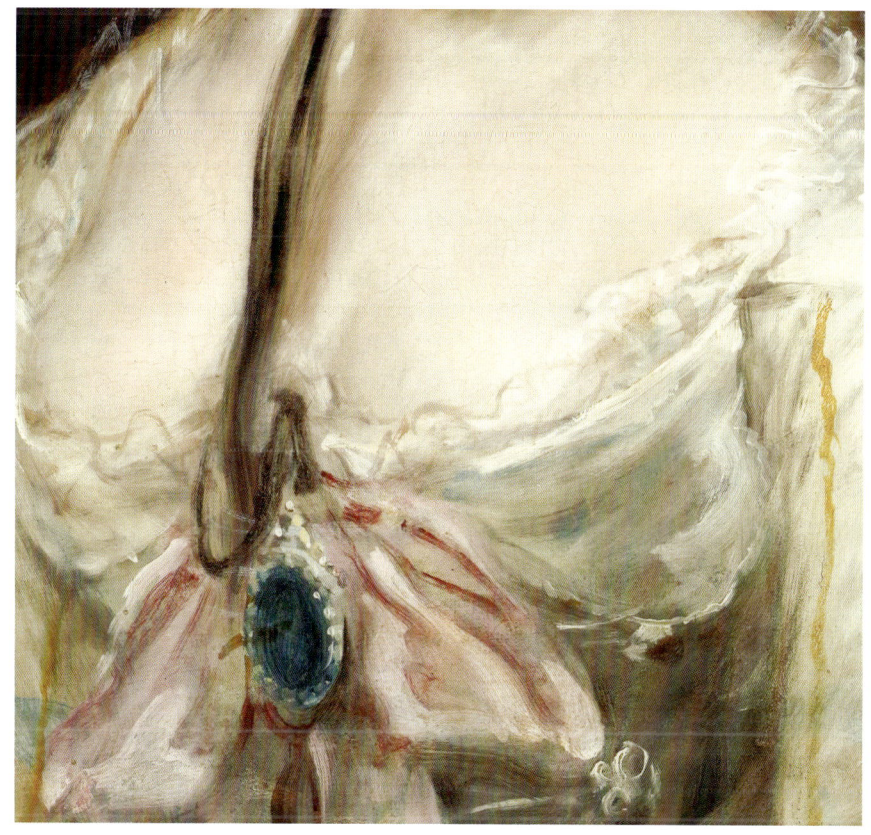

FIG. 13
Detail of
Grace Dalrymple Elliott
(cat. 21)

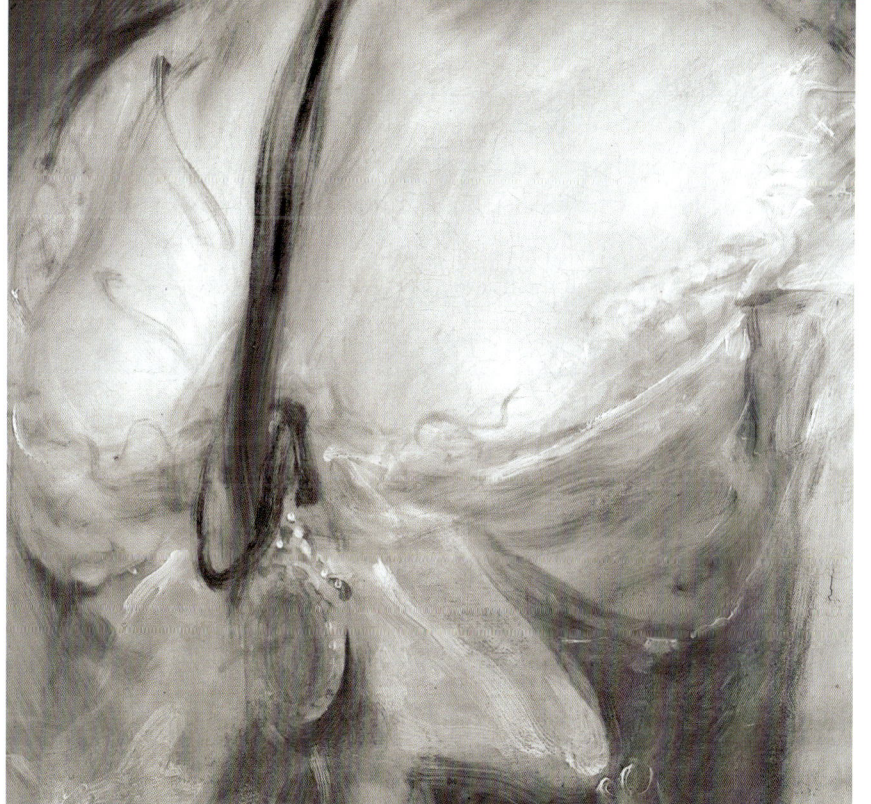

FIG. 14
Infrared reflectogram
of detail of dress in
Grace Dalrymple Elliott
(cat. 21)

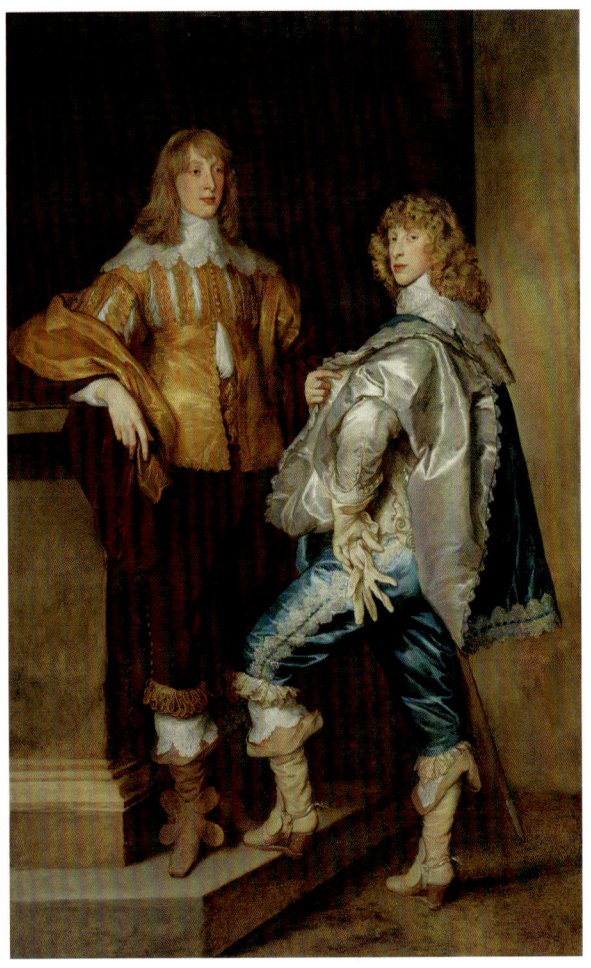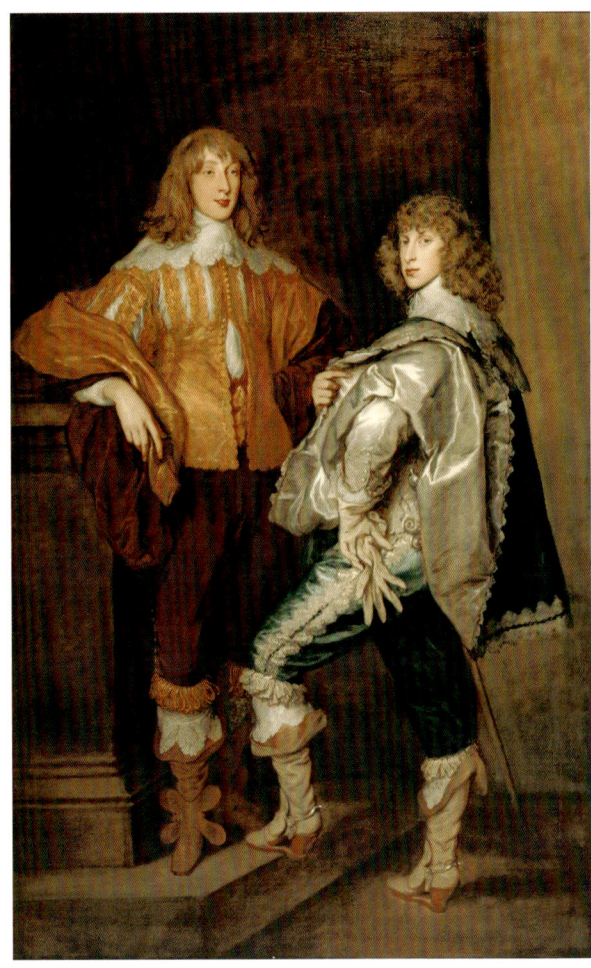

Lessons from the Past

How did Gainsborough's rendering of fabrics evolve so spectacularly between his early conversation pieces and his later works? Gainsborough's family connections to cloth and clothing industries brought him close to the materiality of fashion, and some have speculated that his study of the great art collections in England catalyzed a revolution in his painting technique.[54] Both his collecting habits and copies after Old Master paintings speak to his engagement with his predecessors: His personal collection upon his death included portraits by Anthony van Dyck, Peter Lely, Cornelius Janssen, Peter Paul Rubens, Diego Velázquez, and Bartolomé Esteban Murillo.[55] Gainsborough's copies appeared to fulfill different functions, and although they signify a considerable investment of time and materials, he likely kept them in his studio as references.[56] He must have had strong feelings regarding the efficacy and instructive potential of such copies, as both he and his apprentice, Gainsborough Dupont, executed replicas after Van Dyck's *Pembroke Family*.

Gainsborough's production of three copies (one full-length and two head studies) after Van Dyck's *Lord John Stuart and His Brother, Lord Bernard Stuart* (fig. 15) warrants particular consideration for insights into what he achieved through the act of copying.[57] Arguably, the

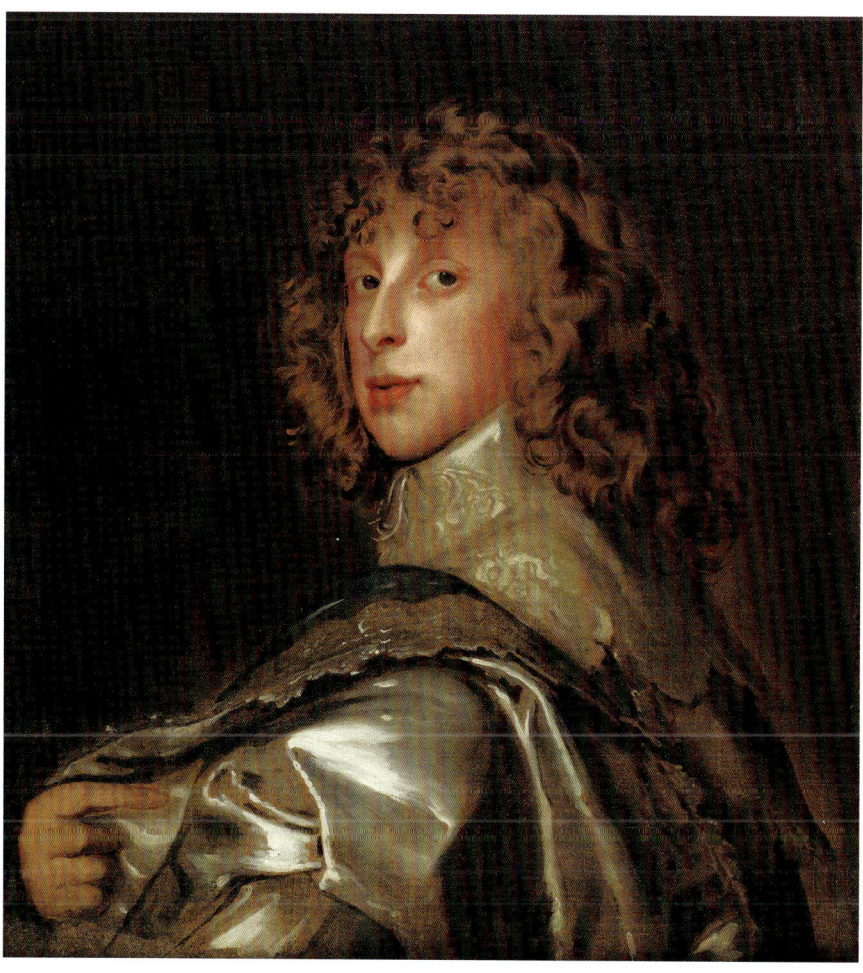

costumes worn by the brothers in Van Dyck's painting provided the impetus to copy: Van Dyck masterfully conveyed their varied sheens and textures and the translucency and intricacy of the lace detailing, while employing a rich, complementary palette.[58] Comparison of the full-scale copy (fig. 16) and the Gainsborough's House version (fig. 17) with Van Dyck's original yields insights into Gainsborough's working process and perhaps his intentions in creating these copies.[59] He did not create precise replicas but instead explored different coloristic effects in each painting.[60] The result is a radically different effect and overall coloration in Gainsborough's versions, which have a warmer tonality overall. While the lace collar in the full-scale version incorporates tinges of yellow and blue to modulate the white swirls, as does the Van Dyck, the palette seems to be pared down in the version that focuses on *Lord Bernard Stuart*, and the work appears less finished. Gainsborough improvised the design of the collar in each version, while remaining convincing and conveying a sense of spontaneity. These copies evidence Gainsborough's studied attempts to imbue his depictions of drapery with the appearance of effortless simplicity and to increase his speed of execution.

Fashion Trends

One of Gainsborough's distinguishing features as a portraitist was his inclination to portray up-to-the-moment fashions, in stark contrast to the exhortations of Joshua Reynolds in his discourses.[61] Anecdotal evidence suggests that Gainsborough was asked to portray specific costumes and that he was at times called upon to adjust or amend his work. As early as 1760, a series of letters by George Lucy document changes that he specified while he was sitting for Gainsborough. On April 5, Lucy complained about the portrait Gainsborough had begun, bemoaning that "unless he alters it much for the better, it will scarcely deserve the carriage, I think to have the dress altered as well as the face."[62] Following his next sitting with the artist, on April 12, Lucy noted that "the dress is to be entirely altered, a blue cloth coat with a little gold embroidery, which the painter thinks will give a little more life, and make it look much better."[63] Some of Gainsborough's letters specify revisions to other portraits. One such letter implies that a 1765 portrait of Lord Darnley's ward, Theodosia Magill, was returned to the artist for amendments.[64] Other letters from 1767 indicate that the Duchess of Marlborough at Woburn wished for a fur-lined mantle to be added to her portrait, which Hugh Belsey investigated and did, in fact, deem to have been an addition.[65]

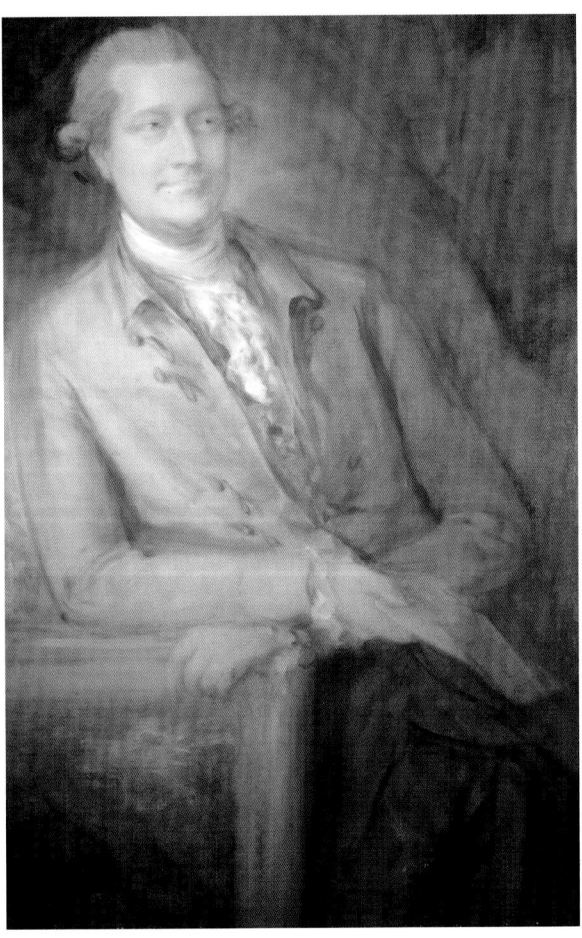 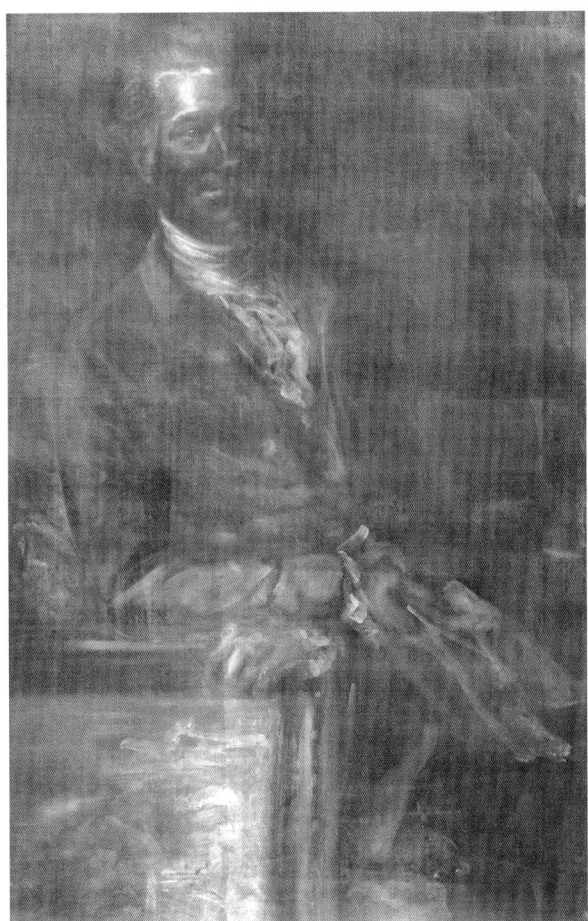

Perhaps the most famous and extensive example of revision is that of the double portrait *Elizabeth and Mary Linley*, dated 1772/85 (Dulwich Picture Gallery, London). Gainsborough modified the painting significantly, reworking Mary's likeness and modifying both women's outfits and demeanors to reflect changes in fashion in the 1780s.[66] Around the same time, between 1785 and 1787, Gainsborough also altered a full-length portrait of Elizabeth Sheridan (cat. 23), painting over his initial presentation of her as a shepherdess complete with bonnet, basket of flowers, and shepherd's crook, a depiction that received pointed criticism.[67] He subsequently modified her garments and features to reflect her elevated social station.[68]

Another later work that seems to have undergone revision, whether or not at the request of the sitter, is a portrait of James Christie (cat. 17). Christie was clearly satisfied with the final image as it hung for many years at his auction house in London. It was purported to have captured his exact likeness.[69] However, at least one reviewer of the Royal Academy exhibition that year found it lacking: "After painting an excellent face, he joins a very bad body to it. There is not that strength of execution, which gives life and motion to a figure. The brush is laid on, as it were, with a trembling hand, and it produces an unharmonious effect."[70]

FIG. 18
Infrared reflectogram
of Christie's torso in
James Christie (cat. 17)

FIG. 19
X-radiograph of the
sitter's torso, with stretcher
bars digitally reduced,
in *James Christie* (cat. 17)

FIG. 20
Infrared reflectogram
of detail of shoe bridging
the canvas seam in
The Hon. Frances Duncombe (cat. 14)

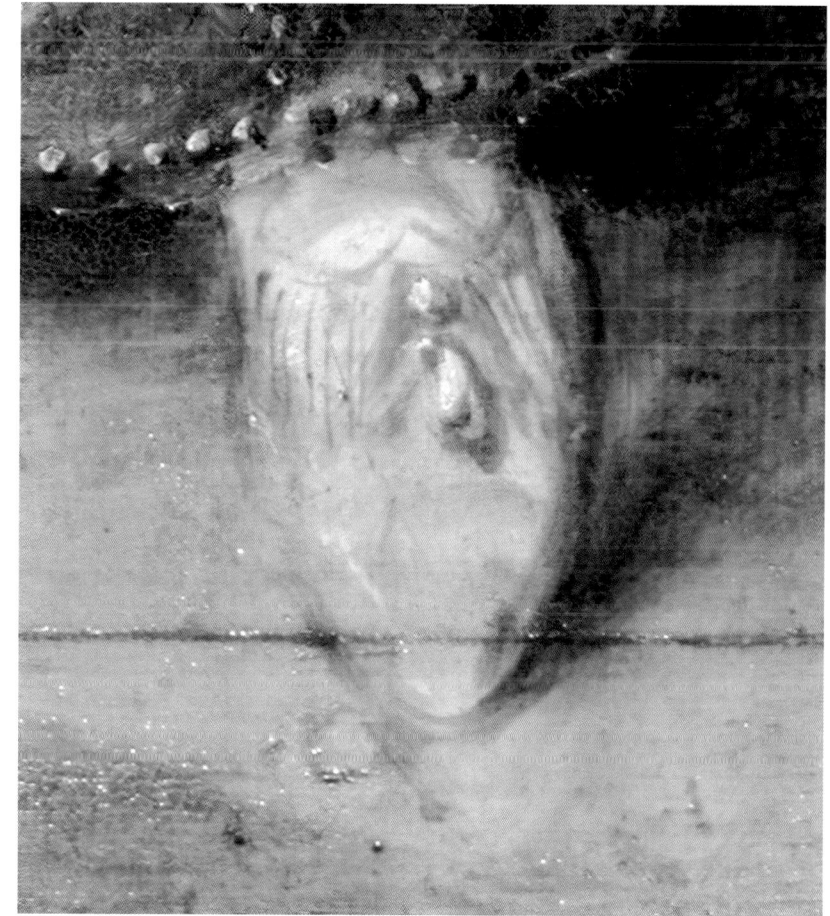

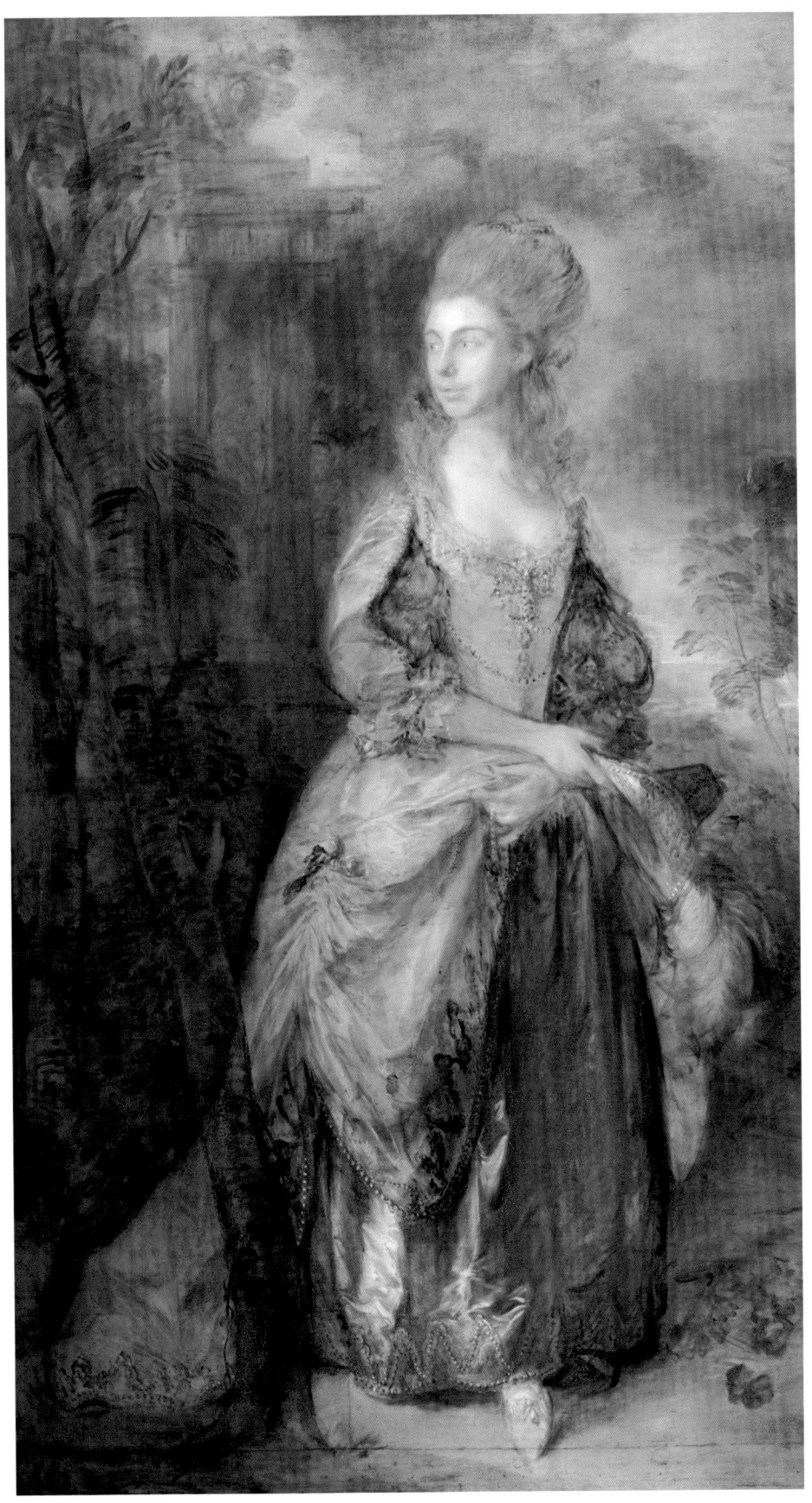

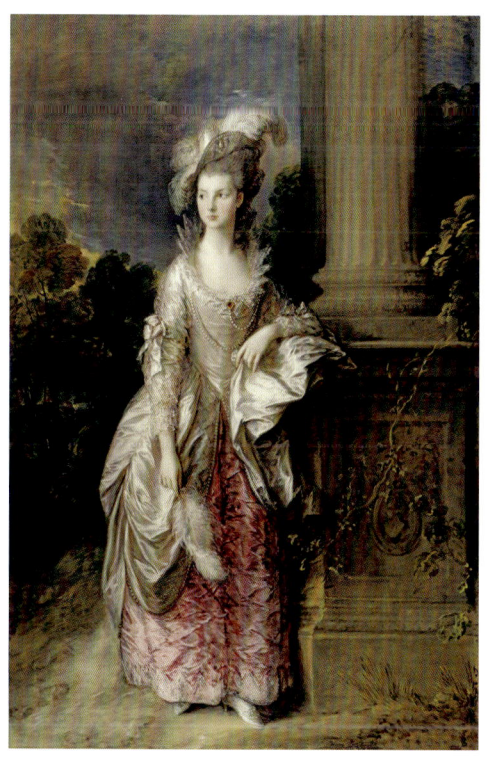

Technical imaging shows that Gainsborough sought ways to make Christie's pose more active and dramatic, and that his revisions resulted in some visual discordance. Infrared reflectography reveals that Christie's proper right arm was shifted left and down to increase the angle of his torso, while his hips were shifted in the opposite direction, to the right edge of the picture (fig. 18). These changes are somewhat visible even on the surface of the picture. The pendant seals swinging from his waist suggest that Gainsborough captured a moment when Christie is in motion, casually leaning against the frame. Furthermore, an X-radiograph reveals that the angle of the paper Christie holds was revised at least once and that he initially had three round buttons spaced along his jacket, later replaced by button-and-loop closures (fig. 19). The resulting effect of these revisions is that the proper right arm and the corresponding side of Christie's chest are more solid and opaque than the proper left half of the costume—even more so than would be warranted by the left side being in shadow. These adjustments, calculated to achieve a more dynamic composition, may have created the "unharmonious effect" derided by the reviewer.

Another painting that Gainsborough seems to have reworked, possibly dramatically, is *The Hon. Frances Duncombe* (cat. 14). The support was lengthened with the addition to the bottom edge of a horizontal strip of canvas several inches wide. This appears to constitute an original expansion, perhaps added to make room for the satin shoe peeking from beneath the sitter's robe (fig. 20).

Distinct linear markings visible in the infrared reflectogram in the lower left corner of the painting, seemingly drawn in a dry medium such as black chalk, raise further questions about the original composition (fig. 21). These marks form a rectangle overlapping the location of the tree in the foreground, possibly suggesting the presence of some sort of plinth. Other faint vertical marks and possible reserves along the left side and in the architectural elements at upper left suggest further modifications. It is possible that these markings indicate a substantial compositional change, such as the removal of an architectural feature in the foreground; the column flanking the figure in *The Hon. Mrs. Graham* (fig. 22), exhibited at the Royal Academy in 1777 and similar in other

FIG. 21

Infrared reflectogram
detail showing underdrawing
and compositional changes in
The Hon. Frances Duncombe (cat. 14)

FIG. 22

Thomas Gainsborough,
The Hon. Mrs. Graham, 1775–77
Oil on canvas
93⅝6 x 60⅝ in. (237 x 154 cm)
National Galleries of Scotland, Edinburgh (NG 332)

aspects to *Frances Duncombe*, comes to mind. Dark marks visible through infrared reflectography at Frances Duncombe's proper right elbow tantalizingly hint that perhaps she initially rested her arm on the same sort of structure, mirroring the pose of Mrs. Graham.

If such a major change did indeed take place, other smaller pentimenti in this area of the painting speak to Gainsborough's reassessment of and subsequent adjustments to the sitter's dress in a way that is both agile and convincing. The trailing train of the skirt seems likely to have been a later addition. The infrared reflectogram also shows that the gathered bustle of the skirt was lowered, necessitating a laborious reworking of the folds that is visible in the X-radiograph. The folly and cluster of trees along the right edge cleverly overlap the perhaps earlier structure, with the late addition of the large tree in the foreground over the top of the dress crucially integrating the sitter into the landscape. Other changes speak to Gainsborough's willingness to make incremental modifications until he deemed the composition just right. Both hands seem to have been reworked, particularly the proper left hand. Initially clutching the strand of pearls, the hand in the final version is more relaxed, with the strand loosely draping from the fingers, pinky extended. The hemline of the dress and contours of the proper left sleeve were adjusted, and the design of the hat appears to have gone through several iterations.

Gainsborough's portraits demonstrate his interest in engaging with fashion in the most expansive, contemporary sense of the word and testify that his skill in depicting the materiality of fashion evolved and grew. Among the definitions of *fashion* in Johnson's *Dictionary* was the broad idea of the "form, make, [or] state of anything with regard to appearance" (see p. 17n.9). In this sense, Gainsborough was a product of his time and of the intersections of industries dedicated to manufacturing. He also was a singular artist who married the physical and the aesthetic in his engagements with fashion. The resulting transcendent portraits are a testament to his versatility as an artist, his intimate knowledge of his materials, his economical technique, and his willingness to innovate and improvise.

NOTES

I am sincerely grateful to Charlotte Hale, Conservator in Charge of the Paintings Conservation Department of the Metropolitan Museum of Art, for her support of this work. This essay is particularly indebted to the technical analysis carried out at the Met—by Silvia A. Centeno, Scientist; Conservators Derek Lintala and Dorothy Mahon; and Evan Read, Manager of Technical Documentation—of three paintings from The Frick Collection: *Sarah Hodges, Later Lady Innes*; *Grace Dalrymple Elliott*; and *The Hon. Frances Duncombe*. The utmost thanks are also due to the author's conservation and curatorial colleagues in Paintings Conservation and the Paintings Department at the J. Paul Getty Museum for supporting the technical analysis of *James Christie*.

1 Gainsborough himself notes this in one of his undated letters to William Jackson; Hayes 2001, 74.

2 It must be acknowledged that Gainsborough's nephew, Gainsborough Dupont, may have had more of a hand in painting draperies in some of Gainsborough's portraits than is commonly recognized, particularly later in his uncle's career; Rayner 2018a, 106–8.

3 For the purposes of this essay, "the arts" encompasses a range of visual arts including drawing, printmaking, painting, and sculpture, largely in alignment with what was represented at the Royal Academy of Arts. However, see note 5 below on the "Polite Arts."

4 Although the society's founding dates to 1754, its transactions were not formally documented until 1783.

5 *Transactions* 1783, 44–45. In the first volume, rewards were given in the "Polite Arts" for charts, maps, and surveys and improvements in crayon, watercolors, inks, and staining marble.

6 Ibid., 9.

7 Ibid., 14–15, 20–21.

8 Ibid., 14–15, 181.

9 Ibid., 62. This number stands in contrast to the approximate totals for Agriculture (£3281), Chemistry (£1391), Colonies & Trade (£2785), Manufactures (£2057), and "Mechanicks" (£2543).

10 Ibid., 48–49. The Society's investment in the arts is further underscored by its reporting of the commission of James Barry to paint a series entitled "The Progress of Human Knowledge and Culture" for the Great Room of the Society; ibid., 60–61.

11 Ibid., 48–49.

12 A. Reynolds in London 2023, 15; Evans 1985, 95, 103–4.

13 Porter 1990, 88.

14 Kirby 1993, 63.

15 Sloman 2002, 70; Whitley [1915] 2016, 277.

16 He formally apprenticed his nephew Gainsborough Dupont in 1772, having briefly worked with other trainees before. See also Whitley [1915] 2016, 35. He also occasionally used other assistants after returning to London; Sloman 2002, 71; Fulcher 1856a, 40.

17 Simon 2013. More than forty paintings by Gainsborough have been

surveyed by the author for physical characteristics, and dimensions of many others have been reviewed.

18 On Gainsborough's practice of painting with loose canvas, see Sloman 2002, 57. For more on standard sizes, see Simon 2013.

19 Belsey 2019, 1: 495.

20 Canvas weight was visually estimated for each of the paintings surveyed by the author (see note 13). A precise thread count was obtained for a subset of these paintings. No examples of a painting by Gainsborough on twill are known to this author.

21 There is somewhat conflicting evidence regarding whether Gainsborough primed his own canvases or purchased them pre-primed. Due to the unusual pink priming color and consistent cusping patterns present on some of Gainsborough's full-length canvases from his Bath period, Glanville (1988, 22) has postulated that Gainsborough primed these works himself. Sloman has further supported the idea that the artist generally prepared his own canvases, particularly larger ones, and that this would have given him freedom to stretch them as suited him; Sloman 2002, 62. While he may have primed his canvases himself under certain circumstances, the stratigraphy of the priming typically identified in samples from his paintings seems to conversely be characteristic of commercial preparation by an artist's colorman. See Rayner and Greenwald (unpublished), 25–30; Rayner 2019, 81–82; Rayner 2018b. Also suggested in Jones 1999, 48. This layer structure suggests that a colorman may have primed those particular works and that Gainsborough may have specified the coloration of the ground.

22 Jones and Townsend 2016, 174, 179.

23 Hypothetically, artists could have formulated their paints this way as well, but the abrupt lessening of the microcissing phenomenon around 1760 supports the idea that it was linked to the use of a proprietary product that perhaps fell out of favor or went out of production; Jones and Townsend 2016, 179–80.

24 "Reynolds's desire to be an independent and quickly successful society painter must have led him to worry less about the soundness or durability of his technique and more about his capacity to concoct the qualities and substance of paint that would encourage clients to bestow praise on his emulation of great masters"; Gent, Roy, and Morrison 2014, 12.

25 Kirby, Spring, and Higgitt 2007, 88; Whitley [1915] 2016, 277–78.

26 Cochineal has been detected through analysis in several of Gainsborough's works, whereas the presence of madder has been more circumstantially identified in *The Hon. Frances Duncombe* (cat. 14). Ultraviolet radiation induces a pinkish fluorescence possibly indicative of madder in the sitter's cheeks, her tear ducts, and in her upper lip; A. Reynolds in London 2023, 28. Notably, apothecary and chemist Robert Dossie remarked in his manual *The Handmaid to the Arts* in 1758 that the preparation process for turning raw cochineal into either pigment or dye was very similar; Dossie 1758, 54–55.

27 Bomford, Roy, and Saunders 1998, 51.

28 Most of these pigments are noted by a contemporary to have been used by Gainsborough; Whitley [1915] 2016, 277–78. Naples yellow and yellow ochre were identified in *Dr. Ralph Schomberg*; Bomford, Roy, and Saunders 1998, 49. Indian yellow was tentatively identified in *The Linley Sisters*; Glanville 1988, 25. Other technical and analytical reports agree with this list.

29 A. Reynolds in London 2023, 28.

30 "Brown pink" was identified in *Rev. John Chafy Playing a Violincello* (1750–52); Jones 1999, 51.

31 Yellow lake was reported in samples of *Pomeranian and Puppy*, (cat. 13); Green 1982, 25. Yellow lake(s) are inferred to be present in samples from *Dr. Ralph Schomberg* (1770); Bomford, Roy, and Saunders 1998, 49–51. *The Linley Sisters* (1772/85) is reported to contain yellow lakes; Glanville 1988, 20, 24.

32 London, Washington, and Boston 2002–3, 29.

33 Reynolds 2023, 26.

34 Lotut 2018.

35 On the first occasion, he wrote, "I am so pleased with both your Remarks, & your Indigo, that I know not which to admire most, or which to think most of immediate use" and, in a subsequent letter, "thanks for the Indigo—a little of it goes a great way"; Hayes 2001, 71, 73.

36 Specialized analytical techniques such as Raman spectroscopy or high-performance liquid chromatography on a paint or pigment sample are required for identification of indigo.

37 Hayes 2001, 71. Gainsborough speaks of using indigo on a paper support in another letter to Jackson (January 29, 1773); Hayes 2001, 111.

38 Kirby 1993, 64. See also Kirby and Saunders 2004, 73–99.

39 Recorded in an unpublished technical report by the author (2016), several ultramarine particles were found in dispersed pigment samples from *Landscape with Peasant and Donkeys* from Gainsborough's House, Sudbury. Verditer was found in *Dr. Ralph Schomberg*; Bomford, Roy, and Saunders

1998, 269. Ultramarine and blue verditer were found in early works by Gainsborough; Jones 2015.

40 London, Norwich, and Newcastle 1997, 8.

41 Munro 2014, 167–68.

42 Ibid., 20; Whitley [1915] 2016, 387; Whitley 1928, 1: 278.

43 Munro 2014, 20.

44 Ibid., 76.

45 Examples of reuse include using the same costume in *The Blue Boy*, *Edward Richard Gardiner*, *Portrait of an Unknown Boy*, and Tate's *Gainsborough Dupont*.

46 London, Washington, and Boston 2002–3, 18, 148.

47 Gainsborough wrote to William Mayhew on March 13, 1758: "You please me much by saying that no other fault is found in your picture than the roughness of the surface, for that part being of use in giving force to the effect at a proper distance, and what a judge of paintings knows an original from a copy by"; Hayes 2001, 10.

48 Solkin 2001, 104–5.

49 "The mask of artifice that created the fashionable face was extraordinarily elaborate and recipes for eighteenth-century beauty would appall a modern cosmetologist"; Gunn 1973, 110.

50 *Art of Beauty* 1760, 32.

51 Gunn 1973, 110, 115.

52 "Cinnabar is composed of brimstone and mercury. When it is reduced to a subtle powder, in a marble mortar, it acquires so lively and so high a color, that it is called vermillion. Some Ladies mix it with paint, wherewith they rub their cheeks which is very dangerous; for by using it frequently they may lose their teeth, acquire a stinking breath, and excite a copious salivation"; *Art of Beauty* 1760, 32–33.

53 Solkin 2001, 95.

54 London, Washington, and Boston 2002–3, 33.

55 Several notable copies after Van Dyck remained in Gainsborough's studio upon his death, including *The Pembroke Family* and *Lord John and Lord Bernard Stuart*; *Editorial* 1944, 108–10, Whitley [1915] 2016, 322. *Editorial* 1944, 108–10 notes that his posthumous collection contained twelve copies the artist made after Old Master paintings, although according to Waterhouse, at least twenty copies are known to have existed; Waterhouse 1958, 124–25. Whitley ([1915] 2016, 358) also describes several notable copies after Van Dyck remaining in Gainsborough's studio upon his death, including *The Pembroke Family* and *Lord John and Lord Bernard Stuart*. See also Mould 2006, 45–54.

56 Mandy 2016, 8.

57 The sole, full-scale copy resides in the Saint Louis Art Museum (cat. 6), while two smaller studies of *Lord Bernard Stuart* can be found in a private collection and in Gainsborough's House, Sudbury.

58 Mandy 2016, 13. Gainsborough's three copies date to the mid-1760s through the early 1770s.

59 Warm thanks to Melissa Gardner, Judy Mann, and Hannah Segrave of the Saint Louis Art Museum for providing high-resolution images of the painting in their collection for study purposes.

60 The ground color of the Gainsborough's House version is a light brown similar to that used by Van Dyck. In contrast, the full-scale version employs a pink ground, which, characteristically, along with the initial outlines and warm underlayers, he left exposed in many places, such as in Lord Bernard Stuart's gray costume and lace collar. Van Dyck, instead, had used a cool gray paint layer as a midtone in the jacket and collar; Mandy 2016, 14.

61 "However the mechanic and ornamental arts may sacrifice to fashion, she must be entirely excluded from the art of painting; the painter must never mistake this capricious changeling for the genuine offspring of nature, he must divest himself of all prejudices in favor of his age or country; he must disregard all local and temporary ornaments, and look only on those general habits that are everywhere and always the same. He addresses his works to the people of every country and every age"; Reynolds 1908, 52–53.

62 Sloman 1997, 327.

63 Sloman 1997, 327. Belsey suggests that the change was rather drastic, indicating that the sitter previously wore a red suit and that it was repainted blue; Belsey 2019, 2: 569.

64 Belsey 2014, 303.

65 Belsey 2014, 303.

66 Glanville 1988, 18.

67 Christensen and Luciano 2013, 240.

68 Ibid.

69 Whitley [1915] 2016, 135, 181–82.

70 London 1778, 4.

FASHION AND CLASS

"A CONDITION ABOVE THE VULGAR"

Be it known then, that the human Species are divided into two sorts of People, to wit, High *people and* Low *people.... High People signify no other than People of Fashion, and low People those of no Fashion. Now, this word* Fashion, *hath by long use lost its original Meaning, from which at present it gives us a very different Idea: for I am deceived, if by Persons of Fashion, we do not generally include a Conception of Birth and Accomplishments superior to the Herd of Mankind; whereas, in reality, nothing more was originally meant by a Person of Fashion, than a Person who drest himself in the Fashion of the Times.*

—Henry Fielding, 1742

FASHION TOUCHED ALL RANKS of Georgian society in Britain and its colonies, from the monarch dictating rules of court dress to harvesters, dyers, and weavers serving the supply chain. Across this spectrum, when one referred to people "of fashion"—or "fashionable" people—it was not simply about how people dressed. By 1742, the term "of fashion" had come to refer to a social condition "superior to the Herd of Mankind"; it carried an inflection synonymous with reputation, quality, and terms that have since shed, especially in North America, connections to class, such as "gentle" (which retains hints of class in forms like "gentleman" and "genteel") and "polite."[1] Keeping up

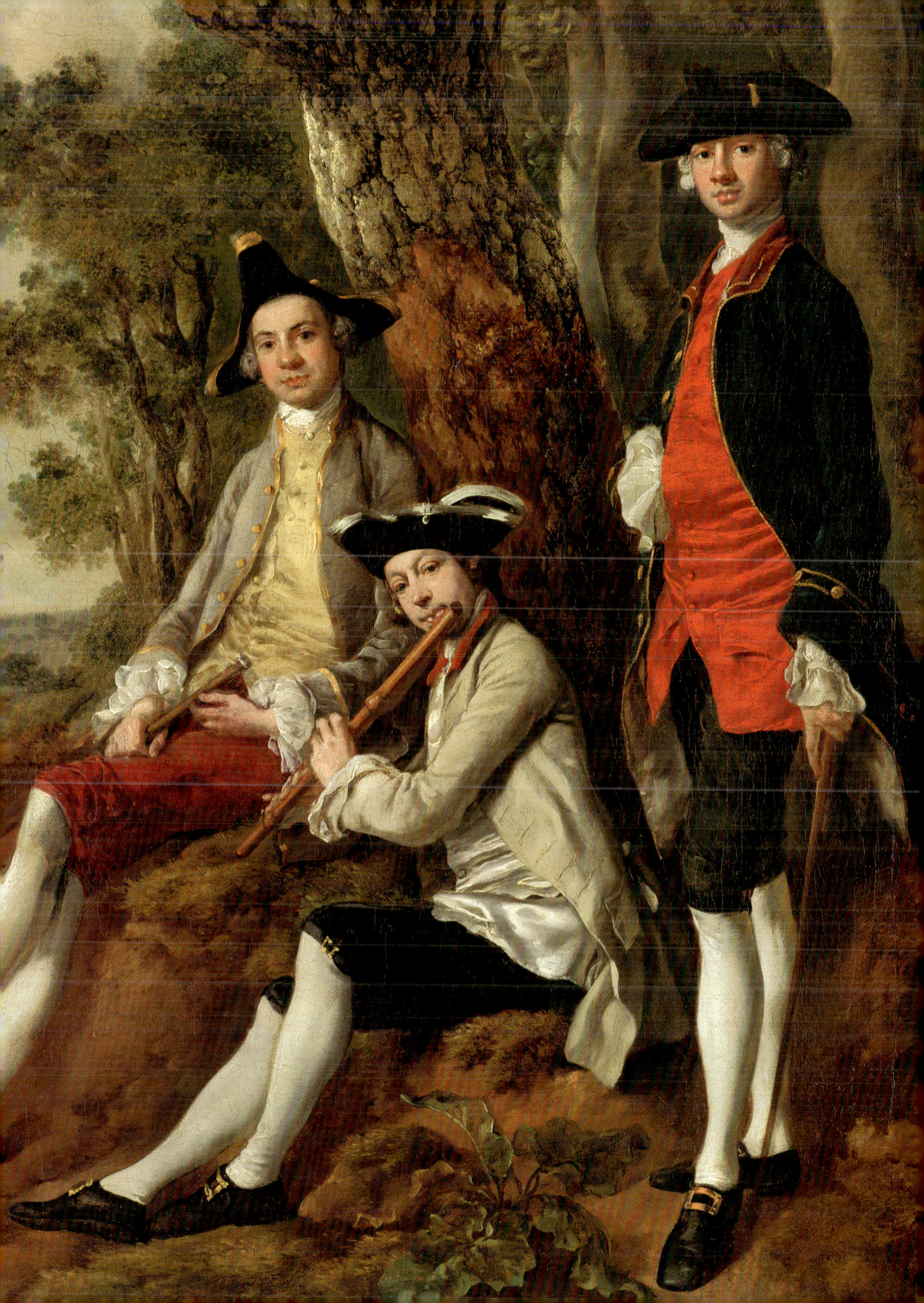

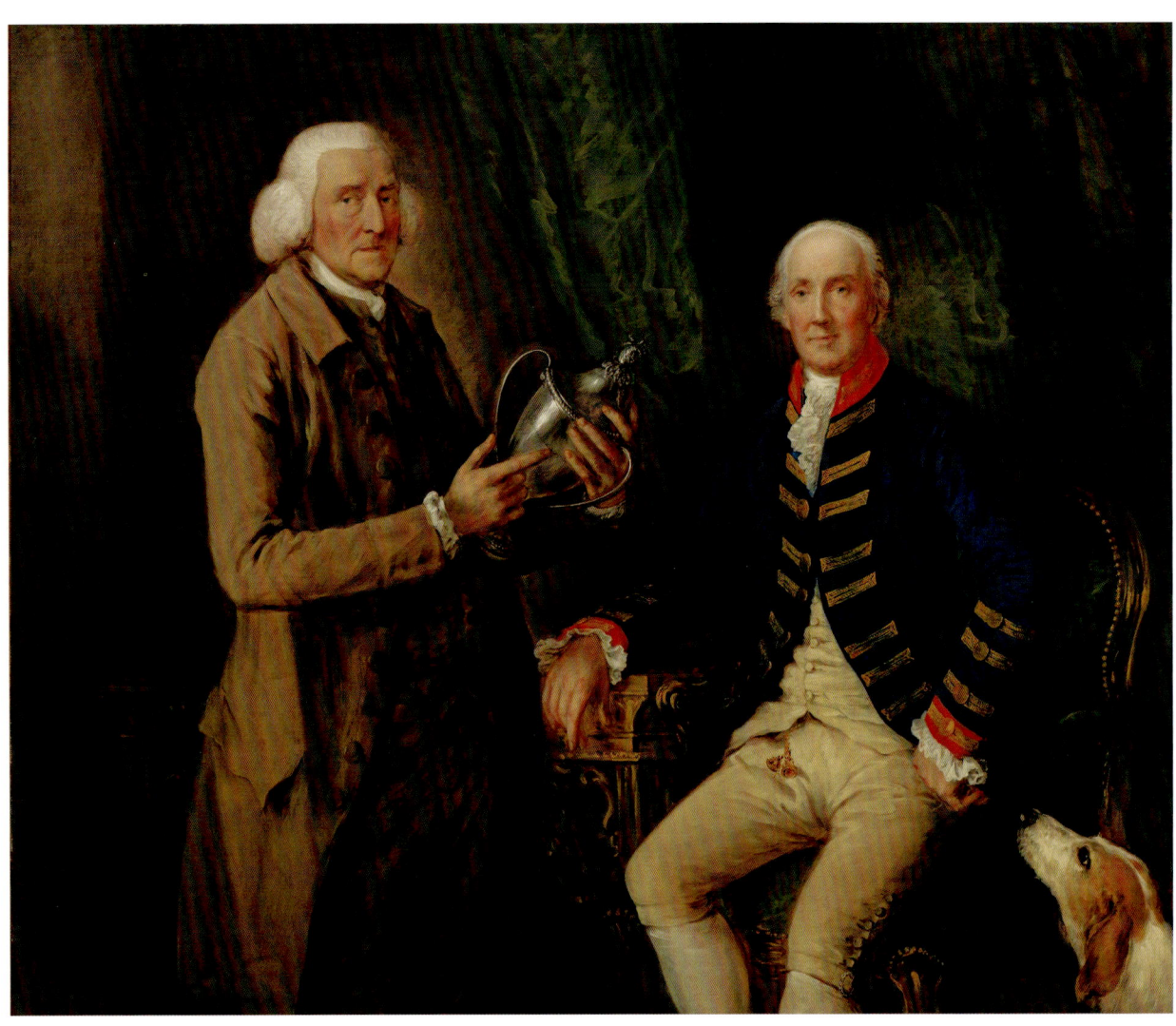

FIG. 23
Thomas Gainsborough
William Anne Hollis, 4th Earl of Essex,
Presenting a Cup to Thomas Clutterbuck of Watford, ca. 1784–85
Oil on canvas
57½ x 68¼ in. (146.1 x 173.4 cm)
J. Paul Getty Museum, Los Angeles (72.PA.2)

with trends in attire was a privilege of this group, who had the material means to do so. It was also associated with traits like trustworthiness and honor. Sources from criminal court records to auction catalogues attest to an understanding of being "of fashion" as having good character and worth.[2] The designation of being "of the first fashion" applied to the upper reaches of this class. Samuel Johnson's *Dictionary*, meanwhile, gives a distinct place to the "fashionable" in British society, describing a uniform group neatly sandwiched between the "vulgar" and "nobility."[3] In reality, of course, the situation was not so tidy.

The relation between strict hierarchies, on the one hand, and social mobility, on the other, has long made the British class system a subject of intrigue and fascination. While members of the upper classes may have sought to preserve the illusion of a static social structure (from which they benefited), social ascension happened often enough, and especially dramatic ascents from the "vulgar" to "nobility"—such as the famous case of George Romney's impoverished muse, Emma Hart, who became Lady Hamilton—fueled the ambition to climb.[4] One's status could change swiftly for better or worse with marriage, divorce, fluctuations in wealth and reputation, and approval (or disapproval) by persons of influence. Social rises and falls propelled countless narrative plots in contemporary literature, theater, and gossip columns.

Over the century, the "middling classes" swelled for various economic reasons, including colonial exploitation and the mounting fortunes of tradesmen who served a growing and increasingly wealthy clientele.[5] As more people acquired the means to emulate their social superiors in manner and attire, they did just that.[6] The writer Soame Jenyns described a never-ending race in which "everyone is flying from his inferiors, in pursuit of his superiors who fly from Him with equal alacrity."[7]

The social dynamic fueled cycles of fashion, for dress conveyed social rank—which is not to say that people always dressed according to their rank.[8] England abandoned sumptuary laws in the early seventeenth century not because people stopped caring about social dress codes but because the laws were neither followed nor effectively enforced.[9] Trespassing perceived bounds of social station—especially in dress—was frowned upon but common enough.[10] In the satirical words of eighteenth-century poet Richard Owen Cambridge, who equated the forces of fashion on dress with those on language, women, especially, cast off fashions "continually," as soon as they found them "prophaned by any other company but one step lower than themselves in their degrees of politeness."[11] It was not just the middle classes. Over the course of the eighteenth century, the peerage doubled, in part because well-positioned individuals successfully petitioned the monarch to create or re-create titles to affirm their ascent.[12] Precise rankings within the five degrees of the peerage—from dukes through barons, oldest titles to newest—were made available for reference in annually published lists, which recorded individual changes in social status that occurred every year.

Portraits became "probably one of the greatest opportunities for social mobility of the period."[13] As artists offered a wider variety of sizes, types, quality, and thus price points, portraits became accessible to a greater number and range of clientele. As Rouquet observed, portraits were a form of social currency: "It is the polite custom," he wrote, "even for men, to present one another with their pictures," and "especially the ladies, make it one of their chief amusements."[14] For those running the race of social mobility, Gainsborough and his fellow society painters visualized their aspirations, shaping, asserting, and inventing aspects of identity and status. Portraiture played a part in social dynamics, and it mattered where it was displayed, with whom it was associated, and by whom it was seen.[15] Though painted portraits were by and large a privilege of the powerful and wealthy, Gainsborough had the capacity to bestow qualities "of fashion" on almost anyone, especially on those close to him, members of his family, and himself. Portraiture was a means by which artists and their subjects could reinforce, resist, or break rules of social order.

In everyday life, Charles Howard, 11th Duke of Norfolk, deliberately dressed below his station, with "shabby old clothes, lack of hair powder and a threadbare coat of dirty plum-colour"; his "studied neglect of dress" was calculated to "excite inquiry" about his status and "then surprise by the answer."[16] When it came to his portrait, however, Gainsborough presents the duke in black Van Dyck dress that connected him to ancestors painted by Van Dyck a century earlier, and he painted the duke's third cousin and heir dressed the same way (see cat. 25 and p. 72). Gainsborough visualized traditional social codes in images like his double portrait of William Anne Hollis, 4th Earl of Essex, and Thomas Clutterbuck (fig. 23). The composition commemorates the occasion of the earl presenting a silver cup to his friend and thus appears more officious and overtly hierarchical than Gainsborough's typical society portraiture.[17] It shows the earl in Windsor uniform, emphasizing his role as Lord of the Bedchamber to George III, who invented the uniform for members of the royal family and household. The earl sits majestically, while Clutterbuck, himself from a prominent, but untitled, Watford family, stands deferentially in his brown suit, looking as devoted as the dog.

Gainsborough conveys subtler social distinctions in the group portrait *Peter Darnell Muilman, Charles Crokatt, and William Keable* (cat. 1), probably commissioned by the father of one of the two depicted landowners, Muilman and Crokatt. The conversation piece grants the musician and painter Keable, seated at center, the privilege of appearing alongside his wealthy associates.[18] Details of dress that declare Keable's lower rank, such as his jacket that lacks the costly trim of the others, would be easy for modern viewers to miss. Casting him as the performer for the company, Gainsborough pictures Keable in the midst of blowing into his flute, resulting in a facial distortion that, though subtle, would be unthinkable in portraits of people like the Muilmans or Crokatts.[19]

Unlike Reynolds, Gainsborough does not appear to have produced portraits featuring servants as secondary (and often anonymous) figures. *Ignatius Sancho* (cat. 9), Gainsborough's only known portrait of a servant and of a Black figure, is a far cry from such hierarchical images and seems to be the only independent portrait of a servant of the period painted by a major artist.[20] Through a remarkable series of events, Sancho, who was born into enslavement, came to be employed as butler to Mary Churchill, 2nd Duchess of Montagu, in the late 1740s.[21] Sancho would have known the portrait of Mary Churchill with her servant Charles Manwell (see fig. 47), the latter dressed in Montagu livery and pictured in subservience to the duchess, though, unusually, looking out to the viewer.[22] In 1768, Sancho traveled to Bath as valet to George, Duke of Montagu, where the duke, his wife (Mary, Duchess of Montagu, daughter of the Mary Churchill mentioned above; see cat. 8), and their daughter, Elizabeth, sat for portraits by Gainsborough. Extraordinarily, Sancho also sat for his portrait. By this time, although he worked as a servant, Sancho had published musical compositions and was earning a reputation as a man of letters. Whether it was a gift from his employers or from Gainsborough—who had mutual friends with Sancho through their musical circles—or given by the artist in exchange for something musical from Sancho, as Gainsborough was known to do, the portrait effaces any clue to Sancho's servitude and presents him as a gentleman in pose and attire.[23] Dressing Sancho in a blue coat and

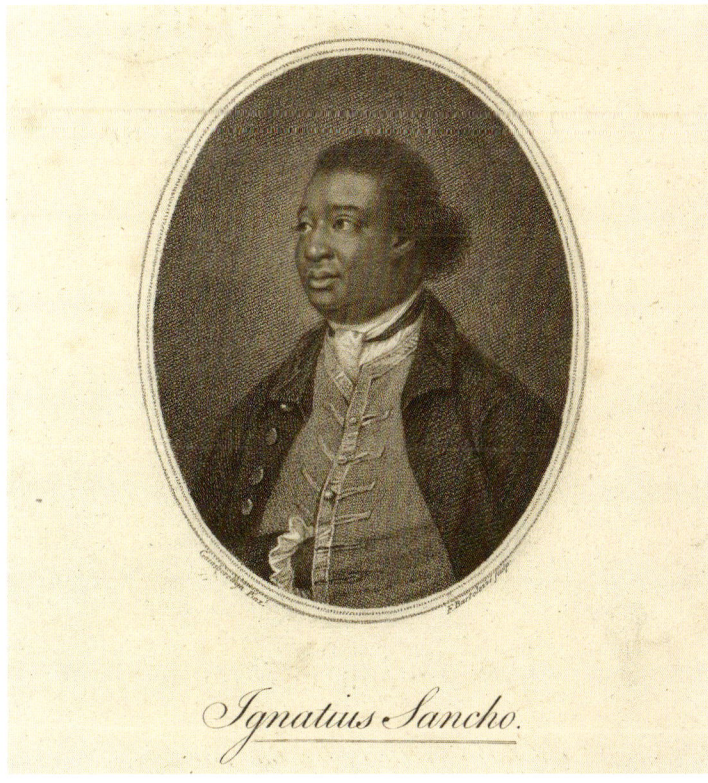

Ignatius Sancho.

FIG. 24
Francesco Bartolozzi
(after Thomas Gainsborough)
Ignatius Sancho, 1802
Engraving
3½ x 2¾ in. (89 x 70 mm)
The Metropolitan Museum
of Art, New York
(17.3.756-2151)

gold-trimmed waistcoat, Gainsborough suppresses Sancho's role as a servant to highlight him as a respectable society figure no different in stature than the artist's paying clientele. When Sancho's letters were published in 1782, Gainsborough's portrait served as the book's frontispiece (fig. 24). Sancho's portrait points to the complexity of identity in which people have more than one persona and to the constructive power of portraiture to erase or elevate aspects of a life.

In the 1760s, the spa town of Bath was a hotbed of social diversity.[24] Though individual portraits of them were few and far between, free Black men and women were part of eighteenth-century British society. Many, formerly enslaved, worked as servants like Sancho, who appears to have been one of the most famous Black people in London by the end of his life. He was an outspoken abolitionist and lived to see slavery outlawed in Britain in 1772 (though not formalized in Parliament until 1807, and in its colonies in 1833).[25] What contemporaries may have thought of Gainsborough depicting the Duke of Montagu's valet as a gentleman—as a dignified composer and man of letters—is unknown. Derisive comments about Black people in Britain and Europe—such as those written by contemporaries close to Gainsborough, like Philip Thicknesse—are chilling reminders of the social realities and injustices of the moment, no matter how Gainsborough dignifies Sancho in paint; in this climate, Sancho's portrait may not have been widely praised or even widely seen.[26] Who would have seen the portrait is an open question. If the artist had displayed it in his Bath showroom, it did not generate any known commentary, and no mention of it is made in his surviving correspondence. It seems to have gone directly to Sancho's family, with whom it remained until 1820.

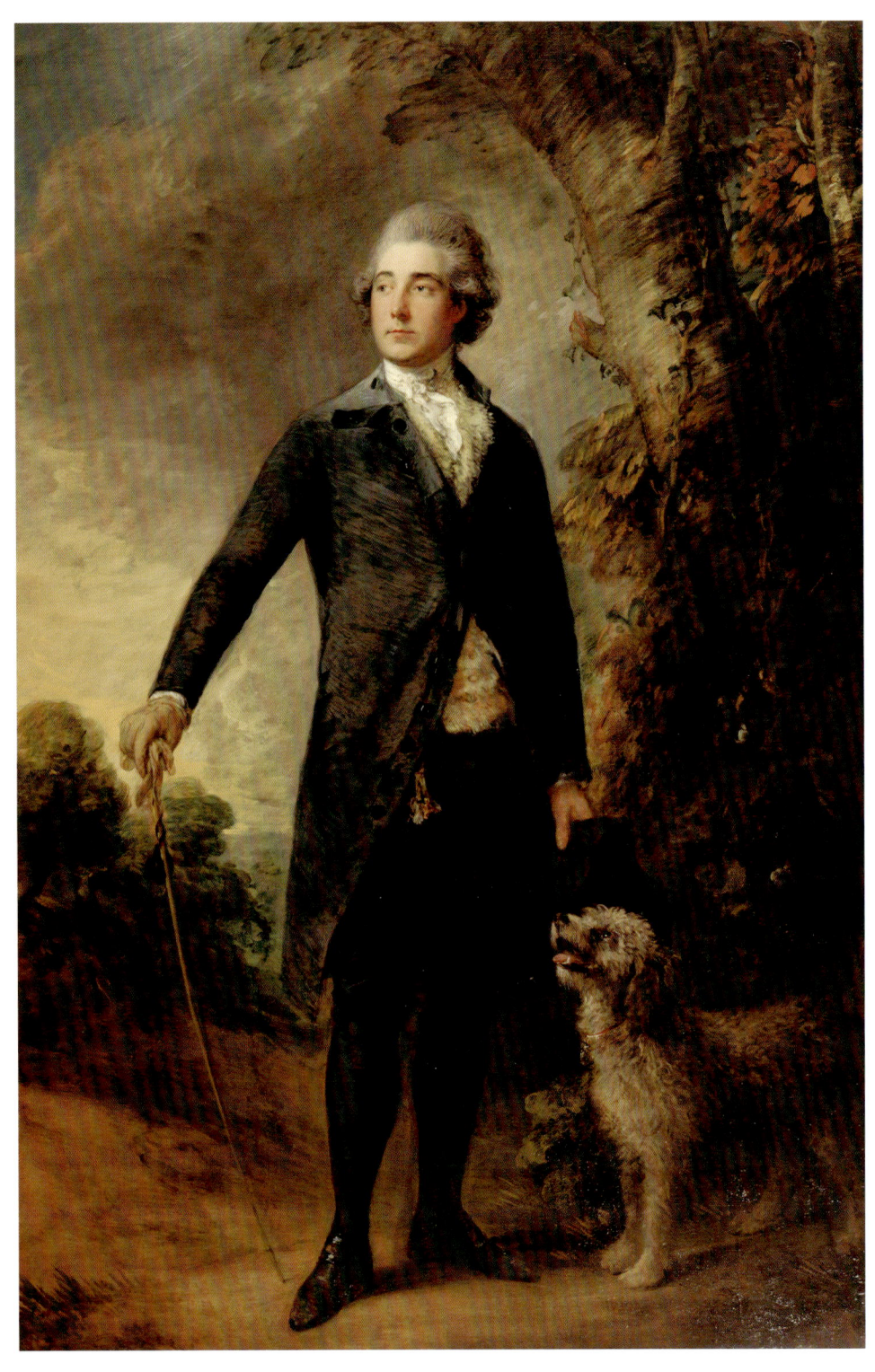

FIG. 25

Thomas Gainsborough

The Revd. Sir Henry Bate Dudley, 1st Bt., 1780

Oil on canvas, 88 x 59 in. (223.5 x 149.9 cm)

Private collection (L01438)

Portraiture's ability to transform a servant into a gentleman was worrisome to those who sought to protect a clear, visual hierarchy of British society. Public exhibitions of contemporary art emerged as a new phenomenon for the burgeoning British School of artists during Gainsborough's life and invited a new anxiety around society portraiture, as artists' and sitters' social aspirations were visualized in works shown in public spaces for several months each year. Beginning in 1760 with Society of Artists exhibitions and subsequently in the various halls used by the Royal Academy, every spring, artists moved paintings out of private showrooms into public venues to vie for attention in crowded displays alongside works by their peers.[27] Reflecting the market, portraiture was the leading type of work on display.[28] As in other public spaces—opera houses, assembly rooms, and outdoor promenades—people came to the exhibitions to see and be seen; they performed rank and status in person and on the walls.[29] The exhibitions brought artists greater exposure, as well as criticism in the form of reviews published in daily newspapers.[30] Ranging from poetic praise to attacks on artists and their sitters, the reviews reveal the extent to which critiques of society figures extended to portraits of them and how rules of social decorum applied to painted likenesses. As they can today, social dynamics in the real world affected the display of art, such as when the hanging committee of 1772 rejected Gainsborough's portrait of Lady Waldegrave—whom George III had just banished from court—for fear of offending the king.[31] Gainsborough sums up the power of social class in the public display of portraits when he writes to his friend William Jackson about his portrait of him, hung "a mile high" at the exhibition, musing, "I wish you had been [created] a Lord before my sending the Picture," as then the Secretary of the Academy "would have taken care you had been in sight."[32]

The *London Chronicle* complimented the attendees of the opening of the inaugural Royal Academy exhibition on April 27, 1769, as "persons of the first fashion."[33] Contemporary writings and images affirm that, over the course of the monthslong exhibition, the halls were sites of social mixing among the classes. Art critics typically published their texts anonymously or under pseudonyms, but the known writers—such as Rev. Henry Bate, who signed some of his reviews "Guido" and later became Sir Henry Bate Dudley—counted among the fashionable set. Even before his creation as a baronet he appears in a portrait by Gainsborough not in the modest attire of a clergyman, indistinguishable from all of Gainsborough's other reverends, but as a fashionable gentleman (fig. 25). Art criticism mingled with personal politics and class perspectives. For the most part, reviews focused on evaluating artistic merit, often creating hierarchies among artists and pitting them against each other, as many critics did to Gainsborough and Reynolds. When criticism veered toward evaluating the subjects of the portraits, however, it became clear that it was largely from a privileged social position that the reviewers (presumably exclusively male) presented their opinions. The cover of anonymity emboldened some writers to criticize subjects—even those of elevated rank—without fear of reprisal.[34] It is not unlike online trolling today.

Because printed catalogues rarely identified the subjects of portraits, it was up to viewers to recognize the individuals masquerading beneath the trappings of fashion and conventions of portraiture. Critics published the identities in newspapers, providing crucial insight into the social dynamics at play on the exhibition walls for anyone who failed to recognize the portraits' "originals." One type of sitter incited particularly pointed criticism: women of questionable reputation who were represented in their portraits as ladies of the first fashion. Critics deplored the appearance on the exhibition walls of images of such women alongside and indistinguishable from those who, according to public opinion, possessed indisputable social standing and moral rectitude.[35] According to Whitley, French visitors were "shocked at the indelicacy," quoting an unidentified writer: "In Paris . . . such portraits would on no account be admitted; the name of the King is a sufficient check upon them to keep a just decorum in *his* Academy."[36] Gainsborough bucked expectations for such "just decorum," seeming even to have taken advantage of the publicity such women drew to his art.

Newspapers were teeming with gossip about Grace Dalrymple Elliott when Gainsborough submitted portraits of her to the Royal Academy exhibitions of 1778 and 1782. At the time of the first—a full-length painting of her in profile, in which she wears fashionably high hair and fantastical Van Dyck–style dress (cat. 18)—she was fresh from divorce following her affair with Lord Valentia and was keeping company with George, 4th Earl of Cholmondeley. Critics of the exhibition acknowledged her scandalous reputation but were otherwise highly complimentary. The writer for the *General Evening Post* praised Gainsborough's portrayal of her beauty and was inclined to forgive any errors of the "unfortunate lady."[37] The *Morning Chronicle* hinted at the artist's own questionable reputation in being visited by, and a favorite of, women like Elliott and other so-called "demi-reps."[38] The term, not included in Johnson's *Dictionary*, referred to a type of married woman who had affairs with other men in exchange for social and financial security.[39] Bate, writing for the *Morning Post*, used the euphemism "filles de joye" (women of pleasure) to describe Elliott and others painted by Gainsborough that year, evoking John Cleland's popular (and many times banned) pornographic novel *Fanny Hill, or, Memoirs of a Woman of Pleasure* (1748), about a fifteen-year-old girl entering the world of the demi-reps. In 1776, an expanded and illustrated French edition was published with the title *Fille de joie*.[40] Real and fictional demi-reps both titillated and incited censure, yet even in the gratuitously lascivious pages of Cleland's novel one gets a sense of the social and financial limitations on eighteenth-century girls and women, even within the fashionable class.

Critics were less forgiving in 1782, when Gainsborough exhibited a more intimate portrait of Elliott (cat. 21), who had just given birth to a child, reportedly fathered by the Prince of Wales but raised in the household of Lord Cholmondeley. Shedding the historicizing Van Dyck dress and modest profile pose of the earlier, grander image, she wears her own clothes and faces straight out, the bust format placing her in much closer proximity to the viewer. Her look is seductive, with eyes trained forward and lips parted, the neckline of her dress tracing the curves of her breasts and a nearly invisible kerchief draped across her chest. Critics of the earlier portrait had quoted the poetry of Alexander Pope, speculated about the artist's own morals, and referred to modern theater in their indulgent praise for the "unfortunate" subject of the painting. Now they were terse and dismissive: "A wanton countenance; and such hair; good God!"[41]

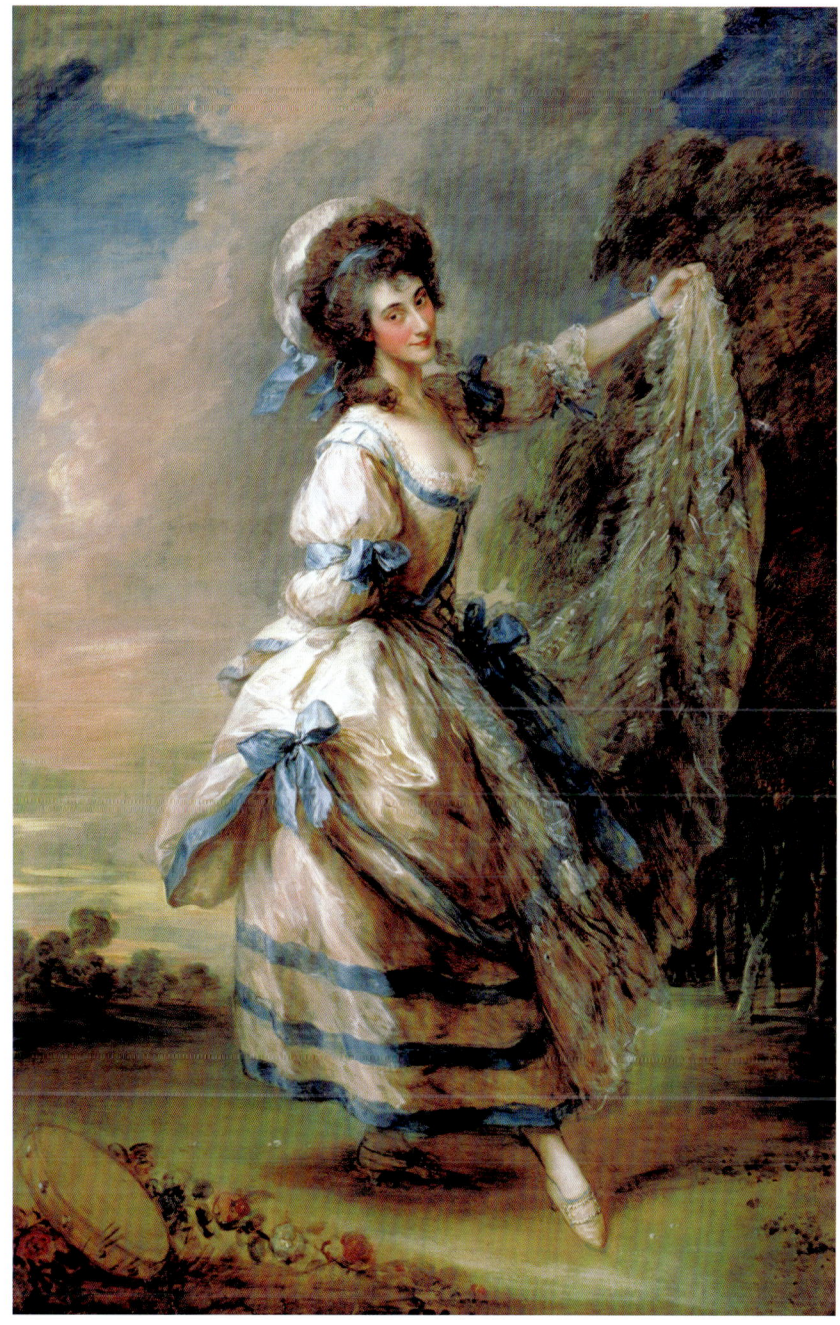

FIG. 26
Thomas Gainsborough
Giovanna Baccelli, exhibited 1782
Oil on canvas
89¼ x 58½ in. (226.7 x 148.6 cm)
Tate, London (T02000)

It was clear that Gainsborough, in his pursuit of likeness, had crossed a line. According to the *Public Advertiser*, while Gainsborough's depiction of the Italian dancer (and mistress of the 3rd Duke of Dorset) Giovanna Baccelli in mid-dance (fig. 26) was a "good moral likeness," *Grace Dalrymple Elliott* was not: "The *Eyes* are too characteristic of her Vocation."[42] Gainsborough broke the rules of social decorum in conveying Elliott as a demi-rep so blatantly. It was bad enough that a portrait of such a woman would sully the space in which were displayed images of dukes and duchesses; it was worse that the portrait did not attempt to mask her.

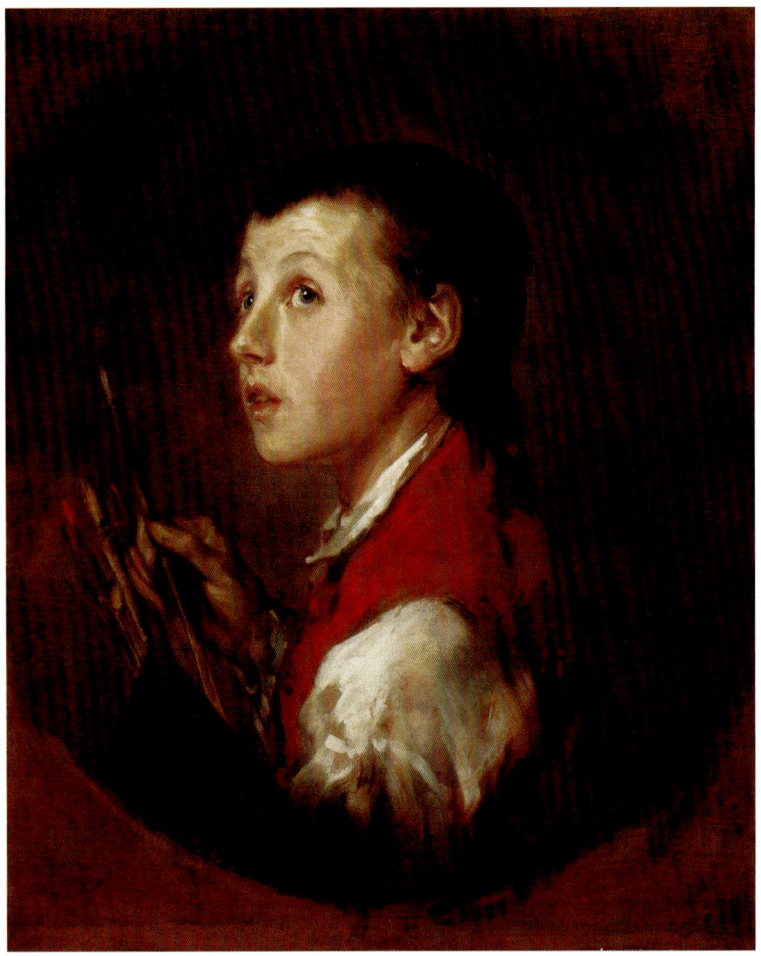

FIG. 27
Thomas Gainsborough
The Pitminster Boy, ca. 1768–69
Oil on canvas
23¹⁵⁄₁₆ x 19¹³⁄₁₆ in. (60.8 x 50.4 cm)
Gainsborough's House, Sudbury;
on loan from a private collection (L0003)

❖

Gainsborough painted an unusually large number of family portraits—some thirty or so canvases, about a dozen of which depict his wife, his daughters, and himself—presumably for personal reasons, including experimentation and display in his own showrooms.[43] Not all of his familial sitters would have been able to afford portraits by a professional society painter. In the fluid circumstances of artist's models, members of Gainsborough's family, especially his daughters, could play polite young gentlewomen as easily as they could rustic peasants.[44] He sent none of his family pictures to Royal Academy exhibitions, though the youth holding paintbrushes known as *The Pitminster Boy* (fig. 27)—possibly that shown in 1769 as *Portrait of a Young Boy*—has been suggested to depict his nephew Gainsborough Dupont; *The Blue Boy*, exhibited as *Portrait of a Young Gentleman* in 1770, has also been suggested to depict Dupont (see fig. 43).[45]

Gainsborough's own social status was complicated by his closeness to the upper classes. His apprenticeship at age thirteen suggests he was not the recipient of a generous annuity from his wealthy late uncle, as has been proposed.[46] His father's bankruptcy in the 1730s indebted him to local Sudbury debtor Bernard Carter, whose relatives Gainsborough painted in the conversation pieces *Mr. and Mrs. Carter* (see fig. 37) and *Mr. and Mrs. Andrews* (cat. 2). As Mark Bills notes, the Gainsborough family's obligation to the Carters begs the question of the nature of these commissions.[47] Gainsborough employed servants and referred disparagingly to his "cowardly footman," who was afraid to step outdoors in fear of being pressed into naval service.[48] His great rival Reynolds outranked him with his positions as founding president of the Royal Academy (for which George III knighted him in 1769) and Painter in Ordinary to the King from 1784. Gainsborough's scornful complaints about "gentlemen" to his friend William Jackson suggest that he felt excluded from this class:

> There is not such a set of Enemies to a real artist in the world as they [gentlemen] are, if not kept at a proper distance. . . . They think . . . they reward your merit by their company and notice. . . . They have but one part worth looking at, and that is their Purse. . . . If any Gentleman comes to my House, my Man [footman] asks them if they want me (provided they don't seem satisfyed with seeing the Pictures) and then he askes what they would please to want with me; if they say a Picture Sir please to walk this way and my Master will speak to you; but if they only want me to bow & compliment Sir my Master is walk'd out.[49]

To his patrons, Gainsborough may have feigned modesty regarding his family's social class, such as when he wrote to Dr. William Dodd, whose wife had sent a dress to the Gainsborough household, that there was "no one here fit for such an elegant dress."[50] His wife, however, may have disagreed. Margaret Burr was the illegitimate daughter of the 3rd Duke of Beaufort, and her marriage to Gainsborough in 1746 brought her a £200 annuity from the duke's estate, although Gainsborough's continued financial struggles are well recorded (see cat. 15). One can only wonder how the couple saw the ironic fact of her descent, though illegitimate, from the 2nd Earl of Gainsborough.[51] Family connections of her "secret" paternity may have brought socially elevated clients to her husband, such as the Duke and Duchess of Rutland, Margaret's first cousins (and the same Duchess of Rutland who complained of Reynolds painting her wearing a "bedgown"; see p. 20).[52] The Rutlands were, however, much closer to Reynolds, who painted a number of family portraits and helped to build the duke's art collection.[53]

It is clear from the portraits they left behind that Gainsborough and his wife saw themselves as people of fashion. His early *Portrait of the Artist with His Wife and Daughter* (see fig. 54) pictures his young family no differently than his paying clientele at the time. Contemporary descriptions suggest that he presented himself and his circumstances like those of a gentleman.[54] According to Thicknesse, Gainsborough knew "how to act, and think, like a gentleman, as he does to contemn [*sic*] and despise those who dare treat him in any other light."[55] One anecdote describes Margaret Gainsborough defending a particular choice of dress—the subtext being that she might be seen to be dressing above her station—with the memorable statement, "I have some right to this, for . . . I am a prince's daughter" (cat. 15).[56] The story suggests a tension in the Gainsboroughs' lives around the status they strived to attain, his subordinate relationship to paying clients, and the unrecognized nobility into which she had been born. In all but one early self-portrait (of debated attribution), Gainsborough presents himself not as a painter working for his living but dressed as, and with the air of, a man of the first fashion (cat. 24). This dual sense of self may well have motivated him to paint people like the servant Sancho, the eccentric entertainer Merlin (cat. 20), musicians like Abel (cat. 12), and social outliers like Grace Dalrymple Elliott, who represented the complexity and multiplicity of social identity and portraiture's power to disrupt.[57]

NOTES

1   Fielding 1742, 1: 168. Langford 1989, 71, on "the ambiguous term," politeness: "It was naturally associated with the possession of those goods which marked off the moderately wealthy from the poor, the trappings of propertied life. It also included the intellectual and aesthetic tastes which displayed the continuing advance of fashion in its broadest sense. But most of all it affected the everyday routine and rules of social life, from matters as trivial as the time at which one dined, and the way one ate one's dinner, to matters as important as the expectations and arrangement of partners in marriage." On other terms related to fashion as class, such as beau monde and ton ("tone"; from bon ton and haut ton), see Greig 2013.

2   For example, from a case of an alleged theft of a snuffbox, January 15, 1719: "The Prisoner [Elizabeth Coleburn] produced her Mistress and several Persons of Reputation and Fashion who gave her an Extraordinary Character. The Jury acquitted her"; Trial of Elizabeth Coleburn 1719.

3   Johnson's definitions of "fashionable": "1. Approved by custom; established by custom; modish. 2. Made according to the mode. 3. Observant of the mode. 4. Having rank above the vulgar, and below nobility." On the "vulgar," see Klein 1995, 365–6. An error in the 1768 edition of Johnson's Dictionary defines fashion as a condition "of" (rather than "above") the "vulgar," underscoring the human labor of compositors who typeset each page and who, though ideally having a "tolerable Genius for letters" and being fluent in Latin and Greek, were considered closer to the ranks of the "vulgar" than of "fashion." See Campbell 1969, 120–24, and a court case of July 11, 1750, involving composer Richard Noke: Trial of Thomas Mayo 1750.

4   Vickery 2009, 136: "Ladies were not to dress or decorate above their station, but nor were they to descend in manners or modes from their eminence, for in so doing they undermined respect for rank and brought the whole social edifice into jeopardy. They were fully implicated in what E. P. Thompson called 'the theatre of power,' so crucial to the maintenance of a deferential society." On the "theatre of power," see Thompson 1974.

5   Langford 1989, 70: "Legal records . . . confirm the impression created by contemporary comment, that the middle ranges of society benefited as much as any by the creation of new wealth, and that their conditions of life changed substantially." On the growing middle classes and art patronage, see Solkin 2015, 110–12. Buck (1979, 94), points to G. F. A. Wendeborn's observation (1791, 1: 193) of "the splendid manner in which many of the shopkeepers live, and the short time in which some of them acquire fortunes."

6   Langford 1989, 67: "Nothing unified the middling orders so much as their passion for aping the manners and morals of the gentry more strictly defined, as soon as they possessed the material means to do so."

7   Langford (1989, 67) quoting Jenyns 1790, 2: 93.

8   Buck 1979, 13: "The view that dress expressed status in society was an unchallenged commonplace of the eighteenth century." Langford 1989, 66–67: "It was a common observation that in England the appearance of a gentleman was seemingly sufficient to make him one, at least in the sense of his acceptance as such by others." Dressing downwards usually reflected the carelessness afforded by high rank, as parodied in Gunnersbury 1776, 90: "This gentleman, however, had a patrimonial title, which he thought a sufficient apology for the carelessness of his appearance." Fanny Burney (2001, 67) described in 1776 seeing the Duchess of Devonshire in "such an undressed and slaternly [sic] manner" that had she "not had a servant in superb Livery behind her, she would certainly have been affronted," as in, mistaken for a "loose woman" or prostitute.

9   On sumptuary laws in England, see Buck 1979, 186–87.

10 A. Reynolds in London 2023, 44: "Blurring of class boundaries was a source of frustration for those who considered clothing a fundamental indicator of social status, resulting in complaints of deliberate deception and disruption of the natural order." Klein (1995, 374) refers to "a sort of social 'transvestitism,' people wearing the 'wrong' clothing for their social estate," a common complaint in early eighteenth-century Britain. Buck 1979, 109 cites London Magazine 1783, 128–29: "Luxury in the dress of our female servants and the daughters of farmers and many others in inferior stations who think a well-chose cotton gown shall entitle them to the appellation of young ladies is highly prejudicial both to the landowner, the farmer and the public."

11 Cambridge 1803, 439.

12 Buck 1979, 13. Among Johnson's Dictionary (1755) definitions of "peer": "A nobleman: of nobility we have five degrees, who are all nevertheless called peers, because their essential privileges are the same."

13 Pointon 1984, 187.

14 Rouquet 1755, 33, 36. He also observes (45): "Indeed it is amazing how fond the English are of having their pictures drawn; but as peoples fortunes are more upon a level in England than in any other country, and as the very best painters take only ten or twelve guineas for a bust, this moderate price is no hindrance to the custom of frequently making a present of one's picture."

15 For example, regarding Ann, Duchess of Grafton and the place of portraiture in retaining, after her separation from the Duke of Grafton, "her footing in fashionable society," see Vickery 2009, 142.

16 Robinson 1995, 171.

17 The earl commissioned the painting for Clutterbuck to commemorate the earl's presentation of a silver cup to his friend in a gesture of esteem and gratitude; Belsey 2019, 1: no. 318.

18 Vaughan 2002, 53, argues that conversation pieces "are intended to show the polite modes of deportment and address that marked off those in society from the lower orders. While ostensibly displaying people in carefree social gatherings—taking tea, conversing in a club or simply strolling in a park—they were precisely staged statements of the sitters' status and ambitions."

19 J. Chu in Chu 2017.

20 G. Waterfield and A. French in London and Edinburgh 2003–4, 38, discuss servants in portraiture especially from 1745 as linked to the promotion of an image of loyal servants as exemplars and the singularity of Gainsborough's Ignatius Sancho.

21 Among numerous biographies of Sancho, see King et al. 1997 and The Cambridge Companion to Ignatius Sancho, forthcoming.

22 Buccleuch and Queensberry 2022, 29. See C. Powell in Aljoe and Huang 2025, which discusses the coterie of Black people associated with the

Montagu household and portraits of them. Though Sancho's exact term of employment is unknown, Powell outlines what is known of Sancho's association with the Montagu family, beginning in his childhood working for John, 2nd Duke of Montagu (1690–1749) and leaving service in 1773 or 1774. Thanks to Scott MacDonald and Crispin Powell for providing information on the current attribution of this work.

23 Fulcher (1856a, 149) offers examples demonstrating that Gainsborough "bestowed inconsiderately" money and pictures on his friends and associates.

24 A satirical view of Bath's mixed society in 1771 is described in Tobias Smollett's *Expedition of Humphry Clinker* (Smollett 2015, 43): "Every upstart of fortune, harnessed in the trappings of the mode, presents himself at Bath . . . Clerks and factors from the East Indies, loaded with the spoil of plundered provinces; planters, negro-drivers, and hucksters, from our American plantations, enriched they know not how; agents, commissaries, and contractors, who have fattened, in two successive wars on the blood of the nation; usurers, brokers, and jobbers of every kind; men of low birth, and no breeding, have found themselves suddenly translated into a state of affluence . . . all of them hurry to Bath, because here, without any further qualification, they can mingle with the princes and nobles of the land." See also Langford 1989, 107.

25 On Sancho as the most famous Black person in London in the late 1770s, see Chater 2009, 39; on Black populations in eighteenth-century, see Chater 2009, 35–73 and 85–88; on observations by Carl Moritz, who traveled to England from Germany in 1782 and regarded the presence of several Black people "simply as interesting members of society," Chater 2009, 87.

26 Gerzina (2022, 33–77) explores Sancho's place in British society as "a black man wholly at home in England and English society, while at the same time amusedly aware of his position as both insider and outsider" (68). A decade after the 1777 publication of Thicknesse's travelogue (*A Year's Journey through France and Part of Spain*), he inserted a letter in the 1788 edition and subsequent editions, apparently written in England, that praised the French king's "wise" decision to deport "all the negroes, mulattoes, etc." and expressed his beliefs that Black people were "of a lower order," disparaging their appearance, intellect, and character, over twelve pages; Thicknesse 1789, 2: 101–12.

27 Gainsborough exhibited works at the Society of Artists exhibitions between 1761 to 1768 and at the Royal Academy, as a founding member, from 1769 to 1783 with a hiatus between 1772 and 1777. He also exhibited at the short-lived Free Society of Artists exhibitions. His exhibitions at his showroom at Schomberg House in London also drew commentary from the press. On the beginnings of public exhibitions in England see M. Hallett and S. Turner in London 2018, 13–25, and on the Royal Academy exhibitions, M. Hallett in London 2018, 29–41.

28 London 2018, 31, 40.

29 Brewer 1997, 348: "Culture was characterised by an emphasis upon social display: cultural sites were places of self presentation in which audiences made publicly visible their wealth, status, social and sexual charms. The ostensible reason for an individual's presence at a cultural site—seeing the play, attending an auction, visiting an artist's studio, listening to a concert—was often subordinate to a more powerful set of social imperatives."

30 On the proliferation of reviews, see M. Hallett and S. Turner in London 2018, 20.

31 Hamilton 2017, 213. Belsey (2019, 1: 401) suggests the portrait he catalogues as no. 404 may be the portrait in question. See also Perry 2007, 65–66, on Gainsborough's withdrawal of portraits in 1782 due to social friction among the people they represented.

32 Gainsborough to William Jackson, June 9, 1770; Hayes 2001, 76.

33 M. Hallett and S. Turner in London 2018, 13.

34 For example, the writer of the *Morning Chronicle*, April 25, 1778, criticizes Lord C------[understood to be Chesterfield] by stating that "the countenance of the portrait has all the insensibility and want of meaning for which the original is remarkable." In 1780, Bate was found guilty of libel against the Duke of Richmond for printing, as editor of the *Morning Post*, accusations of treason signed by "An Inquirer."

35 Perry 2007, 71–72.

36 Whitley [1915] 2016, 216.

37 *General Evening Post*, April 30–May 2, 1778.

38 *Morning Chronicle*, April 25, 1778. Some confusion around the exhibited portraits arises from the identification in Graves 1905, 192, of the

sitters of no. 114 "Portrait of a lady; whole length (*Mrs. Elliott*)" and no. 115 "Portrait of a lady; half length (*Miss Dalrymple*)," which presumably are not referring to the same Grace Dalrymple Elliott (though Williamson 1972, 168, suggested that the bust portrait was shown alongside the full-length in 1778 as number 115). Mysteriously, the writer for the *Morning Chronicle*, April 25, 1778, names "Miss Dalrymple" and "Clara Haywood," among the demi-reps painted by Gainsborough that year, but leaves unnamed "another well-known character of the same stamp."

39 The meaning of "demi-rep" can be gleaned from the epigraph to [Edward Thompson], *The Demi-Rep* (Thompson 1756): "Where Matrimony veils the incestuous Life, / and Whore is sheltered in the name of Wife." The satire, *Memoirs of a Demi-Rep of Fashion* (Gunnersbury 1776), describes the entanglement of social class, financial struggle, and moral reputation in the world of demi-reps, especially 1: 56–57, and the complex relationship of demi-reps to prostitution (1: 83). Even before his move to London in 1774, Gainsborough, along with Reynolds, was seen as a favorite portraitist to such women; see Stevens 1772, 29.

40 *Morning Post and Daily Advertiser*, April 27, 1778: "The portraits which he has exhibited on this occasion consist chiefly of *filles de joye*, and all are admirable likenesses, No. 114, particularly being that of the beautiful Mrs. [Grace Dalrymple] E[lliott]."

41 *London Courant*, May 9, 1782.

42 *Public Advertiser,* May 2, 1782. Conway 2001, 40–41: The criticism of the 1782 portrait of Mrs. Elliott "highlights the concern that female portraiture must represent an abstraction of virtue in order to become eligible for public display." On Giovanna Baccelli and Gainsborough's portrait fueling public interest in her, see Perry 2007, 68.

43 On family portraits, see London and Princeton 2018–19. On Gainsborough showing portraits of his assistant Dupont in his showroom as following the example of Reynolds, who displayed portraits of his assistant Giuseppe Marchi to emphasize to his clients his ability to capture likeness, see Sloman 2002, 78–79.

44 On an 1824 reference to a painting by Gainsborough of his daughters "in the garb of peasant girls," suggesting that a fragment in the Ashmolean Museum, Oxford, is what remains of the painting, see D. Solkin in London and Princeton 2018–19, 113.

45 Sloman 2013.

46 Bills 2018, 17–25, on Gainsborough's early life and family.

47 Bills 2018, 20. On Gainsborough's father's bankruptcy, see Tyler 1997/98, 55, 64.

48 Hayes 2001, 133.

49 From Gainsborough to William Jackson, September 2, 1767; Hayes 2001, 42. Langford 1989, 65: "There seemed no shortage of Englishmen, or, as it was often said, Englishwomen, whose prime ambition in life was to rise higher up the social ladder. Above all, there beckoned the lure of acceptance into that great and growing, yet tantalizingly unattainable, class composed of gentlemen and their ladies."

50 Gainsborough to Dr. William Dodd, November 24, 1773; Hayes 2001, 120.

51 Sloman (2002, 147) illustrates a family tree showing Margaret Gainsborough's descent and connections to members of the Noel and Price families who sat for portraits by Gainsborough.

52 Sloman 2002, 116.

53 See Sloman 2002, 179 and Belsey 2019, 2: no. 785.

54 Postle 2002, 26; Rosenthal 1999, 77.

55 Thicknesse 1770, 97.

56 Cunningham 1829–33, 1: 334–35, cited by Sloman 2002, 24n.15, who (correspondence, 2025) suggests caution around Cunningham's reliability. Belsey (2002, 25) argues that Margaret's annuity had a negative aspect: "It questioned Gainsborough's ability to support his family and, despite the stigma of illegitimacy, it furnished Mrs Gainsborough with social aspirations which were to [remain] at odds with those of her husband's background."

57 Vaughan 2002, 81: "He never became too grand to forget this [that he still made his living principally as a fashionable portrait painter] and retained close friendships with others in the service industry. Perhaps it was this that spurred him to paint the direct and sympathetic portrait of the 'African Man of Letters', Ignatius Sancho, in 1768."

FASHION, PORTRAITS, AND TIME

Fashion, let it consist of false or true taste, will have its run,
like a runaway Horse.

— Thomas Gainsborough, 1768

Fashion in the widest sense of the word is change.

— Anne Buck, 1979

EARLY MODERN EUROPEAN PORTRAITS often bear the Latin inscription *aetatis suae . . .* (at the age of . . .), pinning the painting to a moment in the sitter's life (e.g., fig. 28). In this way, the artist seems to stop time, wielding the power of painting to hold the subject at this age in perpetuity. In Gainsborough's day, it was not customary to inscribe society portraits with sitters' ages. Nevertheless, portraits had much to do with time.[1] Critics marveled at the impression of immediacy, of instantaneous translation of human into paint, in Gainsborough's brushstrokes. Reynolds suggested that Gainsborough's "unfinished manner" contributed "to that striking resemblance for which his portraits are so remarkable."[2] Reports that portraits such as

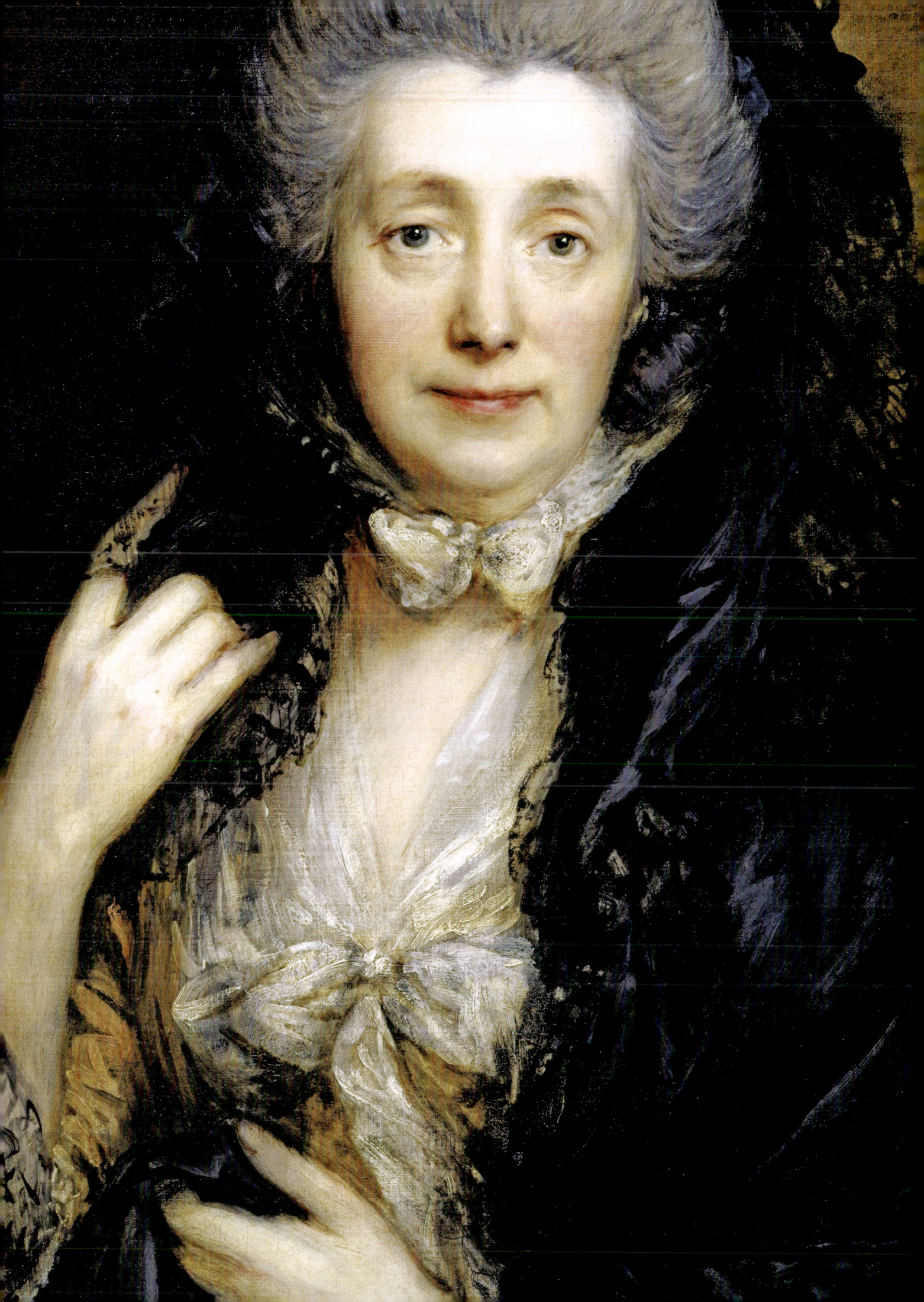

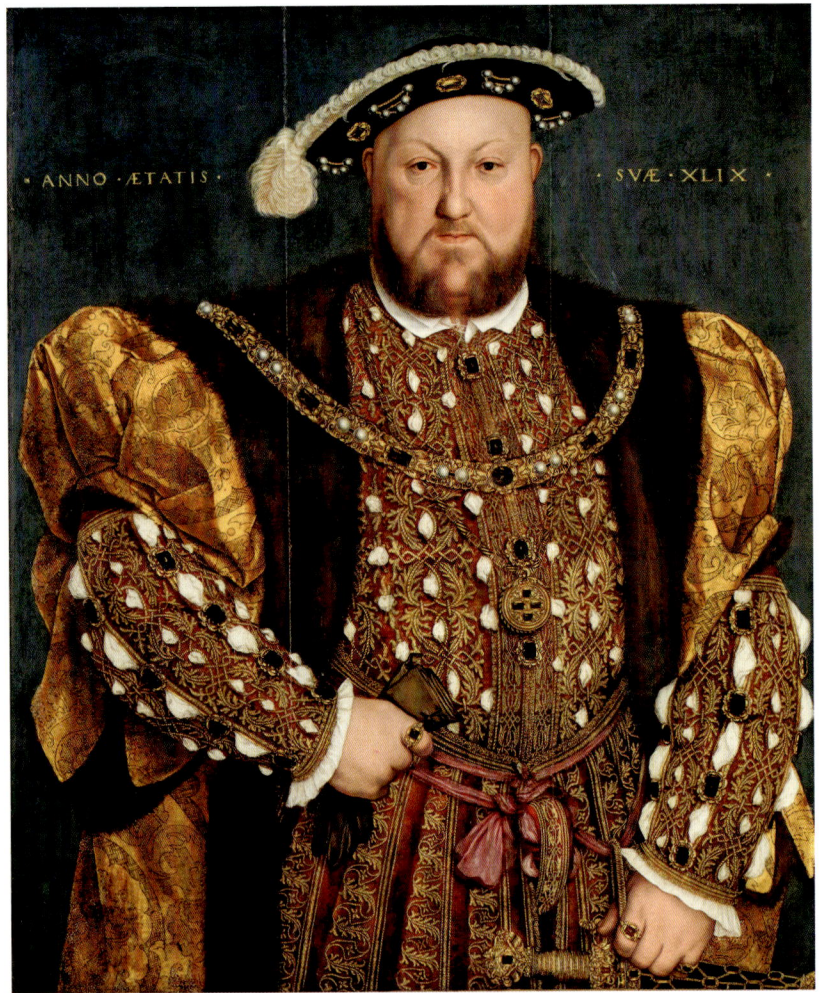

ANNO · ÆTATIS ·   · SVÆ · XLIX ·

FIG. 28
Hans Holbein the Younger
Henry VIII, 1540
Oil on wood
34¹³⁄₁₆ x 29⁵⁄₁₆ in.
(88.5 x 74.5 cm)
Palazzo Barberini, Rome (878)

FIG. 29
Thomas Gainsborough
Penelope, Viscountess Ligonier, 1770
Oil on canvas
94½ x 61¾ in.
(240 x 156.8 cm)
The Huntington Library,
Art Museum, and Botanical
Gardens, San Marino (11.29)

Ignatius Sancho (cat. 9) and *Samuel Linley* (cat. 16) were painted in sittings of under two hours, whether true or not, cast them as direct impressions of their sitters. This was in contrast to Gainsborough's more labored constructions, such as his full-length paintings of Lord and Lady Ligonier (fig. 29), which, the artist complained, held him hostage for a month.[3]

In Gainsborough's oft-quoted 1771 letter to Lord Dartmouth, he asserts that likeness is best achieved by posing sitters in modern dress and that it is a "misfortune" that "cannot be helped" that the resulting portraits are "soon out of fashion and look awkward."[4] The speed with which fashions—and thus portraits depicting them—went out of style varied. Formal wear, for example, changed more slowly than other types of clothing.[5] Court dress was deliberately outdated, decorum requiring that those who appeared at court did so in attire that was behind the times.[6] The German theologian and historian Gebhard Friedrich August Wendeborn was presumably exaggerating when he observed, in 1786, that "the fashions [in England] alter in these days so much that a man can hardly wear a coat two months, before it is out of fashion."[7] Opinions sometimes differed about what was on trend at what time; there are conflicting views, for example, about the trendiness of Robert Andrews's hat (cat. 2).[8]

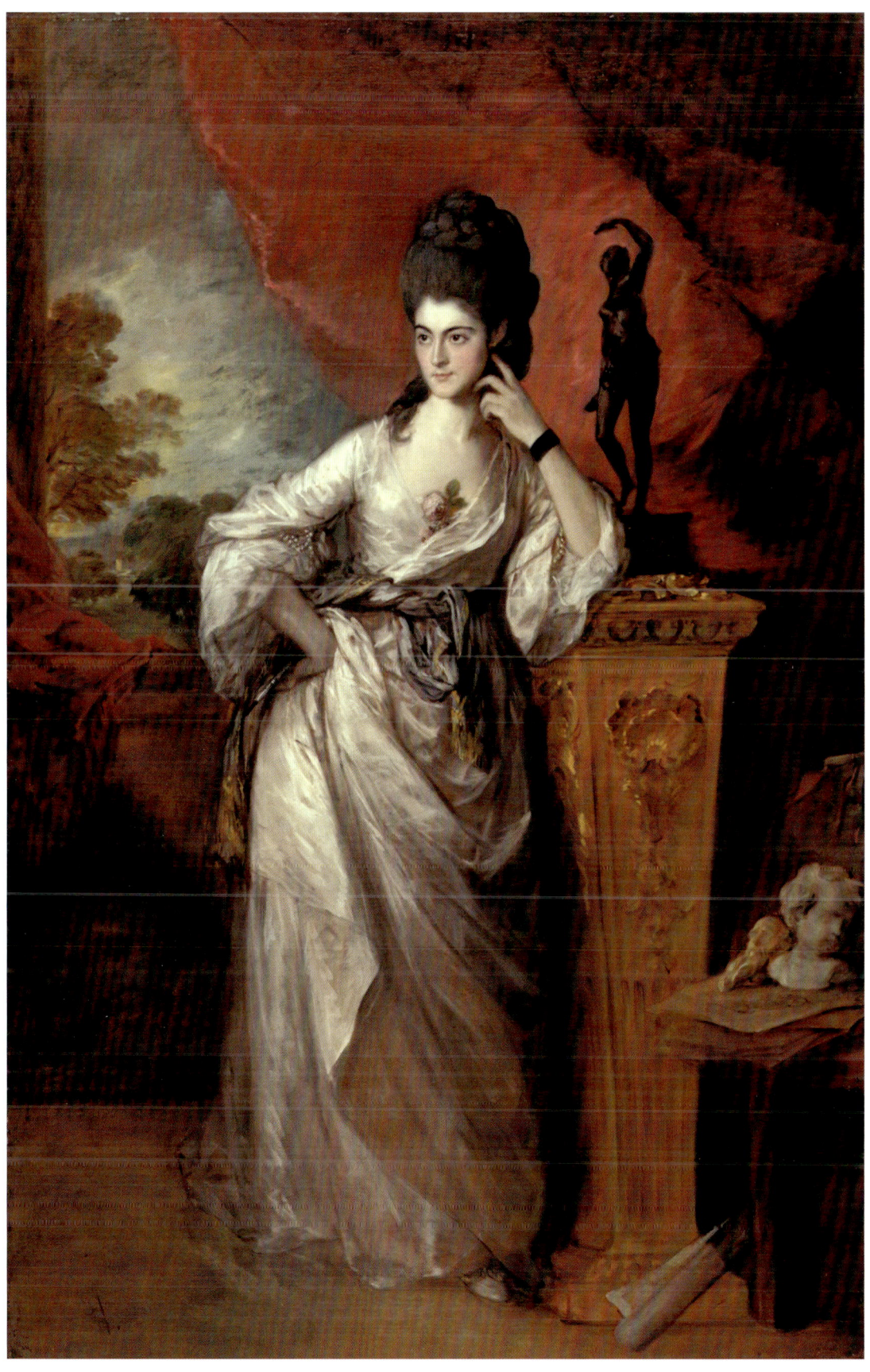

As today, people could be deliberately retro in their dress; Gainsborough's portrait of James Freeman, for instance, presents the subject in clothes some thirty years out of date (fig. 30). Hugh Belsey proposed that such resistance to modern fashion aligns with the generally sober dress preferred by Nonconformists—Englishmen like Freeman who did not conform to the doctrines and practices of the Church of England.[9]

"Quick" and "slow" are, of course, relative terms and may well have been very different experiences in eighteenth-century Britain, when a portrait painted in under two hours might have seemed nearly as instantaneous as the click of a camera today. One can now travel between London and Bath in under three hours by car (under two by train), whereas the fastest time in Gainsborough's life was twenty-four hours.[10] Yet it was a trip he made often enough. The experience of time for Gainsborough and his contemporaries may be hard to imagine from the perspective of the twenty-first century, such as when, in 1752, Britain finally adopted the Gregorian calendar that other European nations had been using since 1582. Britain's Julian calendar was by then eleven days behind, so when the nation switched calendars on September 2, 1752, it was immediately followed by September 14, 1752, and Gainsborough and his compatriots lost eleven days overnight.[11] Printed annual almanacs and calendars conveyed the rhythms of the year in Britain and its colonies, tracking holidays, moon cycles, court sessions, and much more, including lists of how many years away one was from major historical events, such as the creation of the earth (5,731 years in 1782).[12] Social "seasons" dictated how and where Gainsborough's fashionable clientele spent their days; the London season ran from November to March, and that at Bath—where a master of ceremonies presided over daily itineraries—ran from October to May.[13]

The fashionable set planned wardrobes accordingly. Women especially (and their milliners and tailors) competed to debut the season's latest styles, established primarily by Parisian designers and circulated through Europe and its colonies in the form of fashion dolls, plates, and, later, magazines. Varying by region and class, certain types of dress were appropriate for day and others for evening. Commenting on the disparity between how the British dressed in the morning versus in the evening, the French writer François de la Rochefoucauld described staying in a Suffolk country house in 1784, where, beginning at breakfast (9 o'clock), "the ladies are fully dressed with their hair properly done for the day" and at "4 o'clock precisely . . . you must present yourself in the drawing room with a great deal more ceremony than we are accustomed to in France."[14]

Pressures of time shaped Gainsborough's working life. He painted furiously to satisfy client demands during seasons in Bath and London and, beginning in 1760, to meet deadlines for annual exhibitions at the Society of Artists and later the Royal Academy.[15] Without a deadline, he could take months to complete a portrait, such as *Mrs. Graham* (see fig. 22), which seems to have occupied him on and off for about a year.[16] It is no wonder that he pictured her in Van Dyck dress, for such a protracted gestation for the portrait would not have suited the cycles of modern fashion. Critics were watching: The *Morning Herald*, for instance, reported in 1785 that Gainsborough was working on a portrait of the actress Sarah Siddons and that in it she wore "the new stile [*sic*] of drapery" in a dress that was "particularly *novelle*" (p. 13).[17]

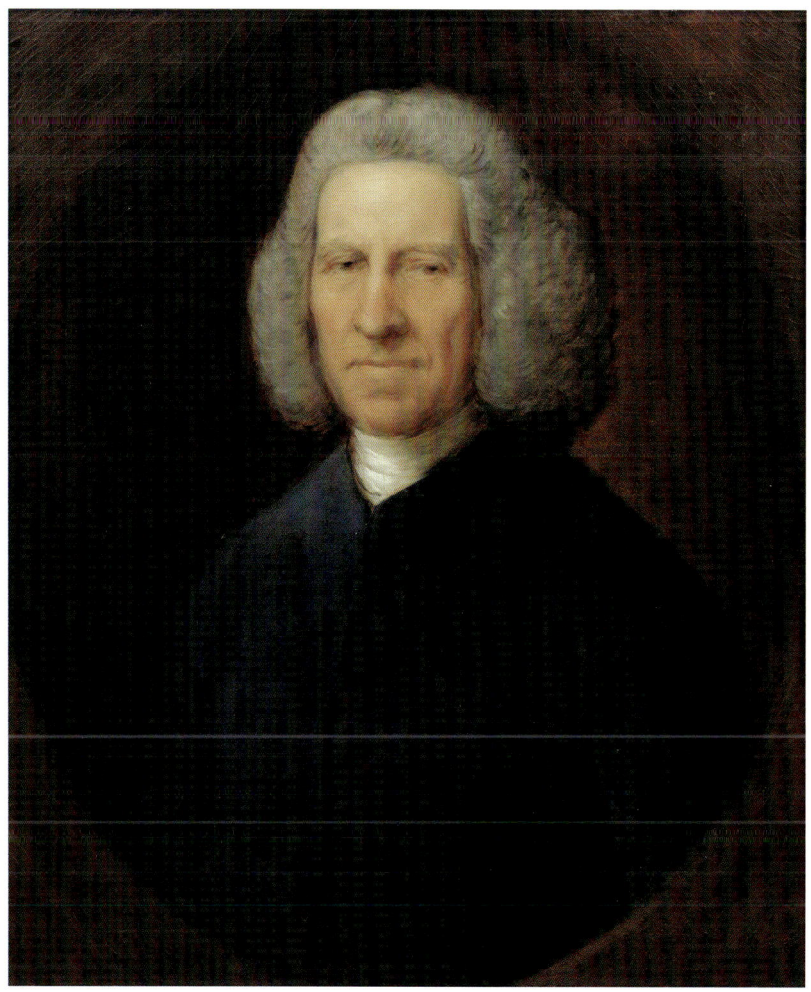

The pocket watch was an element of fashion that signaled mastery over one's time, as well as affluence and, as technology advanced, ever greater command of knowledge and science, regardless of whether the wearer needed it in his daily life (usually he did not).[18] Women owned watches, but few painted portraits of Gainsborough's time show women wearing them (notably, one is included among the accessories of an extant fashion doll from the period; see fig. 5).[19] A similar trend in the ownership of clocks for the home suggests that instruments of time and technology tended to be in the male domain and possibly even considered "unfeminine."[20] Watches were such an indispensable part of male fashion that some men wore pieces that did not actually tell time but simply suggested the form of a watch, to create an association with the timepiece as a status symbol.[21] Gainsborough's portraits imply watches but do not depict them. They show watch chains, from which hang seals (used to impress the wearer's monogram and other devices into wax), while the timepiece itself is understood to be tucked into a fob, or a shallow pocket in the waistband (still sewn into some trousers today).[22] In Gainsborough's stark portrait of George III (fig. 31), the chain and seals fall straight down from beneath his waistcoat, mirroring the stillness of the composition, while in *James Christie* (cat. 17), they tumble to the right, as if Gainsborough has captured the auctioneer in motion.

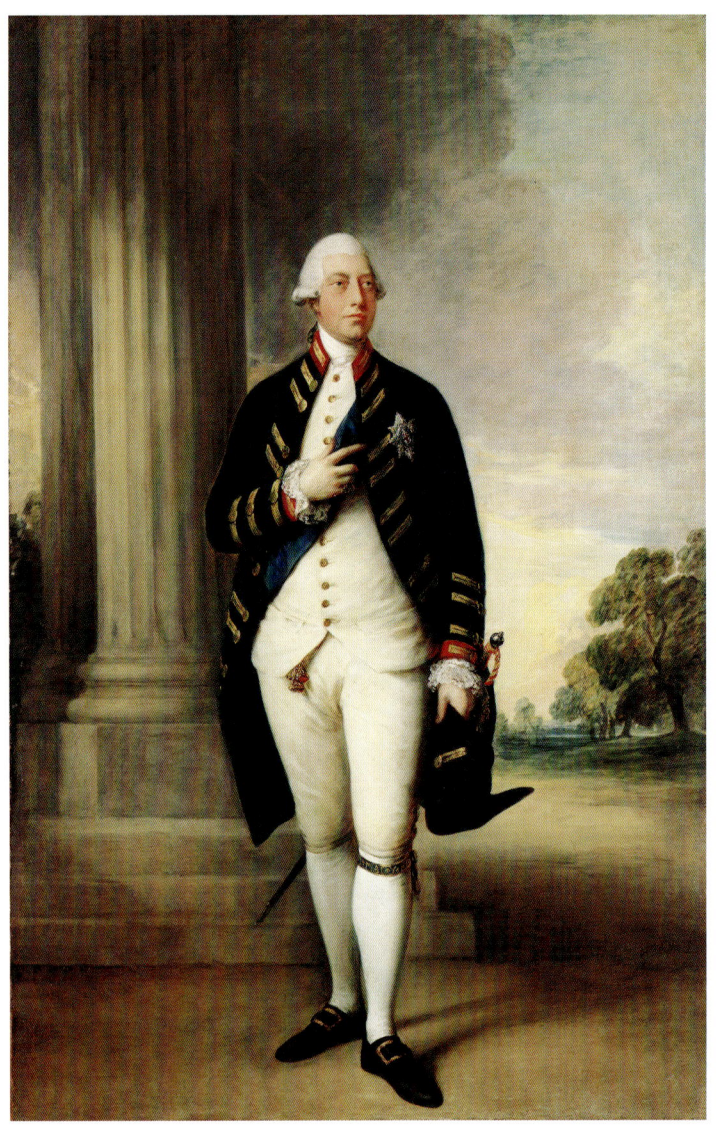

FIG. 31
Thomas Gainsborough
George III, 1780–81
Oil on canvas
94 x 62½ in. (238.8 x 158.7 cm)
Royal Collection Trust, London (RCIN 401406)

    Watches were among the most common items reported stolen among men's articles. In 1775, highwaymen robbed Gainsborough of a watch, "the inside case made of metal, and the outside case covered with shagreen."[23] He had been traveling with Johann Christian Bach (whose court testimony recounted the thieves crying, "Stop, your money or your watch!" before seizing both).[24] When it came to recovering Gainsborough's watch at the courthouse, his twenty-one-year-old nephew Dupont arrived to claim it, explaining that his uncle had borrowed it from him.[25]

The impermanence of fashion meant that tailors and dressmakers were constantly stitching and unstitching and adding, removing, and replacing layers to refresh garments. Clothing at all levels of society was designed with change in mind.[26] The style of dress in *Sarah Hodges, Later Lady Innes* (cat. 4), for example—called a *sacque* dress (or dress *à la française*)—was made from gathered fabrics at the back that could be let out to create different shapes and sizes as the wearer's needs changed.[27] Gainsborough showed that portraits could be similarly adaptable over time. Many reasons prompted him to repaint them years after their making—from births and deaths to new titles and other shifts in identity, and above all his clients' desire to keep up with changing tastes.[28] No evidence confirms how much he charged for such alterations, if anything; on several occasions, he offered to make modifications for free.[29] He also made alterations to other artists' portraits and vice versa.[30] Even after Gainsborough's death, artists endeavored to keep his portraits up to date: John Raphael Smith engraved his 1781 portrait of the Prince of Wales in 1783 (figs. 32, 33), republished it in 1785, and after Gainsborough died in 1788 republished it again in 1789 (fig. 34) and 1813 with adjustments to reflect the aging face and broadening body of the subject.[31]

Repainting was one solution to portraiture's problem with fashion and time, but it was not a profitable one. Complementary updates to completed portraits were hardly ideal for an artist who already complained about the portraits he had to make. Gainsborough appears to have sought other ways to avoid the trap of modern fashion: Like other artists of the era, he turned to fancy dress. The matter was not, however, a simple binary between modern and non-modern attire. Reynolds hints at the complexity of the matter when, while prescribing in his *Seventh Discourse* "a general air of the antique" to bring dignity to a portrait, he concedes that it should also have "something of the modern for the sake of likeness."[32] And so Reynolds championed concoctions of women clad in vaguely classical garments evoking an imagined Greco-Roman past while wearing high-piled hairstyles of the 1770s. Gainsborough's defense of modern dress in his 1771 letter to Lord Dartmouth, together with his exacting portrayals of attire, can obscure the fact that he did not always precisely record how people dressed; as artists do, he augmented, embellished, and invented clothing, sometimes mixing historical elements with modern styles.[33] His words and convincingly rendered clothes should be considered alongside his decades-long experiments with Van Dyck dress. Indeed, he exhibited his most emphatic endorsement of non-modern dress, *The Blue Boy*, at the Royal Academy in 1770, the year before he wrote to Dartmouth about the virtues of modern fashion.

"Fancy" and "fancied dress" were not rigidly defined terms, though they applied principally to antique-style or generally "exotic" garments. Cataloguers of the 1770 Royal Academy exhibition, for instance, designated Gainsborough's portrait of Penelope Ligonier (see fig. 29) as a *Portrait of a Woman in a Fancied Dress*.[34] Meanwhile, the showstopping Van Dyck suit of Gainsborough's *The Blue Boy* went unremarked, the painting displayed simply as *Portrait of a Young Gentleman*.[35] The artist himself made no explicit mention of Van Dyck dress in his surviving correspondence. In terms of specific costumes, he refers only to "the foolish custom of Painters dressing people like scaramouches,"[36] the stock *commedia dell'arte* character—invoked hyperbolically to make his point about "fancied Dress taking away Likeness" from a portrait.[37]

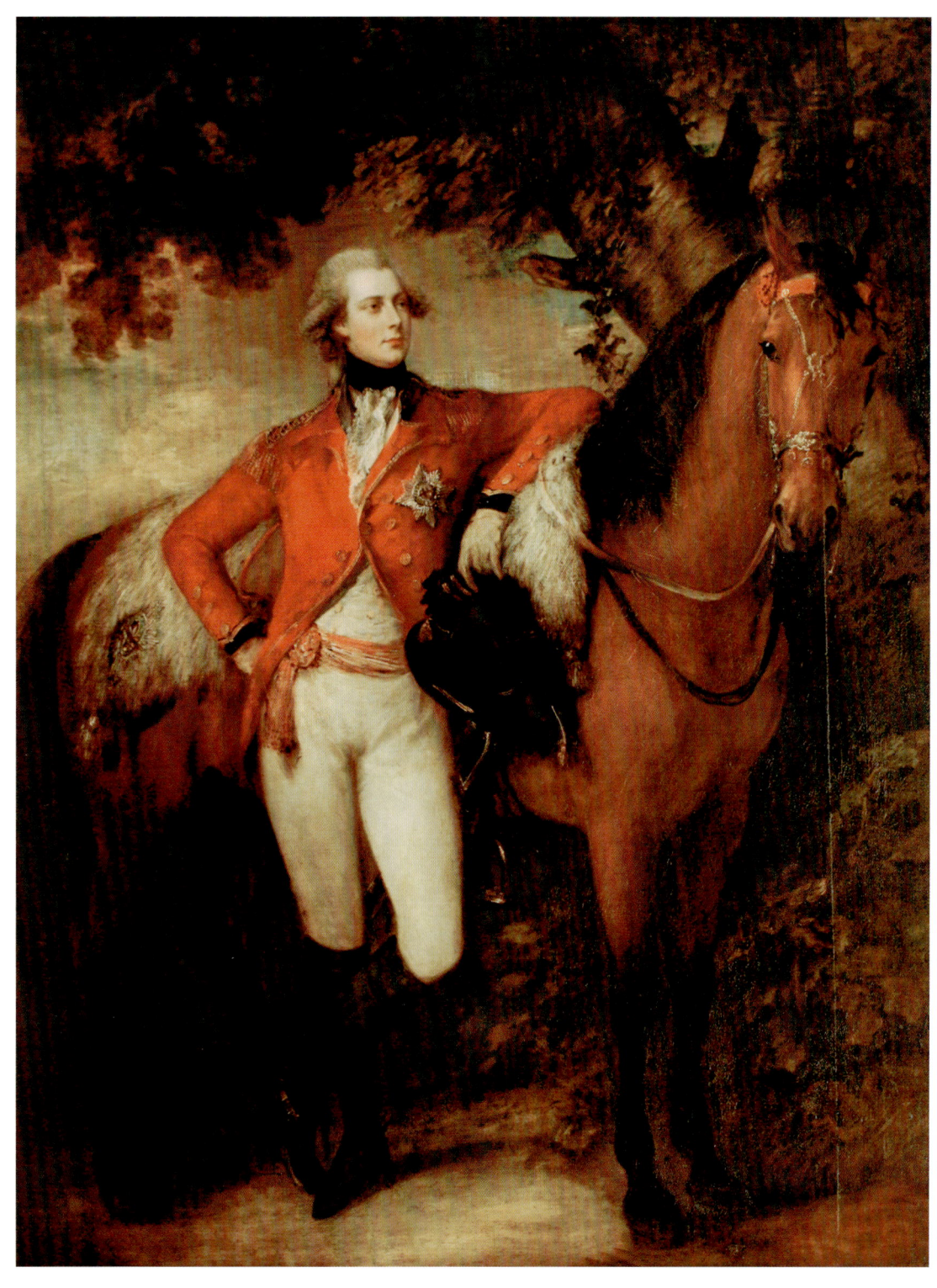

FIG. 32
Thomas Gainsborough
Prince of Wales, ca. 1782
Oil on canvas
98⁷⁄₁₆ x 73¼ in. (250 x 186 cm)
Waddesdon Manor, Waddesdon, Aylesbury (2258)

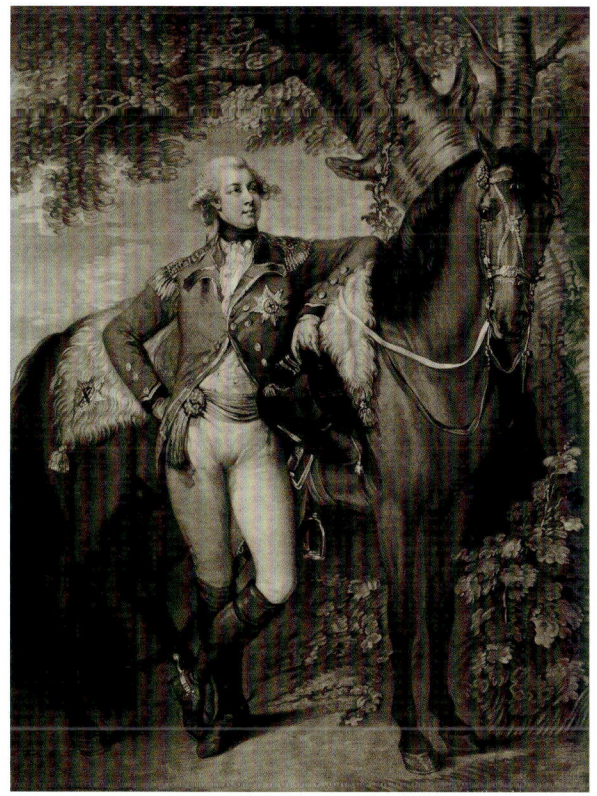 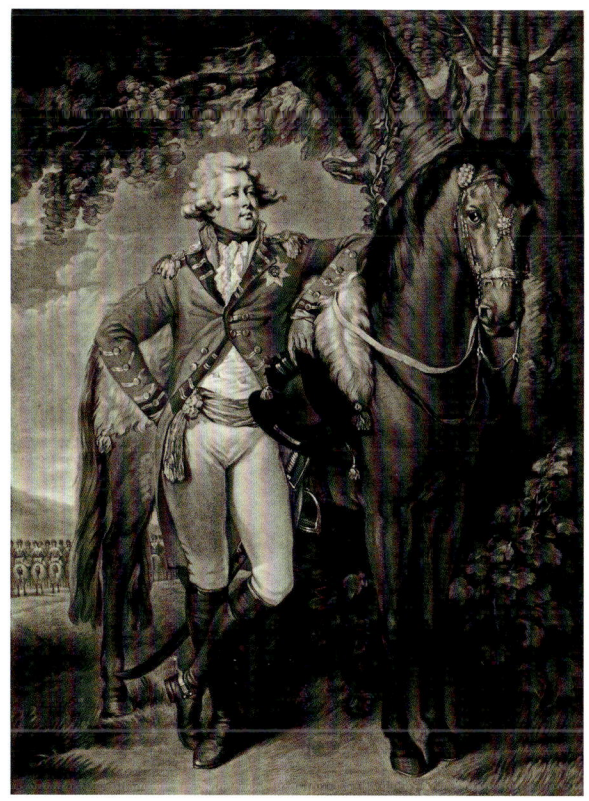

FIG. 33
John Raphael Smith (after Thomas Gainsborough)
Prince of Wales, 1783
Engraving
25¹¹/₁₆ x 17⅞ in. (652 x 454 mm)
The British Museum, London (1902,1011.5066)

FIG. 34
John Raphael Smith (after Thomas Gainsborough)
Prince of Wales, 1789
Engraving
26 x 18 in. (661 x 457 mm)
The British Museum, London (1902,1011.5063)

Van Dyck dress was one of many styles that could fall under the category of "fancy" and one of a great many varieties of masquerade costume, which was part of Georgian social life. In 1742, Horace Walpole described the effect of seeing at a masquerade "quantities of pretty Vandykes, and all kinds of old pictures walked out of their frames."[38] In 1770, Fanny Burney records encountering at a masquerade a crowd of nuns and friars, a witch, Punch, an Indian queen, Dominoes (masked and hatted figures clad in hooded gowns), shepherds and shepherdesses, "a Persian," "two or three Turks," and "an old Dutchman."[39] She, meanwhile, donned a "meer fancy dress," which she described as a "close pink Persian *vest* . . . covered in gauze" and a mask.[40] Among the signature social events of the era, masquerades, or masques, offered participants momentary liberation from the rigidity of social codes and hierarchies, taking them out of their everyday lives. Playing characters in costumes and masks gave Burney courage: "But for my *mask*," she wrote, "I could scarce have had courage to appear."[41] Perhaps, in portraiture, non-modern dress had the potential to empower sitters in a similar way.

Alluding broadly to seventeenth-century portraiture by Rubens, Van Dyck, and Peter Lely, Van Dyck dress offered rich and poignant associations for British portraiture in Gainsborough's day.[42] It recalled the pre–Civil War England immortalized in portraits of Charles I's court and connected Gainsborough's patrons with a grand English lineage of the previous century, whether his sitters were from established families (see cat. 25) or were recently created peers and *nouveaux riches*.[43] Gainsborough could associate his sitters with a grand history without dressing them in head-to-toe Van Dyck: He could evoke the tradition with just a "tooth-edged lace collar or a single slashed sleeve."[44] For Grace Dalrymple Elliott, whose scandalous reputation drew wide scrutiny, the whiff of Van Dyck style in Gainsborough's full-length portrait of her may have contributed to keeping her critics at bay in a way that contemporary clothing—worn in her later portrait—did not (see cats. 18 and 21). In *The Hon. Frances Duncombe* (cat. 14), her pearl-laden, electric-blue dress in Van Dyck style seems to exaggerate and outdo the pictorial lineage she grew up with, as an orphan, among the Bouverie family at Longford Castle.

In 1776, Reynolds referred to Van Dyck dress as an outdated, though lingering, trend: "We all very well remember how common it was a few years ago for portraits to be drawn in this fantastick dress; and this custom is not yet entirely laid aside."[45] Van Dyck–style elements may have made their way into contemporary fashion, but they did not endure.[46] Over the course of three decades, Gainsborough probed the possibilities of Van Dyck dress, in whole and in part, to transcend the tyranny of modern fashion, to travel through time, and connect to a nationalist past, suggesting that, for him, Van Dyck dress was not a passing trend.[47] The full-length portrayal in a full Van Dyck suit of Bernard Howard, heir apparent to the 11th Duke of Norfolk (whom Gainsborough painted earlier in a similar Van Dyck suit), may have been the last portrait he painted before his death (cat. 25), while a personal work, the head of Gainsborough Dupont with its Van Dyck collar sketched out under foppish hair (cat. 10), was rumored to have been on his easel when he died. Through all this nostalgic costuming, his signature painting style marked his portraits as products of the eighteenth century, the painter marshalling the past to establish himself at the forefront of an emerging British school of art.[48]

❖

Jean André Rouquet described portraiture as a frivolous fashion followed by Britain's social-climbing, superficial society. While Gainsborough seems to have shared this sentiment, he also showed that portraiture had the power to be much more: a means to transgress social boundaries, a vehicle for exchange among friends and entrepreneurs, and, especially toward the end of his life, a force in the human battle against time. The care he invested in mapping time's passage manifests in portraits like *Margaret Gainsborough* (cat. 15) and *Mary, Duchess of Montagu* (cat. 8). Lavishing time on articulating fine lines and the topography of aged faces, he honors the dignity of older age and records both likeness and years lived.

According to an early anecdote, the parents of Master John Heathcote (cat. 11) had lost their other children to illness and begged Gainsborough to paint the child's portrait before they lost him too. The story has been evoked in modern scholarship to reflect the artist's compassion. The family's tragedy may have reminded him of his own; his early family portrait (see fig. 54) is said to record the likeness of his first daughter, Margaret, who died barely a toddler. Death was all around. Gainsborough's *The Gravenor Family* (cat. 3) presents the wife and daughters of John Gravenor, who did not make a similar record of his late first wife and

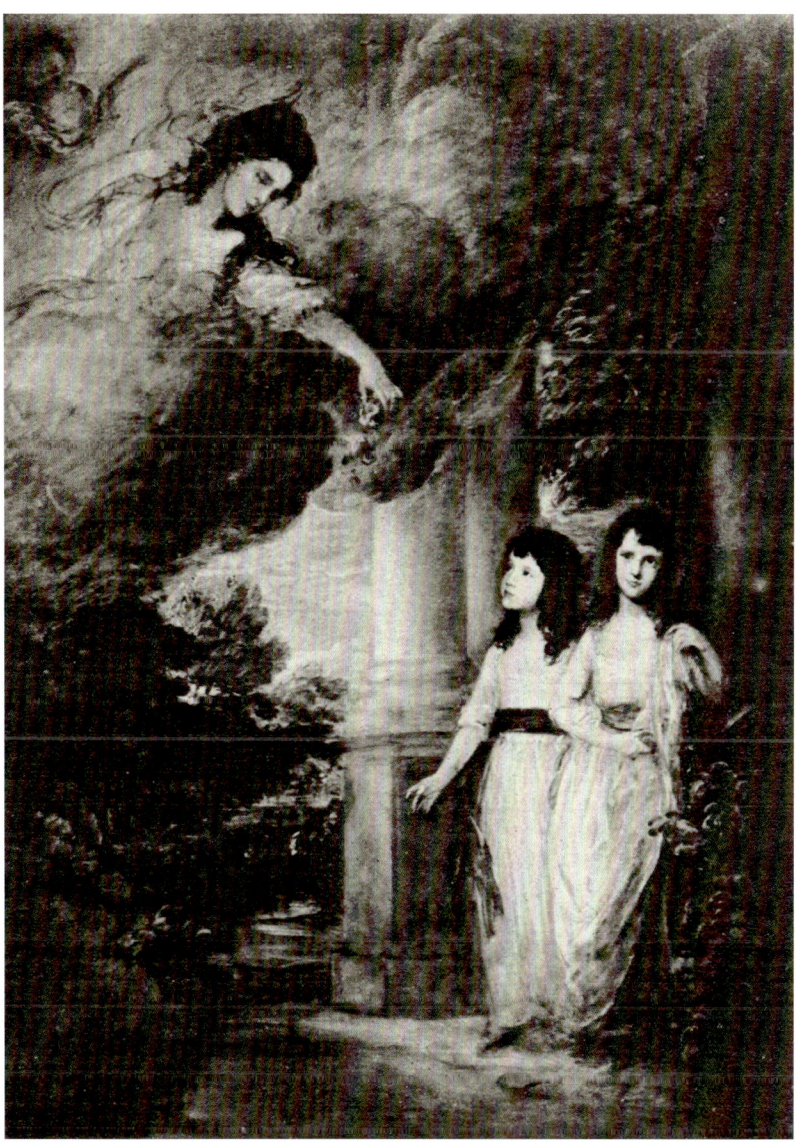

FIG. 35
Photograph of Gainsborough's *Mrs. Sloper Spiritualized
and Two Girls* from *The Illustrated London News*,
December 11, 1920

73

their son, who died in childhood. Gainsborough painted his bust of Samuel Linley (cat. 16) just in time, as the teenager—dressed in his uniform as a midshipman in the Royal Navy—died soon after, in the midst of his first voyage. Gainsborough's portraits of Samuel and his elder brother, who drowned a few months before Samuel's death, must have taken a new and painful place in the Linley family's life after their passings. A self-portrait Gainsborough had intended to present to his friend Abel (cat. 24) was too late to be received, as Abel died before Gainsborough could give it to him. It is said to be unfinished.

Perhaps more than any other work by Gainsborough, *Mrs. Samuel Moody* (cat. 19) represents the nature of portraiture as both fleeting fashion and a matter of life and death. What began as a stylish presentation of Samuel Moody's new wife—with hair piled high in the 1770s fashion and toying with a string of pearls at her neck—was transformed into a memorial. When she died shortly after the birth of the couple's younger son, her widower brought the portrait back to Gainsborough to paint the children in (and the pearl necklace out), creating a vision of the mother with her boys that was possible only in paint. A few years later, Gainsborough accepted an "uncommon" commission to depict a "spiritualised" maternal figure—her identity is debated but clearly she was already deceased—looking down from a cloud bed upon two young girls (fig. 35).[49] Since Gainsborough was adamant about his preference for painting from life, one must wonder who or what served as his model for the ghostly figure. The triple portrait was cut into fragments in the early twentieth century, disconnecting the union.

When the formerly enslaved African Olaudah Equiano (1745–1797), who bought his freedom in England in 1766 and became a respected man of letters, first encountered a painted portrait belonging to his "master," he was afraid. The picture "appeared constantly to look at me," he wrote. "At one time I thought it was something relative to magic; and not seeing it move, I thought it might be some way the whites had to keep their great men when they died, and offer them libations as we used to do our friendly spirits."[50] As a maker of portraits, Gainsborough knew better than anyone that they were simply pigments suspended in medium, laid with brushes on linen for well-to-do Brits to trade as social currency. Yet surely, he also saw them as Equiano first did, as a way to "keep" those who have passed. Two months before his death, seemingly aware of his limited time, he wrote with precision about his own image. "It is my strict charge," reads the unaddressed letter, "that after my decease no plaster cast, model, or likeness whatever be permitted to be taken: But that if Mr. Sharp, who engraved Mr. Hunter's Print, should chuse to make a print from the ¾ sketch which I intended for Mr. Abel painted by myself, I give free consent."[51] Why he chose the self-portrait meant for Abel over any other is unknown; his surviving daughter did not perceive it to be his closest likeness (see cat. 24). For Gainsborough, this portrait's lack of finish and its intention for a friend may have offered something poignant at the end of his life: an impression of a painter still at work, a perpetual work in progress. Gainsborough's portraits served many functions for the men, women, and children who sat for him, each likeness he committed to paint becoming, in the end, a way to keep them alive—enduring testaments to lives as fleeting as fashion.

NOTES

1 Gainsborough's *Self-Portrait* (Houghton Hall) is inscribed on the back, in a nineteenth-century hand, "Painted by Thomas Gainsborough at Ipswich about the year 1754 (2nd sitting of himself) aged 28", Belsey 2019, 1: no. 369.

2 Reynolds 1959, 259.

3 Gainsborough to James Unwin, July 10, 1770; Hayes 2001, 78. Sloman (2004, 319) suggests "Gainsborough's ability to catch a likeness within a very short space of time commended him to the pleasure-seeking clientele of Bath. Resort visitors feared being 'fatigued' by lengthy portrait sittings, and one Bath artist was so anxious for employment he advertised portraits from no sittings at all, although these cost more than his usual price."

4 Hayes 2001, 89–90.

5 Buck 1979, 17.

6 Ribeiro 1995, 62.

7 Wendeborn 1791, 1: 193, 224, quoted in Buck 1979, 94.

8 Rosenthal 1999, 17.

9 Belsey 2019, 1: 332.

10 Hayes 2001, 81.

11 On calendar reform in England, see Poole 1998.

12 See Morriello 2023, 244–46. Vickery 2009, 108, discusses the use of account books, diary, and pocket book.

13 A character in Tobias Smollett's 1771 *Expedition of Humphry Clinker* describes Bath's grueling social schedule: "We have musick [*sic*] in the Pump-room every morning, cotillons every fore-noon in the rooms, balls twice a week, and concerts every other night, besides private assemblies and parties without number"; Smollett 2015, 45.

14 Quoted in Buck 1979, 59. La Rochefoucauld 1933, 28.

15 Whitley ([1915] 2016, 166) recounts Gainsborough trying to meet the exhibition deadline, promising a Thomas Stratford that "he will touch up certain works for him when he comes to town, but . . . at the moment his hands are full, as the pictures for the Exhibition must be packed up and despatched [*sic*] in the course of the following week."

16 Belsey (2019, 1: 410) cites a letter from Mrs. Neale to Mary Graham dated June 1775, though without clarity on which portrait of Mrs. Graham it refers to: "Gainsborough has not advanced your picture a single stroke, and sais [*sic*] he has no thoughts of finishing it within twelve month, if he did not add that it shall be the compleatest of pictures, I should cry at the delay."

17 *Morning Herald*, April 1, 1785.

18 Vickery 2009, 264: "A watch was above all a prestigious piece of male jewellery, often adorned with extra decorative seals. Adult success, enviable affluence and a command of technology were all embodied in a silver watch."

19 William Hogarth's *Miss Mary Edwards* (The Frick Collection, New York), which showcases her watch, is an important exception.

20 Vickery 2009, 263.

21 Cummins 2010, 38.

22 On seals as fashionable and necessary accessories for men, especially landed letter writers, see Clifford 2004, 121–23.

23 Trial of Henry M'allester and Archibald Girdwood 1775.

24 Idem.

25 According to Whitley ([1915] 2016, 143), the artist had borrowed the watch from Gainsborough Dupont, then only twenty-one years old, who claimed it as his property at the trial. Gainsborough does not seem to have appeared at the trial and both of the accused were acquitted on the charge; however, found guilty of theft against Bach, one of the men was hanged. Whitley ([1915] 2016, 404–5) recounts an anecdote regarding Gainsborough's drinking and almost losing his watch.

26 Buck 1979, 183.

27 Ribeiro 1995, 54.

28 Among many examples of Gainsborough's reworked portraits are *The Byam Family* (Andrew Brownsword Art Foundation, on loan to Holburne Museum, Bath), which featured complete costume changes and the addition of their child (Postle 2002, 27; Belsey 2019, 1: no. 140), and *William Lynch* (Muskegon Museum of Art, Michigan), the uniform of which Gainsborough repainted after the Eastern Battalion of the Suffolk Militia was disbanded in 1763 (Belsey 2019, 2: no. 609).

29 Gainsborough, writing to Richard Stevens, January 28, 1768: "I am sorry sir I have not been so happy in Mrs. Awse's Picture as to give satisfaction to yourself and friends. . . . If at any time you should have a convenience of bringing Mrs. Awse's Picture with you to Bath I shall very willingly make any alterations which you or Mrs. Awse may think proper, without any additional charge" (Hayes 2001, 50).

30 Gainsborough reworked a portrait of John Meller, originally painted in the 1720s (Belsey 2019, 2: no. 627), and one of Reynolds's studio assistants appears to have repainted the attire in Gainsborough's *Mrs. John Hudson* (Wallington Hall, Northumberland); see Belsey 2019, 1: no. 510.

31 A. Griffiths in London 1978, no. 170. Russell 1926, 304–7, no. 1308.

32 Reynolds 1959, 140. Pointon 1993, 114.

33 Ribeiro 1995, 73–74.

34 Belsey 2019, 2: 549: "The confection that the sitter wears and her pose are best described as Turkish."

35 London 1770, no. 85. Van Dyck dress was also variously understood. Though modern scholars have described a pair of portraits of the sons of Archibald Hamilton (Belsey 2019, 1: nos. 435, 436) as donning Van Dyck dress, the *Morning Herald* (December 30, 1786) describes them differently: "Two of the Sons of Lord Archibald Hamilton are charming portraits; —the elder brother is in a Vandyke habit, and his hair in a style to comport with the drapery;—The other is in a modern dress."

36 Gainsborough to William, 2nd Earl of Dartmouth, April 18 [1771]; Hayes 2001, 90.

37 Gainsborough to William, 2nd Earl of Dartmouth, April 13, 1771; Hayes 2001, 90.

38 Walpole (1974, 338–39) describes the diversity of costumes as "an assemblage of all ages and nations" and that it would have "looked like the day of judgment, if tradition did not persuade us that we are all to meet naked." On Van Dyck dress as masquerade wear and in portraiture, see Nevinson 1964, Ribeiro 1977, Cherry and Harris 1982, and Ribeiro 2002, 245–82.

39 January 10, 1770. Burney 1907, 1: 70–77.

40 Burney 1907, 1: 71.

41 Idem.

42 On Gainsborough and the "habit of Rubens's wife," see Belsey 2019, 1: no. 325. MacLeod (2001) discusses the continuity of Peter Lely's portraiture.

43 Cherry and Harris 1982, 305.

44 Cherry and Harris 1982, 300. Woodall (1963, 24) addresses the variants of Van Dyck dress that veered far away from their prototypes.

45 Reynolds 1959, 138–39. Cherry and Harris (1982, 291) point out that shaky knowledge of historical dress led generally to any dress of the 1630s being called "Van Dyck dress" in Gainsborough's time.

46 Cherry and Harris 1982, 301. Sloman 2002, 116.

47 Sloman (2013, 237) suggests that Gainsborough kept a Van Dyck–style masquerade suit in his painting rooms as one appears almost exactly in various portraits. Cherry and Harris 1982, 292, discuss Gainsborough's varied use of Van Dyck style in his portraits.

48 Reynolds (1959, 248) commemorated Gainsborough shortly after his death: "If ever this nation should produce genius sufficient to acquire to us the honourable distinction of an English School, the name of Gainsborough will be transmitted to posterity, in the history of art, among the very first of that rising name."

49 On the debates around the subjects of the portrait, which was cut into three fragments, see Belsey 2019, 1: 406. Whitley ([1915] 2016, 324) identifies the maternal figure as the late Mrs. Sloper, who is to be "spiritualized" in the representation, and her two surviving daughters.

50 Equiano 2003, 63.

51 Fragment, no addressee, June 15, 1788; Hayes 2001, 175. Gainsborough wrote to Reynolds (July 1788) acknowledging the end of his life and wishing for a final meeting; Hayes 2001, 176.

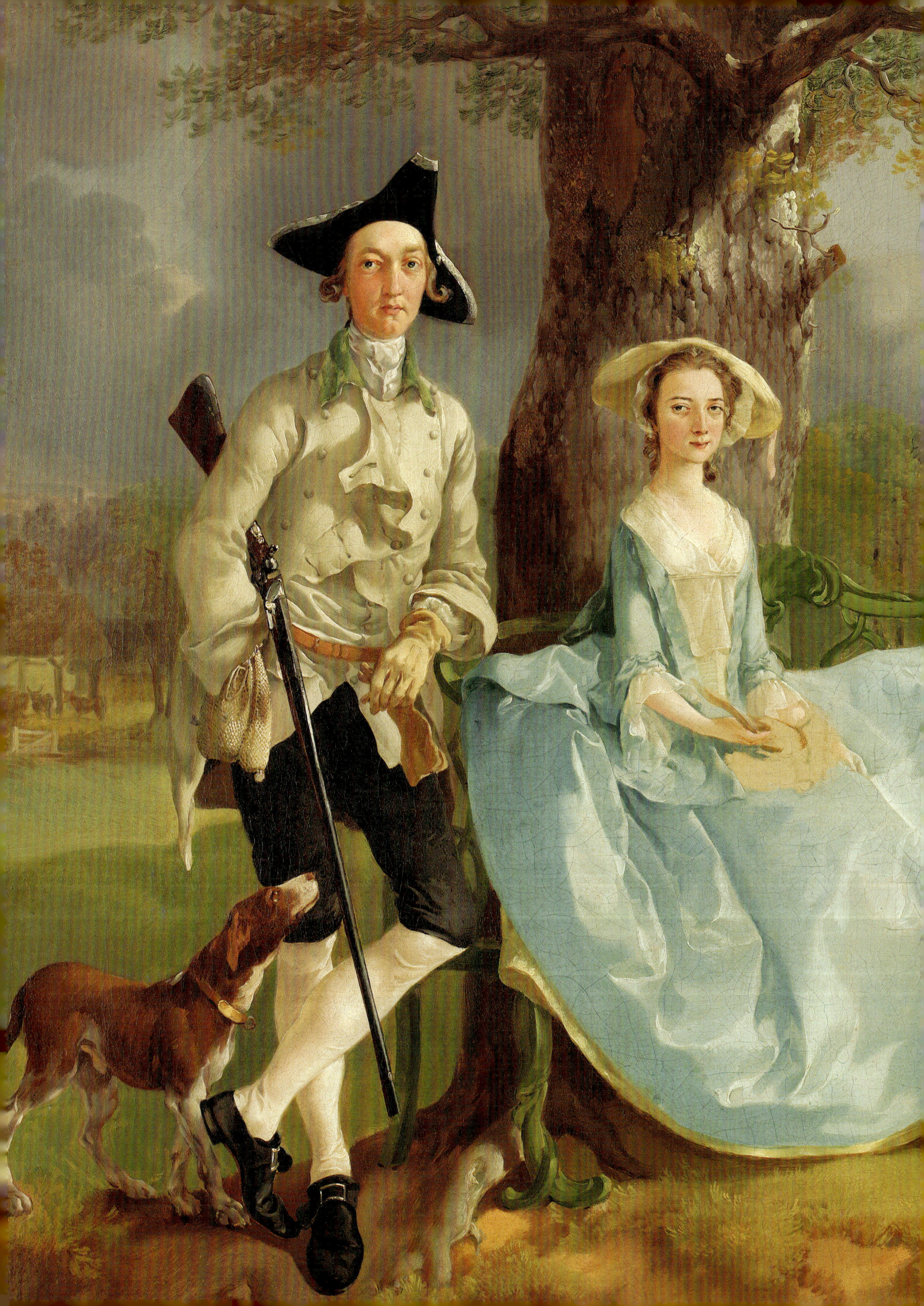

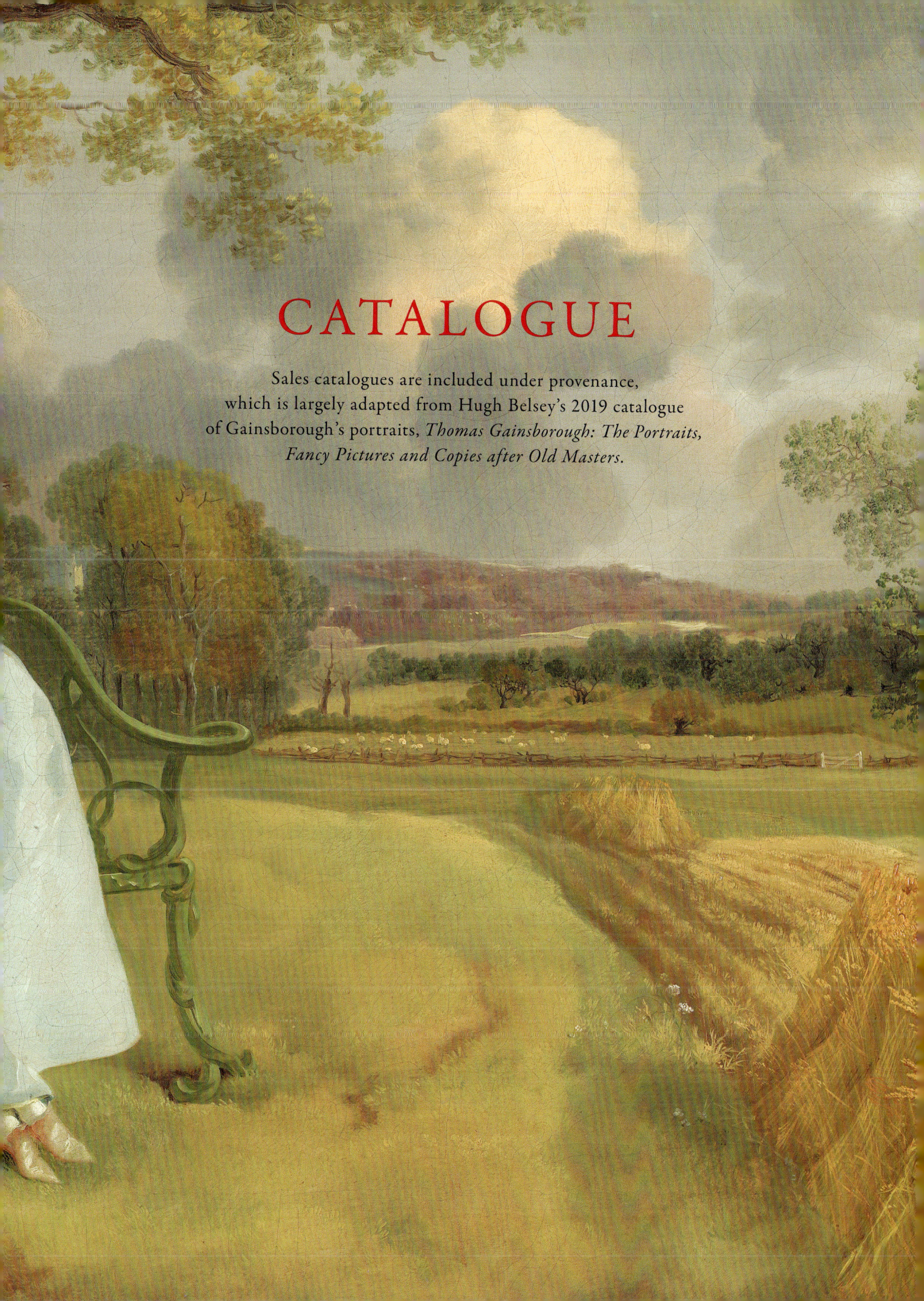

CATALOGUE

Sales catalogues are included under provenance,
which is largely adapted from Hugh Belsey's 2019 catalogue
of Gainsborough's portraits, *Thomas Gainsborough: The Portraits,
Fancy Pictures and Copies after Old Masters.*

CAT. 1

PETER DARNELL MUILMAN, CHARLES CROKATT, AND WILLIAM KEABLE

CA. 1750

Oil on canvas
30⅛ x 25¼ in. (76.5 x 64.2 cm)
Tate, London; Purchased jointly with Gainsborough's House, Sudbury,
with assistance from the National Heritage Memorial Fund, the Art Fund,
and the Friends of the Tate Gallery, 1993 (T06746)

THIS CONVERSATION PIECE (a type of small-scale group portrait popular in Britain from the 1720s to 1750s) was probably painted soon after Gainsborough—newly married and aged twenty-one—returned to Sudbury from his apprenticeship and early work in London. It retains strong stylistic similarity to portraits by Francis Hayman, with whom he had studied and worked in the capital city.[1] A label once affixed to the back of the painting (with an inscription written after 1789) identifies the three sitters as Peter Darnell Muilman (1730–1766), Charles Crokatt (1730–1769), and William Keable (?1714–1774), though it does not indicate which figure is which.[2] Muilman and Crokatt were born into wealthy merchant families from Amsterdam and Charles Town (present-day Charleston, South Carolina), respectively, who had in 1749 acquired estates—and thus the status of landed gentry—in Essex.[3] Keable was a local Suffolk painter and musician some fourteen years their senior. Why the three men are pictured together is unknown, as are the circumstances of the commission. It has been suggested that the father of either Crokatt or Muilman ordered the painting to commemorate the new status of their immigrant family as landed gentry in England. It may also have been commissioned to mark, or in anticipation of, the engagement of Crokatt to Muilman's sister Anna, through whom the painting descended; they married in 1752.[4] Keable may have been his companions' music or drawing teacher, his inclusion here representing the families' culture and access to these arts, as well as, perhaps, the sitters' friendship.[5]

78

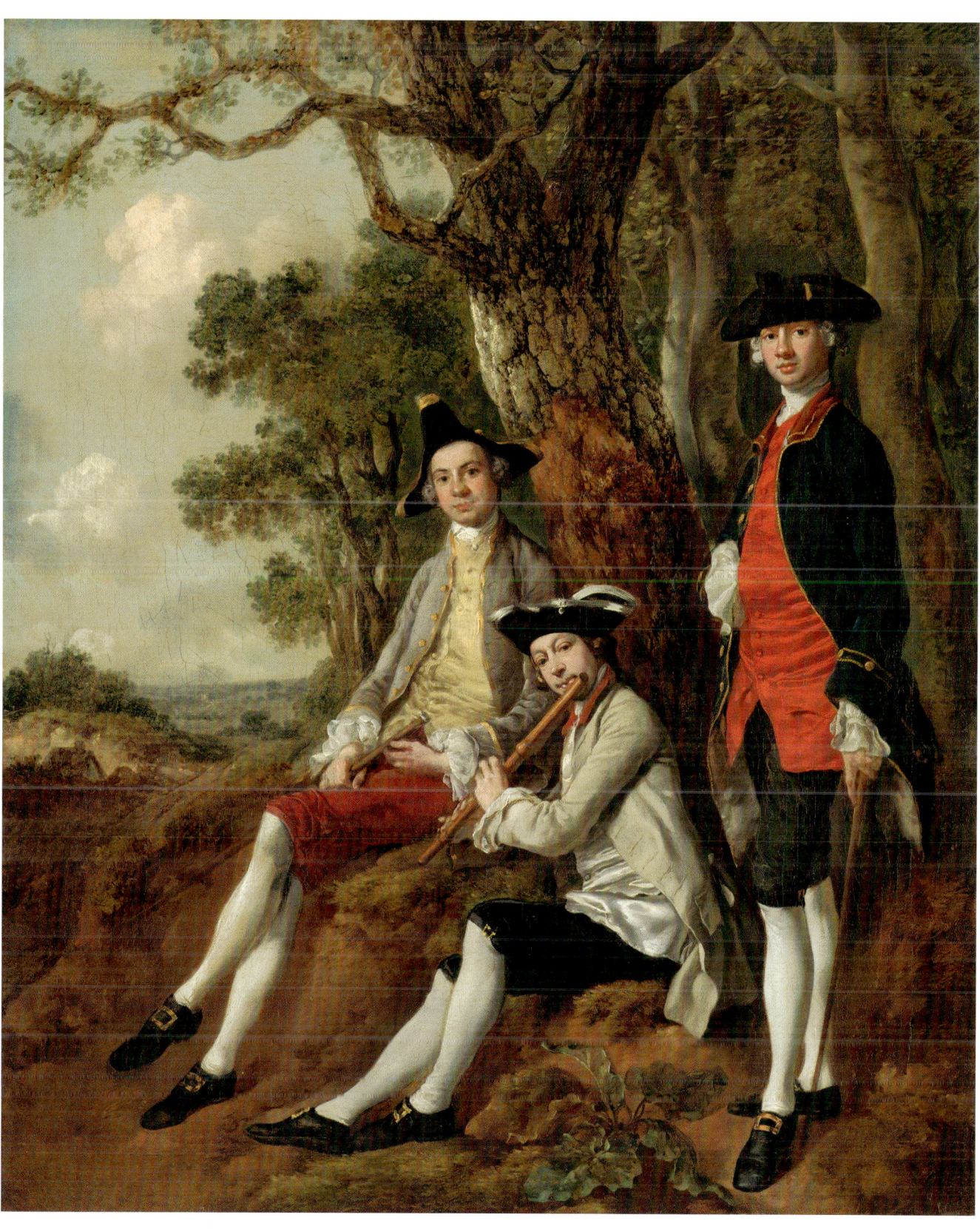

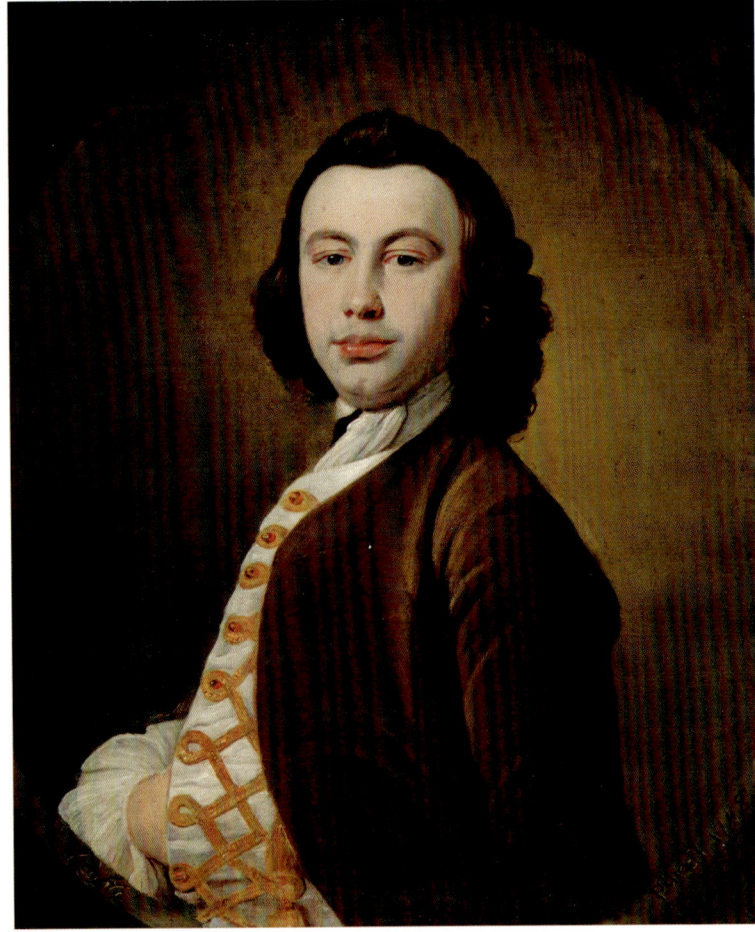

FIG. 36
William Keable
Self-Portrait, 1748
Oil on canvas
30⅛ x 25 in.
(76.5 x 63.5 cm)
Yale Center for
British Art, New Haven;
Paul Mellon Collection
(B1976.7.47)

The figure playing the flute is no doubt Keable, based on the musician's resemblance to a self-portrait by Keable at the Yale Center for British Art (fig. 36).[6] Moreover, the act of blowing into the instrument creates a facial distortion that, however subtle, would have been deemed inappropriate for portraits of gentlemen of the standing of Muilman and Crokatt.[7] The flanking figures, adorned with powdered wigs, coats with gold trim, and gold decoration on their tricorns (in contrast to the natural hair, untrimmed coat, and silver hat decoration on the central figure) must be Muilman and Crokatt. Which one is which has not been securely determined; however, one contemporary described Crokatt as "a very pretty young fellow" and Muilman, "from what I have seen, and heard of him," as "not quite so agreeable as could be wished," leading scholars to identify the figure on the left as Crokatt, with Muilman—exhibiting more "hauteur"—on the right.[8]

The suggestion (from the label on the back) that Keable painted the figures and Gainsborough the landscape has been challenged since at least 1927.[9] Examination by Tate conservators confirms that the face of Keable is painted differently than the rest of the composition, but no evidence explicitly supports attribution to another hand.[10] While scholars generally agree that the entire composition is by Gainsborough, there is tentative acceptance of the possibility that Keable had a hand in the work, perhaps in his own self-portrait. Acknowledging that there may be "a grain of truth" to the label's claim of multiple hands, Martin Postle emphasizes the collaborative nature of portraiture in the period.[11]

An avid amateur musician, Gainsborough painted musicians throughout his career (see cat. 12). One of his group portraits (now lost) of the Ipswich Musical Club included a self-portrait of him playing the violin.[12] Gainsborough may have met Keable in artistic and musical circles, but the nature of his relationships with Muilman and Crokatt is unknown. They were close in age, and there is some evidence to suggest that Muilman may have later encountered the artist in Bath before his early death in 1766.[13] Crokatt committed suicide in 1769. Keable moved to Italy and died there.

PROVENANCE

Charles Crokatt's wife, Anna Crokatt (née Muilman, 1733–1783); by descent to their daughter Emilia Boucherett (née Crokatt, 1761–1831); by descent to her son, Ayscoghe Boucherett (1792–1857); by descent to Frederick Barne (1801–1886); by descent to Miles Robin Barne (b. 1940); his [anonymous] sale, Sotheby's, London, July 14, 1993, lot 49; where bought by Hazlitt, Gooden and Fox jointly for Gainsborough's House and Tate.

SELECTED LITERATURE

Waterhouse 1953, 116–17; Waterhouse 1958, no. 747; London 1977 (unpaginated), under no. 13; Lindsay 1981, 40; Hayes 1982, 1: 35; B. Allen in New Haven and London 1987, 40; Belsey 2002, 26–29; H. Belsey in London and Sudbury 2003, no. 2; Postle 2002, 17–19; Perkins 2002, 12–14; Sloman 2002, 35, 47, 68, 235; D. Perkins in London, Washington, and Boston 2002–3, no. 21; Chu 2017; Hamilton 2017, 82, 83, 92–93; Retford 2017, 150; Belsey 2019, 2: no. 666.

SELECTED EXHIBITION HISTORY

Norwich 1948, no. 19; Bath and other cities 1949, no. 6; London 1953a, no. 12; London 1956–57, no. 211; Norwich 1961, no. 9; Sudbury 1961, no. 4; Ferrara 1998, no. 3; Charleston 1999, no. 1; London, Washington, and Boston 2002–3, no. 21; London and Sudbury 2003, no. 2; Hamburg 2018, no. 25.

MR. AND MRS. ANDREWS

CA. 1750

Oil on canvas
27½ x 47 in. (69.8 x 119.4 cm)
National Gallery, London; Bought with contributions from
The Pilgrim Trust, the Art Fund, Associated Television Ltd.,
and Mr. and Mrs. W. W. Spooner, 1960 (NG6301)

LAUDED AS "one of the most arresting and original pictures of the eighteenth century,"[14] this painting has been described as a "triple portrait" of Robert Andrews, his wife Frances, and the farmland they owned at Auberies, outside Sudbury, which Gainsborough articulated precisely enough that modern scholars claim to be able to identify the still-standing oak tree under which the couple sits.[15] The distant church has been identified as St. Peter's in Sudbury. Born in the same year, Robert Andrews and Gainsborough both attended Sudbury Grammar School, but they were not social equals. Besides the significant wealth of the Andrews family, Frances's relatives had loaned money to Gainsborough's family after his father's bankruptcy in the 1730s.[16] Gainsborough also painted a portrait of Frances's parents, *Mr. and Mrs. Carter* (fig. 37), which, together with the present portrait, raises the question of the nature of his social relationships with the families and of these commissions, for which no documents are known.[17] Frances and Robert married in 1748, a date with which the present portrait has been associated. It has also been argued that on the basis of dress the portrait may be closer to 1750, and specifically in the early autumn, as suggested by the newly reaped cornfield and Robert's hunting attire.[18] In 1750, the will of Frances's father passed to Robert (not to Frances) a moiety of land that had been sold by Robert's ancestors, reuniting the vast land in the background of the painting into a single estate.[19]

Modern scholars have described *Mr. and Mrs. Andrews* as "radical" and "eccentric," the first English conversation piece to assign equal prominence to portrait and landscape, the latter

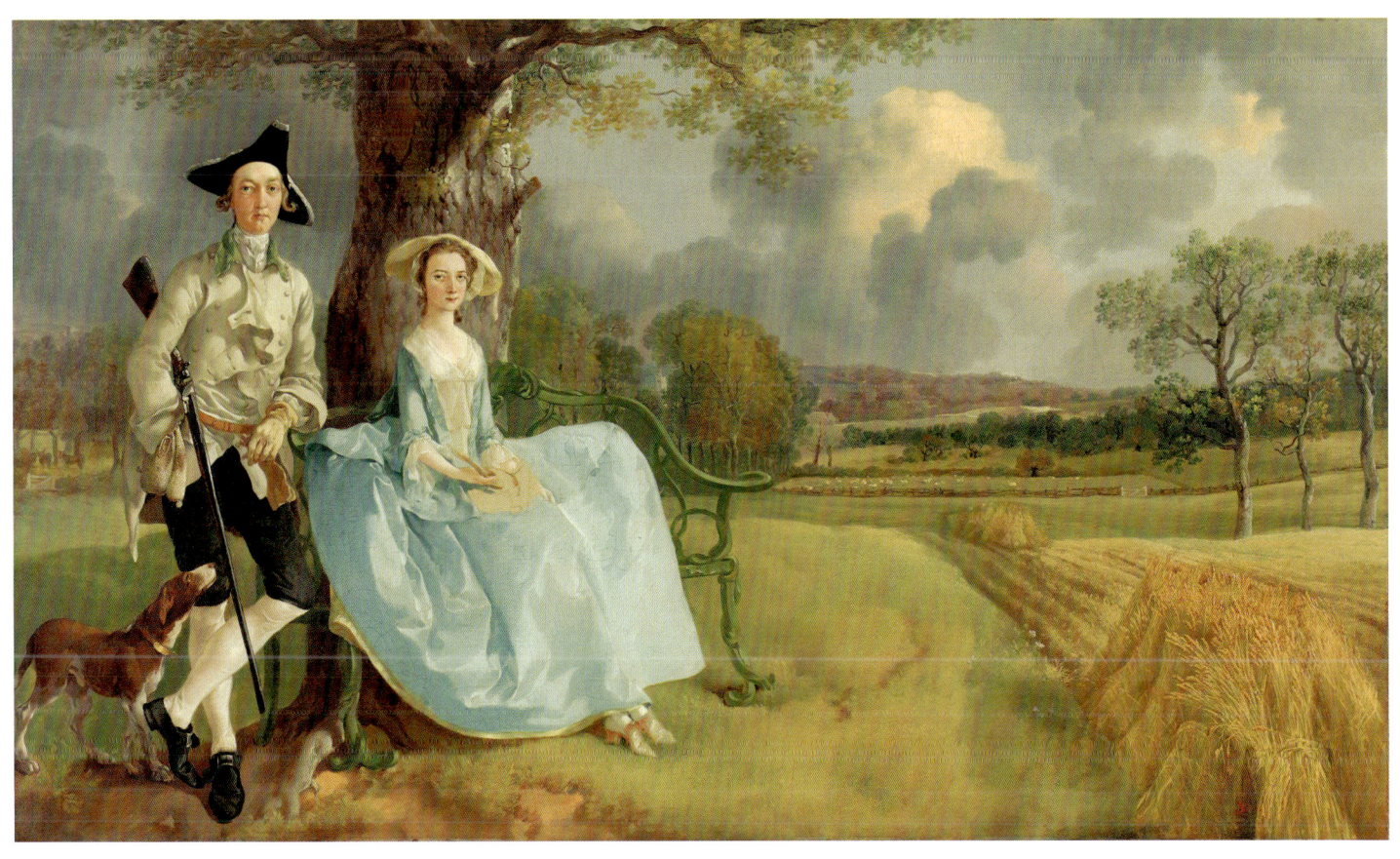

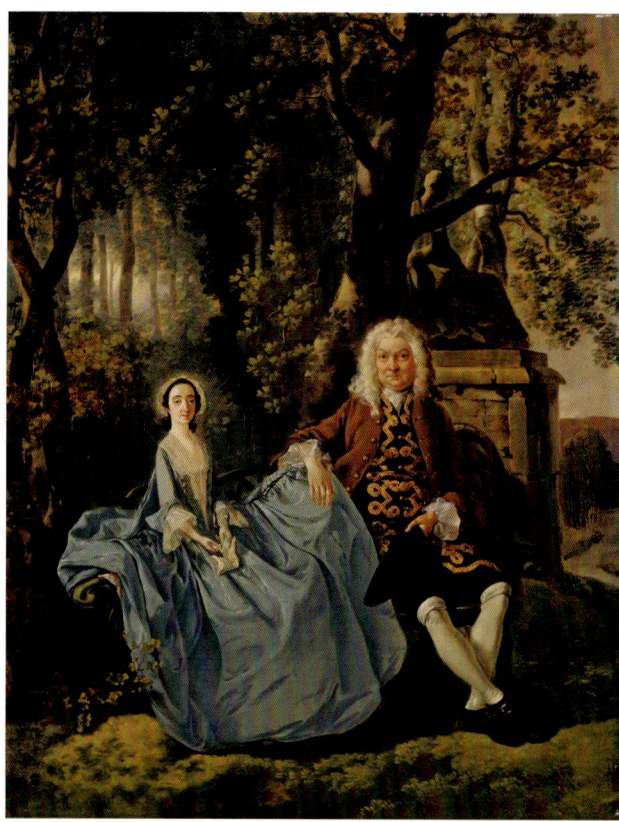

FIG. 37
Thomas Gainsborough
Mr. and Mrs. Carter, ca. 1747–48
Oil on canvas
35 15/16 x 27 15/16 in. (91.2 x 71 cm)
Tate, London (T12609)

FIG. 38
Gerard Donck
Jan van Hensbeeck, His Wife and a Child,
probably 1630s
Oil on wood
29 15/16 x 41 13/16 in. (76 x 106.2 cm)
The National Gallery, London (NG1305)

of which is not a conventional park or garden but productive farmland.[20] Seventeenth-century Dutch precedents such as Gerard Donck's *Jan van Hensbeeck, His Wife and a Child* (fig. 38) offer a historical comparison.[21] It has been argued that the emphasis on land in the earlier Dutch portraits had to do with national identity as a united republic.[22] For *Mr. and Mrs. Andrews*, the land is personal. Robert may well have requested from Gainsborough this expansive view that showcases his farmland and modern farming techniques, such as the field ploughed in regular furrows; this is also one of the few instances in which Gainsborough painted enclosures in a landscape.[23] Meanwhile, details such as the corn stacks and sheep may also allude to the couple's prosperity and fertility. Ann Bermingham draws attention to the myth of labor—the illusion that Robert is an independent producer of goods from his land—in Gainsborough's presentation of the pair alone with their agrarian holdings, which are marked with "visible signs of the labor performed by the invisible men and women who work the farm."[24]

Robert's shooting dress, with bags of powder and shot hanging from his pocket, and hunting dog underscore his status as a landowner.[25] Frances's hooped dress—accessorized with a straw hat (called Leghorn after the characteristic fine straw weaving in Livorno, Italy, then anglicized as "Leghorn") in the *bergère* style, and pink satin mules—highlights her modishness.[26] The unfinished passage in Frances's lap has been suggested to have been intended for a pheasant, left incomplete as a joke between the artist and sitters regarding Robert's shooting skills. It has also been proposed that the only reason to leave a space on Frances's lap would be

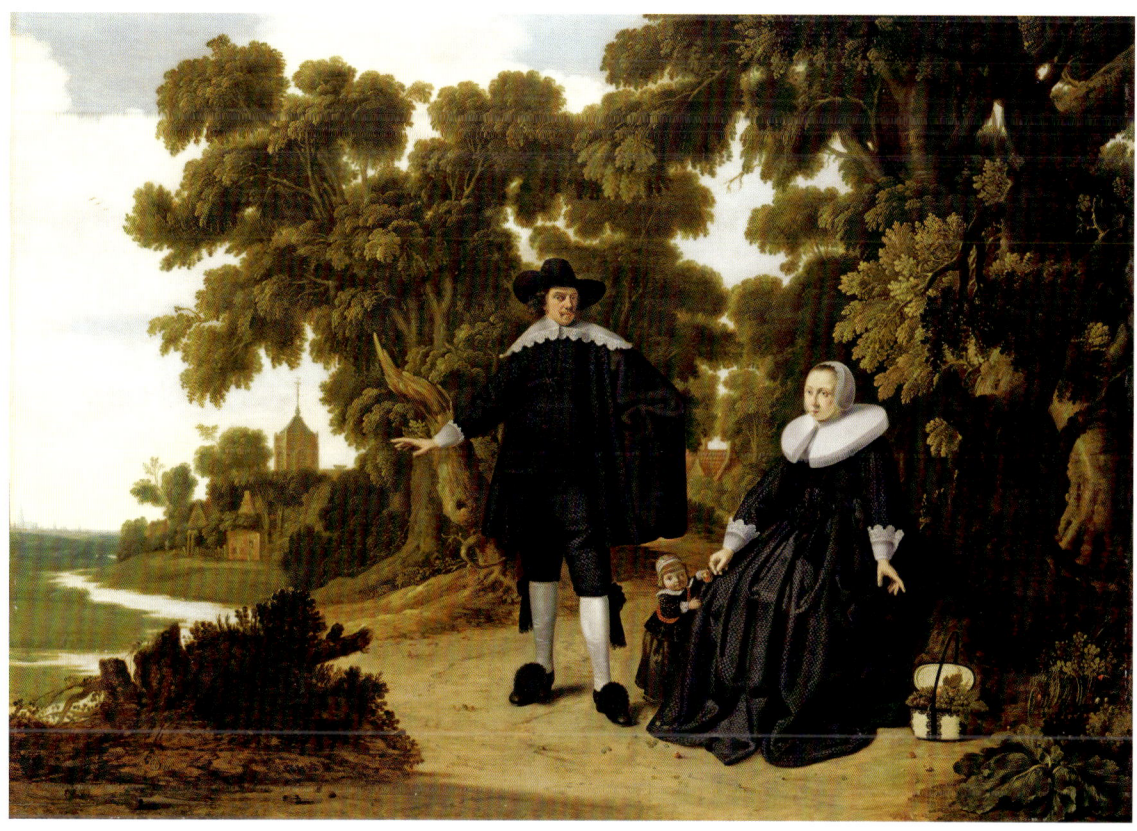

to anticipate a child (they would have nine children, the first in 1751).[27] Despite the unresolved passage, the painting was delivered to the Andrews family, with whom it remained until 1960.

PROVENANCE

By descent through the sitters' daughter Sophia (b. 1763), who married Christopher Barton Metcalfe, to Mrs. Walter Metcalfe; purchased by Louis Willoughby Andrews (b. 1831), great-grandson of the sitters; by descent to Gerald Willoughby Andrews (b. 1896); his sale, Sotheby's, March 23, 1960, lot 59; from which purchased by Agnews for Paul Mellon (1907–1999); purchased by the National Gallery, May 1960.

SELECTED LITERATURE

Armstrong 1898, 204; Armstrong 1904, 257; Estrangin 1930, 39; Williamson and Sassoon 1931, 24, pl. LXXI; Fry 1934, 69–71; Sitwell 1936, 15, 67–69, 101; Tinker 1938, 73; Waterhouse 1953, 3; Waterhouse 1958, 17, 52; *National Gallery* 1962, 25–26; Waterhouse 1962, 174; London 1963a, 28–29, no. 6301; Ripley 1964, 12–14; Berger 1972, 106–8; Williamson 1972, 18, 212; Herrmann 1974, 94; Hayes 1975, 41, 203, no. 12; Burke 1976, 213; Potterton 1976, 9–13; Goodison 1977, 80–81; Lindsay 1981, 26, 28; Waterhouse 1981, 135; Hayes 1982, 1: 67–71, 252, Rosenthal 1982, 42; Corri 1983, 214; Bermingham 1986, 28–33, 41, 201n.45; Cormack 1991, 4, 7, 10, 14, 34, 46, no. 8, 52 under no. 11, 72 under no. 21; Bensusan-Butt 1992/93, *passim*; Kalinsky 1995, 16, 40, no. 5, 44 under no. 7, 48 under no. 9, 120, no. 45; Foister 1997, 9; Rosenthal 1997, 39–40; Egerton 1998, 37–38; Asfour and Williamson 1999, 49–52, 56, 71, 133–34; Rosenthal 1999, 10, 17–18, 130, 133, 189–90; Shawe-Taylor 1999, 128–30, 205; Belsey 2002, 32, 41–43; Postle 2002, 15–16, 71–72; Vaughan 2002, 37, 52–57, 210; Govier 2010, 10, 12, no. 7; Solkin 2015, 114, 116; Retford 2017, 149–51, 305; Belsey 2019, 1: no. 20.

SELECTED EXHIBITION HISTORY

Ipswich 1927, no. 26; Brussels 1929, no. 63; Manchester 1934, no. 19; Amsterdam 1936, no. 38; London 1936, no. 93; London 1937, no. 277; Paris 1938, no. 43; Lisbon and Madrid 1949, no. 18; Hamburg and other cities 1949–50, no. 44; London 1953a, no. 5; Rotterdam 1955, no. 31; Montreal 1967, no. 38; Paris 1981 no. 4; Madrid 1988–89, no. 24; London 1991, no. 21; London, Washington, and Boston 2002–3, no. 18; Hamburg 2018, no. 24.

THE GRAVENOR FAMILY

CA. 1754

Oil on canvas
35½ x 35½ inches (90.2 x 90.2 cm)
Yale Center for British Art, New Haven;
Paul Mellon Collection
(B1977.14.56)

WITH HIS WIFE AND TWO YOUNG DAUGHTERS, Gainsborough moved from Sudbury to the larger Suffolk port city of Ipswich in 1752, hoping to advance his career in a bigger market. It is unclear how he met John Gravenor (1700–1778), an apothecary who became a prominent Ipswich politician. Though the dating of the present portrait has been debated, Gravenor's appointment as bailiff in 1754 is a likely occasion for him to commemorate with a family portrait and suits the apparent ages of his daughters as depicted here.[28] Gainsborough shows Gravenor with his second wife, Ann Colman, and their daughters Ann, in pink, and Elizabeth, in white.[29] The stiff bodices and panniers (hoops worn beneath skirts to create wide silhouettes) of the dresses make the female figures appear somewhat awkward as they sit, stand, and recline on the ground; as was conventional for conversation pieces, the artist makes "no concessions to any fears of dirt or damp."[30] The girls hold flowers and wheat in their hands and skirts, while their mother grips a fashionable Leghorn hat. John stands with the poise of a dancing master, striking the gentleman's pose of tucking the right hand into the waistcoat.

The brook on the left and wheat field at right are presumably meant to symbolize fecundity and fertility.[31] The figures have been criticized for their stiffness, a quality that has been attributed to Gainsborough's use of lay figures in the studio.[32] The portrait appears close in

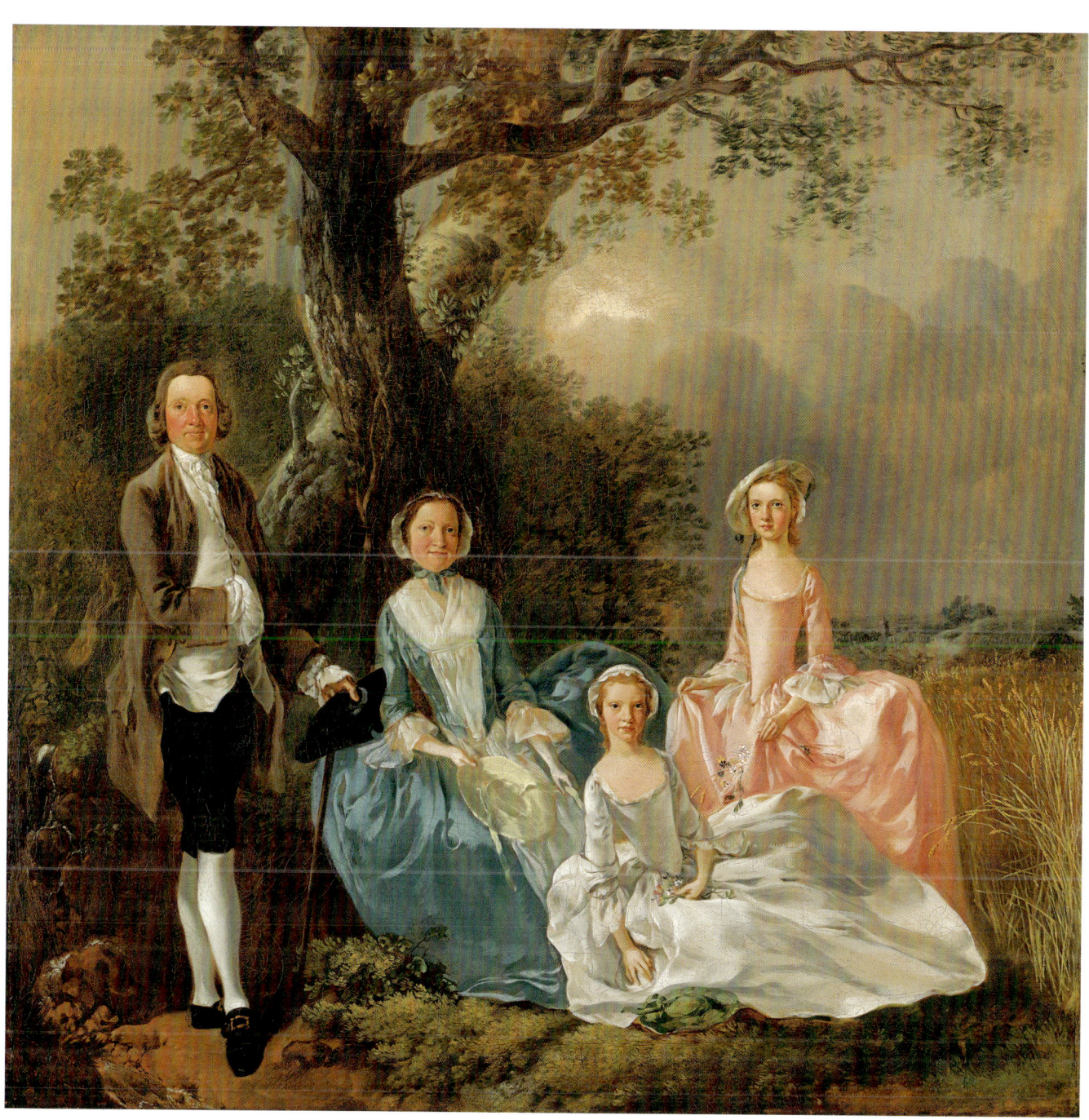

style and composition to paintings by Gainsborough's teacher, Francis Hayman, with scholars citing Hayman's *Jacob Family* as a close model (fig. 39). That Gainsborough could revert to a retrospective mode after creating his singular and innovative *Mr. and Mrs. Andrews* (cat. 2) suggests the flexibility of his style and his willingness to adapt to his patrons' preferences at this early stage in his career.[33] Technical examination reveals handling in the present painting that the artist would carry through to his more mature works, such as exploiting the translucency of paint to create the effect of shimmering fabrics.[34] The vogue for conversation pieces was by this time waning in England's major cities. *The Gravenor Family* is one of the last of this type that Gainsborough would paint until his return to small-scale group portraiture, updated with his signature style, in his late career (see fig. 7).[35]

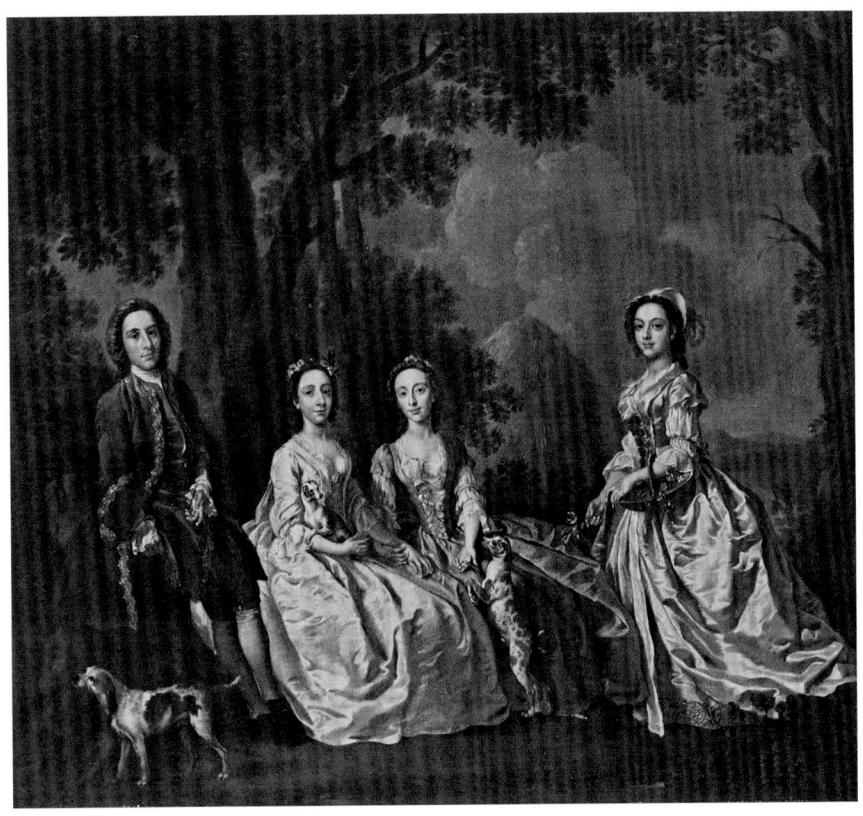

FIG. 39
Undated photograph of Francis Hayman
The Jacob Family, ca. 1745
Oil on canvas
40 x 42½ in. (101.6 x 107.95 cm)
Location unknown

PROVENANCE

By descent to John and Ann Gravenor's daughter, Ann, who married Thomas Gladwin of Ipswich;
by descent to their daughter, Dorothea (b. 1765), who in 1790 married John Stanislaus Townshend (d. 1826) of Hem House
and Trevalyn Hall, Denbighshire, by descent to their great-grandson Major John Sydney Townshend (1886–ca. 1936);
his trustees' sale, Sotheby's, July 19, 1972, lot 41; where bought by Colnaghi; Sir Nigel Broakes (1934–1999), Wargrave Manor, Berkshire;
on offer through Colnaghi from December 1974; purchased by the Yale Center for British Art, 1977.

SELECTED LITERATURE

Davis 1972, 556; Wraight 1974, 152–53; Hayes 1975, 203; E. D'Oench in New Haven 1980, 19, 72, no. 55; Lindsay 1981, 26;
Cormack 1985, 96; Allen 1991, 141, 154; Cormack 1991, 52, no. 11; Bensusan-Butt 1993, 76; Rosenthal 1997, 39–40; Jones 1997, 19, 21, 22,
25; Rosenthal 1999, 127, 130; Belsey 2002, 50–51; Vaughan 2002, 53, 56; R. Jones and M. Postle in London, Washington, and Boston 2002–
3, 29–31; Shawe-Taylor 2009, 148; Howard 2010, 48; Webster 2011, 114–15; Retford 2017, 17, 150; Belsey 2019, 1: no. 412.

SELECTED EXHIBITION HISTORY

Milan 1975, no. 34; New Haven 1980, no. 55; Paris 1981, no. 3; London 1987–88, no. 153; Sydney, Brisbane, and Adelaide 1998 , no. 15;
New Haven and San Marino 2001–2, no. 13; London, Washington, and Boston 2002–3, no. 20;
New Haven and London 2007–8, 257, no. 35.

SARAH HODGES, LATER LADY INNES

CA. 1759

Oil on canvas
40 x 28⅝ in. (101.6 x 72.7 cm)
The Frick Collection, New York
(1914.1.58)

SARAH HODGES (1737–1770) was the only child and heir of Thomas Hodges, Esq., and Sarah Peacock of Ipswich, Suffolk, where Gainsborough had been building his portraiture practice since about 1752. This portrait is among the last he painted there before moving his family out of East Anglia and west to the fashionable spa town of Bath in late 1759. Though his immersion in the great Old Master collections around Bath, especially at Wilton House and Corsham Court, would not take place until after his move, he was in Bath for up to six months in late 1758 and appears to have returned to Ipswich with new ambition.[36] The present painting has been seen as a "transitional" work between Gainsborough's more stiffly painted conversation pieces and his mature life-size portraits. It is among the first to show overt allusions to Van Dyck in handling, color, and the motif of a female sitter holding a rose.[37] Thomas Hodges may have commissioned it to celebrate his daughter's twenty-first year, and Gainsborough could have painted it shortly before or after his monthslong stay in Bath. Its imagery, symbolizing the sitter's blossoming youth with a rosebud in her hand and a rose unfurling in the bush at left suggesting the promise of maturity, would have been suited to a portrayal of an unmarried heiress.[38] Sarah wed Captain William Innes in 1766 and became Lady Innes after he inherited his brother's baronetcy in 1768.[39] Lady Innes died in 1770 at age thirty-three, shortly after the birth of her second daughter.[40]

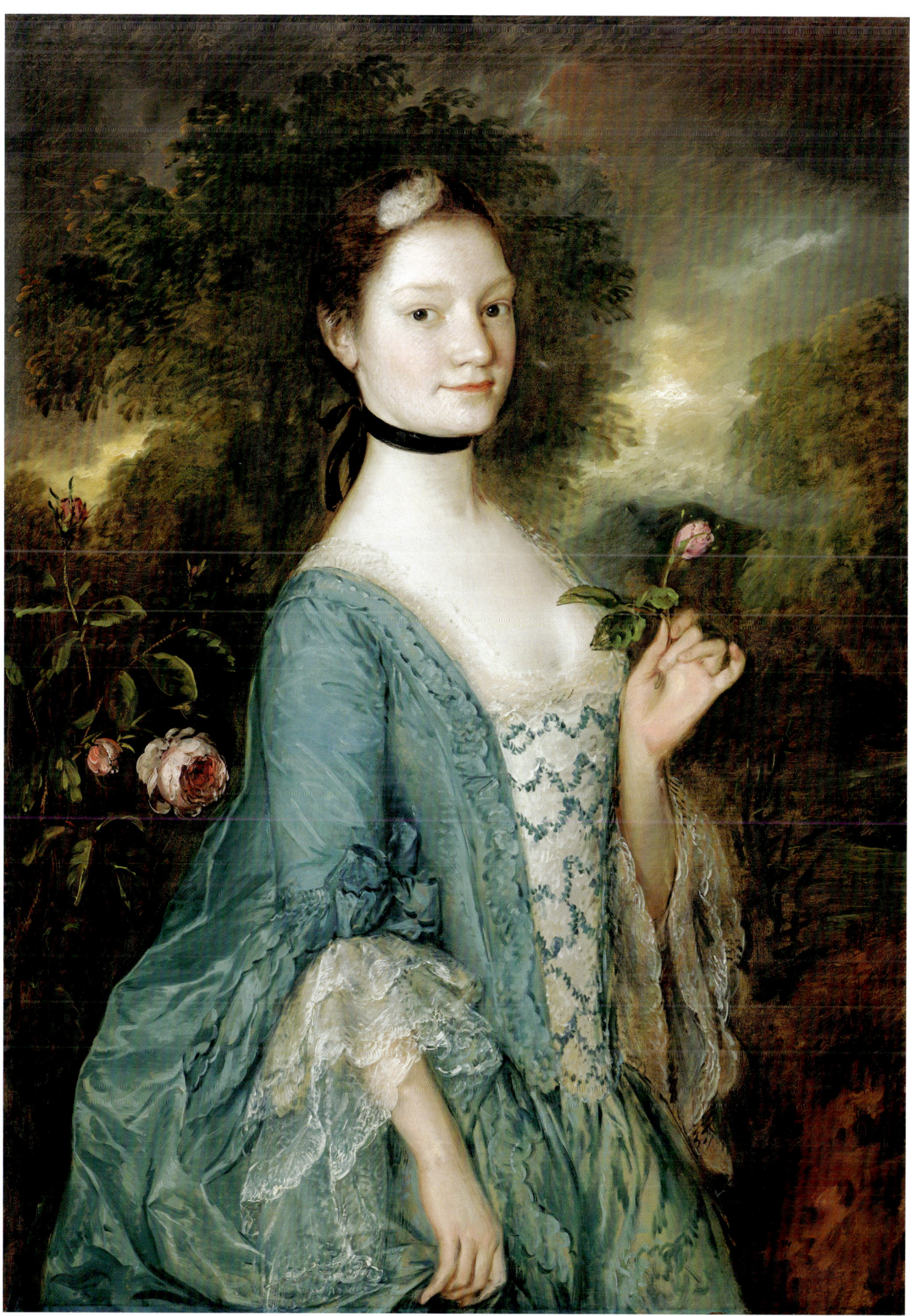

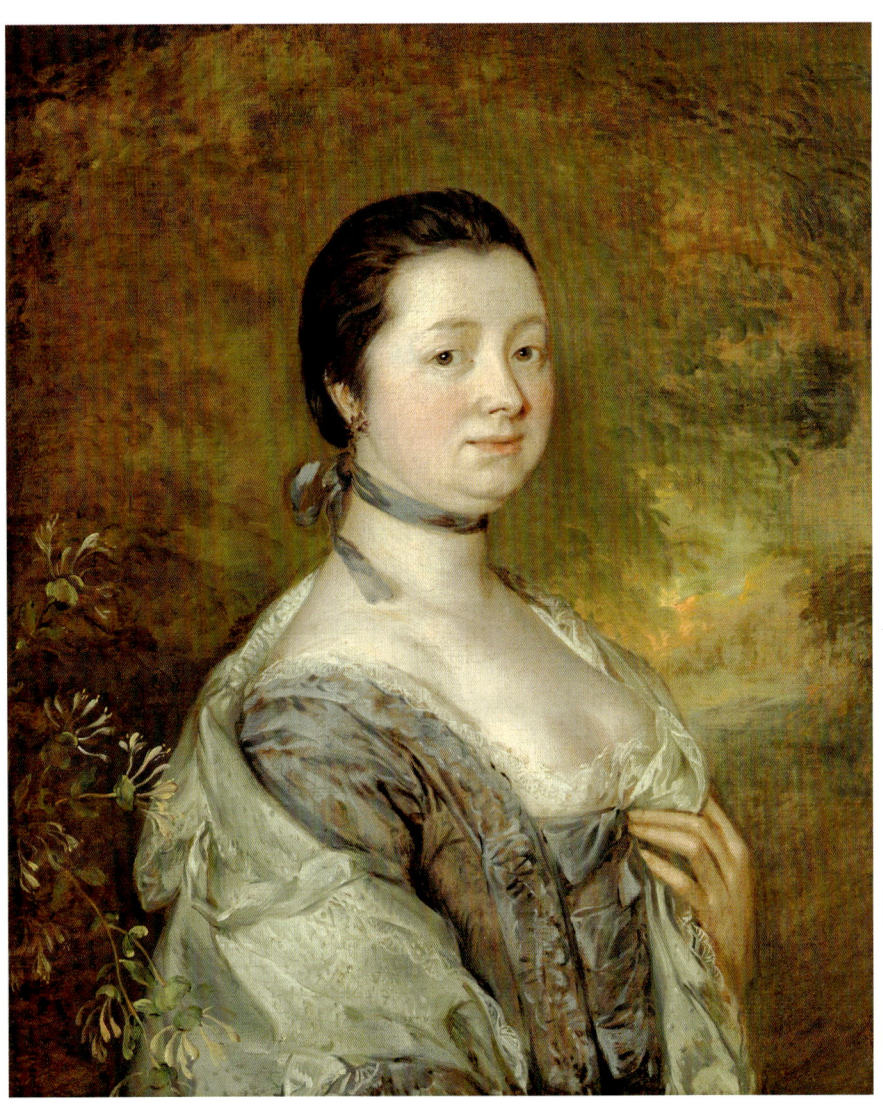

FIG. 40
Thomas Gainsborough
Margaret Gainsborough, ca. 1758–59
Oil on canvas
29¹⁵⁄₁₆ x 25 in. (76 x 63.5 cm)
Staatliche Museen zu Berlin (2200)

Adorned with a black choker and white feather pompom on her natural hair, she wears a blue watered-silk dress *à la française* (or *sacque*, characterized by pleated fabric cascading from the neckline at the back), its front opening covered by a stomacher (triangular piece of fabric) decorated with blue scalloping.[41] Though it has been suggested that the portrait shows, well before the famous *Blue Boy* of 1770, that "Gainsborough had run counter to Sir Joshua Reynolds's aversion to blue as the predominant note in a portrait,"[42] Aileen Ribeiro observes that such blue silk dresses were popular and appear in portraits of the 1750s and 1760s.[43]

The dramatic sky and landscape setting anticipate the highly achieved, monumental outdoor environments he would paint in Bath, such as in *Mary, Countess Howe* (cat. 5). Gainsborough demonstrates his range of paint handling in the portrait, from the feathery strokes for the face to the tightly painted flowers that recall Dutch seventeenth-century still lifes to the looser rendering of her hands and fabric of her dress. Noting the unusual proportions of the canvas, Belsey proposed that it was made for a particular location, such as over a mantel; the meticulous detailing of the flowers, meanwhile, suggests it was meant to be appreciated from up close.[44]

Around the same time, Gainsborough painted a portrait of his wife (fig. 40) wearing a similar style dress (with lace edging around the neckline, ruched robings along the open front, and stomacher) on a standard-sized canvas.[45] Which one was painted first is uncertain, but similar compositional features, such as the leafy background that haloes the head and presumably symbolic flora (in Margaret Gainsborough's case, honeysuckle), present the possibility that Gainsborough worked on his wife's portrait both as a personal creation and to experiment with ideas he put to use in commissioned works.[46]

PROVENANCE

Presumably by descent to Sir James Innes, 11th Baronet, Ipswich; anonymous sale (presumably George Knight Erskine Fairholme, Esq.), Christie, Manson & Woods, London, June 3, 1876, lot 35; probably with Thomas Humphrey Ward, London, from whom purchased by Agnews, 1892, and subsequently by Charles Sedelmeyer, 1893; Joseph Critchley Marrin, Norfolk, England; his sale (*De la Rue and others*), Christie's, London, June 16, 1911, lot 79; sold jointly to Colnaghi and Knoedler; J. H. Dunn, Surrey, England, 1911; Knoedler, Frick, 1914.

SELECTED LITERATURE

Art Journal 1911, 423–24; Bridge 1919–20, 85; Baker 1933, 110; Wilenski 1934, 122, 127; Waterhouse 1953, 61; Waterhouse 1958, 75, no. 395; Hayes 1965, 70; Davidson 1968, 42–44; Hayes 1975, 207–8, no. 34; Heilmann 1978, 223; Lindsay 1981, 44; Cherry and Harris 1982, 296; Hayes 1982, 1: 84–85; A. French in London 1988b, 23 under no. A1; I. Lumsden in Fredericton 1991, 13–14; Cormack 1991, 18; Ribeiro 1995, 54; Rosenthal 1999, 147–48; Sloman 2002, 46; Vaughan 2002, 71–72; Allen 2005, 10; Honegger 2011, 87; Hamilton 2017, 114; Belsey 2019, 1: no. 519.

SELECTED EXHIBITION HISTORY

London 1911, no. 7; Paris 1913, no. 10; New York 1914b, no. 18.

MARY, COUNTESS HOWE

1763–64

Oil on canvas
94¹⁵⁄₁₆ x 60¾ in. (243.2 x 154.3 cm)
English Heritage, Kenwood House, London;
The Iveagh Bequest

ONE OF GAINSBOROUGH'S earliest full-length portraits of a female subject, this portrait has been seen as a turning point in the artist's style, where he leaves behind the "bumpkin air" of his earlier work to attain the sophistication of his maturity.[47] The transition was suited to his move to Bath, the fashionable spa town west of London. Lord and Lady Howe traveled to Bath in December 1763, seeking relief in Bath's waters for Lord Howe's gout, a lifelong affliction. (In 1788, they would become Earl and Countess Howe, the titles by which their portraits are traditionally known.)[48] That autumn, Gainsborough had just recovered from a severe illness that kept him bedridden for weeks and much reduced in his ability to paint.[49] By March of 1764, he boasted to a friend of having recovered his lost revenue, having by then completed more than a dozen portraits; a "Whole length" he lists among these works may refer to this portrait or to the pendant of the countess's husband (fig. 41).[50]

Born into a landowning family, Mary Hartopp (1732–1800) ascended to the aristocracy upon her marriage in 1758. Her husband, Richard Howe, was a celebrated naval officer who inherited his family's Irish viscountcy.[51] The portraits were probably commissioned for their London home on Grafton Street. The couple had visited Bath in 1760, at which time Gainsborough seems to have painted a bust portrait of Lord Howe.[52] In December of 1763, they returned to Bath with elevated status: Mary, now in her early thirties, had given birth to the first of three daughters, and Richard had been appointed a Lord of the Admiralty (he would become treasurer of the Navy in 1765).[53]

Gainsborough shows his subject dressed at the height of fashion from head to toe, from the Leghorn straw hat in the *bergère* or pastoral style to her high-heeled black shoes fastened with brass or gold buckles.[54] The artist lavished attention on the depiction of her dress, a "nightgown" (loose-fitting dress) of pink silk over which a lace apron is tied (hers is

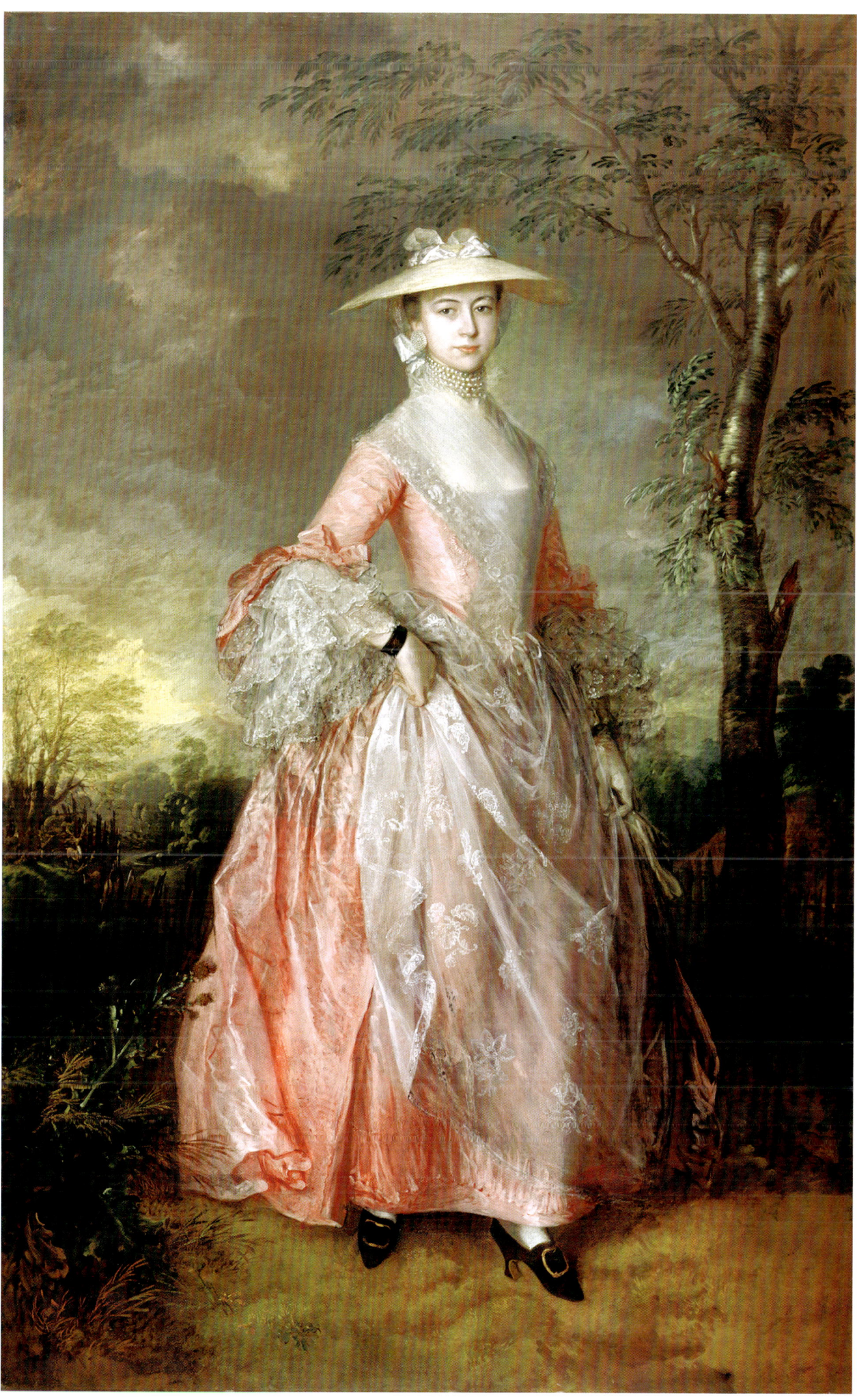

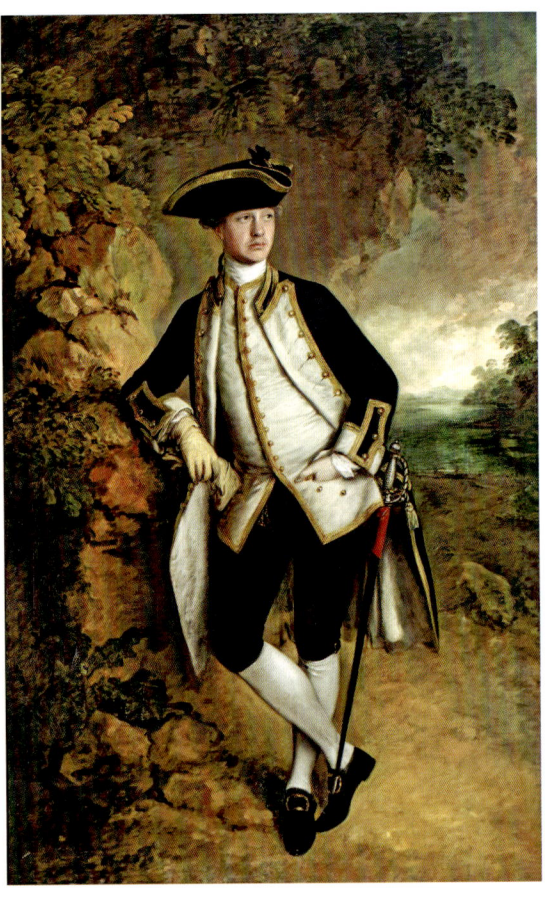

FIG. 41

Thomas Gainsborough
Richard, 1st Earl Howe, 1763
Oil on canvas
95 x 60¾ in. (241.2 x 154.3 cm)
Trustees of the Howe Settled Estates

FIG. 42

Thomas Gainsborough
A Woman with a Rose, ca. 1763–65
Black chalk and stump and white chalk on gray-green paper
18¼ x 13 in. (464 x 330 mm)
The British Museum, London (1855,0714.70)

decorative, unlike aprons worn for work), which is appropriate attire for informal activities like taking a walk. Triple lace *engageantes* (false, or detachable, sleeves) hang at her elbows, while black wristbands contrast with her pale skin, and her gloved left hand dangles the other glove. A diaphanous fichu (or kerchief) veils her chest. She wears shield-shaped earrings and five strings of pearls, an extravagance that relies on specialist skills of drilling the gems and stringing them, typically on horsehair.[55] The artist has portrayed Mary as if in mid-step, her swishing skirt about to catch the nettle at left while her apron folds back against itself, demonstrating a highly sophisticated rendering of translucent layers.

Several drawings have been associated with the portrait, though none is a direct study.[56] In a sheet showing a similarly dressed woman walking in profile with arm akimbo (fig. 42), the artist applied white chalk in a way that anticipates the lace apron in the painting. Numerous pentimenti (seen with the naked eye and through infrared reflectography and X-radiography) emphasize the artist's efforts to achieve the final composition—her proper right shoe, for instance, shifted slightly to the right. Meanwhile, in the distance at left, a group of stags rests by a rustic fence that continues behind Countess Howe in the background at right.

The little that is known of the sitter's personality is gleaned from biographies of her husband. She was "a most affectionate wife, watching over her Lord in all his illnesses, accompanying him wherever he went; and when employed afloat, it was her special care that everything

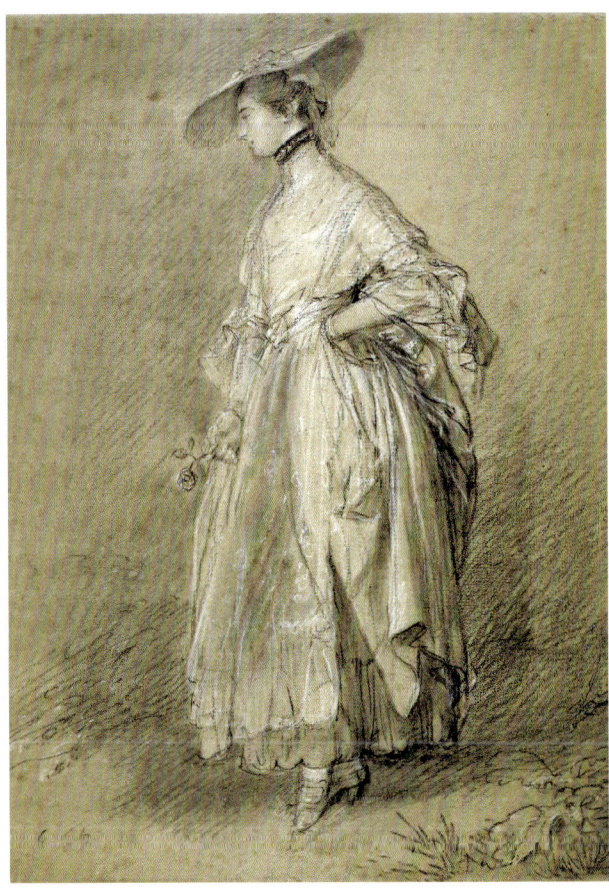

was provided for his convenience and comfort."[57] Later in life, she and her daughters were often visited at their Hertfordshire home by Queen Charlotte and the princesses.[58] While Lord Howe was reported to be "exceedingly temperate in his habits," Countess Howe was "rather particular with regard to the keeping [of] a good table, and at one time had a French cook," an attention to detail perhaps reflected in the exacting style and elegance of her portrait.[59]

PROVENANCE

Bequeathed to the sitter's daughter Louisa, Marchioness of Sligo (1767–1809); by descent to her grandson George John, 3rd Marquess of Sligo (1820–1896); from whom purchased by Richard, 3rd Earl Howe (1822–1900); purchased from him by Agnews, June 12, 1888, and sold on the same day to Edward Cecil Guinness, later 1st Earl of Iveagh; bequeathed by him as part of the Iveagh Bequest to Kenwood House, 1927.

SELECTED LITERATURE

Armstrong 1898, 198; Armstrong 1904, 270; Menpes and Greig 1909, 175; Waterhouse 1953, 60; Waterhouse 1958, 75, no. 387; Waterhouse 1973, 365; Hayes 1975, 38, 211–12, no. 55; Daniels 1981, 112; Waterfield 1981, 1051; Waterhouse 1981, 136; Cherry and Harris 1982, 293; Corri 1983, 236; Mullins 1983, 27; Lavezzari 1983–84, 318; A. French et al. in London 1988b; Postle 1991, 190; Cormack 1991, 18–19, 78, 80 under no. 25, 82 under no. 26; Kalinsky 1995, 16; Ribeiro 1995, 64–65; Parent 1999, 90–91; Rosenthal 1999, 44, 54, 242, 251, 275, 277; Sloman 2002, 46, 58, 86, 88–89, 91, 98; Vaughan 2002, 6, 76, 111, 112, 211; Bryant 2003, 184–93, no. 43; Clifford 2004, 119; J. Bryant in Houston and other cities 2012–13, 16; Hamilton 2017, 207, 227, 239–40; Belsey 2019, 1: no. 507.

SELECTED EXHIBITION HISTORY

London 1908b, no. 21; London 1928, no. 224; Manchester 1928, no. 57; London 1956–57, no. 226; Paris 1981 no. 27; London 1988b, no. A1; London, Washington, and Boston 2002–3, no. 64; Houston and other cities 2012–13, no. 8.

CAT. 6

LORDS JOHN AND BERNARD STUART

AFTER ANTHONY VAN DYCK, CA. 1765

Oil on canvas
92½ x 57½ in. (235 x 146.1 cm)
Saint Louis Art Museum;
Gift of Mrs. Jackson Johnson in memory
of Mr. Jackson Johnson (15:1943)

UNLIKE REYNOLDS, Gainsborough did not travel to study art on the Continent, instead making use of Old Master paintings in English collections and those circulated in prints, including works by artists such as Titian, Rubens, Teniers, and above all Anthony van Dyck.[60] At his death, he left no fewer than seven copies after Van Dyck in his studio (including the present painting), along with Old Master works he had collected.[61] Though he was by no means alone among eighteenth-century artists in his emulations of Van Dyck's portraits, his decades-long experiments with Van Dyck dress set him apart (see, for example, cats. 14 and 25), and critics and peers recognized his singular connection to the seventeenth-century Flemish artist in aspects of brushwork, coloring, and composition as well as poses, costume, and motifs.[62]

This careful, though not slavish, copy after Van Dyck's *Lord John Stuart and His Brother, Lord Bernard Stuart* (see fig. 15)—made to scale after its celebrated prototype—is the largest and most accomplished of Gainsborough's copies after Old Masters.[63] Gainsborough closely observed the original while interpreting it with his own style, including giving it a blonder tonality overall.[64] Though Gainsborough follows Van Dyck's brushwork in general, his swift strokes appear free and loose, suited to the depiction of shimmering fabrics and the brothers' sensational attire, from lace collars to cuffs spilling over heeled boots. His imitation of Van

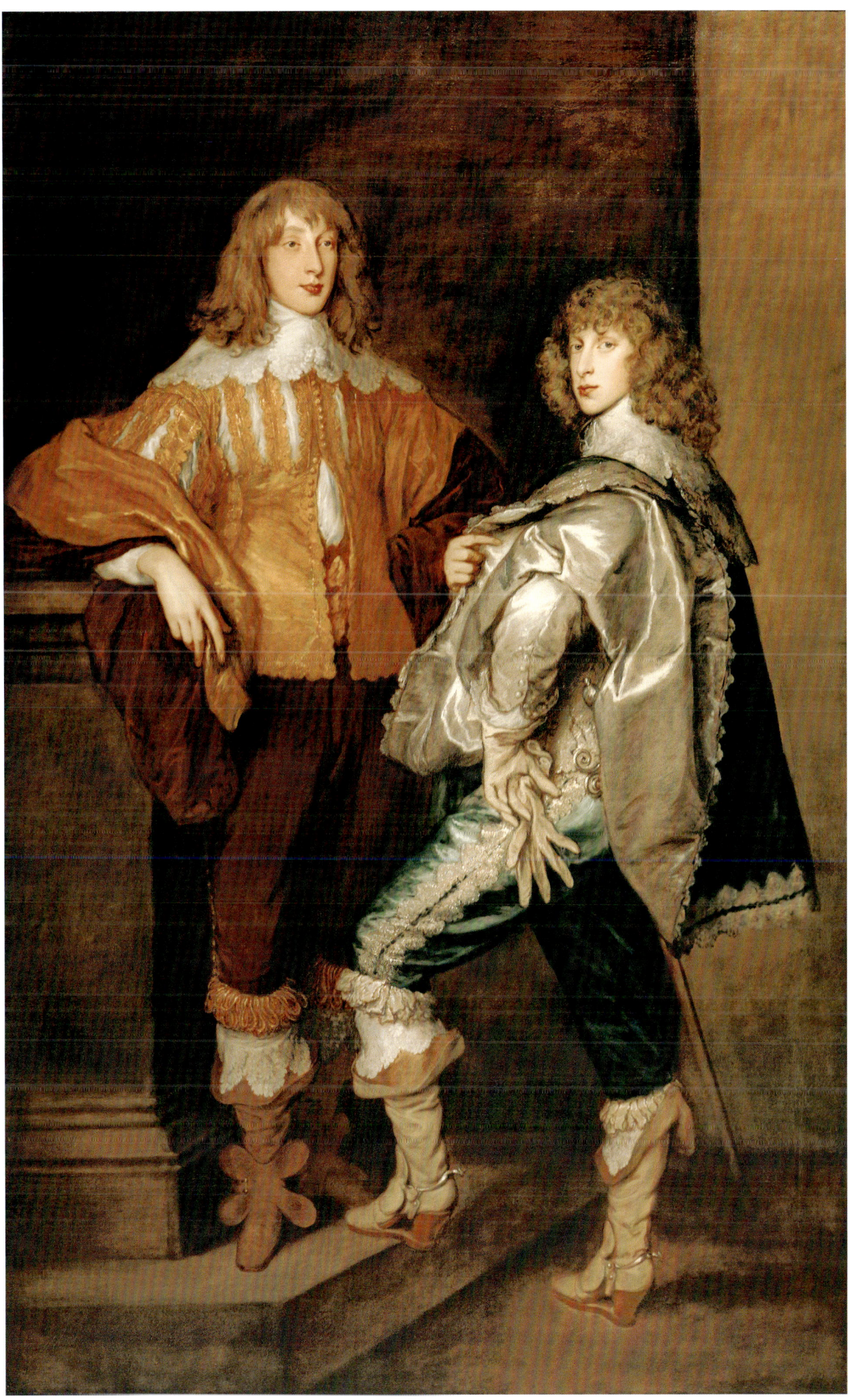

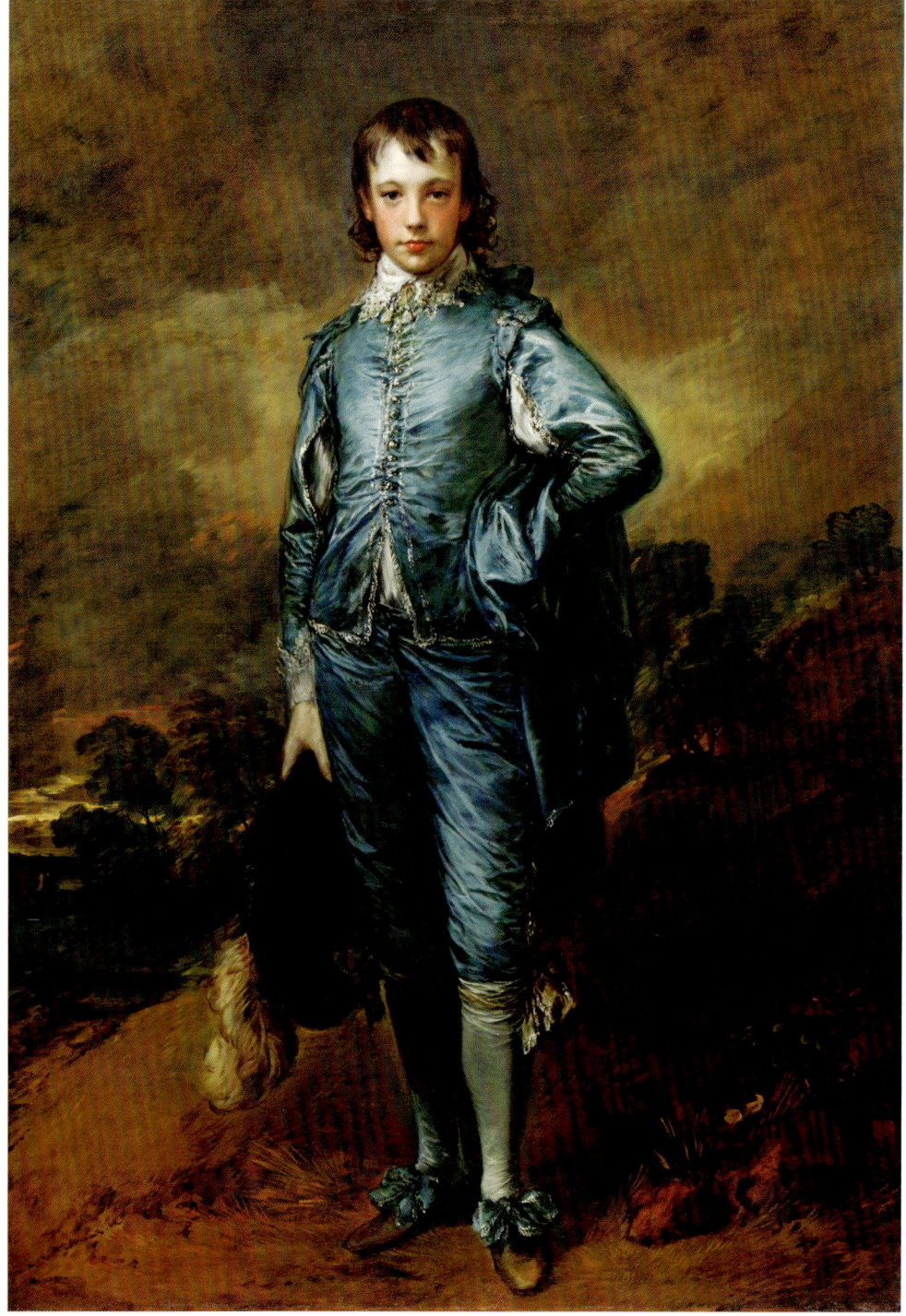

FIG. 43
Thomas Gainsborough
The Blue Boy, 1770
Oil on canvas
70⅝ x 48¾ in.
(179.4 x 123.8 cm)
The Huntington Library,
Art Museum, and
Botanical Gardens,
San Marino (21.1)

Dyck's grandeur in expression and attitude and dynamic posing manifests explicitly in what appear to be personal works, like *Gainsborough Dupont* (cat. 10), as well as his most notable public presentation of Van Dyck style, *The Blue Boy* (fig. 43), at the 1770 Royal Academy exhibition. Some thirty portraits dating from the 1760s through to his last years feature various interpretations of Van Dyck dress.

While the significance of this copy is without doubt, its date—and thus its place and implications for Gainsborough's development as an artist—is uncertain. Scholars agree that Gainsborough made it for his own education and interest, since it remained in his studio at his death.[65] In the 1760s, Van Dyck's original belonged to John, 3rd Earl of Darnley, who resided at Berkeley Square in London and Cobham Hall in Kent. There is no record of Gainsborough visiting Cobham Hall, and he may have seen and studied the painting in London, which he visited with frequency before his move there in 1774.[66] Two Earls of Darnley commissioned portraits from him, though he need not have made the copy around the time of either occasion. In 1765, the 3rd Earl commissioned a portrait of his niece and ward,[67] and in 1785, John, 4th Earl of Darnley (who succeeded to the title in 1781), commissioned a portrait of himself.[68] (The 4th Earl would later purchase the present copy from Gainsborough's posthumous sale in 1789, uniting it with Van Dyck's original in his collection.) Scholars generally agree that an earlier date is more likely, and it would make sense that Gainsborough copied the Darnley Van Dyck before he painted works like *Gainsborough Dupont* and *The Blue Boy*. It is tempting to wonder if Gainsborough borrowed the motif of the gloved hand holding the other glove in *Mary, Countess Howe* (see cat. 5) from Van Dyck's figure of Bernard Stuart, a detail he copied with flair.

The Van Dyck portrait was sold from Cobham Hall in 1904 and Gainsborough's copy in 1925.[69] Correspondence between the art dealer Joseph Duveen and his associates in 1925 records debate over the copy's merits; after the sensational, record-breaking sale of *The Blue Boy* to Henry E. Huntington in 1921, they were eager to see "Gainsboro blue" in other portraits by the artist.[70] Though Gainsborough's copy was described as "quite a powerful thing," the firm did not purchase it.[71] The painting was soon acquired by the wealthy American shoe and boot manufacturer Jackson Johnson of St. Louis, Missouri. Duveen later inquired if Johnson would consider selling the painting, but he did not.

PROVENANCE

Among the contents of the artist's studio sold by Gainsborough Dupont at Gainsborough sale 1789, lot 92;
where purchased by John Bligh, 4th Earl of Darnley (1767–1831); by descent to Ivo Francis Walter Bligh, 8th Earl of Darnley (1859–1927);
his sale, Christie, Manson & Woods, May 1, 1925, lot 20; where purchased by Bromhead, Cutts & Co. Ltd.; Jackson Johnson (1859–1929)
and Minnie Alva Johnson, St. Louis; given by Mrs. Jackson Johnson in memory of Mr. Jackson Johnson to Saint Louis Art Museum, 1943.

SELECTED LITERATURE

Fulcher 1856a, 188; Fulcher 1856b, 192; Bell 1897, 136; Musick 1943, 7–10; Waterhouse 1958, 124; Wark 1974, 45–53; Hayes 1975, 210;
Cherry and Harris 1982, 305; Cormack 1991, 19; Waterhouse 1994, 252; H. Belsey in London, Washington, and Boston 2002–3,
32 under no. 8; M. Myrone in London, Washington, and Boston 2002–3, 168; Brenneman 2003, 90–91n.32; Secrest 2004, 306;
H. Belsey in San Marino 2013, 94; J. Yarker in Belsey 2019, 2, no. 1090; I. Tedbury in London 2022, 65 under no. 4.

SELECTED EXHIBITION HISTORY

London 1908a, no. 203; St. Louis 1927, no. 10; St. Louis 1935, no. 6; London, Washington, and Boston 2002–3, no. 85.

CAPTAIN AUGUSTUS JOHN HERVEY, LATER 3RD EARL OF BRISTOL

CA. 1768

Oil on canvas
91⁵⁄₁₆ x 60¹⁄₁₆ in. (232 x 152.5 cm)
Ickworth House, Suffolk (851720)

Born the second son to a noble family, Captain Augustus John Hervey (1724–1779) began a career in the navy, joining in 1735 at age eleven as a "Captain's Servant." His journals for the years 1746 to 1759 describe a colorful life at sea and on land.[72] Contemporaries regarded the Hervey family as eccentric (an oft-quoted quip was that "God made men, women, and Herveys"). The captain made a fortune through successful missions, among the most important being the 1762 bombardment of Fort Moro, Havana, part of the Seven Years' War; he was honored with dispatching the news to England that year (under the Treaty of Paris, Britain returned control of Havana to the Spanish in 1763). He ended his seafaring career in 1763 as captain of the *Centurion* and served as a Lord of the Admiralty until 1775, when he inherited the earldom from his brother to become the 3rd Earl of Bristol.[73]

Hervey suffered from bouts of poor health and like many contemporaries traveled to Bath for relief from ailments such as gout; he would ultimately die of "gout of the stomach."[74] Gainsborough painted the present portrait in Bath presumably in late 1767 or early 1768, as he sent it to the last exhibition of the Society of Artists in London in the spring of 1768 (as *A Sea Officer*). The details of Hervey's naval uniform are meticulously observed as are the fob hanging from the waist, sword hilt peeking out from his coat, and a pinky ring, "perhaps a Roman seal in a diamond setting."[75] He holds a telescope in his left hand and rests against

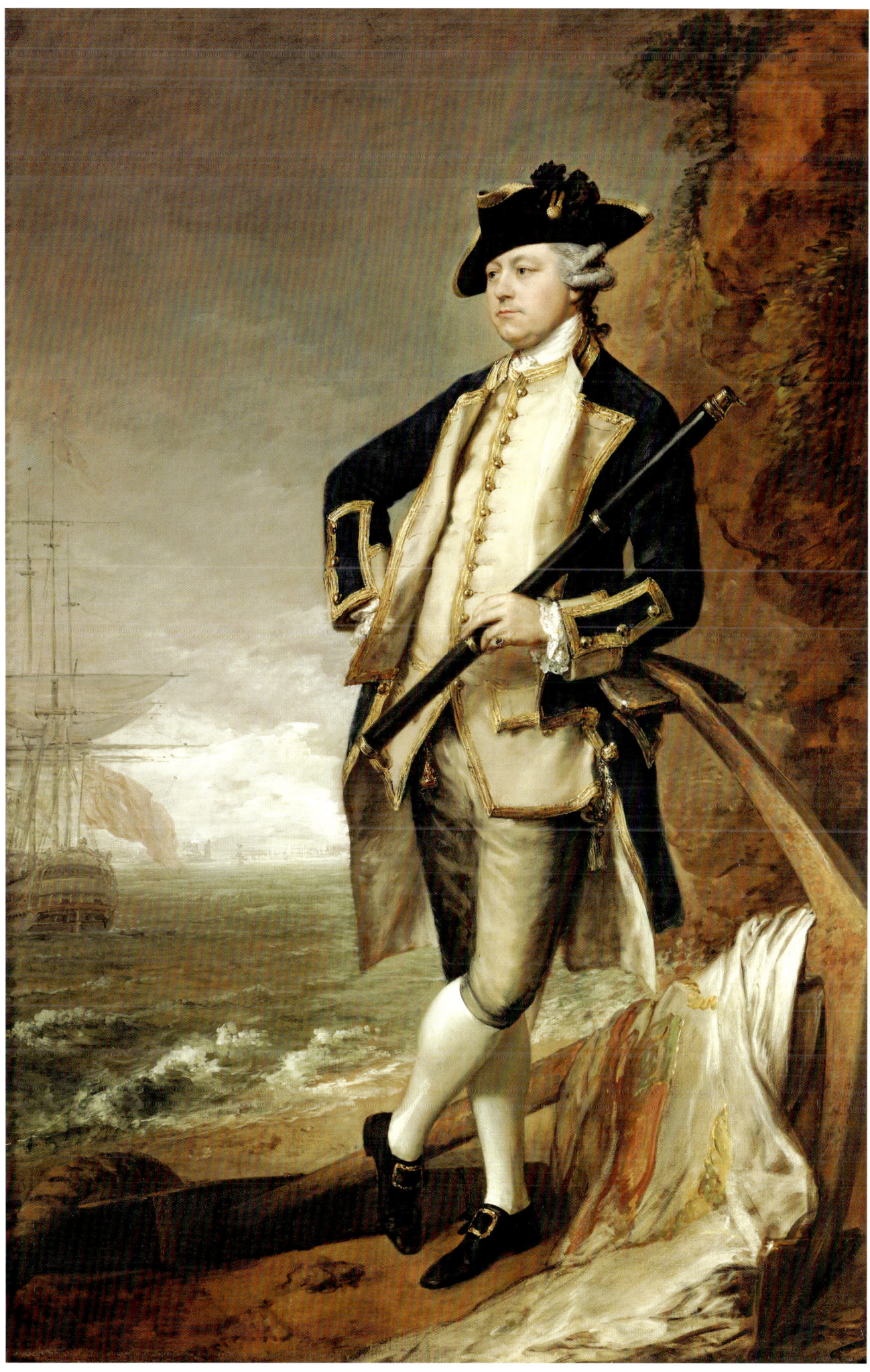

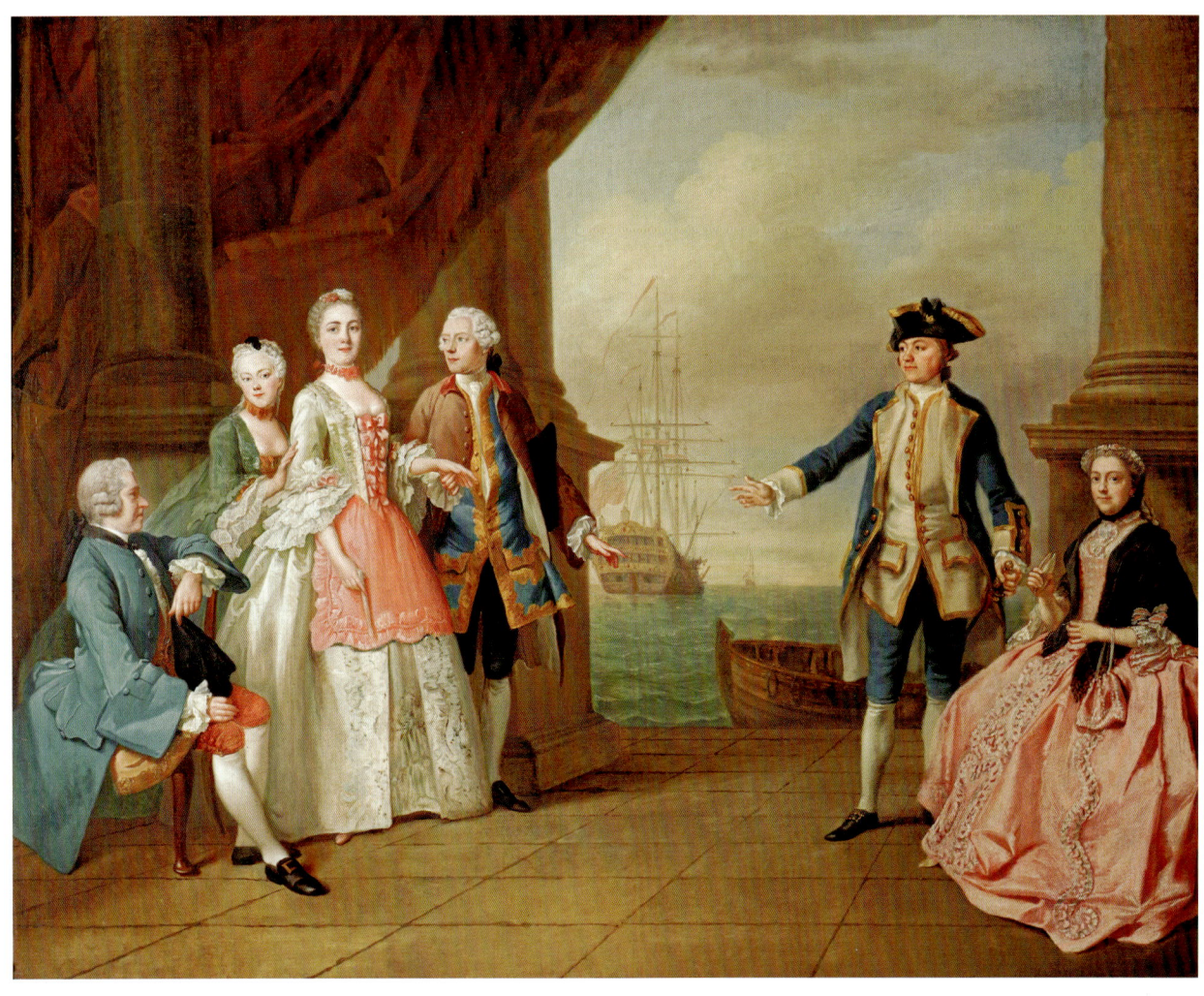

FIG. 44
Hubert-François Gravelot, Jean-Étienne Liotard, and Francis Hayman
The Hon. Mrs. Constantine Phipps Being Led
to Greet Her Brother, Captain the Hon. Augustus Hervey, 1750
Oil on canvas
39 x 49 in. (99.1 x 124.5 cm)
Ickworth House, Suffolk (NT 851727)

an anchor in a pose reminiscent of Van Dyck's *Algernon Percy, 10th Earl of Northumberland* (Alnwick Castle).[76] The Spanish ensign draped over the anchor, the ship, and fort in the distance allude to the events at Havana, by this time six years in the past.

The sitter had many portraits made of himself during his life, and his journals record him gifting these to associates. The present picture resembles, at a monumental scale, Hervey's figure at far right in a group portrait of nearly two decades earlier (fig. 44), begun in Paris and completed in London, with a complex attribution to Gainsborough's teachers, Gravelot and Hayman, Swiss artist Jean-Étienne Liotard, and others.[77] Gainsborough may have seen this group portrait, in which Hervey wears almost exactly the same uniform and bears a similar stance as in the present picture. Susan Sloman observed that the low viewpoint in Gainsborough's portrait, like that of Van Dyck's, creates the imposing effect of the figure and suggests that Gainsborough "added a few inches to the height of the dais on which he placed the sitters' chair in his studio, a relatively small practical adjustment that had a dramatic effect on his portraits."[78]

The occasion of the commission is unknown. At the time of this painting, Hervey's estranged wife of twenty-four years, Elizabeth Chudleigh, was in the process of wedding the Duke of Kingston (in 1774 she would be charged with bigamy but was spared corporal punishment due to her noble title as Hervey's lawful wife).[79] It has been suggested that the portrait was commissioned by the captain's nephew Constantine John Phipps, Lord Mulgrave, who would in the 1780s commission from Gainsborough portraits of himself.[80] Since Horace Walpole states in his annotations of the 1768 Society of Artists catalogue that Lord Bristol's portrait, which he describes as "very good and one of the best modern pictures I have seen," is at Lord Bristol's "in St. James's Square," London, it seems most likely that the sitter commissioned it himself.[81] Hervey left his unentailed property, including this portrait, to his last and enduring companion, Mary Nesbitt, and to his illegitimate son (born to Kitty Hunter), Augustus, who was also painted by Gainsborough and died in naval action the year after his father's death, at age seventeen.[82]

PROVENANCE

Left by the sitter to Mrs. Mary Nesbitt (1742/43–1825), Norwood House, Streatham, Surrey; passed to Hon. Anne Phipps, Lady Murray (d. 1848); her sale, Robins, May 17, 1827, lot 111; bought in; left with the auctioneer, Joseph Robins; sale, Christie's, February 21, 1843, lot 83; bought in; reoffered by Mr. Hoard, at Traveller's Club, May 9, 1835, lot 106; bought in; reoffered, Deacon's Auction Rooms, London, May 9, 1838 (lot unknown); bought by E. H. Locker; offered to Lord Jermyn (later 2nd Marquess of Bristol), then to his father, Frederick William, 1st Marquess of Bristol (1769–1859), who purchased; by descent, accepted with Ickworth House in lieu of death duties and transferred to the National Trust, 1956.

SELECTED LITERATURE

Fulcher 1856a, 69, 140, 181, 211, 212, 220; Fulcher 1856b, 69, 143, 185, 215, 216, 224; Brock-Arnold 1881, 33; Armstrong 1898, 87, 116, 197; Chamberlain 1903, 68; Gower 1903, 51–52; Armstrong 1904, 115, 154–55; Fletcher 1904, 199; Mourey 1905, 48; Willoughby 1906, 210; Boulton 1905, 156; Farrer 1908, 207, no. 44; Menpes and Greig 1909, 2, 79; Whitley [1915] 2016, 78; Dibdin 1923, 90; Stokes 1925, 49; Whitley 1928, 2: 369; Woodall 1949, 61; Waterhouse 1953, 11; Waterhouse 1958, 21, 56; Williamson 1972, 79; A. Wilton in London 1992–93, no. 40; Laing 1995, 32, no. 8; Rosenthal 1999, 12; Sloman 2002, 62; S. Sloman in London 2009, no. 126; Belsey 2019, 1: no. 102; Ostler 2021, 178.

SELECTED EXHIBITION HISTORY

London 1891, no. 360; London 1934, no. 264; London 1963b, no. 18; Brussels 1973, no. 17; London 1980, no. 15; Washington 1985–86, no. 483; London 1992–93, no. 40; London 2009, no. 126.

MARY, DUCHESS OF MONTAGU

CA. 1768

Oil on canvas
49¼ x 39½ in. (125.1 x 100.3 cm)
Duke of Buccleuch, Bowhill House, Scottish Borders;
Lent by the Duke of Buccleuch and Queensberry, K. T.
and the Trustees of the Buccleuch Chattels Trust

THE DUCHESS OF MONTAGU (1711–1775) was about fifty-seven years old when Gainsborough painted this portrait, conceived as a pendant to the half-length he painted of her husband, George (fig. 45).[83] The couple had traveled to Bath several times in late 1767 and 1768—presumably to relieve her ill health—and there commissioned several portraits from Gainsborough.[84] In addition to the pendant pair, Gainsborough also painted the couple's daughter, Elizabeth, as well as another bust portrait of the duchess (fig. 46).[85] There was much to commemorate: Mary and her husband, the 4th Earl of Cardigan, had become Duchess and Duke of Montagu in 1766 (a re-creation of the title after her father, the 1st Duke, had died without a male heir in 1749); and their daughter Elizabeth had just married (in 1767) Henry, 3rd Duke of Buccleuch.[86]

When Horace Walpole got to know Mary in the 1740s (then still Countess of Cardigan), he described growing "every day more in love with" her, praising the "dignity in her way of thinking."[87] Modern scholars have appreciated the dignity with which Gainsborough presents the duchess here, both in her seated posture (facing right to her husband's pendant) and her face, which attests to the artist's ability to convey "beauty without denying the effects of age."[88] Her restrained expression contrasts with the cascade of red fabric behind her and her sumptuous attire: a blue silk *robe à la française* adorned with lace *engageantes* at the elbows, white shawl, lace kerchief covering her chest, and a "fly" headdress tied under her chin that frames her clustered

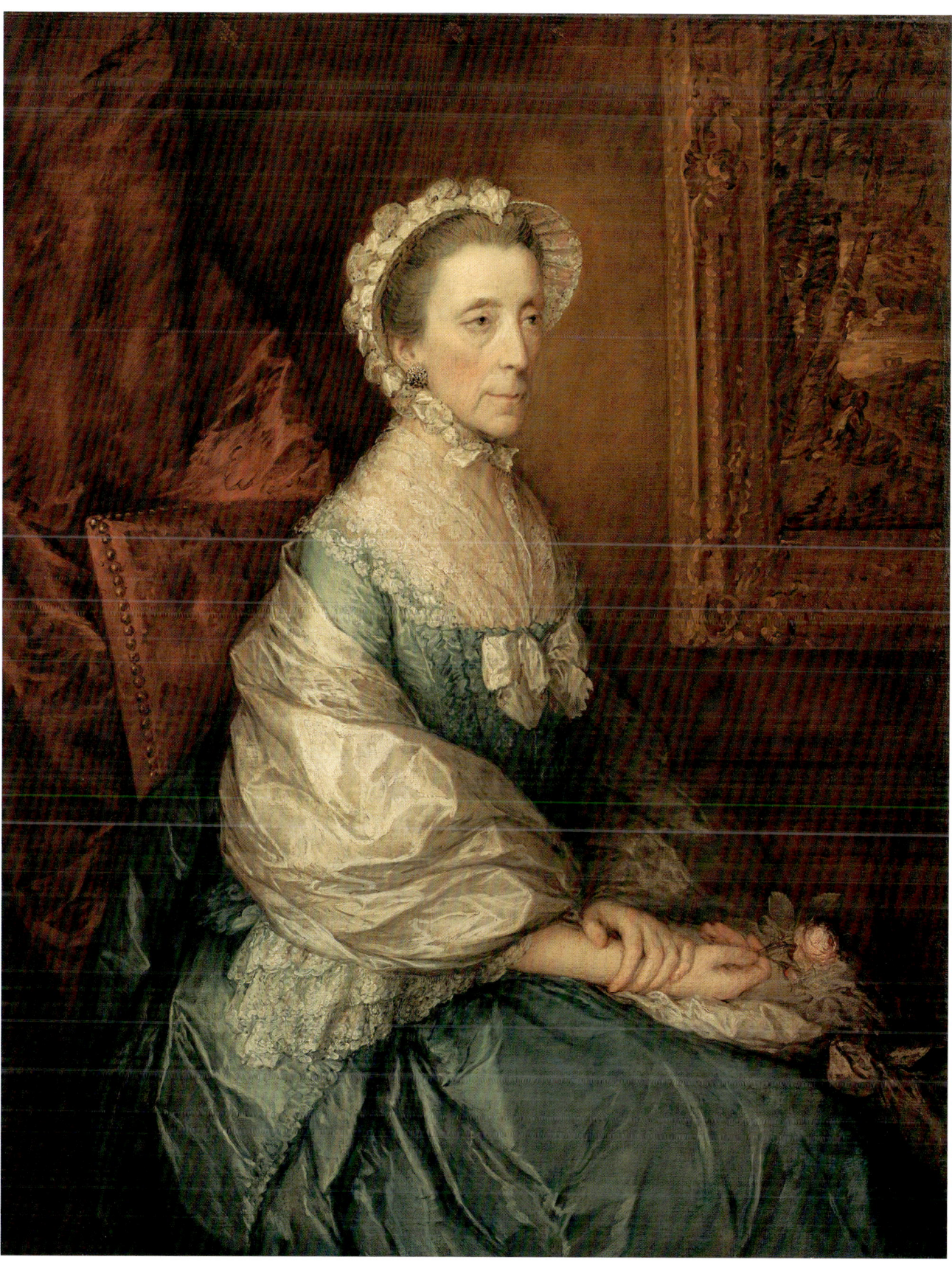

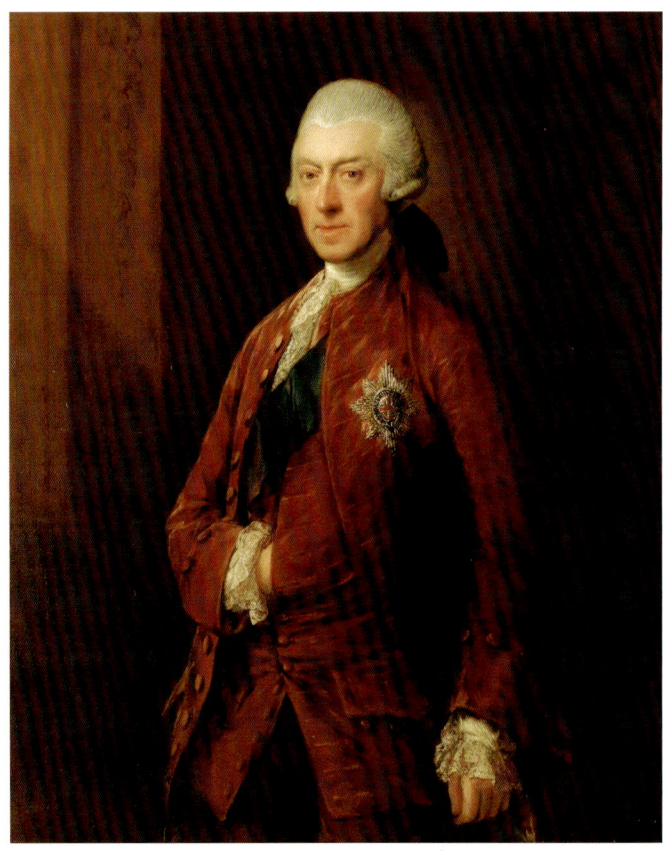

FIG. 45
Thomas Gainsborough
George Montagu, 1st Duke of Montagu, 1768
Oil on canvas
49¼ x 39½ in. (125.1 x 100.3 cm)
Bowhill House, Scottish Borders

FIG. 46
Thomas Gainsborough
Mary, Duchess of Montagu, ca. 1768
Oil on canvas
29½ x 24½ in. (74.9 x 62.2 cm)
Boughton House, Northamptonshire

earring, which would have been made from as many as two hundred individual brilliant-cut diamonds.[89] Mary holds the stem of a rose and rosebud in her lap, a motif from Van Dyck, offering a poignant contrast to the pert flower brandished by the younger Lady Innes (cat. 4).[90]

This is one of some six portraits Gainsborough produced in the late 1750s and 1760s that has a framed landscape painting in the background.[91] Depicting a sketchy figure seated under a tree, the painting-within-a-painting calls to mind Gainsborough's fancy pictures and may allude to the sophistication and art collecting of the duchess's family. Their collection included Rubens's *The Watering Place* (National Gallery, London) and four portraits by Van Dyck that Gainsborough admired (see below).[92] It does not appear that the duke and duchess ever owned one of Gainsborough's landscapes.[93]

In the summer of 1768, Gainsborough wrote to his friend the actor David Garrick, encouraging him to "call *upon any pretence* [sic] any day after next Wednesday at the Duke of Montagus" to "see the Duke & Duchess in my *last* manner," meaning his latest style. He goes on, self-deprecatingly, to suggest that their paintings by Van Dyck and Rubens would justify the visit.[94] Presumably, Gainsborough was referring Garrick to the present picture and its pendant, which may have been delivered to the duke and duchess's London residence—Montagu House (demolished in the twentieth century) in Whitehall—by August of that year, but only partial documentation survives. Payments from the duke's personal accounts indicate that in May 1768 he paid £42 for his portrait (a receipt from Gainsborough specifies that

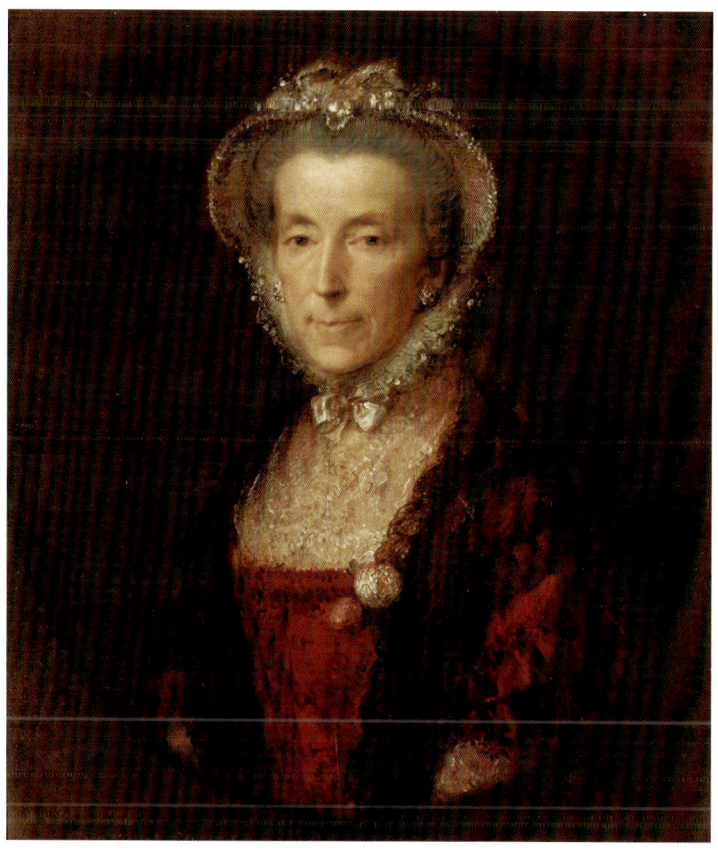

it was a half-length) and on December 6, 1768, he paid £31.10 for "the Duchess's Portrait" (no receipt from Gainsborough for the latter has been found).[95] It is possible that by the summer of 1768, Gainsborough had delivered the half-length pendants and that, when she returned to Bath in November 1768, the duchess sat for the smaller bust portrait (fig. 46). Duchess Mary kept her own accounts and at times divided expenses equally with her husband. She may have paid for the present half-length portrait herself.[96] During this visit to Bath, Gainsborough also painted the duke's valet, Ignatius Sancho (cat. 9). Whether the duke or duchess paid for the portrait of the servant or the artist made it as a gift is not known.

PROVENANCE

By descent.

SELECTED LITERATURE

Waagen 1854, 3: 312; Fulcher 1856a, 209; Fulcher 1856b, 213 (as "w[hole] l[ength])"; Armstrong 1898, 119, 120
(as painted between 1772 and 1777); Fletcher 1904, 72, 113; Boulton 1905, 127, 174 (as painted at end of Bath period);
Menpes and Greig 1909, 73; Scott and Dalrymple 1911, 20–21, no. 39; Whitley [1915] 2016, 81; Millar 1949, 8–9; Hayes 1975, 214, no. 67;
Lindsay 1981, 91; J. Hayes in Washington 1985–86, no. 472; Cormack 1991, 19, 96, no. 33; Cole 1997, 373–74; Rosenthal 1999, 42, 147;
Vaughan 2002, 115; Clifford 2004, 117–18; Hamilton 2017, 241; Belsey 2019, 2: no. 647.

SELECTED EXHIBITION HISTORY

London 1868, no. 858; London 1875, no. 156; London 1936, no. 105; Amsterdam 1936, no. 43;
London 1980, no. 100; Paris 1981, no. 34; Washington 1985–86, no. 472.

IGNATIUS SANCHO

1768

Oil on canvas
29 x 24½ in. (73.7 x 62.2 cm)
National Gallery of Canada, Ottawa;
Purchased 1907 (NGC 58)

IGNATIUS SANCHO (CA. 1729–1780) was an actor, composer, merchant, and literary figure. He was also the first and only known eighteenth-century Afro-Briton to have voted in parliamentary elections and the first to receive an obituary in the British press.[97] Born on a slave ship, Sancho was made to work for three sisters in Greenwich, England, as a child. The sisters gave him the derogatory name (after the comical character Sancho Panza in *Don Quixote*) that he would use thereafter.[98] As a teenager serving the sisters, he met John, 2nd Duke of Montagu, who was impressed with his intellect and welcomed him into his home and library.[99] After the duke's death in 1749, his widow (Mary Churchill, 2nd Duchess of Montagu) hired Sancho as a butler. At her death in 1751, she left Sancho a legacy and annuity (of £70 and £30, respectively), which he reportedly squandered (apparently spending his last shilling at the theater to see David Garrick perform), forcing him to return to service.[100] This time, he worked for the duke's daughter Mary, then Countess of Cardigan (cat. 8), and her husband George, 4th Earl of Cardigan (re-created 1st Duke and Duchess of Montagu in 1766). It was as the valet of George, 1st Duke of Montagu, that Sancho traveled to Bath with his employers in 1768 and sat for this portrait.

Ignatius Sancho is Gainsborough's only known portrait of a Black sitter. During his employment with the Montagus, Sancho would have seen portraits of other Black servants in

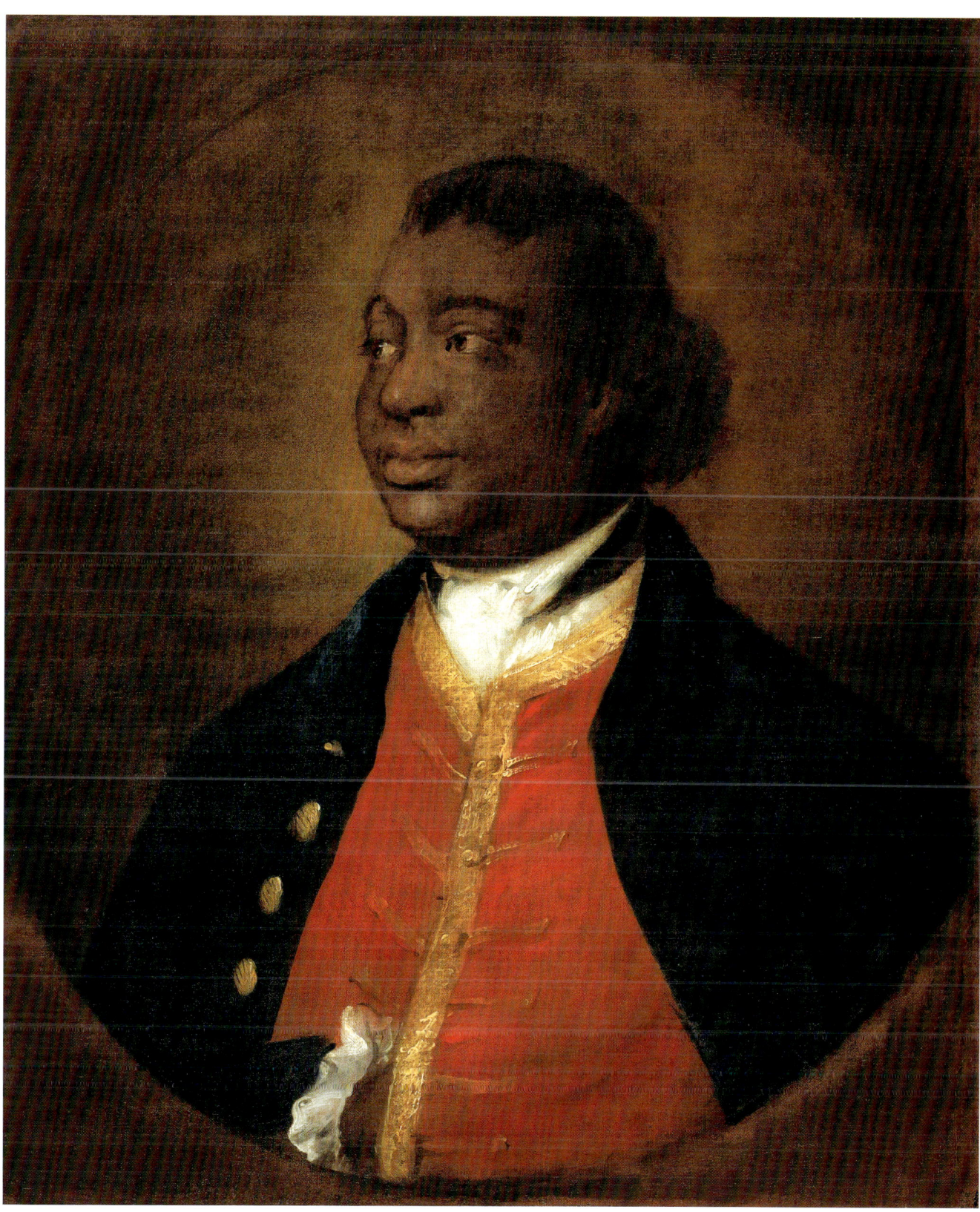

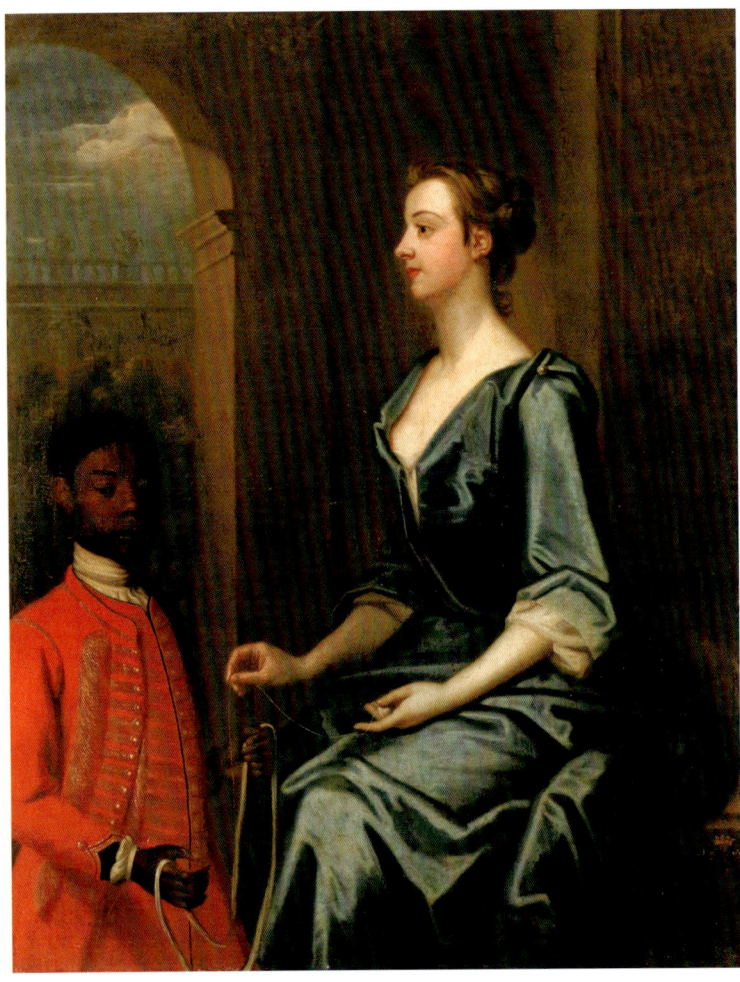

the family's history, such as that of the young Charles Manwell, wearing the green, red, and gold Montagu livery, attending Mary, 2nd Duchess of Montagu (fig. 47).[101] In Gainsborough's portrait, made nearly fifty years later, the artist effaces any trace of Sancho's servitude, instead presenting him in the clothes (dark-blue coat over a gold-trimmed red waistcoat) and pose of a gentleman, with one hand tucked into the waistcoat.[102] The present condition of the picture makes it difficult to evaluate its original appearance; it may have once had highlights and modeling that more emphatically distinguished Sancho's features from the background.[103] Gainsborough had scant experience with painting dark skin tones. Rather than using a lighter-toned background to set off Sancho's skin and hair, such as that in *Samuel Linley* (cat. 16), the artist seems to have picked up a standard-sized canvas prepared with brown ground that he must have had at the ready for his otherwise exclusively white European clients. Francesco Bartolozzi's engraving after Gainsborough's portrait, which served as the frontispiece to the 1782 posthumous publication of Sancho's letters (see fig. 24), may give an idea of the original appearance. Sancho is said to have been well versed in the art of painting, though what he and his contemporaries thought of the portrait is unknown.[104]

An inscription once visible on the back of the painting states that it was made in one hour and forty minutes in Bath on November 29, 1768.[105] This claim of swiftness does not necessarily indicate a lack of care, as Gainsborough was known for expedient painting sessions, including for the queen (see fig. 55).[106] No records of payment for Sancho's portrait have come to light. Gainsborough was at the time charging 20 guineas (£21) for bust portraits.[107] Sancho's wife had given birth to their fifth child in 1768, and with an annual income of about £60 (wages and annuity), Sancho presumably did not pay for the portrait himself.[108] It has been proposed that the portrait was a gift from the duke or duchess, perhaps when she sat for Gainsborough in late 1768 (the duke paid £31.10 for a portrait of the duchess on December 6, 1768, which is more than the fee for a single bust portrait but less than a single half-length and may be a partial or combined payment).[109] It is also plausible that Gainsborough gifted it to Sancho directly. Sancho had been publishing his musical compositions since 1767 and had common musical friends with Gainsborough, who was known to give paintings freely in exchange for music lessons, instruments, and compositions.[110] In 1767, Sancho's employer, Duke George, had purchased copies of Sancho's published music.[111]

Ailing from the gout that eventually contributed to his death, Sancho left the Montagus' service to open a grocery shop in 1773 with financial support from Duke George. An ardent abolitionist, in his writings about slavery, he noted the irony of a former slave making his living by selling goods such as sugar and tobacco from the colonies.[112] The association between the Sancho family and the Montagus continued after Sancho's death. In 1780, Sancho's son William served as bookbinder and bookseller to the duke and duchess's daughter Elizabeth.[113] Gainsborough's portrait appears to have gone straight into Sancho's possession, remaining with his family until 1820.[114]

PROVENANCE

The sitter and his widow, Ann (née Osborne); by descent to their daughter Elizabeth Sancho (d. 1837), who gave it to family friend William Stevenson, FRA (1750–1821); by descent to his son Seth William Stevenson; by descent to Henry Stevenson (1833–1888); his [anonymous] sale, Christie, Manson & Woods, July 9, 1887, lot 138; bought in; reoffered, Christie, Manson & Woods, March 17, 1888, lot 85; bought in; reoffered at Henry Stevenson's posthumous sale, Spelman at 35 Clarendon Road, Norwich, March 21, 1889, lot 220; anonymous sale, Christie's, January 24, 1903, lot 70; bought by Wallis; with Wallis & Son, London; with W. Scott & Sons, Montreal; purchased for the National Gallery of Canada, 1907.

SELECTED LITERATURE

Chambers 1829, 2: 1093; Fulcher 1856a, 110, 219; Fulcher 1856b, 112, 223; Armstrong 1898, 202; Armstrong 1904, 278; Fletcher 1904, 202; Boulton 1905, 178 ; Menpes and Greig 1909, 179; Brown 1913, 16; Baker 1933, 279; Tietze 1936, 183; Hubbard 1948, 80, no. 58; Waterhouse 1953, 95; Hubbard 1957, 112, no. 58; Waterhouse 1958, 88, no. 598; Boggs 1971, 5; Willis 1980, 345, 348, 352, 358; Laskin and Pantazzi 1987, 112–13, no. 58; Lindsay 1981, 90; Honour 1989, 29–30, 308; I. Lumsden in Fredericton 1991, 38; R. King in King et al. 1997, 17, 27, 28–30, 37, Rosenthal 1999, 158, 159, Vaughan 2002, 81; D. Perkins in London, Washington, and Boston 2002–3, 210; G. Waterfield and A. French in London and Edinburgh 2003–4, 38, 49–50, 145–46; Madin 2006, 34, 38–39; Hamilton 2017, 241–42; Belsey 2019, 2: no. 796; E. Chadwick in London 2024, 21.

SELECTED EXHIBITION HISTORY

London 1885, no. 2; Pittsburgh 1919, no. 30; Toronto 1919, no. 30; Bordeaux 1962, no. 188; Detroit 1963, no. 4; Fredericton 1991, no. 8; London 1997 (no cat.); London, Washington, and Boston 2002–3, no. 112; London 2024, no. 6.

CAT. 10

GAINSBOROUGH DUPONT

CA. 1770–72

Oil on canvas
17¹⁵⁄₁₆ x 14¾ in. (45.5 x 37.5 cm)
Tate, London; Bequeathed by Lady d'Abernon, 1954 (N06242)

GAINSBOROUGH DUPONT (1754–1797), virtually the sole assistant to his uncle, was first recorded as Thomas Gainsborough's apprentice in 1772 but was possibly with the artist since childhood.[115] Dupont was the son of Gainsborough's second-eldest sister, Sarah, and her husband, Philip Dupont, both of whom Gainsborough depicted in bust portraits, though evidently not as a pendant pair.[116] Perhaps as a matter of convenience or inspired by his nephew's good looks—possibly both—Gainsborough portrayed him multiple times. Scholars have suggested as many as eight depictions, including one of the young boy holding paintbrushes in the so-called *Pitminster Boy* (possibly the *Portrait of a Young Boy* Gainsborough exhibited at the first Royal Academy exhibition of 1769; see fig. 27) and the model for *The Blue Boy* (exhibited at the Royal Academy in 1770; see fig. 43).[117] The unusual size of the present canvas, smaller than a typical "head" of 30 by 25 inches, and its sketchiness suggest its experimental nature.[118] In the turn of the head, sidelong gaze, falling lace collar, and long, full hair, the painting reflects Gainsborough's study of Van Dyck, especially the figure of Bernard Stuart in his copies after Van Dyck's *Stuart Brothers* (see cat. 6). With the presence of Dupont in the studio demonstrating Gainsborough's ability to capture likeness, the present picture may have offered clients a model after which to imagine their own portraits done in a similar way.[119]

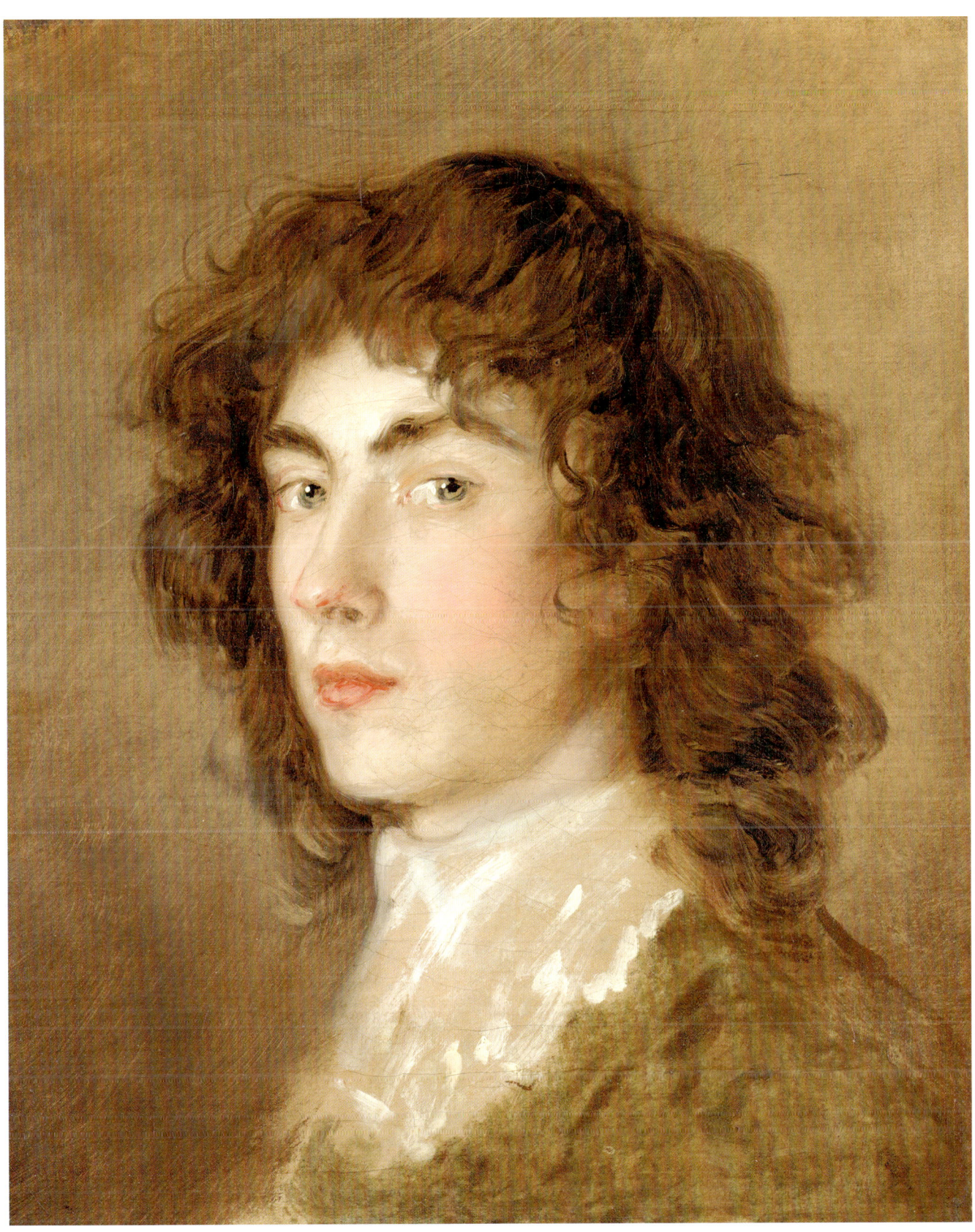

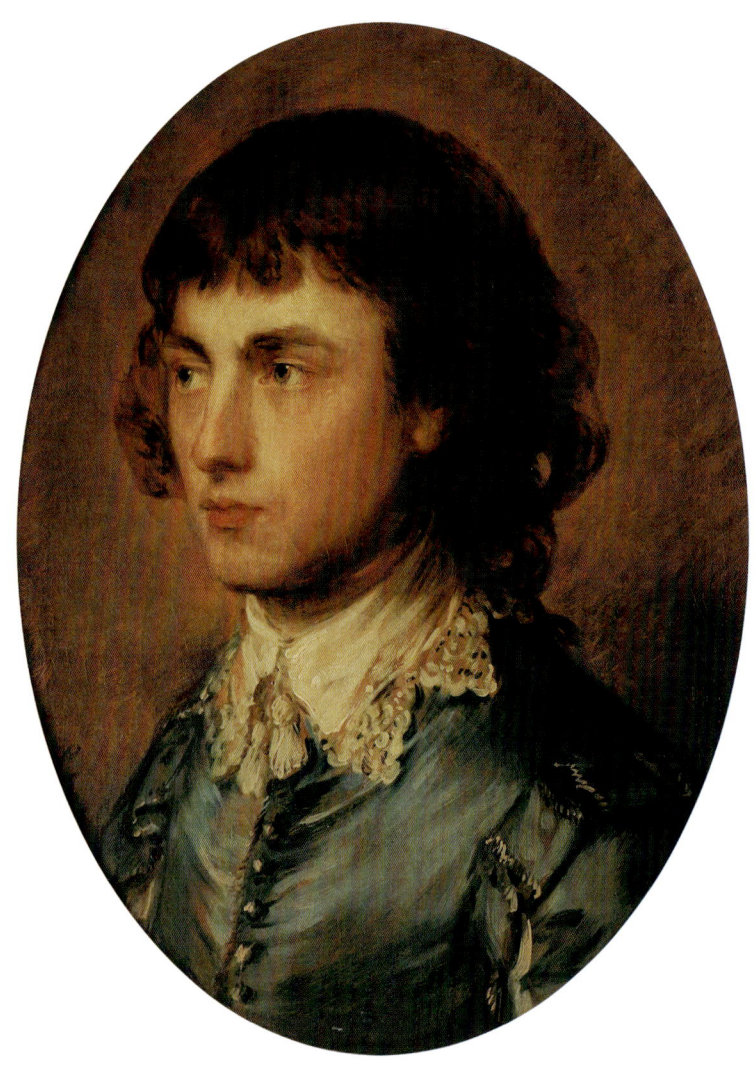

FIG. 48
Thomas Gainsborough
Gainsborough Dupont, ca. 1770
Oil on canvas
20½ x 15⅜ in. (52 x 39 cm)
Waddesdon Manor, Buckinghamshire; on loan from
the Rothschild Family Trust (346.1997)

There have been two matters of confusion around the portrait. The first has to do with an anecdote from Philip Thicknesse describing a portrait of Dupont acquired by Thicknesse himself as having been "the work of one hour"; Susan Sloman's research demonstrated that Thicknesse's portrait is one now at Waddesdon Manor (fig. 48).[120] The conspicuous swiftness in the handling of the present work—which seems to fit the description of being made in an hour—points to Gainsborough's confident, mature style. This, together with its close connection to Van Dyck's *Stuart Brothers*, suggests a date in the early 1770s.[121] The other confusion has to do with an anecdote attributed to Gainsborough's niece, Sophia Lane, describing a portrait of Dupont as the "last head" Gainsborough painted, left "on his easel when he died."[122] Though the present head was probably painted earlier than 1788, given the handling and apparent age of the subject, some scholars have identified this portrait as the one that the dying artist chose to be placed symbolically on his easel, as if the last word on his painterly journey.[123] Sloman, meanwhile, considers the "last head" to be a lost work.[124]

Gainsborough relied on his nephew as a collaborator, assistant, and model for some two decades of his later career.[125] In his will, he also established precautions against Dupont making claims on the studio production after Gainsborough's death.[126] Cultivating a style close to that of his famous uncle, Dupont achieved limited independent renown. He did not present his own work at the Royal Academy until two years after his uncle's death.[127]

PROVENANCE

By descent to artist's grandnephew Richard James Lane (1800–1872); his sale, Christie's, February 26, 1831, lot 54; bought in; sold to George Richmond (1809–1896) before 1856; his posthumous sale, Christie's, May 1, 1897, lot 10; bought by Agnews; purchased by Charles Fairfax Murray (1849–1919), who sold it to Colnaghi for Sir Edgar Vincent (later Viscount d'Abernon, 1857–1941), 1897; bequeathed to the National Gallery by his widow, 1954; transferred to the Tate, 1968.

SELECTED LITERATURE

Fulcher 1856a, 206; Fulcher 1856b, 210; Bell 1897, 10; Armstrong 1898, 123, 152 (erroneously, as having passed through Philip Thicknesse and Lord Bateman), 194; Chamberlain 1903, 181; Gower 1903, 15; Armstrong 1904, 164, 204, 228; Boulton 1905, 290, 312; Menpes and Greig 1909, 19, Whitley [1915] 2016, 349, 373 (as possibly the portrait Mrs. Sophia Lane described as Gainsborough's last portrait); Roberts 1919, 8; Whitley 1928, 206; Waterhouse 1953, 33; Waterhouse 1958, 65, no. 221; Ripley 1964, 41; Williamson 1972, 101; H. Belsey in Sudbury 1988, 64, no. 8; Kalinsky 1995, 74, no. 22; Vaughan 2002, 167; M. Myrone in London, Washington, and Boston 2002–3, no. 87; Sloman 2002, 79, 98; Sloman 2004, 320–22; Sloman 2013, 234, 236; Hamilton 2017, 212; Belsey 2019, 1: no. 287; D. Solkin in London and Princeton 2018–19, 36–49, 177, no. 48; M. McCurdy in London 2022, 53 under no. 1, 55.

SELECTED EXHIBITION HISTORY

Dublin 1861, no. 202; London 1862, no. 132; London 1867, no. 530; London 1885, no. 146; London 1904, no. 25; London 1909–10, no. 96; London 1936, no. 110; Folkestone 1967, no. 59; Sudbury 1988, no. 8; London, Washington, and Boston 2002–3, no. 87; London and Princeton 2018–19, no. 48.

MASTER JOHN HEATHCOTE

CA. 1771–72

Oil on canvas
50 x 39¹³⁄₁₆ in. (127 x 101.2 cm)
National Gallery of Art, Washington;
Given in memory of Governor Alvan T. Fuller
by The Fuller Foundation, Inc. (1961.2.1)

IN GAINSBOROUGH'S TIME, children in the social milieu of his clientele wore the type of loose clothing depicted here, often made of comfortable muslin (plain woven cotton initially imported from India and eventually made in Europe), which reflected Georgian ideals about the liberality and freedom of childhood. Boys were breeched (made to wear breeches) around the age of four and as late as seven.[128] This portrait of John Heathcote (1767–1838) in a serene outdoor setting is at the heart of an anecdote often cited to illustrate Gainsborough's compassion, as well as his strong opinions regarding dress in portraits. As recounted by George Williams Fulcher, who describes the sitter as then being about four years of age:

> Gainsborough chanced to be on a visit in Bath when a destructive sickness was raging in different parts of the kingdom. The parents of Master Heathcote having lost their other children by the epidemic, were anxious to secure a portrait of the one yet spared to them. They applied to Gainsborough, who, however, refused, saying that he had visited Bath for the purpose of recreation; but on hearing the circumstances of the case, he requested Mrs. Heathcote to let him see her son. The next morning, the boy, dressed in a plain white muslin frock with a blue sash, was taken to Gainsborough. "You have brought him simply dressed," he said—"had you paraded him in a fancy costume, I would not have painted him; now I will gladly comply with your request."[129]

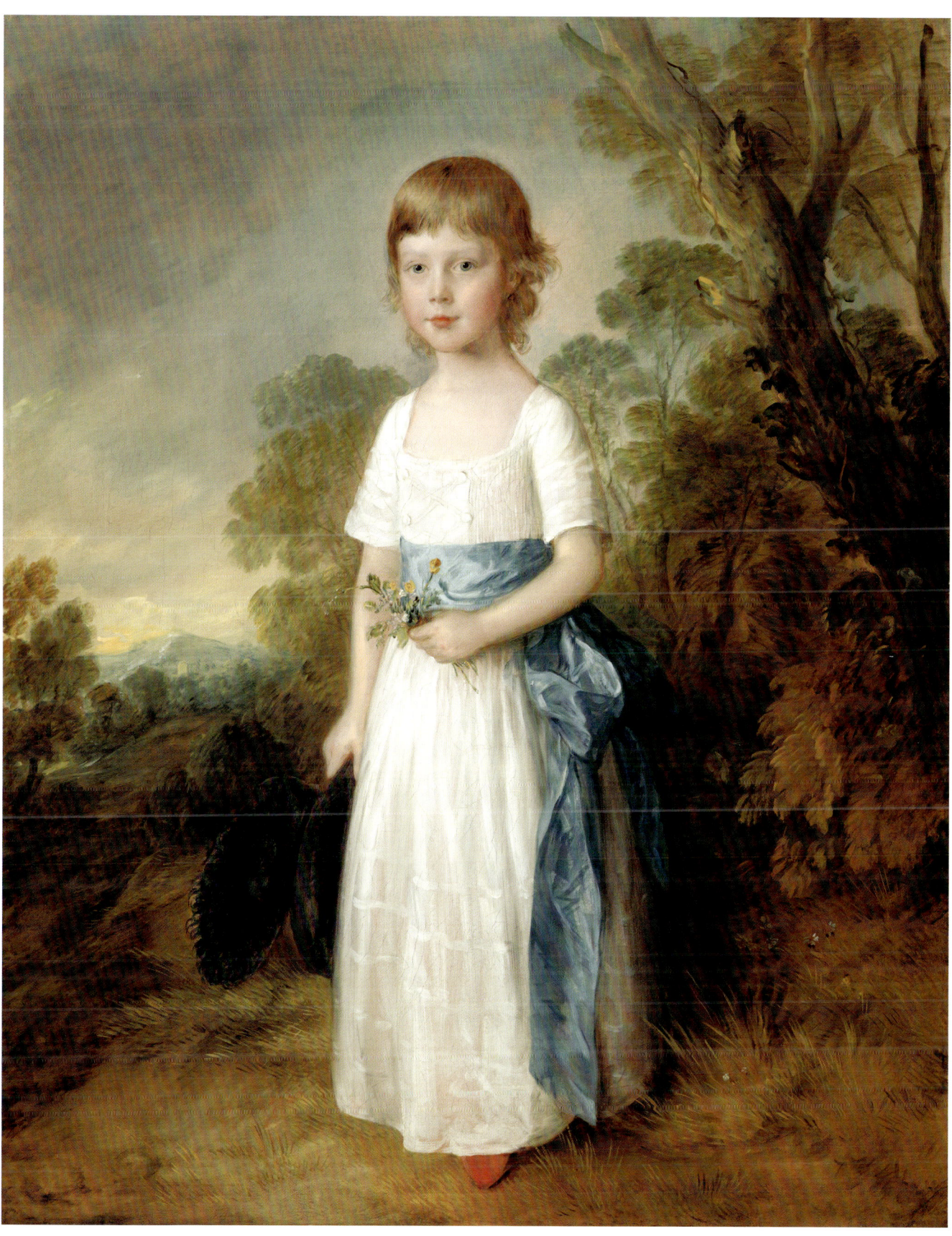

The detail of Gainsborough happening to be on a visit to Bath at this time may be a miscommunication as it contradicts his known biography, which has him living in Bath from 1759 until 1774. Scholars generally agree on dating the portrait to the early 1770s, with a possible *terminus ante quem* of around 1774, when the sitter's only surviving sibling, a sister, was born who, considering the family's circumstances, would presumably have been included in the portrait if it were painted after her birth.[130] The clutch of flowers in John's left hand evokes the blossoms of youth, while the black feathered hat he grips in his right introduces into the composition the signal color of mourning. Black clothing and accessories did not always denote mourning; given the circumstances of the commission, it is possible that the black hat may hint at death and loss. Gainsborough's portrait of another child, *Miss Elizabeth Haverfield* (fig. 49), pictures her in a similar muslin dress (though with a stiffened bodice in place of a sash) and with the identical form of a red shoe peeking out from the skirt; she is draped in a black shawl, also raising the question of whether or not the introduction of black attire into the portrait is significant.[131]

Gainsborough painted about ten independent portraits of children in his career, five of them full-lengths and most, like the present picture, painted on standard-size canvases

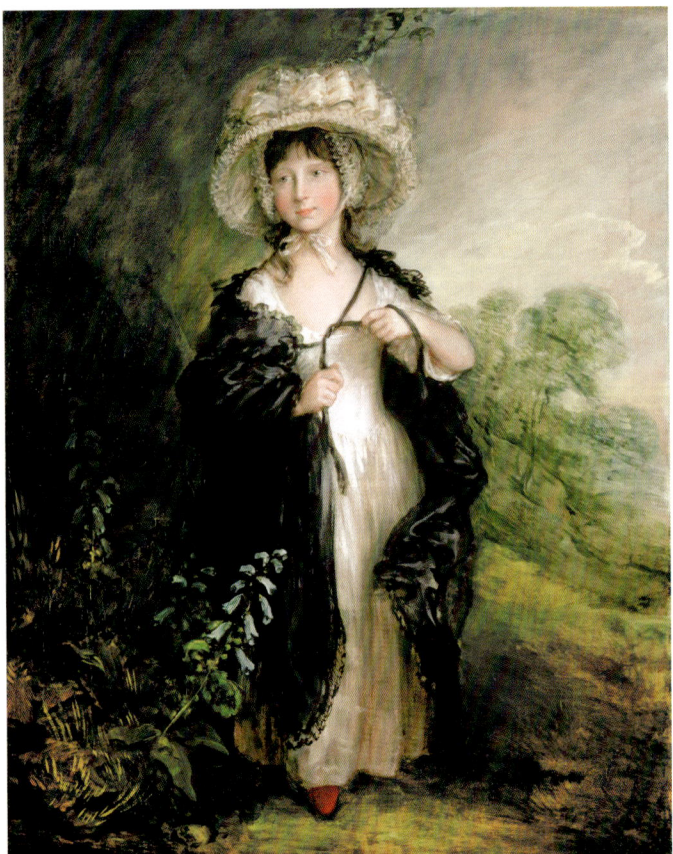

FIG. 49
Thomas Gainsborough
Miss Elizabeth Haverfield,
early 1780s
Oil on canvas
49¹¹⁄₁₆ x 39¾ in.
(126.2 x 101 cm)
Wallace Collection,
London (P44)

typically suited for half-length portraits of adults (50 x 40 inches). In nearly all of them, he presents the subjects wearing similar white muslin frocks, with or without sashes, and with a red shoe emerging from the skirts.[132] Like *Miss Elizabeth Haverfield*, the children are set in idyllic outdoor settings that, like the clothing, reflect contemporary ideals of childhood. In the present work, the peak and building in the far distance at left evoke the Heathcote family's estate in Huntingdonshire. The son of a politician, John followed in his father's footsteps in politics. He also devoted himself to the restoration of his family's home, Conington Castle, where the present portrait once hung in the dining room.[133]

PROVENANCE

Painted for the sitter's parents for their house at Chingford, Essex: by descent to the sitter's grandson John Moyer Heathcote (1834–1912); Conington Castle, Cambridgeshire; purchased from his estate by Agnews, September 24, 1913; purchased by Duveen, October 9, 1913; purchased by Herbert Stern, 1st Baron Michelham (1851–1919), Hellingly, Sussex, 1913; after Michelham's death it was taken to Paris by his widow, Aimee Geraldine (1882–1927); her sale, Hampton and Sons, 20 Arlington Street, London, November 23–24, 1926, 2nd day, lot 292; bought by Captain Jefferson Davis Cohn for Duveen; purchased through Duveen by Alvan T. Fuller (1878–1958), March or April 1927; passed to the Fuller Foundation, Boston; presented by them to the National Gallery of Art, 1961.

SELECTED LITERATURE

Fulcher 1856a, 224; Fulcher 1856b, 228; Bede 1889, 776, 778; Bell 1897, 90; Armstrong 1898, 160, 197; Armstrong 1904, 214–15; Fletcher 1904, 199; Boulton 1905, 278; Menpes and Greig 1909, 154; Borenius 1926, 139; Carter 1926, xliii, xl; Taylor 1951, 22; Waterhouse 1953, 55; Waterhouse 1958, 73; Watson 1969, 56–57; Hayes 1992, 82–84; Secrest 2004, 206, 438; Belsey 2019, 1: no. 472.

SELECTED EXHIBITION HISTORY

London 1864, no. 184; Boston 1928, no. 6; Boston 1939, no. 48; Boston 1959, no. 22.

CARL FRIEDRICH ABEL

CA. 1777

Oil on canvas
88¾ x 59½ in. (225.4 x 151.1 cm)
The Huntington Library, Art Museum,
and Botanical Gardens, San Marino (25.19)

CARL FRIEDRICH ABEL (1725–1787) left his native Germany in 1759 and became chamber musician, with his compatriot Johann Christian Bach, to Queen Charlotte.[134] He composed for and played the viola da gamba, the instrument (a precursor to the modern cello) pictured here resting against his leg. He was one of Gainsborough's closest friends. Gainsborough acquired instruments and musical compositions from Abel, who reportedly exchanged them for art and lived with his walls covered in Gainsborough's drawings.[135] Around 1775, the artist, who painted an earlier half-length of the musician (fig. 50), contributed to the decoration of the concert hall in Hanover Square in which Bach and Abel organized their famous concert series. This portrait may have been intended for that space, though it is not firmly established that it was ever installed there.[136]

Gainsborough presents a dignified image of his friend, whom the diarist Henry Angelo described as "a tall, big, portly person, with a waistcoat under which might easily have been buttoned twin brothers."[137] Seated in a red upholstered chair against a dramatic swath of green curtain, he pauses his pen in mid-composition and rests a hand on a gold snuffbox, possibly one given to him by Frederick William of Prussia.[138] He looks up as if struck by inspiration. "Allegro" is legible on the musical score.[139] A blue lining peeks out from his brown coat, which he wears over a gold waistcoat. Flourishes of white highlight his lace cuffs and powdered

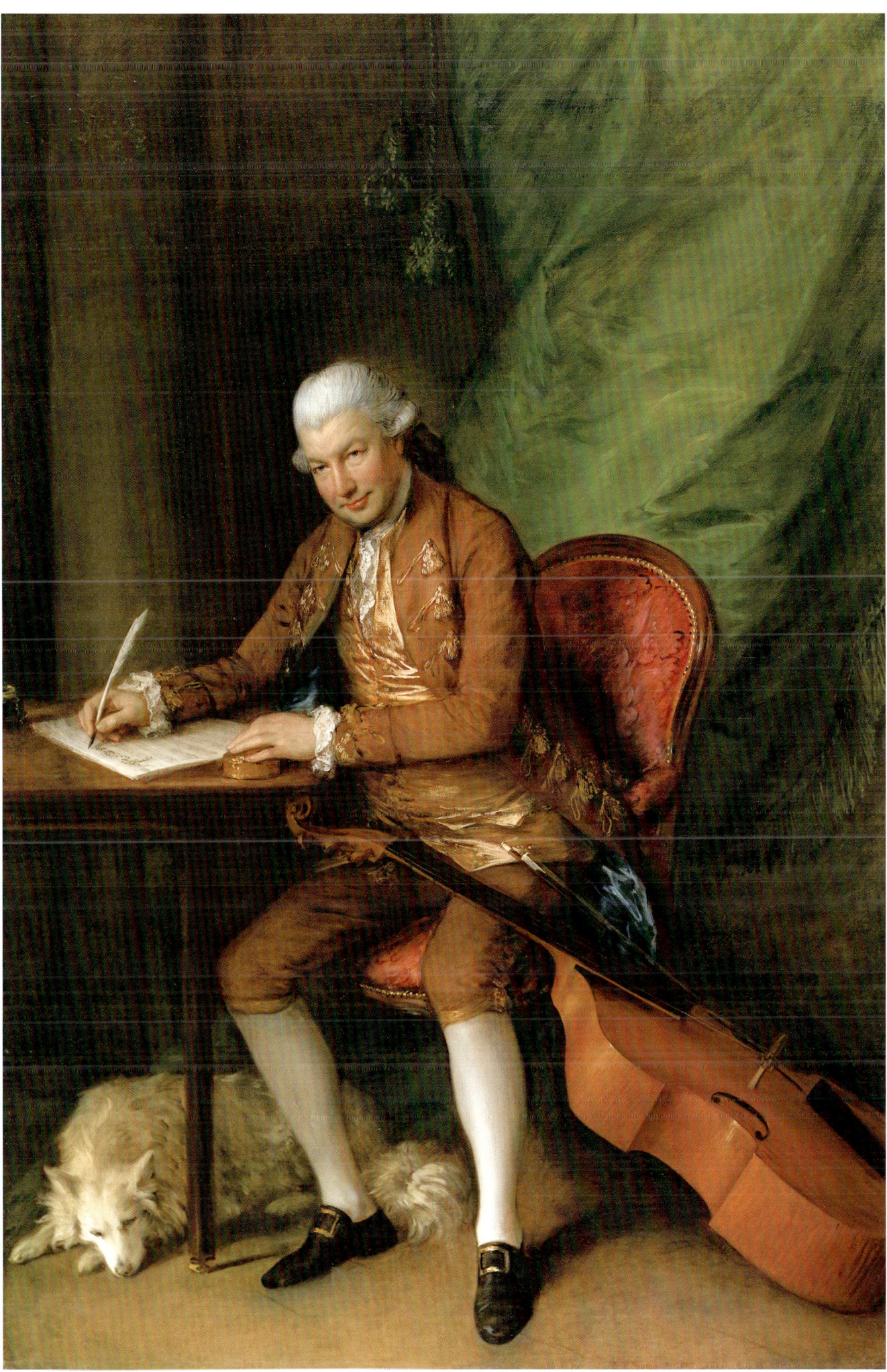

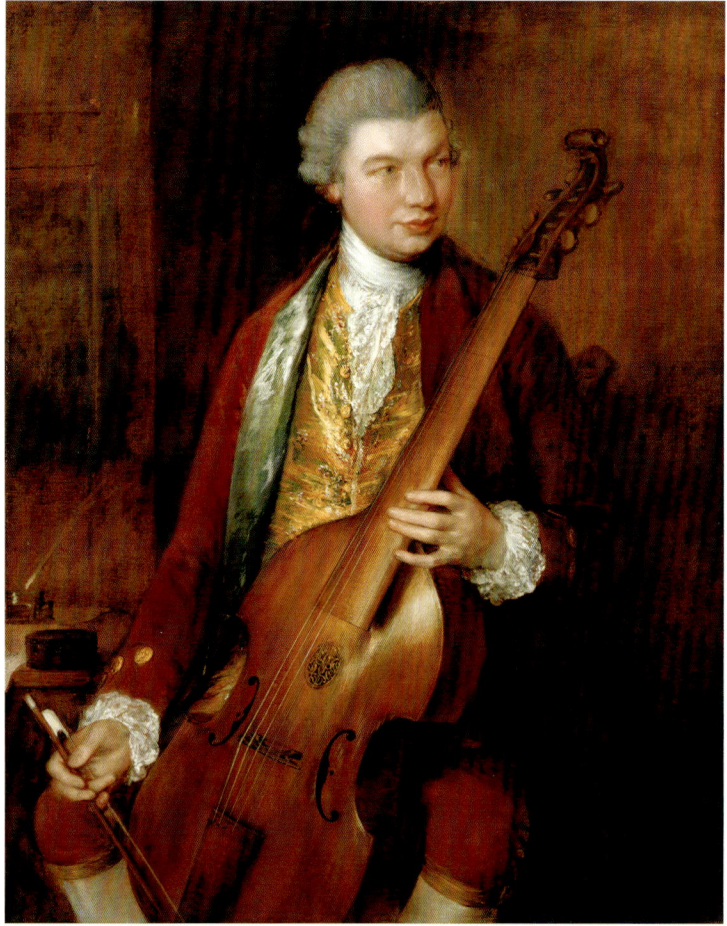

bagwig, while a gold watch chain with seals rests in shadow on his lap. The portrait offers no hint of the financial struggle that plagued him. Under the table, Abel's resting Pomeranian adds domesticity and informality to the scene. Gainsborough devoted an independent portrait to her and her pup, which was given to Abel in exchange for music lessons (cat. 13).

When the *Portrait of Mr. Abel* appeared at the Royal Academy exhibition of 1777—one of the few subjects to be named in the exhibition catalogue—the press raved. The *St. James's Chronicle* applauded the "exceeding good Portrait," observing that "whoever knows the celebrated Musician must pronounce it from Top to Bottom a striking Likeness. Nothing is omitted in this Piece."[140] The *Morning Post* hailed it as "the finest modern portrait we remember to have seen."[141] Singling out the portrait even from among Gainsborough's other works on view that year, the *Morning Chronicle* admired how it combined "with the force of a sketch the high finishing of a miniature"; this was poignant praise for an artist often criticized for lack of finish.[142] As one modern scholar has noted, Gainsborough's *Abel* "illustrates the difference . . . between a portrait by an artist of an intimate and cherished friend, and that of one of a crowd of ordinary sitters, people who merely engage an artist to paint their portraits for a monetary consideration."[143]

The artist planned to give a self-portrait (cat. 24) to Abel, who died before it was done. Abel's posthumous sale included nearly forty works by the artist, predominantly landscapes.[144] The present portrait was not in the sale; it is possible that Queen Charlotte had acquired it by then, as it remained in her possession until her death.[145] Gainsborough expressed his care for his friend on the day of Abel's death. "I shall never cease," he wrote, "looking up to heaven— the little while I have to stay behind—in hopes of getting one more glance of the man I loved from the moment I heard him touch the string."[146]

PROVENANCE

Acquired by Queen Charlotte at an unknown date; her anonymous sale, Christie's, London, May 25, 1819, lot 93; where purchased by Michael Peacock (ca. 1785–1843); George Wyndam, 3rd Earl of Egremont (1751–1837); by descent with Orchard Wyndham, Somerset, to Jane (d. 1876), the widow of George Wyndham, 4th Earl of Egremont (1786–1845); his executor's sale, Christie's, London, May 21, 1892, lot 80; where purchased by C. J. Wertheimer (1842–1911); anonymous sale, Christie's, May 8, 1897, lot 78; bought in; W. Lockett Agnew (1858–1919); purchased by Agnews on July 16, 1909; purchased by Duveen on the same day; who sold it to George Jay Gould (1864–1923), New York; with Duveen in 1925, who sold it on May 15, 1925, to Henry E. Huntington; bequeathed by him to the Huntington Museum, 1927.

SELECTED LITERATURE

Morning Chronicle, April 25, 1777; *Morning Post*, April 25, 1777; *Public Advertiser*, April 26, 1777; *St. James's Chronicle*, April 26–29, 1777; *Morning Chronicle*, August 8, 1788; Edwards 1808, 140; Fulcher 1856a, 107–8, 183, 216; Fulcher 1856b, 109–10, 187, 220; Brock-Arnold 1881, 41, 71; F. G. Stephens in London 1885, no. 46; Bell 1897, 47, 48; Armstrong 1898, 191; Chamberlain 1903, 62, 94, 162–63; Gower 1903, 83–84, 117–18; Armstrong 1904, 257; Fletcher 1904, 195, 222; Boulton 1905, 245, 246–47; Mourey 1905, 64, 96; Whitley [1915] 2016, 168, 170, 315; Roberts 1921, 23–26; Dibdin 1923, 126, 137; Whitley 1928, 323; Baker 1936, 38; Millar 1949, 14; Waterhouse 1953, 1; Waterhouse 1958, 26, 51, no. 1; Millar 1969, 35; Williamson 1972, 137–38, 139, 213; Hayes 1975, 219, no. 89; Wilson 1977, 108; Lindsay 1981, 132; Cyr 1987, 317, 318, 321; Cormack 1991, 25, 27, 106, 120, no. 45, 172 under no. 71; Postle 1991, 240–41; Waterhouse 1994, 257; Kalinsky 1995, 86, no. 28; Rosenthal 1999, 90–93, 112, 244; Asleson and Bennett 2001, 92–100, no. 15 (erroneously as sold in 1787 to Queen Charlotte); R. Asleson in New Haven and San Marino 2001–2, no. 18; Postle 2002, 50–52; Vaughan 2002, 100–101, 112, 135; C. Riding in London, Washington, Boston 2002–3, no. 50; Ingamells 2004, 3, 4; Secrest 2004, 131–32; D. Perkins in Sudbury 2006, 25 under no. 4; Roe 2008, 108, 111, 123, 125; Craven 2009, 325; Holman 2010, 197; Bennett 2013, 277; Hamilton 2017, 295, 319; Belsey 2019, 1: no. 2, 21 under no. 5.

SELECTED EXHIBITION HISTORY

London 1777, no. 135; London 1832, no. 143; London 1885, no. 46; London 1894b, no. 104; London 1897, no. 98; New York 1914a, no. 4; New Haven and San Marino 2001–2, no. 18; London, Washington, and Boston 2002–3, no. 50.

POMERANIAN AND PUPPY

CA. 1777

Oil on canvas
32¾ x 44 in. (83.2 x 111.8 cm)
Tate, London;
Bequeathed by Mrs. Arthur James, 1948 (N05844)

GAINSBOROUGH DEPICTED DOGS in landscape paintings, in fancy pictures, and, above all, in portraits of people, following traditions in European art of presenting dogs as symbols of fidelity and immortalizing the companionship of favorite pets.[147] Noting the "surprisingly large" number of Gainsborough's portraits that include dogs, Ellis Waterhouse found many of the animals "more memorable than their masters."[148] In Britain, independent portraits of dogs—without their owners—conventionally functioned, like those of thoroughbred horses, to map and affirm lineage and to signal the wealth and interests of the animals' owners, especially with respect to hunting dogs.[149] Though this was not a particularly fashionable or lucrative type of portrait, Gainsborough produced throughout his career independent canine portraits, which have been celebrated for their individualized depictions that capture the likeness and personality of the animals as if they were human subjects.

Belsey describes Gainsborough's *Pomeranian and Puppy* as "unquestioningly the most complex and successful of all his dog portraits."[150] An early nineteenth-century source identifies the dog as that belonging to Carl Friedrich Abel and pictured in Gainsborough's portrait of the musician (cat. 12), with her puppy.[151] Presumably, the present work was painted around the same time as the portrait of Abel. As the breed was then rare in Britain, scholars speculate that Abel brought the dog from Germany.[152] The inclusion of the pup nods to the

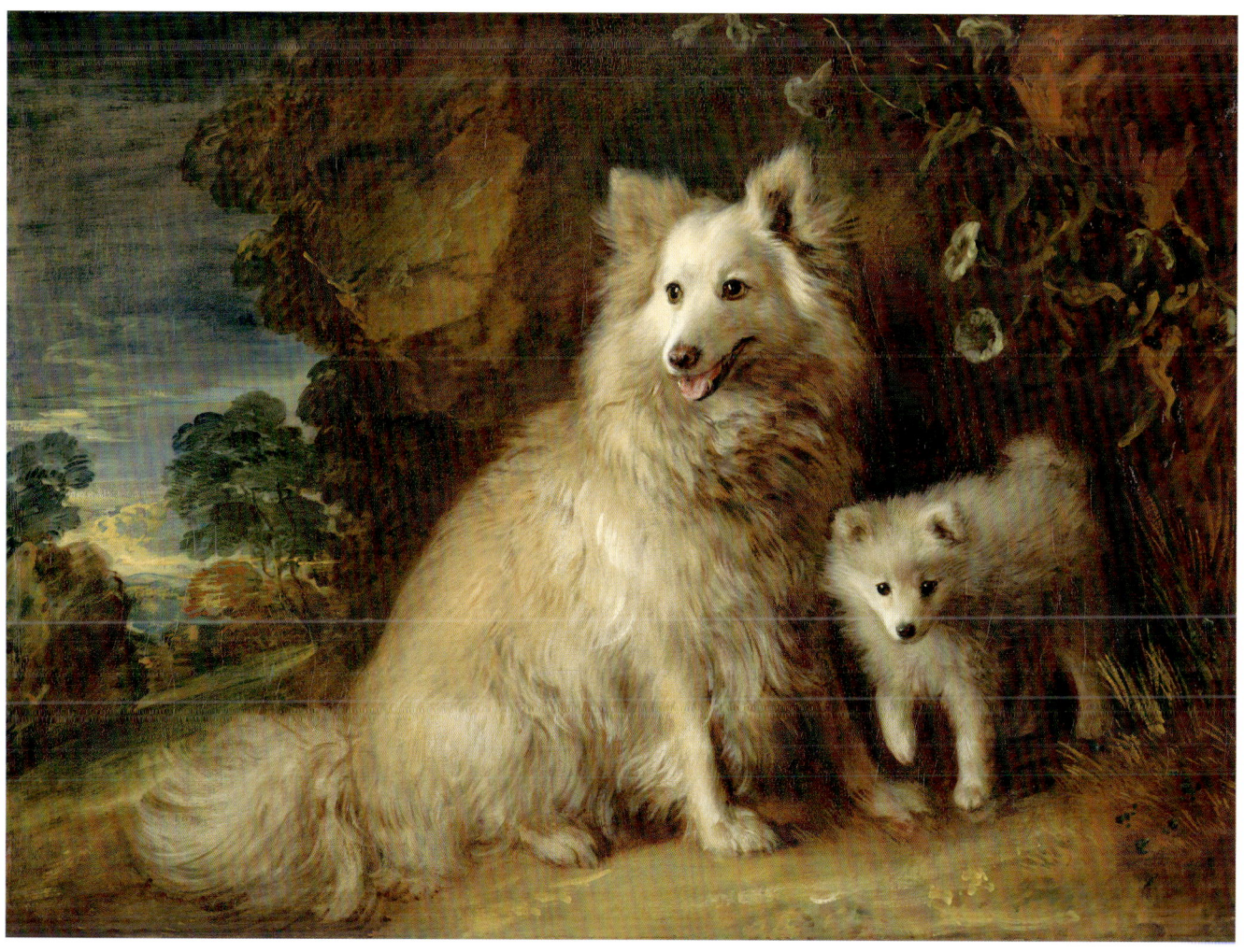

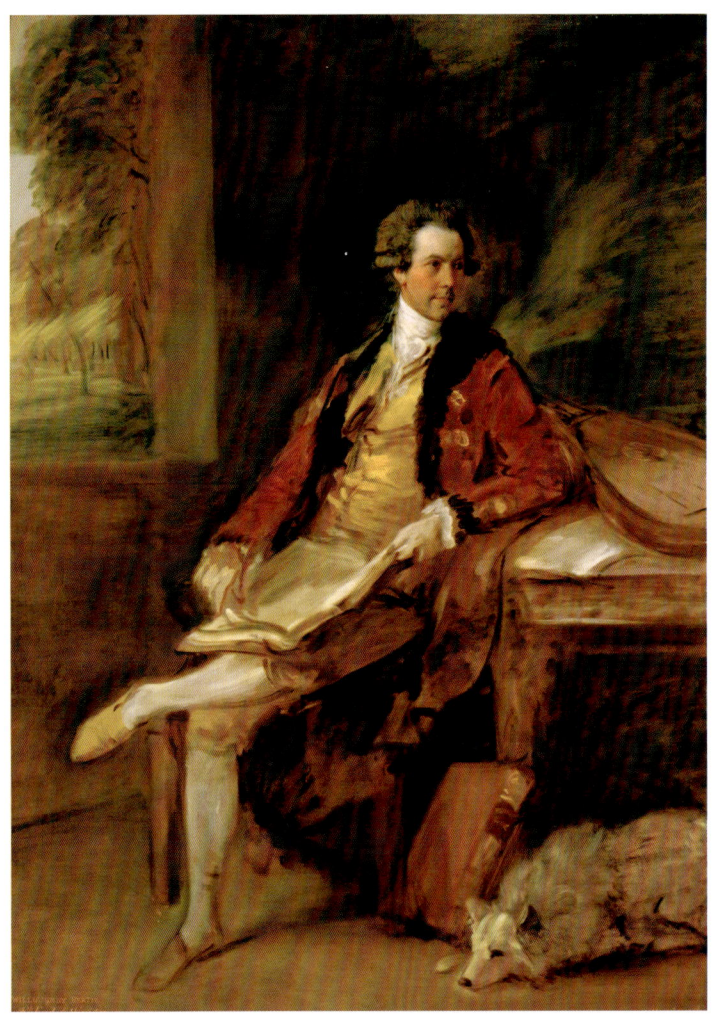

FIG. 51
Thomas Gainsborough
Willoughby Bertie, 4th Earl of Abingdon, ca. 1776
Oil on canvas
82 x 57 in. (208.3 x 144.8 cm)
Private collection

traditional commemoration of lineage and continuation of the bloodline.[153] The Pomeranians that appear in a number of Gainsborough's portraits in the 1770s and 1780s are not likely to have been individual pets belonging to each sitter but rather a motif the artist included to enhance the portraits' aesthetic effects and informality, as in the unfinished portrait of Lord Abingdon (fig. 51), in which a Pomeranian also lies at the sitter's feet.[154] Abel's dog may have been Gainsborough's model and prototype.[155]

Fulcher relays an anecdote in which the portrait, hanging at one point over Gainsborough's mantelpiece when the sculptor Joseph Nollekens visited, inspired Gainsborough spontaneously to model the dog's head in clay.[156] In 1953, Waterhouse erroneously identified the painting over the mantelpiece as *Tristram and Fox* (Tate, London), a mistake repeated by subsequent scholars.[157] Whitley recounts that an early nineteenth-century source claimed that Gainsborough gave the painting to Abel in exchange for lessons on the viola da gamba, and when the painting was first sent to Abel's house, the likeness of the image deceived Abel's dog, who "flew at her own resemblance with such fury that it was found necessary to place the picture in a situation where it was free from her jealous anger."[158] The portrait remained among Abel's possessions and was acquired at his posthumous sale by a fellow musician and friend of Gainsborough, the cellist John Crosdill.

PROVENANCE

Carl Friedrich Abel (1725–1787); his posthumous sale, Greenwood, London, December 12–13, 1787, lot 44; where purchased by John Crosdill (1751–1825); Mr. W. R. M. Thoyts, by 1887; Mrs. Hautenville Cope and Miss Thoyts, London, sale, Christie, Manson & Woods, May 6, 1910, lot 94; bought by C. Davis for John Arthur James (1853–1917); passed to his wife, Mary Venetia Cavendish-Bentinck (d. 1948), who bequeathed it to the National Gallery, 1948; transferred to Tate, 1975.

SELECTED LITERATURE

W. Hazlitt in *The Champion*, July 31, 1814, 247; Smith 1828, 185; Fulcher 1856a, 134, 196; Fulcher 1856b, 137, 200; Armstrong 1898, 209; Chamberlain 1903, 162–64; Whitley [1915] 2016, 400; Waterhouse 1953, 21; Waterhouse 1958, 106, no. 821; Williamson 1972, 134; Lindsay 1981, 128; Green 1982, 17–25; J. Hayes in Ferrara 1998, 84 under no. 11; Vaughan 2002, 182; D. Perkins in Sudbury 2006, 16–17, 20; Belsey 2019, 2: no. 1043.

SELECTED EXHIBITION HISTORY

London 1814, no. 58 (as *Fox Dogs*); London 1876, no. 44 (as *A Pomeranian Dog and Puppy*); London 1885, no. 113; Ipswich 1887, no. 132; London 1953a, no. 51 (as *White Dogs: Pomeranian Bitch and Puppy*); Paris 1981, no. 52; Sudbury 2006, no. 4.

THE HON. FRANCES DUNCOMBE

CA. 1776

Oil on canvas
92¼ x 61⅛ in. (234.3 x 155.3 cm)
The Frick Collection, New York (1911.1.61)

WHEN THE SITTER'S FATHER, Anthony Duncombe (ca. 1695–1763), was elevated to the peerage as 1st Baron Feversham in 1747, she and her half-sister, Anne, were designated with the courtesy title of "The Honourable." By the time Frances was six, she had lost both her parents. Her mother, Frances Bathurst, died nine days after giving birth. Her father, already in his sixties when she was born, remarried but died in 1763. His widow married William Bouverie, 1st Earl of Radnor. It was when Frances (1757–1827) was living with the family of her stepmother and the earl at Longford Castle that Gainsborough first painted her (fig. 52) as part of a suite of bust portraits of the family in 1773.[159] To paint the portraits, Gainsborough stayed at the castle and while there would have seen the family's collection of portraits by Van Dyck with which Frances grew up. Gainsborough presumably painted the present full-length around the time that Frances married John Bowater in late 1775.[160] Gainsborough had been established in London since 1774 and was charging 100 guineas (£105) for full-length portraits. Nothing is known of the portrait's commission, but Bowater, who was notorious for spending and passionate about paintings, is likely to have ordered the monumental portrait of his new wife.[161] None of the portraits Gainsborough painted of the Earl of Radnor's family is as grand—or as ostentatious—as the present picture.

Gainsborough presents Frances as a sophisticated, mature, and elegant figure. He and Frances may have discussed the blue satin Van Dyck–style dress she wears—which may or may not have actually existed—as an allusion to the Bouverie portraits at Longford, perhaps especially to Thomas Hudson's *Harriot Pleydell* (fig. 53), first wife of the 1st Earl and mother of the 2nd Earl, whose Van Dyck dress in her 1749 portrait may have signaled her role in the lineage of

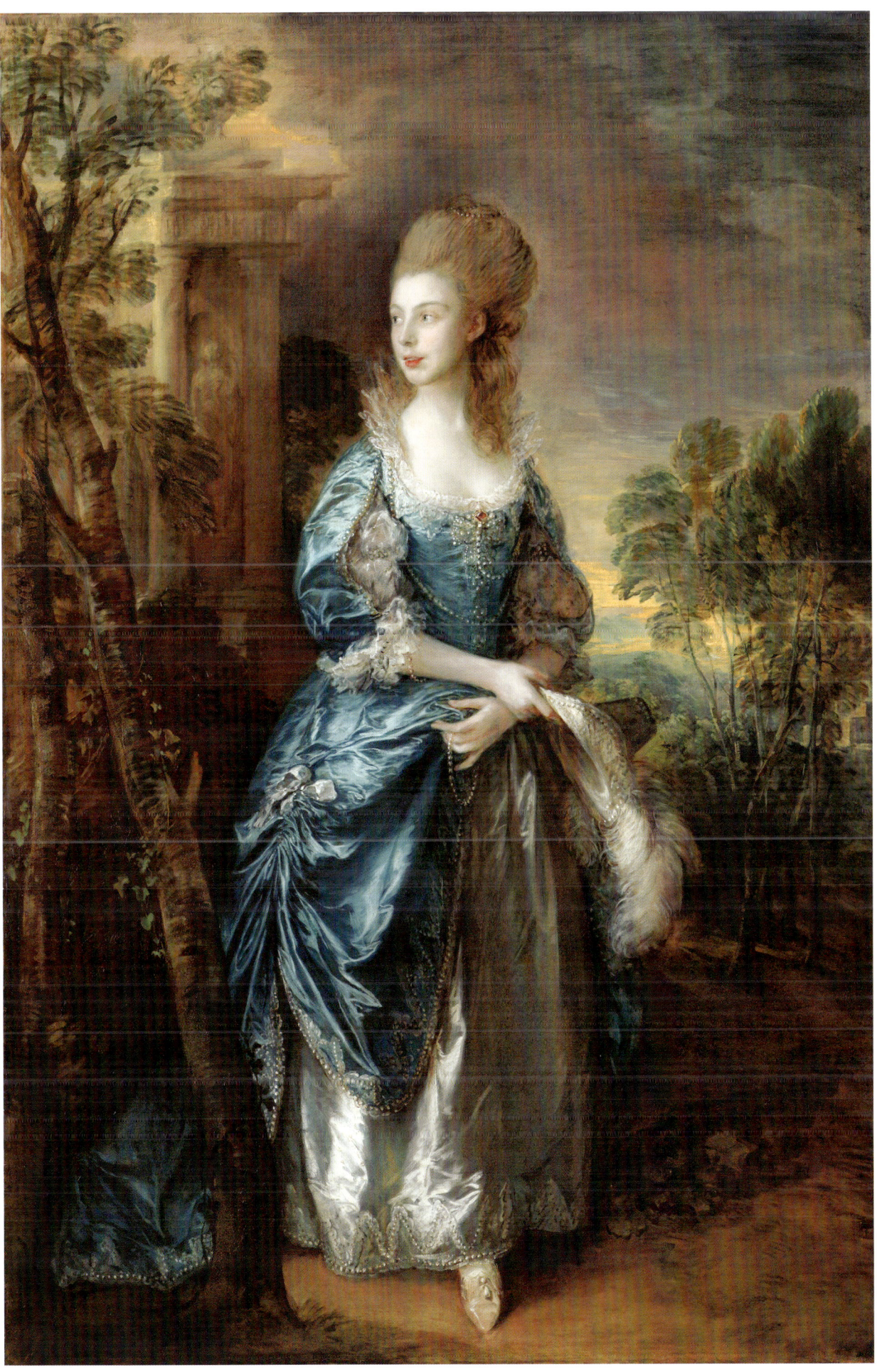

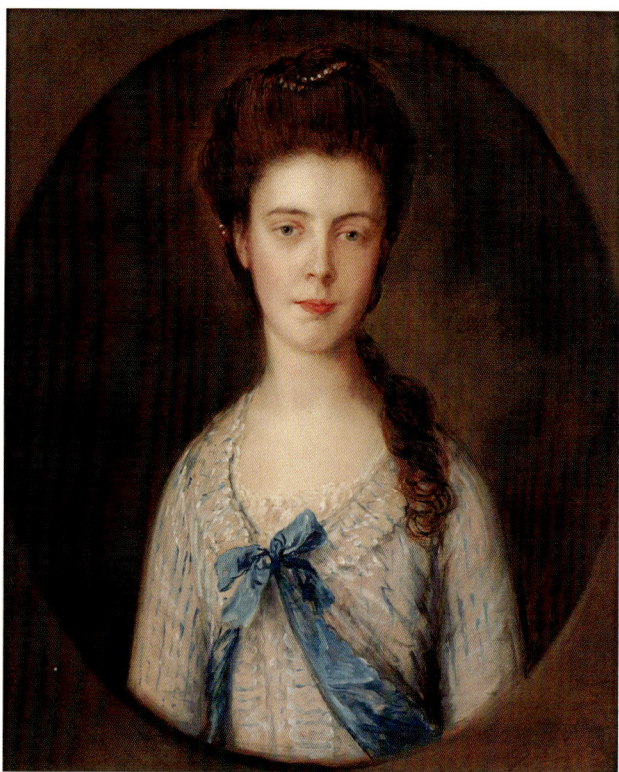

the family.[162] Resplendent in the dress with its dog-tooth collar and embellished with hundreds of pearls, Frances appears extravagant by comparison. She is pictured standing outdoors, her crossed hands gripping her skirt and a feathered hat and a circlet of pearls hanging from her fingers. Red punctuates her lips and the gem nestled at her chest. From beneath her skirts, she points a pink satin shoe, adorned with a teardrop pearl. Behind her at left, a classical building, perhaps a folly, features a sculptural female figure, while at right a rectilinear structure suggests another architectural feature. Outdoor settings are typical of Gainsborough's society portraiture; here, however, the combination of buildings and open landscape seem to more overtly suggest the extensive Leicestershire estates over which Frances presided. The portrait's relationship to Gainsborough's two portraits of the Hon. Mrs. Mary Graham has been a matter of debate; it is possible that the full-length of Mrs. Graham (see fig. 22) was on view in Gainsborough's painting rooms to attract prospective clients—like Frances Duncombe—before it was exhibited at the Royal Academy in 1777.[163]

With John's mounting debt, Mr. and Mrs. Bowater fled to the Continent in August of 1778. Their marriage dissolved (though they never divorced), and John returned to England in 1791, whereupon he started a family with a Sarah Hill before being imprisoned in Fleet prison for debts, around 1806. Frances remained in Bonn, Germany, associated with the court of Maximilian Franz, elector of Cologne and brother of Queen Marie-Antoinette of France. Around the time of the 1793 execution of Marie-Antoinette, Frances fled for England with the elector's chaplain, Abbé Dobeler, with whom she took up residence in her seat at Old Dalby Hall (in separate

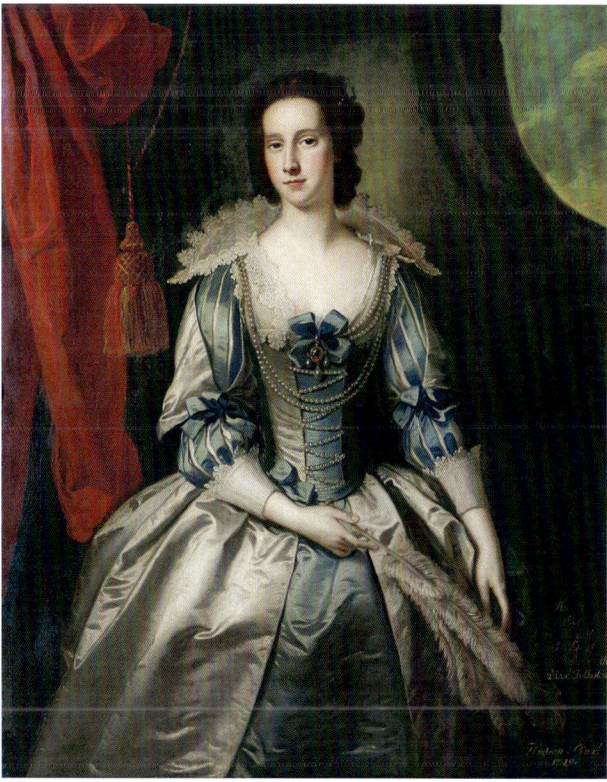

quarters). The present portrait remained at Old Dalby long after her death in 1827. In 1871, it was sold among the contents of the house (reportedly for £6), and was often mistakenly identified as a portrait of her half-sister, Hon. Anne Duncombe, later Countess of Radnor.[164]

PROVENANCE

Passed with Old Dalby Hall to the Rev. William George Sawyer (d. 1871), a descendant of the sitter's aunt Anne, who had married John Sawyer of Heywood, Berkshire, 1827; sold posthumously from Old Dalby Hall in 1871 to "five Jewish dealers from Seven Dials," who sold it to Henry Graves: purchased by Baron Lionel de Rothschild (1808–1879), 1872; purchased from his widow by Agnews, December 6, 1901; bought by C. J. Wertheimer, January 13, 1902; with Duveen in 1911; purchased by Henry Clay Frick (1849–1919), 1911.

SELECTED LITERATURE

Engravings 1874–75, 1: no. 53; Frith 1888, 458–63 (withholds title of portrait, later identified by Roberts 1914); Armstrong 1898, 194 (as *Hon. Anne Duncombe*); Chamberlain 1903, 184 (as *Hon. Anne Duncombe*); Roberts 1906, 140 (as *Hon. Frances Duncombe*, erroneously as in J. Pierpont Morgan's collection); Menpes and Greig 1909, 120–21, 173; Radnor 1909, pt. 2, 84; *American Art News* 1911; *New York Times*, June 13, 1911; Roberts 1912, 152; Roberts 1914, 204–10; Bridge 1919–20, 127; Thieme and Becker 1920, 81 (as "Hon. Mrs. Duncombe"); *New York Times*, May 28, 1921 (as *Anne Duncombe*); *New York Times*, October 20, 1921 (as the *Hon. Anne Duncombe*); Baker 1933, 111; Comstock 1936, 97; Siple 1936, 102; Duveen 1941, no. 275; Waterhouse 1958, 64, no. 217; Davidson 1968, 48–50; Hollander 1971, 484; Reynolds 1971, 410–12; Hayes 1975, 219, no. 92; Fowles 1976, 63–64; Lindsay 1981, 139; Cherry and Harris 1982, 304; London 1982–83, 25; Syer 1987, 257; Hayes 1993, 32; Hall 1994, 271–72; Kalinsky 1995, 80; Ribeiro 1995, 193, 195, 207; Rosenthal 1999, 275–79; H. Belsey in Edinburgh 2003, 52, 54; Secrest 2004, 441; Badea-Päun 2007, 18; A. Ribeiro in Cincinnati and San Diego 2010–11, 136–38; Guillery 2012, 6–7; L. Barnes in West Palm Beach 2015, 98; A. Eaker in New York 2016, 45; Hamilton 2017, 295; Belsey 2019, 1: no. 9; A. Ng in Mizrahi and Ng 2026, 19–65.

SELECTED EXHIBITION HISTORY

London 1873, no. 120 (as *Portrait of a Lady in a Blue Dress*); London 1902, no. 12 (as *The Honble. Anne Duncombe*); London 1907, no. 87 (as *The Hon. Frances Duncombe*); Berlin 1908, no. 23 (as *The Hon. Anne Duncombe*); New York 1914a, no. 1 (as *The Hon. Anne Duncombe*, lent by Henry C. Frick); New York 1914b, no. 7 (as *Lady Anne Duncombe*).

MARGARET GAINSBOROUGH

CA. 1778

Oil on canvas
30³⁄₁₆ x 25⅛ in. (76.6 x 73.8 cm)
The Courtauld, London (Samuel Courtauld Trust) (P.1932.SC.157)

IN JULY 1746, Gainsborough married Margaret Burr (1728–1798) in London, apparently covertly and possibly when she was pregnant. Their baby, Margaret, died in infancy and is probably the child depicted in Gainsborough's early family portrait (fig. 54).[165] How the couple met is unknown.[166] Thicknesse described her as a "pretty Scots girl, of low birth."[167] While the identity of her mother is unknown, documents discovered in 1995 confirm that she was the illegitimate daughter of Henry Somerset, 3rd Duke of Beaufort (1707–1745), from whose estate she received a £200 annuity from 1745 until her death.[168] Financial struggle marked much of Gainsborough's early career, and his wife's annuity helped to keep the family afloat.[169] The extent to which connections to her illegitimate family helped her husband's business is unknown. A few relatives of the Duke of Beaufort sat for him (see p. 59), but the family did not patronize him extensively.

The artist was said to have painted a portrait of his wife annually to mark their wedding anniversary.[170] Fewer than ten depictions of her by his hand are known today, a combination of family portraits and four independent portraits.[171] The present portrait, dated around 1778 on the basis of stylistic comparison and the perceived age of the sitter (around fifty), has been praised as "immensely sympathetic"[172] and "supremely tender,"[173] and as evidence of his affection for his wife after three decades of marriage.[174] Her pose has been compared to

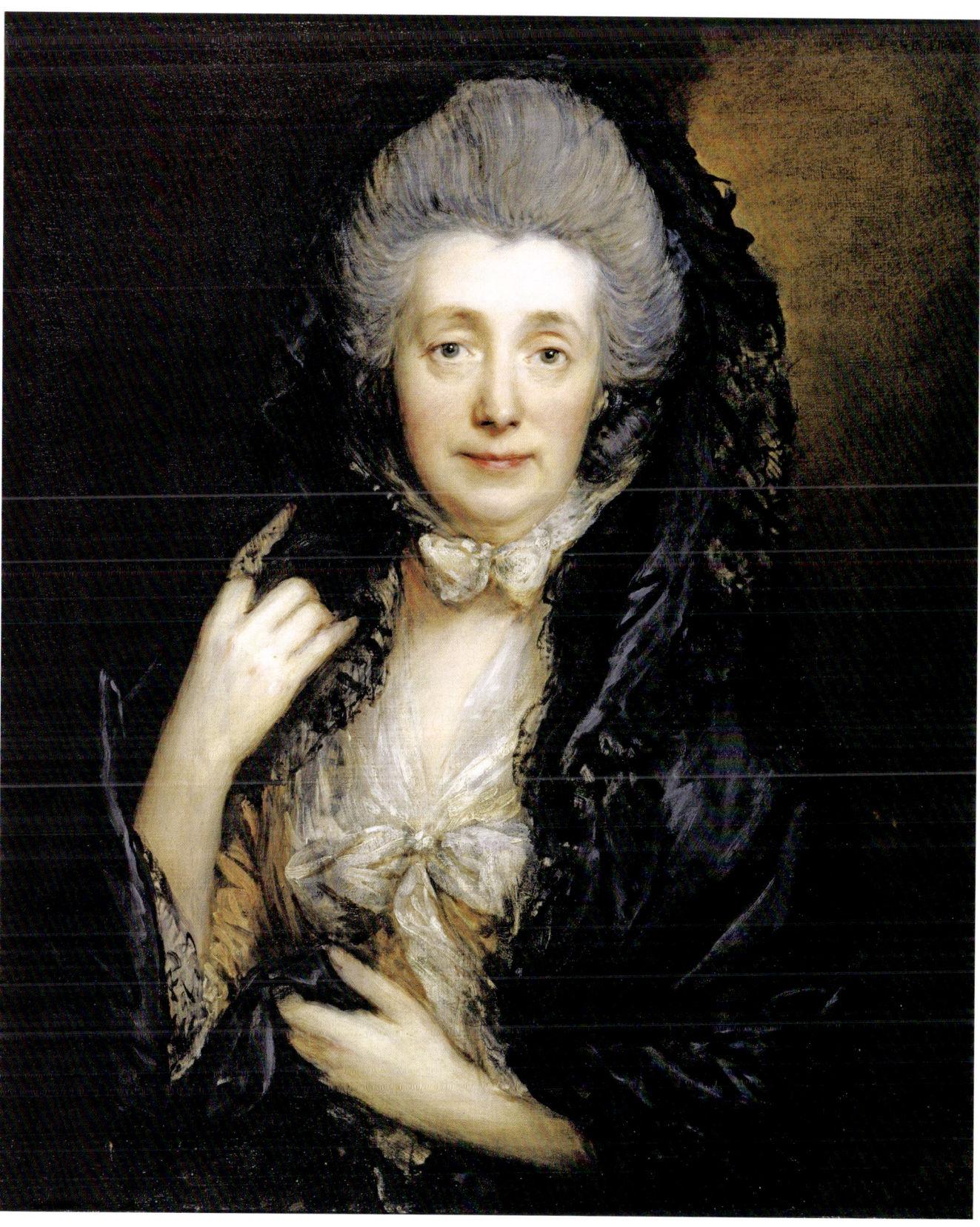

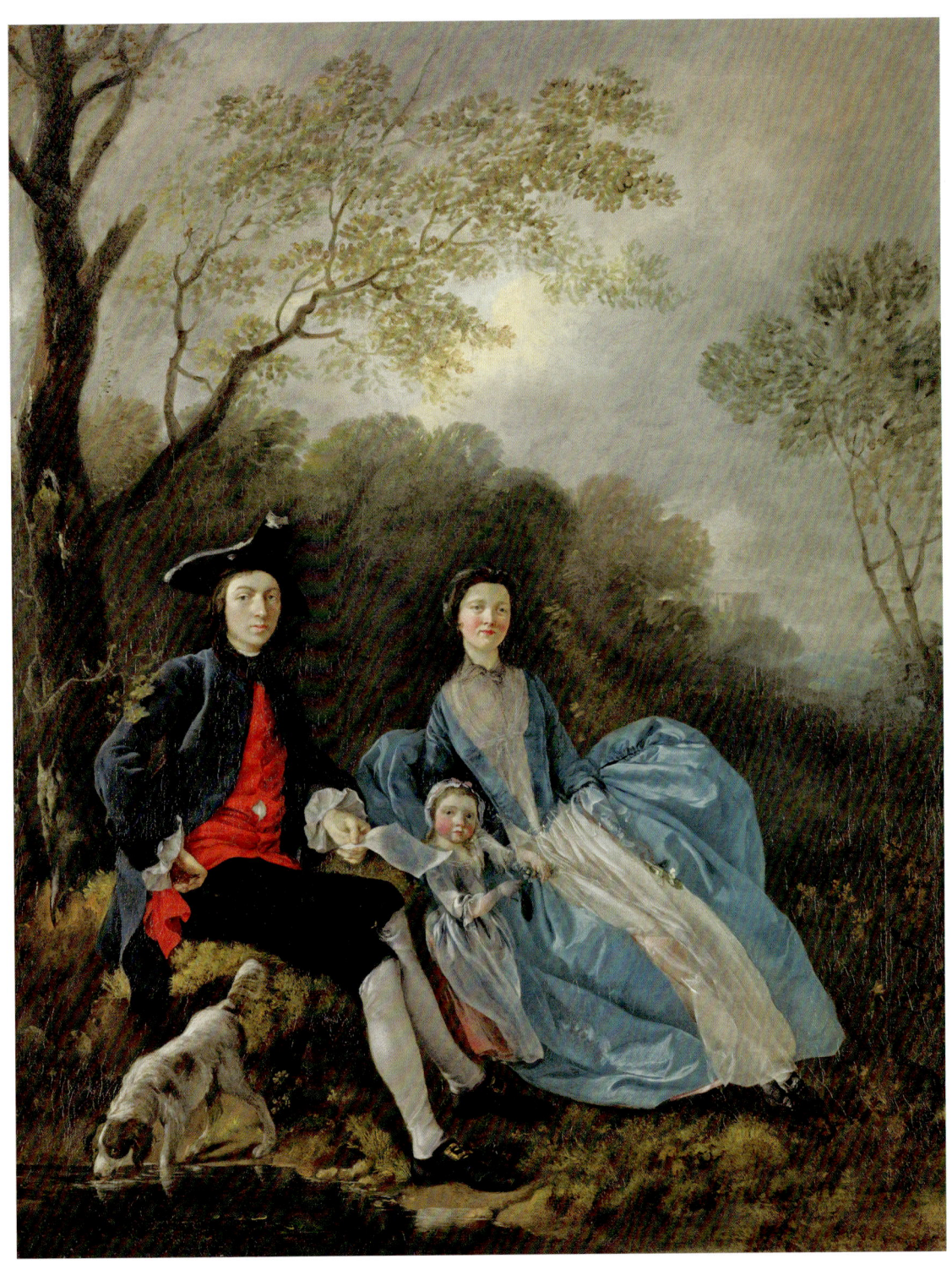

FIG. 54
Thomas Gainsborough
Portrait of the Artist with His Wife and Daughter, ca. 1748
Oil on canvas
36¼ x 27¾ in. (92.1 x 70.5 cm)
The National Gallery, London (NG6547)

136

classical prototypes.[175] John Hayes drew attention to the "lively and unusual" composition, "a highly sophisticated development of the device of the feigned oval—within which the head is frontally set, immediately engaging the spectator's attention."[176] The black mantle encircling her figure intensifies her outward gaze. Dramatically framing her high, powdered hair, pale skin, and white bows tied under her chin and at the bust of her orange dress, the dark garment is at the same time revealed to be made of translucent, delicate lace as she handles it with her raised right hand. Like all of Gainsborough's portraits of his family (with the possible exception of two for which Gainsborough Dupont may have been the model; see p. 58), this portrait was not exhibited at the Royal Academy. It may, however, have hung in the artist's London showroom and, like other personal and "show" pictures, offered as an example that clients could choose. Gainsborough's earlier portrait of her at about age thirty (fig. 40) shares compositional features with commissioned portraits of around the same time, such as *Sarah Hodges, Later Lady Innes,* (cat. 4), suggesting Gainsborough's use of personal portraits as a means to explore qualities, motifs, and moods for paid pictures. In the present portrait, the forceful, direct expression—one that was inappropriate for "ladies of quality," a sort of look that "was to be reserved exclusively for her husband"[177]—anticipates subsequent portraits like the bust of Mrs. Elliott (cat. 21), possibly commissioned by the Prince of Wales, for which Gainsborough would be criticized for the frank portrayal of his subject.

PROVENANCE

By descent to the sitter's grandnephew Richard James Lane (1800–1872); his sale, Christie's, July 7, 1838, lot 172; bought in; sold to William Sharpe (ca. 1805–1865), 1841; by descent to his son William Arthur Sharpe (b. 1847), Highgate, by 1906; purchased from the Sharpe family by Samuel Courtauld (1876–1947), 1921; presented to the Courtauld Institute, 1931.

SELECTED LITERATURE

Fulcher 1856a, 205; Fulcher 1856b, 209; Fletcher 1904, 212; Woodall 1949, 72; Hayes 1975, 219, no. 93; Lindsay 1981, 139–40; Kalinsky 1995, 94, no. 32; Solkin 2000/1; Brown 2001, *passim*; Sloman 2002, 164; Vaughan 2002, 159; Hamilton 2017, 299; Belsey 2019, 1: no. 378.

SELECTED EXHIBITION HISTORY

London 1885, no. 80; London 1906b, no. 16; London 1931, no. 6; London 1934, no. 316; Manchester 1934, no. 57; Amsterdam 1936, no. 42; Bath and other cities 1949, no. 19; London 1980–81, no. 124; Paris 1981, no. 51; Sudbury 1988, no. 15; Ferrara 1998, no. 22; London, Washington, and Boston 2002–3, no. 172; London and Princeton 2018–19, no. 34.

SAMUEL LINLEY

CA. 1778

Oil on canvas
29¹³/₁₆ x 25 in. (75.8 x 63.5 cm)
Dulwich Picture Gallery, London;
William Linley Bequest, 1835 (DPG302)

GAINSBOROUGH PAINTED PORTRAITS of the Linley family of musicians—Thomas Linley, his wife Mary, and their children—in Bath and subsequently in London, where both families moved in the 1770s (see also cat. 23).[178] The present portrait depicts the second son, Samuel (1760–1778). As a child, he performed with his family, singing and playing the oboe, but as a teenager abandoned music for a naval career, serving in the Royal Navy as a midshipman. Gainsborough appears to have painted Samuel on the eve of his first departure, in 1778, on the *Thunderer*, wearing a uniform identified by the white tab with a gold button on the collar of the blue coat, along with a black neckcloth, white shirt, and black waistcoat.[179] Looking off to the left with a somber expression, he appears to wear his own hair, semi-powdered, in a "wig-imitation," with a solitaire, or single pigtail, at the back.[180]

According to an 1858 text by Stephen Poyntz Denning, then curator at Dulwich, the portrait was painted in under an hour, information Denning may have heard directly from the sitter's brother Ozias Linley.[181] The broad strokes that comprise the figure create a sense of unfinish, seemingly "charged with turpentine" to "skim over the canvas," which distinguished Gainsborough's mature style and has been related to Reynolds's praise for Gainsborough in his *Fourteenth Discourse*:

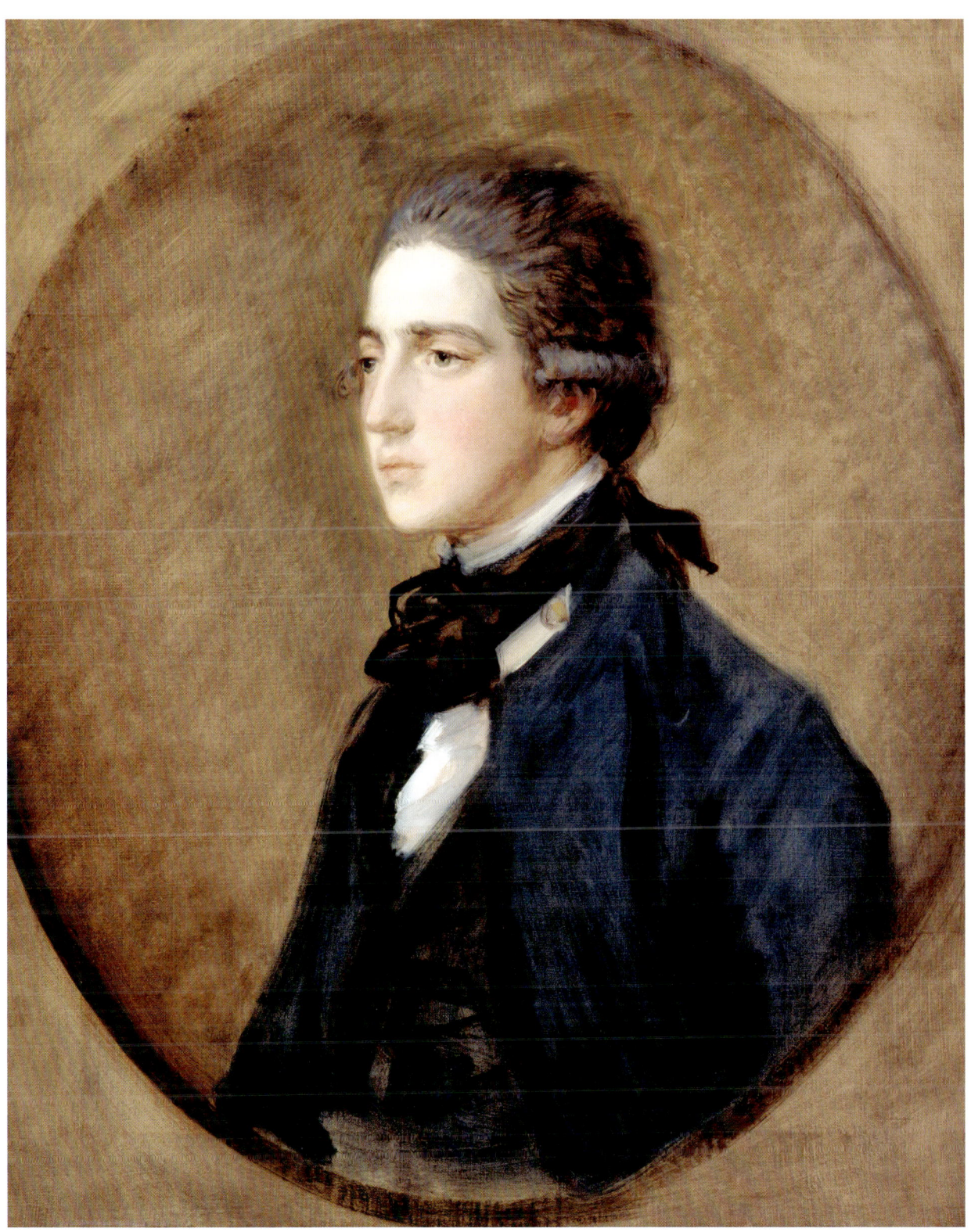

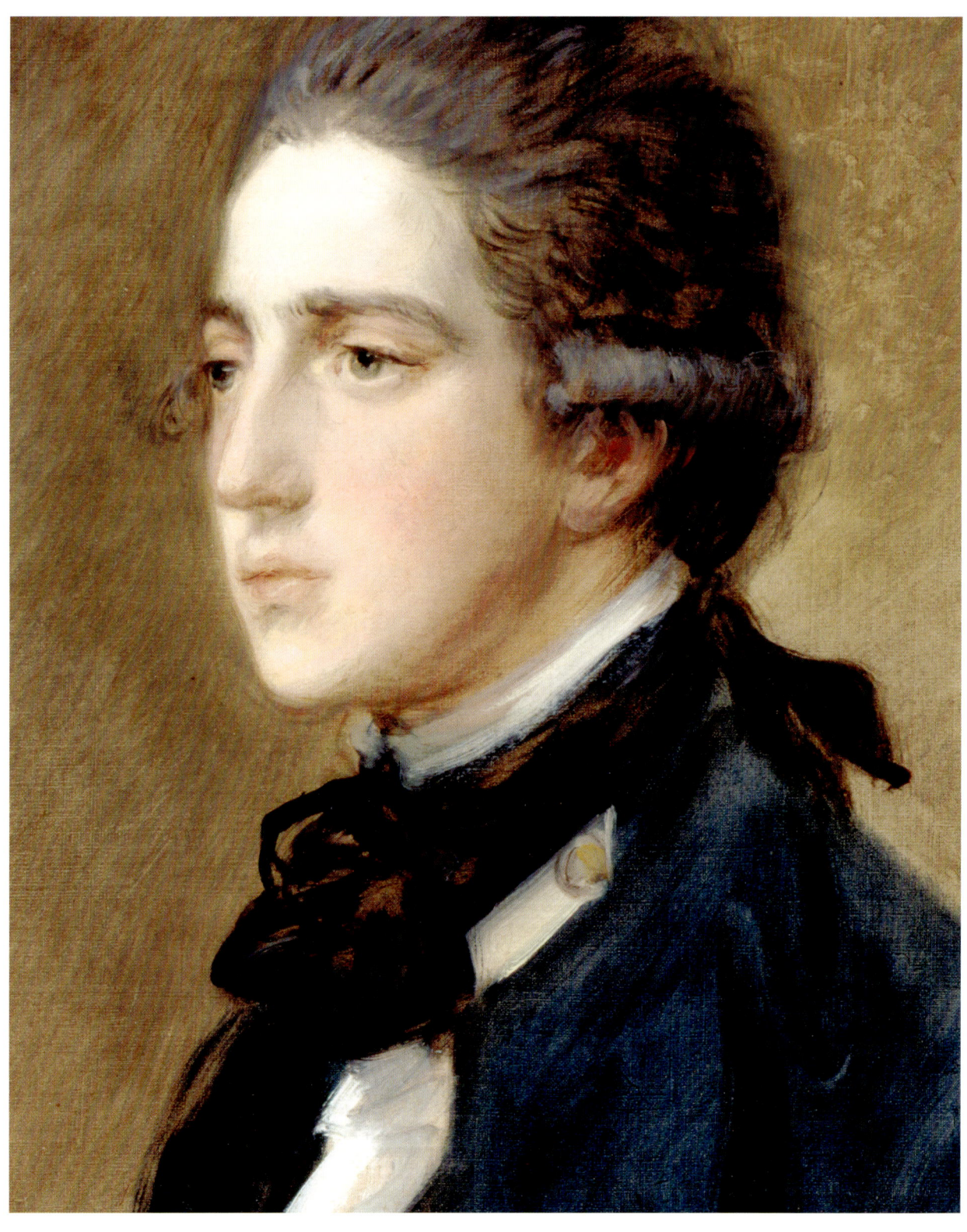

Detail of *Samuel Linley* (cat. 16)

All those odd scratches and marks, which on a close examination, are so observable in Gainsborough's pictures, and which even to experienced painters appear rather the effect of accident than design; this chaos, this uncouth and shapeless appearance, by a kind of magic, at a certain distance assumes form, and all the parts seem to drop into their proper places, so that we can hardly refuse acknowledging the full effect of diligence, under the appearance of chance and hasty negligence.[182]

The background, stippled with a dry brush, appears less finished than is typical for the artist, who also tended to paint feigned oval bust portraits on a dark-brown ground, as he did in *Ignatius Sancho* (cat. 9). It is unclear whether the sitter's father commissioned the portrait or if Gainsborough made it as a gift for the family, as he often did for his friends. Perhaps it was made to commemorate the young man at the start of his naval career. Tragically, Samuel died, aged eighteen, at the time of this first sailing, having been among those who caught fever on the ship.[183] The portrait remained with the Linley family until Samuel's younger brother William bequeathed it to Dulwich in 1835.

PROVENANCE

The sitter's father, Thomas Linley; bequeathed to his wife, Mary Linley, 1795; by descent to their youngest son, William Linley (1771–1835); bequeathed by him to Dulwich Picture Gallery, 1835.

SELECTED LITERATURE

Fulcher 1856a, 222; Fulcher 1856b, 226; Armstrong 1898, 199; Gower 1903, 113–14; Armstrong 1904, 272; Mourey 1905, 96–97; Waterhouse 1953, 69; Waterhouse 1958, 78; Murray 1980, 60; L. Stainton in Washington and Los Angeles 1985–86, no. 9; G. Waterfield in London 1988a, no. 6; Pointon 1993, 133; Ingamells 2008, 132; Belsey 2019, 2: 553–54, no. 588.

SELECTED EXHIBITION HISTORY

London 1947, no. 19; Washington and Los Angeles 1985–86, no. 9; London 1988a, no. 6; Warsaw 1992, no. 11; Bath 1995, no. 17; Madrid and Bilbao 1999, 160–62, no. 43; London 1999, unnumbered.

JAMES CHRISTIE

1778

Oil on canvas
50¼ x 40¼ in. (127.6 x 102.2 cm)
The J. Paul Getty Museum, Los Angeles;
Gift of J. Paul Getty (70.PA.16)

GAINSBOROUGH PRESENTED THIS PORTRAIT of his friend James Christie (1730–1803), founder of the eponymous auction house, at the 1778 Royal Academy exhibition.[184] It was the only one of his eight portraits that year (which included the full-length *Grace Dalrymple Elliott*, cat. 18) whose subject was identified by name in the catalogue, reflecting how well known Christie was in London society. Critics praised the likeness of the sitter's face ("so striking a resemblance, that the name need not have been printed in the catalogue"[185]) while disapproving of the lack of finish in the rest ("it partakes in a degree of unfinished stiffness of the rest . . . he joins a very bad body to it"[186]). Gainsborough apparently gifted the portrait to Christie.[187] Showing the auctioneer as if at work selling art—with paintings and grasping papers—suited the portrait's place in the auctioneer's salesrooms, where it hung until 1846.[188]

Christie is set against a billowing swath of red fabric, with a sketchy tassel at the upper right corner. The framed landscape painting he leans on—perhaps reproducing or evoking one of Gainsborough's own—is a variation on Gainsborough's motif through the 1760s of including framed landscape paintings in the background of portraits. Another ornately framed picture at the left is obscured. Possibly suggesting the Old Master paintings that were Christie's trade, it may allude to the place of Gainsborough's art in the canon of masters. Adorned with a powdered wig and diamond pinky ring, the sitter wears a mauve suit

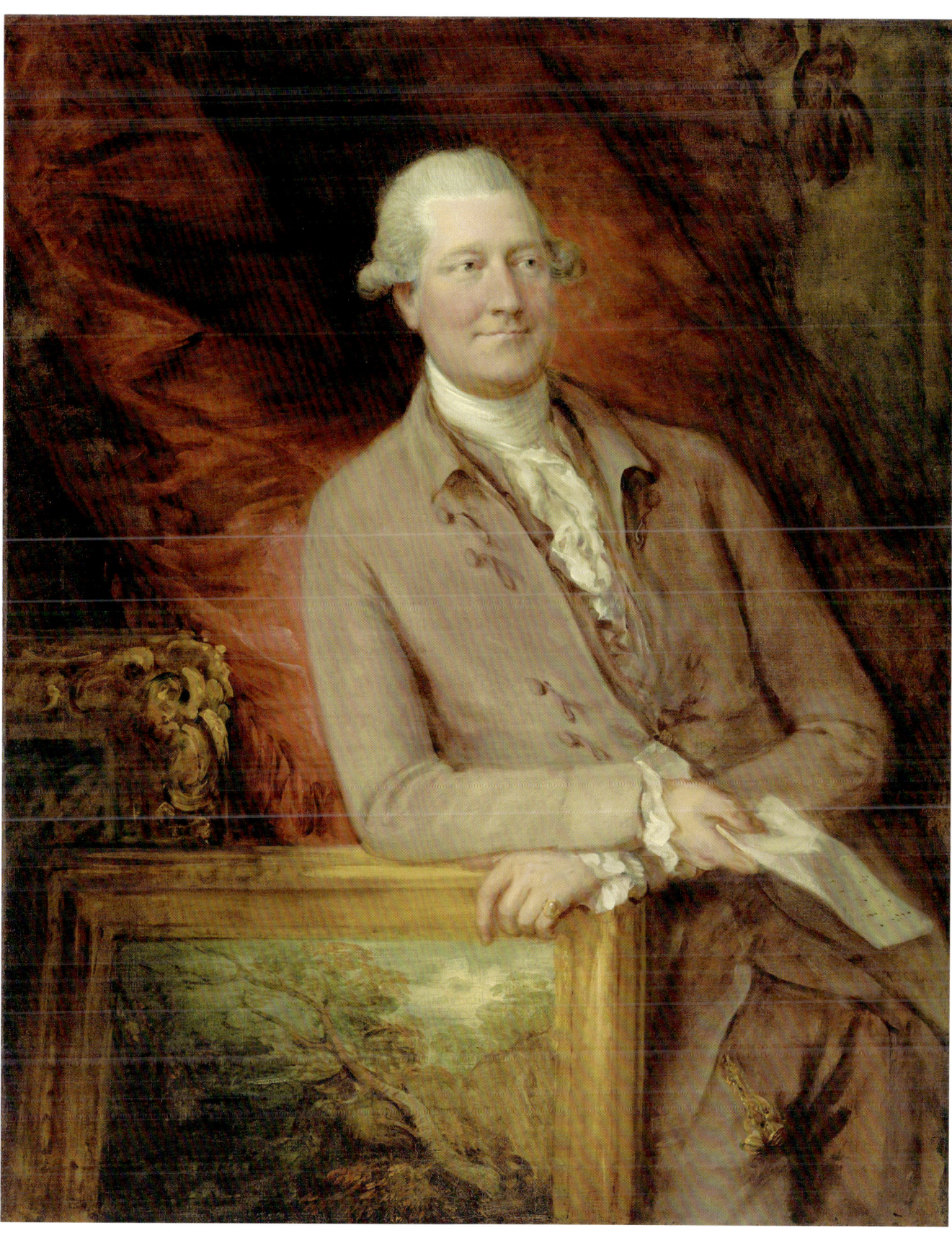

and matching waistcoat, which give the impression of an elongated torso. Recent technical examination reveals changes to the composition that may have contributed to the exaggerated form of the figure, which struck critics as having "an unharmonious effect" (see pp. 43 and 45). Below the waistcoat, a gold watch chain with two seals swings to the right as if Christie has been caught mid-motion.

Like other portraits Gainsborough seems to have given as gifts or in exchange—such as Carl Friedrich Abel's portrait that may have hung in the musician's concert hall (cat. 12) and John Joseph Merlin's that probably adorned the inventor's museum (cat. 20)—*James Christie* represents the subject in the trappings of his profession. This suggests a trend in Gainsborough's practice for making "working" images that advertised the subjects' trade. Surely its installation in Christie's salesroom also promoted the art of Gainsborough, whose frequent and lively presence in the rooms, Christie was reported to have said, increased the auctioneer's commissions by 15 percent.[189]

PROVENANCE

Probably painted to hang in the sitter's salesroom, where it remained until 1846; claimed by the sitter's grandson George Henry Christie (1815–1887), and in his possession by 1856; by descent to his grandson James Archibald Christie, MP (1873–1950), Framingham House, Norwich; his sale, Christie's, May 20, 1927, lot 29; purchased jointly by Colnaghi, Agnews, and Knoedler; purchased by J. Paul Getty, July 23, 1938; transferred to the J. Paul Getty Museum Trust, 1970.

SELECTED LITERATURE

London Evening Post, April 23–25, 1778; *Morning Chronicle*, April 25, 1778; *General Evening Post*, April 30–May 2, 1778; *General Advertiser Morning Intelligencer*, April 27, 1788; Fulcher 1856a, 108, 184; Fulcher 1856b, 110–11, 188; Brock-Arnold 1881, 41; Roberts 1897, 11; Armstrong 1898, 193; Chamberlain 1903, 95; Armstrong 1904, 261; Fletcher 1904, 197; Boulton 1905, 247; Menpes and Greig 1909 123–24; Whitley [1915] 2016, 136, 181–82; Dibdin 1923, 137; Woodall 1949, 74; Waterhouse 1953, 21; Waterhouse 1958, 60, no. 147; Fredericksen 1972, 100, no. 139; J. Hayes in London 1980–81, no. 121; Daniels 1981, 112; Lindsay 1981, 139; Herbert 1990, 133–34, 250–51; Cormack 1991, 24; Rosenthal 1999, 79, 96; C. Riding in London, Washington, and Boston 2002–3, no. 54; Martinez 2009, 140; Pointon 2009, 58, 61; Hamilton 2017, 296; Belsey 2019, 1: no. 181.

SELECTED EXHIBITION HISTORY

London 1778, no. 117; London 1817, no. 137; London 1859, no. 94; London 1867, no. 793; London 1885, no. 67; London 1891, no. 4; Ipswich 1927, no. 52; London 1929, no. 19; Cambridge 1930, no. 29; Cincinnati 1931, no. 2; New York 1931, no. 65; London 1932, no. 1362; London 1937, no. 42; New York 1939, no. 130; Los Angeles 1944, no. 58; London 1967, no. 15; Oakland 1969 (unnumbered); Minneapolis 1972, no. 28; London 1980–81, no. 121; London, Washington, and Boston 2002–3, no. 54.

GRACE DALRYMPLE ELLIOTT

1778

Oil on canvas
92¼ x 60½ in. (234.3 x 153.7 cm)
The Metropolitan Museum of Art, New York;
Bequest of William K. Vanderbilt, 1920 (20.155.1)

GRACE DALRYMPLE (CA. 1754–1823) gained a high profile in British society for having scandalous affairs with prominent men. Her parents, Edinburgh lawyer Hugh (or Hew) Dalrymple and his wife, Grisel Brown, separated when she was a child; her mother was said to have died of a broken heart over her philandering husband.[190] Grace was subsequently raised in a convent in France. In 1771, at age seventeen, she entered a short-lived marriage with Dr. John Eliot, a wealthy physician eighteen years her senior.[191] Her highly public liaison with the married Lord Valentia led to her husband's successful claim in 1776 for divorce and a £12,000 settlement, after which she continued to go by "Mrs. Elliott." Her ex-husband, who was knighted two months after the divorce, provided her with an allowance and, after his death in 1786, an annuity.[192]

Gainsborough submitted the present portrait to the Royal Academy in 1778 at a time when, in the wake of Grace's divorce, the newspapers were reporting on her subsequent and yearslong relationship with George, 4th Earl of Cholmondeley (later 1st Marquess of Cholmondeley), who appears to have commissioned the picture. It was one of eight portraits Gainsborough showed that year[193] and the first of two portraits of Elliott that he would show publicly (see cat. 21).[194] Set in a classicizing architectural space, partly outdoors, Elliott appears as if she has just returned from a walk. Her towering hairstyle reflects contemporary fashion, while her vibrant yellow dress couples Van Dyck style with inventive embellishments suggestive of eighteenth-century masquerade.[195] A slender black ribbon tied around her neck cascades down her décolletage.[196] She draws her skirts toward her torso, a pose that has been described by modern scholars as a

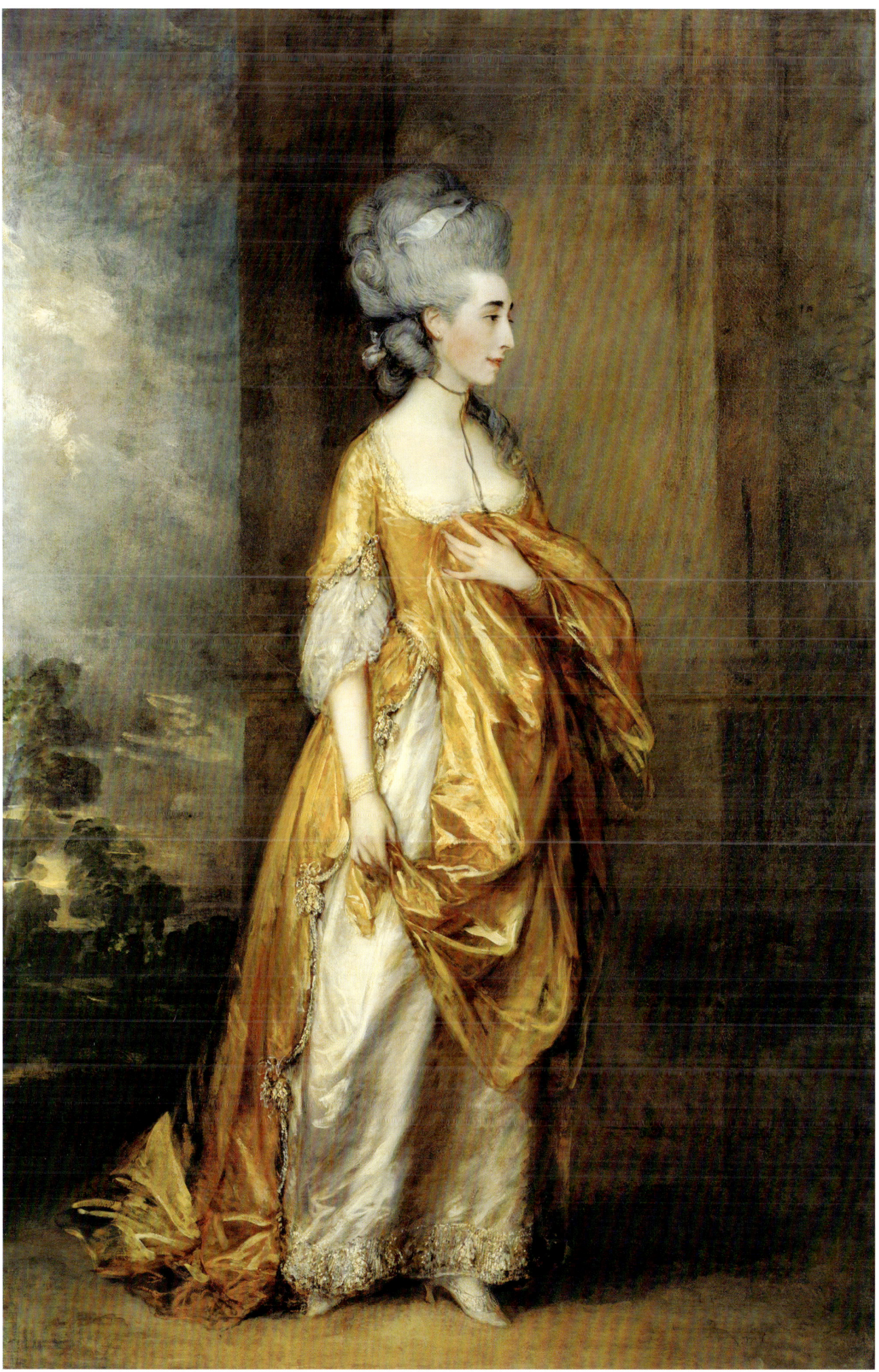

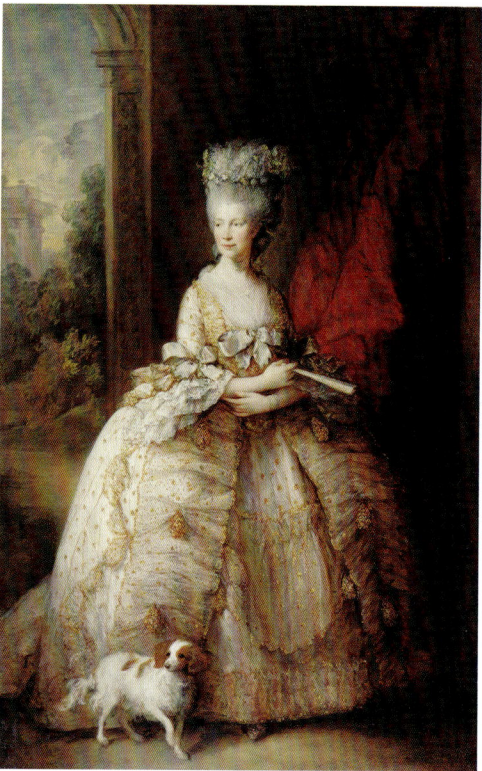

FIG. 55
Thomas Gainsborough
Queen Charlotte, ca. 1781
Oil on canvas
94 x 62½ in. (238.8 x 158.7 cm)
Royal Collection Trust, London
(RCIN 401407)

"gesture of vulnerability."[197] Her face turned to profile emphasizes a sense of modesty. Her figure appears elongated and suits her nickname, "Dally the Tall," a reference to her unusual height.[198] The composition's debt to the portraits of Van Dyck and Lely has been noted.[199] Gainsborough would revive the conceit of a subject returning indoors from a walk for his full-length portrait of Queen Charlotte in 1781 (fig. 55), which includes a small dog.[200] Incidentally, Gainsborough had sketched a small dog into the lower right corner of the present picture before painting it out.[201]

Despite the portrait being shown anonymously at the exhibition, spectators easily recognized Elliott. Her notoriety, combined with Gainsborough's spectacular presentation of her, surely intensified public attention. Mark Hallett suggests that Gainsborough presented *Grace Dalrymple Elliott*, one of six female portraits he submitted that year, in "clothing that is far richer in colour and more flamboyant in style" than the subtler, classicizing portraits by his main rival, Reynolds, and that it stood out in the densely hung hall.[202] *Grace Dalrymple Elliott* inspired extensive critical response. Reviewers agreed on Gainsborough's success in capturing his model's likeness and beauty while remarking on her disreputable status and that of two of his other sitters that year. ("It should seem from this artist's female portraits that he is a favourite among the demi-reps.")[203] One of them offered a sympathetic assessment in which Mrs. Elliott's beauty outweighed her moral shortcomings.[204] They also noted Gainsborough's use of color, with one decrying the "blue tint" of her hair and another suggesting that he was well suited to painting such women known to artificially make up their faces with exaggerated reds and whites.[205] It is unclear if the satirical review in the *Morning*

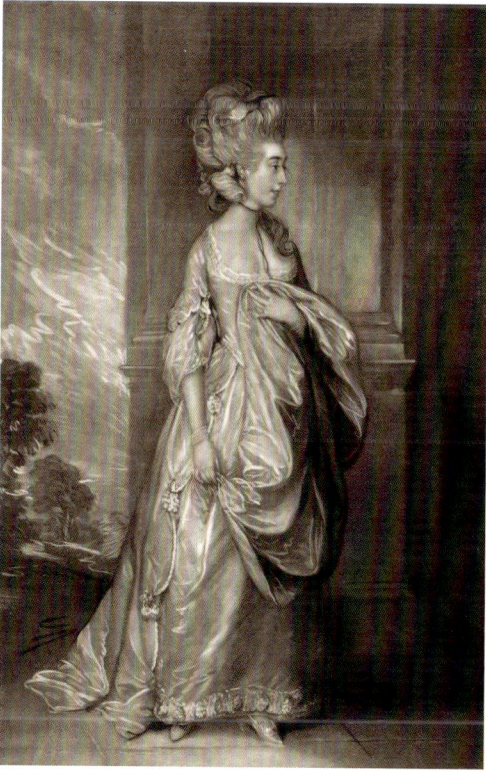

Post (referring to a portrait's body as "cadaverous" and having "lain too long under water") was directed at the present portrait, as has been assumed by some scholars.[206]

The condition of the painting has suffered since the eighteenth century. A sense of what has been lost is suggested by an engraving made soon after its exhibition (fig. 56), showing the flagstone floor on which she walks and a dramatic sky, possibly a colorful sunset.[207]

PROVENANCE

Presumably painted for George James Cholmondeley, 1st Marquess of Cholmondeley (1749–1827); by descent to George Henry Hugh Cholmondeley, 4th Marquess of Cholmondeley (1858–1923), Houghton Hall, who sold it shortly after he inherited the marquisate in 1884; purchased by William K. Vanderbilt (1850–1920), New York, ca. 1885; bequeathed by him to the Metropolitan Museum of Art, 1920.

SELECTED LITERATURE

Morning Chronicle, April 25, 1778; *Morning Post*, April 27, 1778; *General Evening Post*, April 30–May 2, 1778; Fulcher 1856a, 183; Fulcher 1856b, 187; Montezuma 1888, 51; Fairfax Murray 1894, 156 under no. 544; Armstrong 1898, 125, 195; Armstrong 1904, 166–67, 264; Fletcher 1904, 211; Boulton 1905, 174, 249; Graves 1905, 192; Bleackley 1909, 213; Menpes and Greig 1909, 128; Whitley [1915] 2016, 179–83, 216; Vanderbilt Bequest 1920, 270; Tatlock et al. 1928, 1: 52 under no. 81; Waterhouse 1953, 37, 124; Waterhouse 1958, 66, no. 239; Davidson 1968, 56; Williamson 1972, 145–46, 213; Hayes 1975, 222 under no. 103; Burke 1976, 216; Lindsay 1981, 139; Cherry and Harris 1982, 296, 302–3; Cormack 1991, 19, 27, 28, and 124, no. 47; Baetjer 1999, 14, 36–39; Gockel 1999, 24; Rosenthal 1999, 96, 277; Conway 2001, 40; C. Riding in London, Washington, and Boston 2002–3, no. 52; Manning 2005, 18, 19, 22–23, 205; Baetjer 2009, 102–4, no. 45; Craven 2009, 120; B. Leca in Cincinnati and San Diego 2010–11, 60, 100, 105, 132; Brewer 2011, 570–71; Hallett 2014, 274–75; The Hague 2015, 80 under no. 15; Chu 2016, 58n.27; Hamilton 2017, 296–97; Belsey 2019, 1: no. 312.

SELECTED EXHIBITION HISTORY

London 1778, no. 114; London, Washington, and Boston 2002–3, no. 52 (shown in Washington and Boston only); Cincinnati and San Diego 2010–11 (unnumbered).

MRS. SAMUEL MOODY
AND HER SONS, SAMUEL AND THOMAS

CA. 1779, REWORKED CA. 1784

Oil on canvas
92⅛ x 60¹¹⁄₁₆ in. (234 x 154.2 cm)
Dulwich Picture Gallery, London;
Gift of Captain Thomas Moody, 1831 (DPG316)

AT AGE TWENTY-SIX, Elizabeth Moody (1756–1782) died from complications of tuberculosis while taking the "cure" at Bristol Hot Wells in December of 1782.[208] Her sons, Samuel and Thomas, were twenty months and eight months old, respectively. The boys pictured here are in white muslin dresses with sashes (conventional for boys and girls of the period; see cat. 11) and are apparently older than the infant and toddler were at the time of her death.[209] This discrepancy combined with visible pentimenti and a "slightly clumsy" right hand of Mrs. Moody prompted scholars to wonder if the children were later additions.[210] In 1989, X-radiography of the portrait confirmed that Gainsborough had originally painted Elizabeth Moody alone, probably around the time of her marriage in 1779 to Samuel Moody and before the births of Samuel, in 1781, and Thomas, in 1782. The initial composition appears to have been similar to that of *Mrs. Peter William Baker* (fig. 57) in features like the pose of the figure walking toward the left with head turning right and the shape of the landscape, with the dark mass at left that opens out to a distant view at the center.[211]

Evidently, Samuel Moody brought the portrait back to Gainsborough in the year or two after Elizabeth's death (judging from the apparent age of the toddlers). Adding the figures of the children as they appeared then, and not at the age they were when she died, Gainsborough painted over her right arm, which had originally reached upward to toy with a pearl necklace. Painting

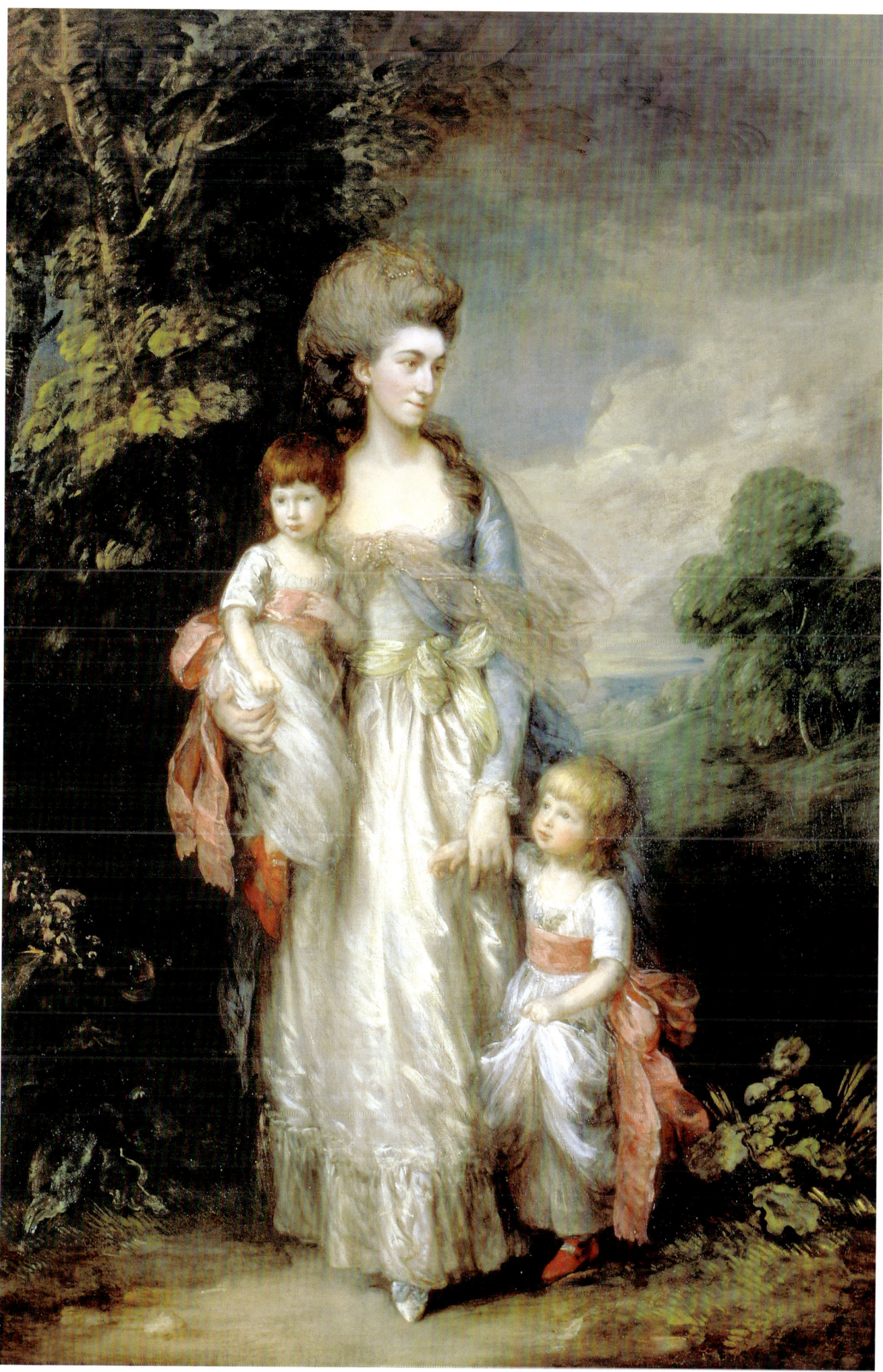

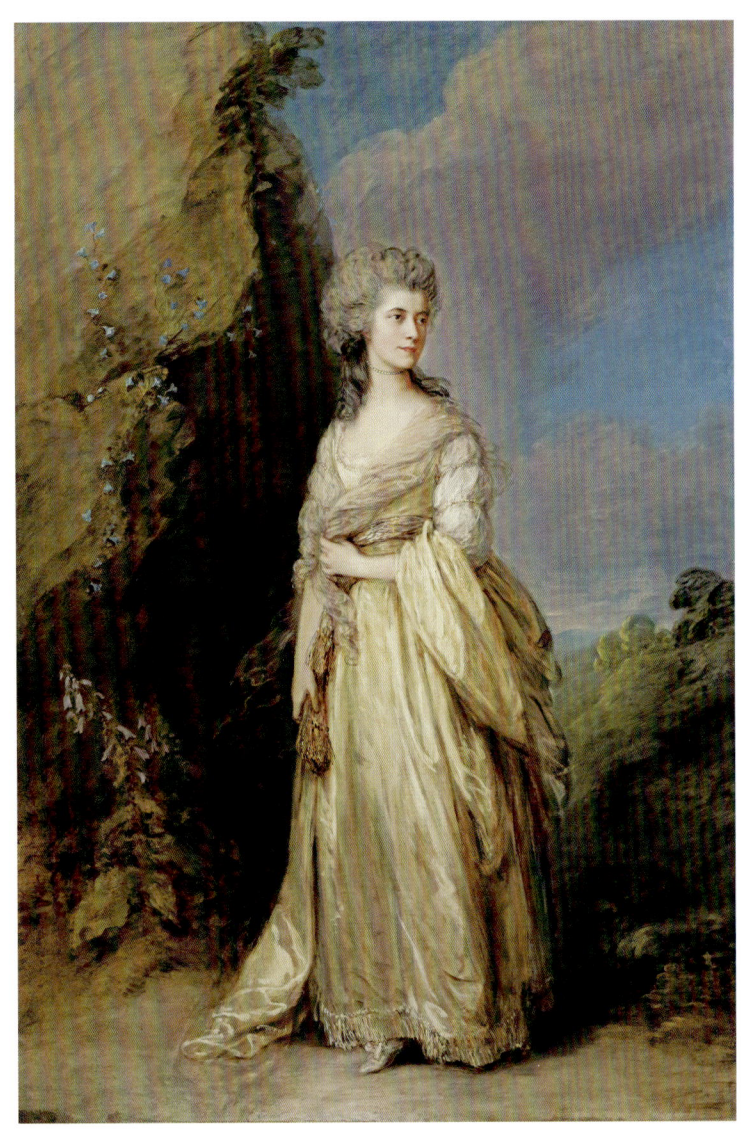

FIG. 57
Thomas Gainsborough
Mrs. Peter William Baker, 1781
Oil on canvas
89⅝ x 59¾ in. (227.6 x 151.8 cm)
The Frick Collection, New York (1917.1.59)

out the necklace, the artist augmented her hands to carry the figure of Thomas, the younger, red-headed boy, and hold the arm of Samuel at her side. Gainsborough thus transformed a fashionable portrait of a newlywed in a Turkish-style dress and modishly piled hair into a memorial image, visualizing a reunion of the boys with their late mother.[212] Samuel Moody remarried in 1786 and fathered four more children. At his death in 1808, he bequeathed the portrait to his younger son from his first marriage, Thomas, who reportedly had an aversion to his stepmother and left the painting to Dulwich Picture Gallery to prevent her children from inheriting it.[213]

PROVENANCE

The sitter's husband, Samuel Moody; bequeathed by him to their son Captain Thomas Moody, October 1808; presented by him to Dulwich Picture Gallery, September 1831.

SELECTED LITERATURE

Fulcher 1856a, 222; Fulcher 1856b, 226; Armstrong 1898, 199; Gower 1903, 119–20; Armstrong 1904, 274; Fletcher 1904, 140; Mourey 1905, 64, 96; Waterhouse 1953, 77; Waterhouse 1958, 82, no. 498; Murray 1980, 60, no. 316; Lavezzari 1983–84, 321–22, 323; A. Sumner in London 1995, no. 12; Ingamells 2008, 206; Belsey 2019, 2: no. 654.

SELECTED EXHIBITION HISTORY

London 1947, no. 22; London 1995, no. 12; Madrid and Bilbao 1999, no. 44.

JOHN JOSEPH MERLIN

CA. 1781

Oil on canvas
30 x 25 in. (76.2 x 63.5 cm)
Engilsh Heritage, Kenwood House, London;
Purchased with the assistance of the Art Fund, and Victoria
and Albert Museum and the Friends of Kenwood

BORN IN HUY, near Liège, Belgium, Jean-Joseph Merlin (known in England as John Joseph or simply Joseph Merlin, 1735–1803) was an inventor who worked in London for the clockmaker John Cox before opening Merlin's Mechanical Museum.[214] Among his inventions and patents were a *rôtisseur* (a type of Dutch oven), a version of roller skates, a wheelchair called a Gouty Chair (an example of which is at Kenwood House), and a range of other mechanical devices.[215] Gainsborough's brothers, who were also inventors, may have been a possible connection to the sitter. Merlin's involvement in music, however—playing, tuning, and inventing instruments like the compound harpsichord—surely brought him into Gainsborough's circle. In 1780, the artist had exhibited his portrait of Johann Christian Fischer (fig. 58), in which the keyboard instrument Fischer plays is inscribed MERLIN LONDONI FECIT (Merlin of London made it).[216] A showman known for dressing in bizarre costumes, Merlin was a regular visitor to the home of musicologist Charles Burney, described with amusement in the diaries of Burney's daughter Fanny. Writing of a dinner at Mrs. Thrale's in June of 1781, Fanny recounts Merlin's favorable comparison of the present portrait with a portrait of her father by Reynolds:

> During the desert [*sic*], mention was made of my father's picture, when this ridiculous creature [Merlin] exclaimed "Oh! for that picture of Dr Burney, Sir Joshua Reynhold [*sic*] has not taken pains, *that is*, to please me! I do not like it. Mr Gainsborough has done one much more better of me, which is very agreeable indeed. I wish it had been at the Exhibition, for it would have done him a great deal of credit indeed."[217]

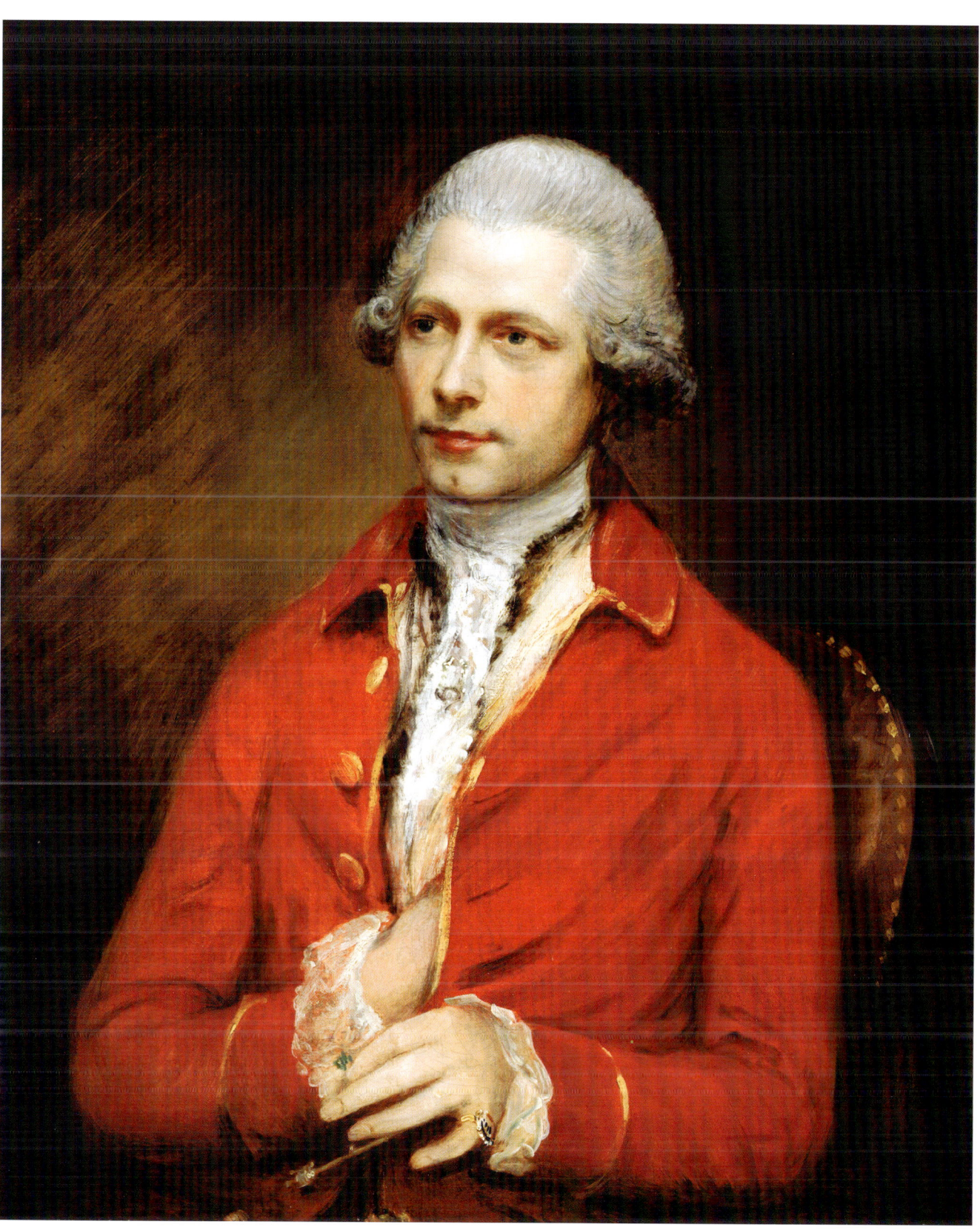

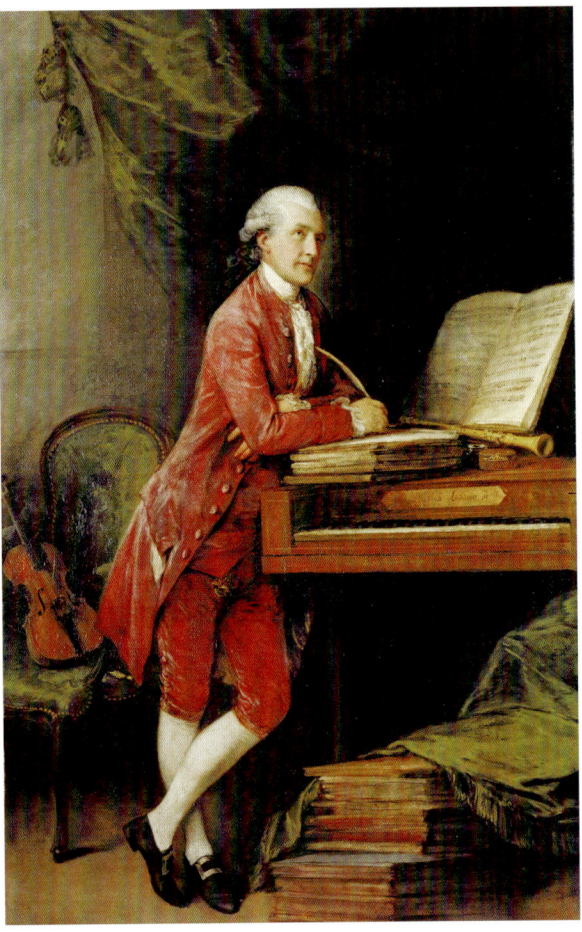

FIG. 58
Thomas Gainsborough
Johann Christian Fischer,
exhibited 1780
Oil on canvas
90³/₁₆ x 59⅜ in.
(229 x 150.8 cm)
Royal Collection Trust,
London (RCIN 407298)

Gainsborough exhibited Merlin's portrait at the academy the following year.[218] The *London Courant* praised it as a "capital" picture.[219] A record of payment of £10 10s from Gainsborough to Merlin in 1783 suggests an ongoing association between the two.[220]

Seated and wearing a powdered wig, a red jacket with lace cuffs, a fur-lined waistcoat, and a jeweled brooch at his cravat, Merlin appears here as a gentleman. One hand tucks into his waistcoat, and the other suspends by a green thread from his index finger the single clue to his remarkable livelihood: his invention known as Merlin's Scales for Gold Coin.[221] A pocket-sized instrument for weighing currency, it was marketed to protect gentlemen from being deceived by compromised or counterfeit coins.

The circumstances of the commission are unknown. As a foreigner, merchant, and entertainer, Merlin may be counted among the subjects Gainsborough portrayed who were on the margins of polite society, including actors, musicians, and courtesans.[222] Fanny Burney's reference to him as "this ridiculous creature" reveals how he was perceived. It has been suggested that the portrait was intended for display in Merlin's museum, just as that of James Christie (cat. 17) was presumably meant to hang in Christie's salesroom.[223] A second version, much looser in handling and in compromised condition, has been called an "unfinished duplicate" and may have been produced for the sitter's family.[224] Merlin's will did not list a portrait among his personal belongings; since his museum remained open for some years after his death, it may have been among its contents.[225] At some point in the nineteenth century the portrait was mistakenly thought to depict the violinist Felice de' Giardini, who was an associate of Gainsborough and also a subject of one of his portraits. In 1977, Lindsay Stainton correctly identified the subject on the basis of known depictions of Giardini and Merlin, especially the resemblance between the present portrait and George Perfect Harding's engraving of Merlin accompanied by an illustration of the inventor's "mechanical chariot" (fig. 59).[226]

PROVENANCE

Robert William Buss (1804–1875); with Alfred Clint (1807–1883); purchased by E. J. Chapman (1801–1854), 1846; by descent to John Chapman Walker; purchased from him by Agnews, April 9, 1888; purchased from them by Major Frank Shuttleworth (1845–1913), April 20, 1888; by descent to his widow, Dorothy Shuttleworth (1879–1968); by descent to Princess Hohenlohe-Langenburg (née Shuttleworth); purchased by English Heritage / Iveagh Bequest by private treaty sale, 1983.

SELECTED LITERATURE

London Courant, May 1, 1782; Armstrong 1898, 196 (as *Felice de Giardini*); Armstrong 1904, 267 (as *Felice de Giardini*); Menpes and Greig 1909, 136; Whitley [1915] 2016, 213, 219–20; Waterhouse 1953, 48 (as *Felice de Giardini*); Waterhouse 1958, 70, no. 312 (as *Mr. Giardini* [?]), 81, no. 480, Joseph Merlin (as "Untraced"); Williamson 1972, 164–65; L. Stainton in London 1977, no. 11 (identifying Kenwood picture as *John Joseph Merlin*); Lindsay 1981, 154; Hayes 1983, 98, 100; A. French in London 1985, no. A1; Bryant 2003, no. 47; Bauwens 2004, 22; Hamilton 2017, 340; Belsey 2019, 2: no. 630.

SELECTED EXHIBITION HISTORY

London 1782, no. 43 (as *Portrait of a Gentleman*); London 1882, no. 271 (as *Felice de' Giardini*); London 1885, no. 156 (as *Felice de' Giardini*); London 1906a, no. 78 (as *Felice de' Giardini*); London 1953b, no. 6 (as *Felice de' Giardini*); Bedford 1954, no. 10 (as *Felice de Giardini*); London 1977, no. 11 (as *John Joseph Merlin*); London 1985, no. A1; Houston and other cities 2012–13, no. 11.

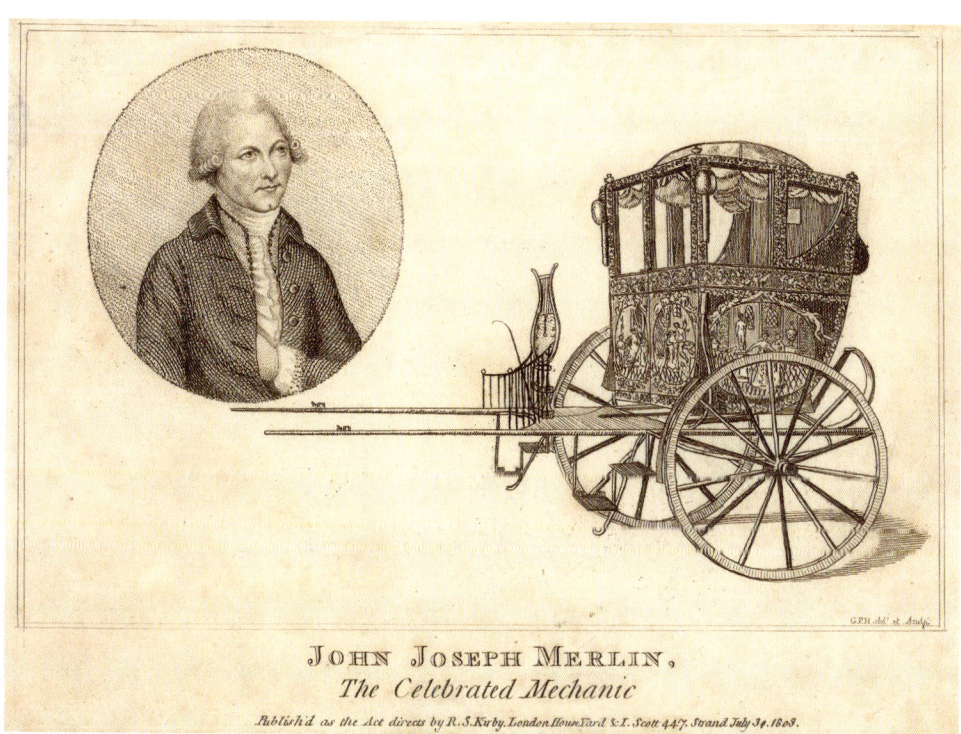

FIG. 59
George Perfect Harding
John Joseph Merlin, 1803
Mixed-method engraving
5⅛ x 8¾ in.
(131 x 221 mm)
National Portrait Gallery,
London (NPG D5252)

GRACE DALRYMPLE ELLIOTT

1782

Oil on canvas
30⅛ x 25 in. (76.5 x 63.5 cm)
The Frick Collection, New York (1946.1.153)

In 1782, Gainsborough submitted his second portrait of Grace Dalrymple Elliott to the Royal Academy, this time a bust-length painting more intimate than his first submission (see cat. 18). Abandoning the profile pose of the earlier full-length, Gainsborough here depicts the subject facing her viewer straight-on with shoulders nearly square.[227] She wears contemporary attire: Lace spills over the deep neckline of her striped dress, which follows the contours of her breasts. Strokes of translucent white paint indicate a diaphanous fichu gathered over her chest, while a black ribbon dangles from her neck to meet a blue locket, fixed to her dress above a pink bow.[228] A nearly identical black ribbon appears in Gainsborough's full-length of her, but the dramatic effect here of the black contrasting against white skin—amplified by the close, frontal view of her body—is much more pronounced. A similar contrast is achieved on her face, where her dark eyebrows and beauty spot, possibly a patch (a piece of velvet adhered to the skin), stand out against her flesh, heavily rouged at the cheeks.[229] These effects may record her actual made-up appearance, as well as the painter's enhancement or invention; the ties between cosmetics and a portraitist's paints were a common topic of discussion.[230]

Critics were not kind in their remarks about the portrait, one of nine that Gainsborough exhibited that year. Where they had been forgiving of Elliott's notoriety when praising the

158

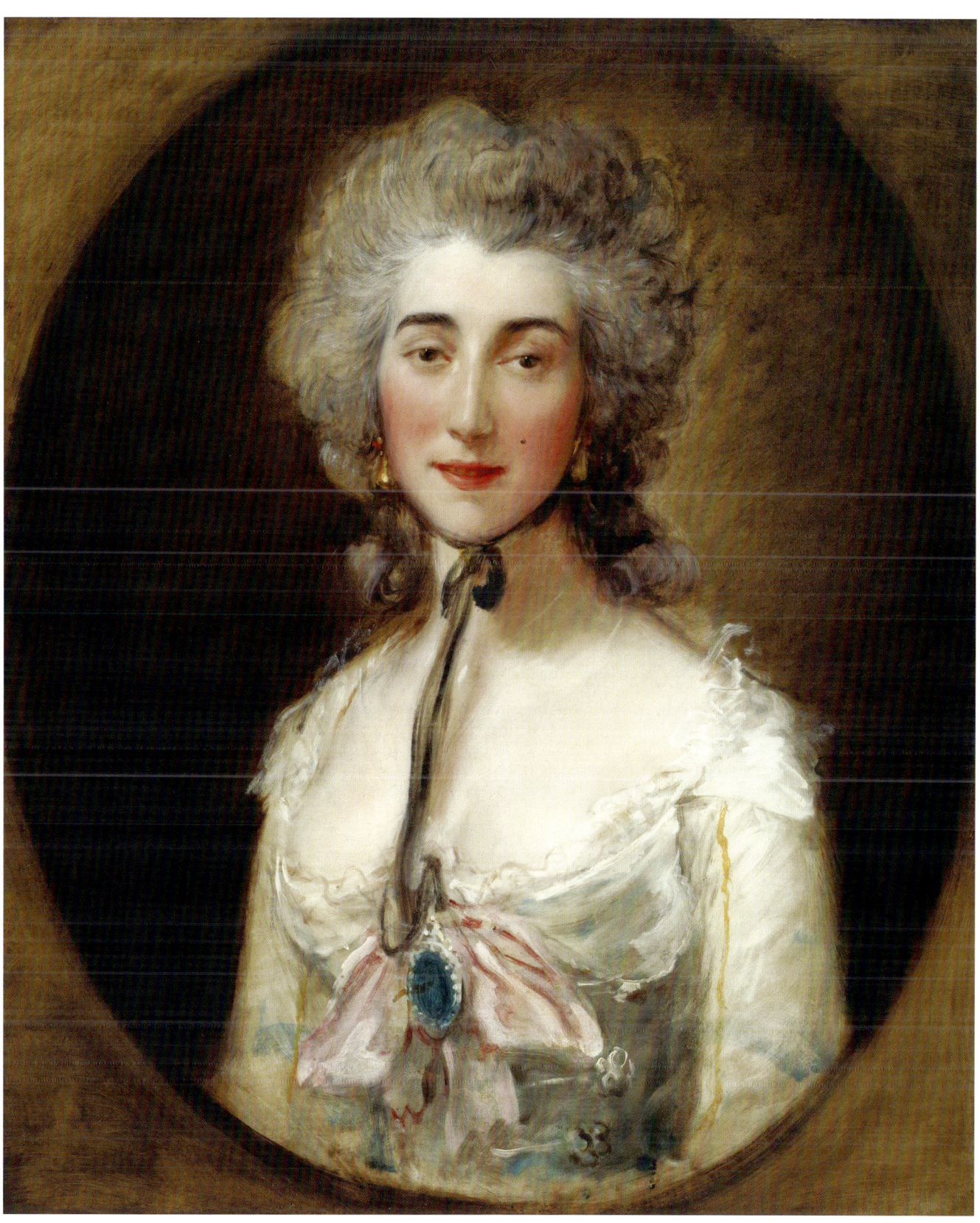

full-length of her in 1778, now they were blunt: "A wanton countenance; and such hair; good God!"[231] The change in reception may be attributed in part to Gainsborough's advancement in the intervening years, having attained royal patronage, the highest milestone of a society portraitist.[232] Among his submissions in 1782 was a full-length of the Prince of Wales (see fig. 32), whose royal status magnified by contrast the disreputable station of sitters like Elliott, and especially her being portrayed so intimately, without the veil of modesty in pose and vaguely historical Van Dyck dress of her earlier picture. Worse yet, Gainsborough's portraits of the prince and of Elliott went on public display just weeks after she had given birth to a daughter, the father of whom was claimed to be the prince, though the child was raised in the household of the Earl of Cholmondeley.[233] In the context of society gossip, Gainsborough's portraits of them became a spectacle—and drew consternation.[234] The transparency and frankness of Gainsborough's presentation of Elliott elicited criticism that revealed contemporary expectations for female portraiture to represent virtue, at least in the public sphere, and especially under the auspices of the Crown. One critic summed it up by praising Gainsborough's *Giovanna Baccelli* (fig. 26, a portrait of the Duke of Dorset's mistress in mid-dance) as a "good moral likeness," while *Mrs. Elliott* was "*not* a good moral Likeness; —the *Eyes* are too characteristic of her Vocation."[235]

Two nearly identical lists of paintings made by Gainsborough for the Prince of Wales suggest that the present portrait may have been commissioned by the prince, who was notorious for extravagant spending and amassing large debts; it is unclear if he paid for it or if it was delivered to him.[236] The early provenance of the picture is unknown. It may have been in the possession of Elliott's daughter, Georgiana, who married a son of the 3rd Duke of Portland and predeceased her mother. Grace Dalrymple Elliott lived most of her life in France from 1786, recording (though not always believably) her adventures and torments during the events of the revolution in *Journal of My Life during the French Revolution* (published posthumously in 1859). She died in Ville d'Avray, outside of Paris.

PROVENANCE

Probably commissioned by George, Prince of Wales; either passed to the sitter's daughter, Georgina Augusta Frederica Seymour (1783–1813), who in 1808 married Lieutenant Colonel Lord William Charles Augustus Cavendish-Bentinck (1780–1826), or purchased in France by John, 5th Duke of Portland (1800–1879); by descent to William, 6th Duke of Portland (1857–1943); purchased from him by Duveen, July 1930; sold to The Frick Collection, May 1946.

SELECTED LITERATURE

Morning Herald, May 1, 1782; *Public Advertiser*, May 2, 1782; *London Courant*, May 9, 1782; Fulcher 1856a, 119, 185; Fulcher 1856b, 119, 189; Fairfax Murray 1894, xii, 155–56, no. 544; Armstrong 1898, 125–26, 195; Chamberlain 1903, 108, 186–89; Gower 1903, 121; Armstrong 1904, 166–67, 264; Fletcher 1904, 211; Boulton 1905, 173–74; Bleackley 1909, 217; Menpes and Greig 1909, 136; Whitley [1915] 2016, 213, 216; *Art News* 1946, 35; Waterhouse 1946, 276; Woodall 1949, 74; Waterhouse 1953, 37; Waterhouse 1958, 66, no. 240; Davidson 1968, 54–57; Millar 1969, 1: 35 under no. 773; Williamson 1972, 164, 168; Hayes 1975, 221–22, no. 103; Lindsay 1981, 19, 151, 153; Cormack 1991, 124 under no. 47; Kidson 1999, 77 under no. LL 3668; Conway 2001, 40–41; Solkin 2001, 115–16; Secrest 2004, 132–34, 441; Manning 2005, 18, 22–23, 197, 205; Perry 2007, 68–70; Baetjer 2009, 102 under no. 45; B. Leca in Cincinnati and San Diego 2010–11, 133; Brewer 2011, 571; Ribeiro 2011, 194–96; D. Cholmondeley in Houston, San Francisco, and Nashville 2014–15, 139; Chu 2016, 58; Hamilton 2017, 341; Belsey 2019, 1: no. 313.

SELECTED EXHIBITION HISTORY

London 1782, no. 184 (as *Portrait of a Lady*); London 1862, no. 116 (as *Portrait of Mrs. Elliot* [*sic*]); London 1885, no. 110 (erroneously describes full-length portrait); London 1894a, no 131; London 1909, no. 135; Leeds 1936, no. 26; London 1936, no. 10 (erroneously states the sitter was "later a well-known figure as Mme. de St. Alban"); Ipswich 1927, no. 74; New York 1940, no. 13; Montreal 1942, no. 87; New York 1942, no. 389; Providence 1945, no. 70 (erroneously dated 1778); The Hague 2015, no. 15.

MRS. FITZHERBERT

CA. 1784

Oil on canvas
29⅞ x 25 in. (75.9 x 63.5 cm)
Fine Art Museums of San Francisco;
Museum purchase, Mildred Anna Williams Collection (1941.19)

Twice widowed by age twenty-five, Maria Smythe (1756–1837) was the granddaughter of a baronet, raised Roman Catholic, and educated at a convent in France.[237] As was customary, after her second husband's death in 1781, she retained her most recent married surname. In the early 1780s, she caught the attention of the young George, Prince of Wales (the future George IV), who in 1782 reportedly fathered a child with Grace Dalrymple Elliott (cat. 21). In 1785, however, the twenty-three-year-old heir to the Crown secretly married Maria, then twenty-nine. The union scandalized the press, public, and royal family, in large part because of her Catholic faith, and it was considered invalid under the Royal Marriages Act of 1772, which required consent from the monarch and privy council.[238] Their morganatic marriage—entitling Maria to none of the titles and privileges of her husband's rank—was tempestuous. Nonetheless, they continued to socialize together—even after his lawful marriage in 1795 to Caroline, Duchess of Brunswick—until his death in 1830.

One of several paintings of Fitzherbert made by the period's leading artists—including Reynolds and Romney—Gainsborough's portrait shows her against red drapery with a glimpse of landscape at far left. These elements and her gesture—the raised arm touching a finger to her temple, reflecting a trend in female portraiture informed by the cult of "sensibility" or feeling—recall an earlier portrait by Gainsborough, *Miss Elizabeth Tyler*, which was

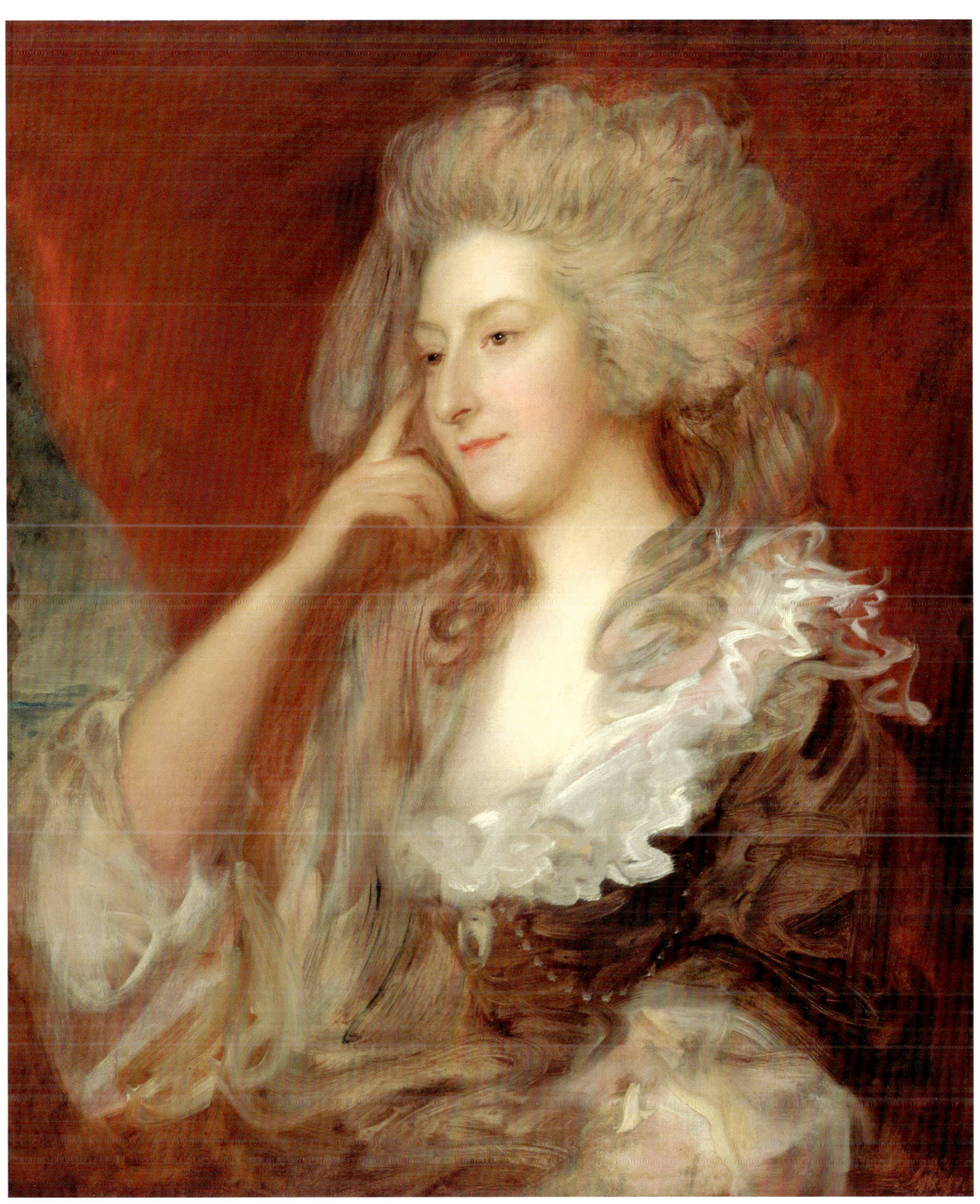

also commissioned by a lover (fig. 60).[239] Reflecting Gainsborough's practice, the face (and much of her hair) in *Mrs. Fitzherbert* appears more finished than the rest of the composition. The loose strokes that compose her dress, with its jagged lace around her neckline and full white sleeves, exemplify the artist's signature style and give a sense of informality and intimacy, as if she were only loosely dressed. Though unfinished, the forms are legible, including a miniature suspended from the neckline of her dress, connected to a string of pearls; this presumably represents a portrait of the prince.[240]

"A Head of Mrs Fitzherbert delivered unfinished by His Highness's orders" appears on a list of thirteen paintings by Gainsborough for the Prince of Wales, next to the date "May 1784" (presumably when it was delivered) and with a value of £31.[241] The prince retained the portrait until his death, when his successor, William IV, sent it to Mrs. Fitzherbert in Brighton.[242]

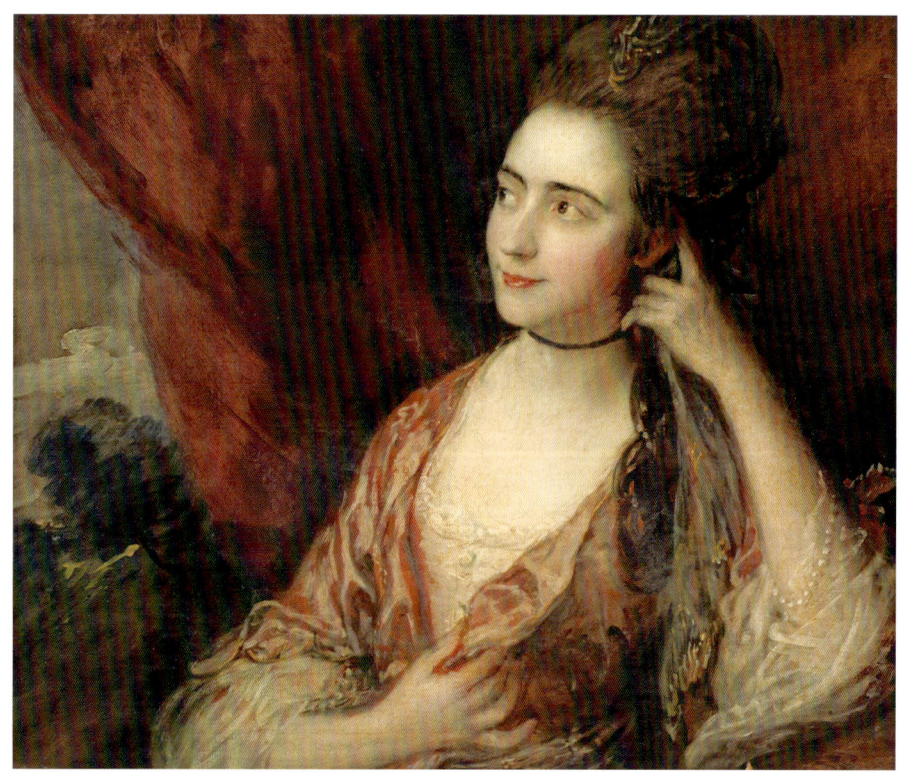

FIG. 60
Thomas Gainsborough
Miss Elizabeth Tyler, 1775
Oil on canvas
24 x 30 in. (60.9 x 76.2 cm)
Private collection

PROVENANCE

Delivered to the Prince of Wales, 1784, and recorded in store at Carlton House (no. 327), 1816;
sent by William IV to the sitter in Brighton, October 5, 1830, bequeathed by the sitter to Hon. Mary Georgiana Emma (Minney) Seymour
(d. 1848), who in 1825 married Colonel George Dawson-Damer, 1837; bequeathed to her daughter, Georgiana Augusta Charlotte Caroline
Dawson-Damer (d. 1866), who in 1847 married Hugh, 3rd Earl Fortescue (1818–1905), Castle Hill, Devonshire; sold to Arthur Sanderson
(1846–1915), Edinburgh, ca. 1895; purchased jointly by Knoedler and Trotti & Cie, March 19, 1907; purchased by John F. Talmage, Jr.
(1875–1943), New York, December 31, 1909; repurchased by Knoedler, February 1912, and sold to Sir James Dunn (1874–1956), London;
jointly purchased by Knoedler, Colnaghi, and Scott and Fowles, July 2, 1914; purchased by J. Horace Harding (1863–1929), New York,
February 1917; his widow's sale, New York, Parke Bernet, March 1, 1941, lot 60; bought by Knoedler and sold to the Mildred Anna
Williams Collection; presented to the Legion of Honor by Henry K. S. Williams (d. 1944) in memory of his wife.

SELECTED LITERATURE

Monkhouse 1897, 35; Armstrong 1898, 195; Gower 1903, 120; Armstrong 1904, 265; Fletcher 1904, 198; Mourey 1905, 64;
Menpes and Greig 1909, 173; Mourey 1909, 87; Comstock 1941, 31–32; Davisson 1946, 26, 28; Waterhouse 1946, 276; Waterhouse 1953, 39;
Millar 1969, xxvi, 35; Goldyne 1980, 123–25; I. Lumsden in Fredericton 1991, 13–14; Walker 1992, 97; A. Ribeiro in Cincinnati
and San Diego 2010–11, 138; Hamilton 2017, 341; Belsey 2019, 1: no. 331.

SELECTED EXHIBITION HISTORY

London 1868, no. 821; London 1885, no. 10; London 1891, no. 85; London 1894a, no. 73; London 1908c, no. 15;
New York 1912, 15 (unnumbered); Paris 1913, no. 9; Cincinnati 1931, no. 11; San Francisco 1933, no. 12; New York 1936, no. 14;
Hartford 1937, no. 35; Dallas 1938, no. 6; San Francisco, 1939–40, no. Y-95; Santa Barbara 1951, no. 8; Minneapolis 1952 (unnumbered);
Birmingham and Toronto 1995, no. 21; Cincinnati and San Diego 2010–11, 32 (unnumbered).

CAT. 23

MRS. SHERIDAN

PROBABLY 1783, ALTERED BETWEEN 1785 AND 1787

Oil on canvas
86½ x 60½ in. (219.7 x 153.7 cm)
National Gallery of Art, Washington;
Andrew W. Mellon Collection (1937.1.92)

A CELEBRITY "ALL HER LIFE," Elizabeth Linley (1754–1792) was trained, like her siblings, by her father, Thomas Linley, and as a child began performing in concerts in Bath and London (see cat. 16).[243] Her beauty and voice attracted wide interest, as well as scandal. The press and public were so fascinated with her love life that a play on the topic of her suitors was staged at London's Haymarket in 1771.[244] Pursuit by one particularly troubling suitor prompted her to flee to France in 1772; she did so in the company of family friend and playwright Richard Brinsley Sheridan, whom she married after they returned to England in 1773. Sheridan forbade her to perform publicly and limited her to private concerts for the nobility. He was notoriously unfaithful, and the marriage was not a happy one. They had one son, Tom, and Elizabeth later had a child with Lord Edward Fitzgerald.[245] She died of tuberculosis at age thirty-eight. Four portraits of Elizabeth by Gainsborough's hand survive, though exactly how many times he depicted her is unclear.[246]

Conflicting descriptions of the painting seen in Gainsborough's rooms at Schomberg House in the mid-1780s created confusion and led to speculation that a portrait of Mrs. Sheridan in pastoral dress has been lost. Scholars debate whether this is the full-length that Gainsborough exhibited at the Royal Academy in 1783 (described as showing her "under the umbrage of a romantic tree" accompanied by objects "descriptive of retirement"),

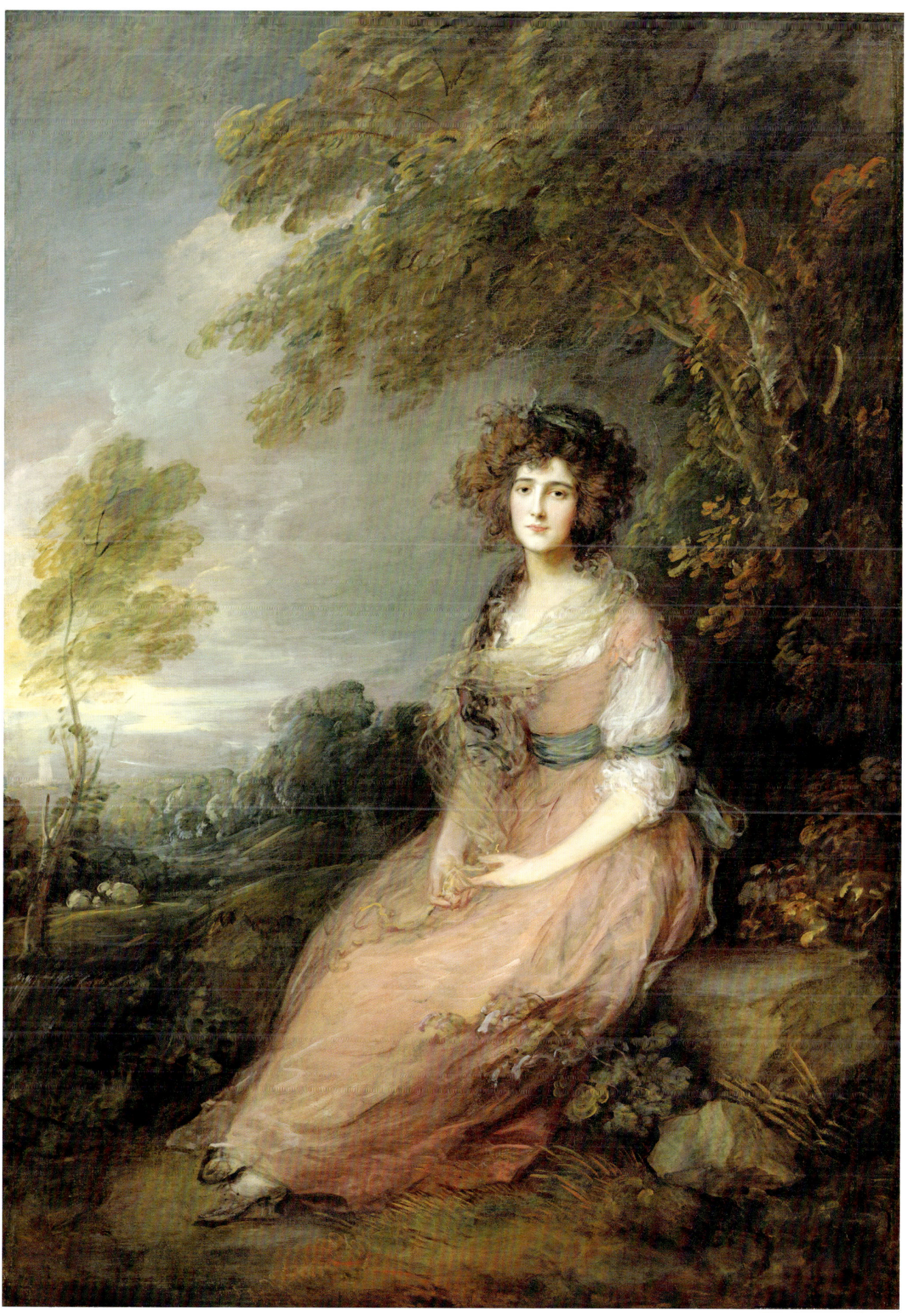

which he then reworked and exhibited at Schomberg House in 1786, or if the 1783 picture was a distinct, now-lost work.[247] Dorothy Richardson, who saw a portrait of Elizabeth in Gainsborough's rooms on March 7, 1785, described "Mrs Sheridan sat upon a bank, with a French Dog at her feet the face beautiful & expressive the Landscape part, a River & Cascade."[248] By January 1786, Elizabeth's sister-in-law referred to Gainsborough having "alter'd the idea of making her a Peasant."[249] In December of that year, Henry Bate Dudley described the painting as a work in progress, that it was "to assume an air more pastoral than at present it possesses, by the introduction of some lambs."[250] Finally, in March of 1788, *The World* refers to Gainsborough's *Mrs. Sheridan* as "compleat."[251] Technical examination reveals that Gainsborough made substantial changes to the portrait, such as removing pastoral elements (basket, shepherd's crook, lamb or other snouted animal, and a *bergère* hat tied under the sitter's chin with a bow).[252] Criticism of the 1783 portrait as "by no means successfully imagined" may have inspired him to make changes.[253] Such extensive changes over several years were not uncommon for Gainsborough—who in 1786 also made considerable modifications to the 1772 portrait of Elizabeth and her sister Mary (Dulwich Picture Gallery)[254]—but the number of changes he seems to have made to *Mrs. Sheridan* from 1783 to 1788 mark this portrait as a particularly labored composition.

Mrs. Sheridan has been praised as heralding a "new style" of romantic portraiture that Thomas Lawrence (1769–1830) would subsequently "take to its furthest lengths."[255] Embedding the figure in the natural setting, with wind tossing her hair and drapery as it does the leaves and branches, Gainsborough fuses the genres of portraiture and landscape more so than in any other monumental full-length. Though Ellis Waterhouse described it as unfinished, with "the hands being merely laid in," the sensitive treatment of the face and diaphanous shawl twirling in the breeze suggest that the painting as Gainsborough finally left it was what satisfied the artist after a long period of rethinking and reworking. Like many of his portraits of his musical friends, it may have been made as a gift to the sitter or her family.

PROVENANCE

Purchased by Mrs. Edward Bouverie (1750–1825), Delapre Abbey, Northampton, a friend of the sitter; descended to General Edward Bouverie (1789–1871); his posthumous sale, Christie's, March 2, 1872, lot 40 (according to a letter from Michael Hall in the National Gallery curatorial files, 27 February 2002); purchased by Baron Lionel de Rothschild (1807–1879), Tring Park, 1872; by descent to his grandson Lionel, 2nd Baron Rothschild (1868–1937); purchased through Agnews by Duveen, November 17, 1936; sold to the Andrew W. Mellon Educational Trust in 1937; presented to the National Gallery of Art, 1937.

SELECTED LITERATURE

Probably *Morning Herald*, March 30, 1783; probably *Public Advertiser*, May 29, 1783; *Public Advertiser*, April 13, 1785; *Morning Post*, April 28, 1786; *Public Advertiser*, April 28, 1786; *Morning Herald*, December 30, 1786; Fulcher 1856a, 123, 124, 185, 222; Fulcher 1856b, 125, 127, 189, 226; Brock-Arnold 1881, 43; Armstrong 1898, 126, 135, 168, 171, 176, 178, 180–81, 185, 187, 202; Chamberlain 1903, 61, 109–10, 184–85; Gower 1903, 5–6, 62, 114; Armstrong 1904, 169, 182, 226, 230, 238, 240, 244, 250, 253, 279; Fletcher 1904, 144; Boulton 1905, 147–48, 218–19, 259, 313; Menpes and Greig 1909, 96, 138, 159, 160, 163; Whitley [1915] 2016, 13, 223, 226, 227, 228–231, 269, 270, 288, 291, 297; Dibdin 1923, 67, 157, 160; Stokes 1925, 99; Woodall 1949, 82; Waterhouse 1953, 97–98; Waterhouse 1958, 89, no. 613; Williamson 1972, 169, 171, 187–88, 189, 191–92; Hayes 1975, 46, 225, no. 119; Paulson 1975, 218, 228; Lindsay 1981, 157, 170, 183; Hayes 1982, 167, 169; Lavezzari 1983–84, 314; L. Stainton in Washington and Los Angeles 1985–86, 60 under no. 9; Dorment 1986, 123–24; N. Kalinsky in London 1988a, 76–77, no. 3:14; Cormack 1991, 28, 164–65, no. 67; Hayes 1992, 103–6; Hayes 1993, 30, 32; Kalinsky 1995 18, 78, 118–19, no. 44; Rosenthal 1999 244–45, 247; Asfour and Williamson 1999, 53, 219–20; Vaughan 2002, 181–83; Secrest 2004, 356–57, 438; Perry 2007, 156–58; H. Belsey in San Marino 2013, 73, 76–77; Christensen and Luciano 2013; Perry, Retford, and Vibert 2013, 134; Belsey 2019, 2: no. 814.

SELECTED EXHIBITION HISTORY

Probably London 1783, no. 140 (as *Portrait of a Lady*); London 1873, no. 35; London 1886, no. 103; Saltaire 1887, 128; London 1936, no. 8; London 1980–81, no. 129; Paris 1981 no. 57; London 1988a, no. 3:14; Paris and London 2006–7, no. 135 [exh. London only]; Cincinnati and San Diego 2010–11 (unnumbered); London 2011 (unnumbered).

THOMAS GAINSBOROUGH

CA. 1787

Oil on canvas
30⅞ x 25⅜ in. (77.3 x 64.5 cm)
Royal Academy of Arts, London;
Given by Miss Margaret Gainsborough, 1808 (03/1395)

THIS IS THE LAST of Gainsborough's self-portraits. Over his career, he produced independent self-portraits in five types, some of which are known in several copies. An early portrait of debated attribution, which may depict him at the age of thirteen, is the only one that presents him as an artist at work, holding a brush and palette.[256] The others, along with an early family portrait (see fig. 54), portray him as a gentleman in pose and attire.[257] In the present work, he wears a green jacket over a striped orange-and-white waistcoat and a cravat tied with a bow.[258] It is unclear if his hair is powdered or naturally gray (at the time, he was sixty). His daughter Margaret presented the portrait to the Royal Academy of Arts in 1808.

In an unaddressed note dated June 15, 1788—some six weeks before he died—Gainsborough reveals that he had intended the portrait, which he refers to as a "sketch," for his friend Carl Friedrich Abel (cat. 12). Abel died on June 20, 1787, before Gainsborough delivered it. In the same note, he declares his wishes for the legacy of his image after his death, writing:

> It is my strict charge that after my decease no plaster cast, model, or likeness whatever be permitted to be taken: But that if Mr. Sharp, who engraved Mr. Hunter's Print, should chuse to make a print from the ¾ sketch which I intended for Mr. Abel painted by myself, I give free consent.[259]

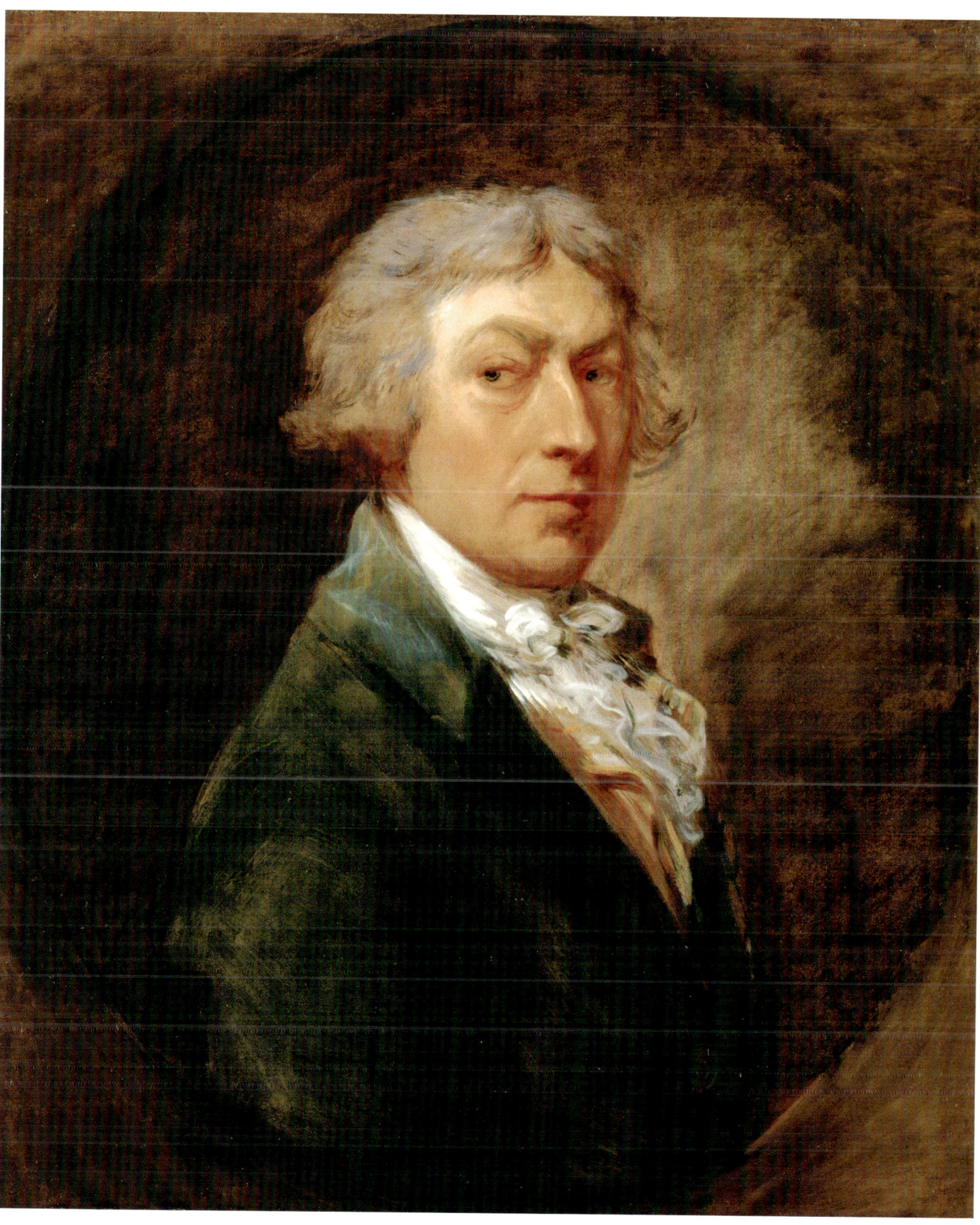

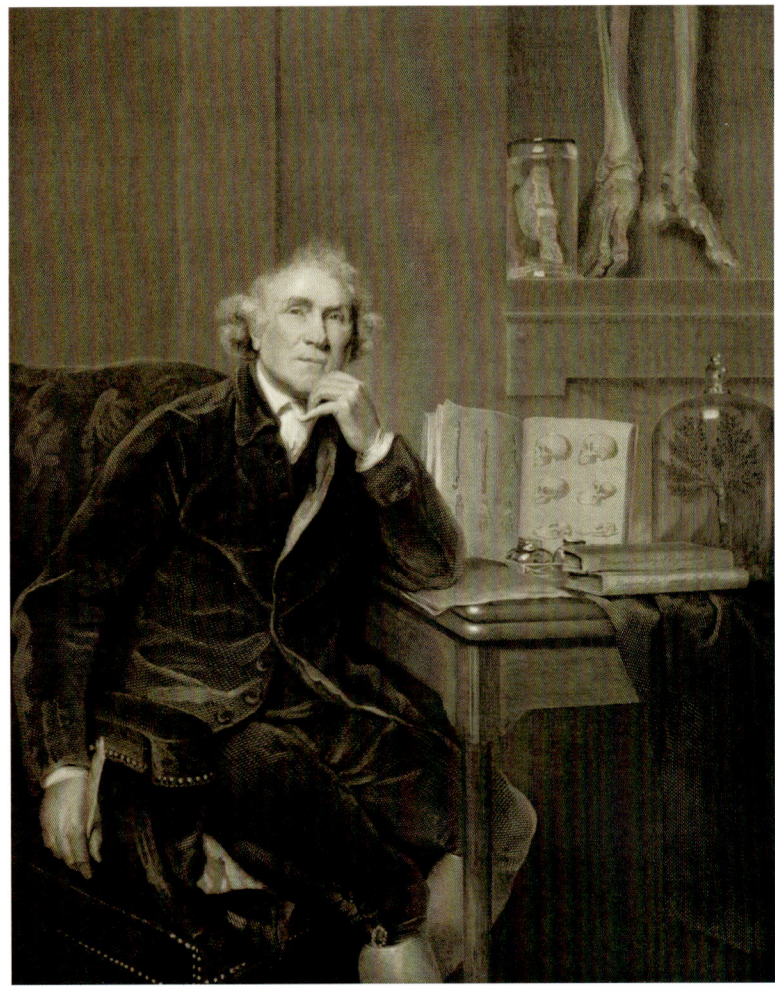

FIG. 61
William Sharp (after Joshua Reynolds)
Dr. John Hunter, 1788 (1786)
Line engraving
19⅞ x 15⅜ in. (504 x 390 mm)
National Portrait Gallery, London
(NPG D36394)

FIG. 62
Thomas Gainsborough
Self-Portrait, late 1760s
Oil on canvas
30³⁄₁₆ x 25 in. (76.6 x 63.5 cm)
The Courtauld, London
(P.1932.SC.100)

Gainsborough refers to William Sharp's engraving after Reynolds's portrait of John Hunter (a doctor who attended Gainsborough at the end of his life), published earlier that year (fig. 61).[260] Presumably, he deemed Sharp's print to be an effective translation of its painted prototype, which was a constant challenge to his own paintings.[261] Selecting this "sketch" for Abel implies that Gainsborough preferred it over his other self-portraits, though it appears that his daughter Mary did not. Ten years after Gainsborough's death, when his friend Francesco Bartolozzi took up the task of engraving it, Mary sent a different self-portrait of her father's (possibly the one now in the Courtauld, fig. 62) to the engraver, citing a better likeness with regard to "the nose, etc."; the Courtauld portrait is much more finished in appearance than the present work.[262] Bartolozzi's engraving was not particularly successful, though Gainsborough's swift style was notoriously difficult to reproduce. Perhaps more than any other by Gainsborough, the present picture offers a likeness of the man while also exemplifying his art in the deft, loose brushwork that became his signature.

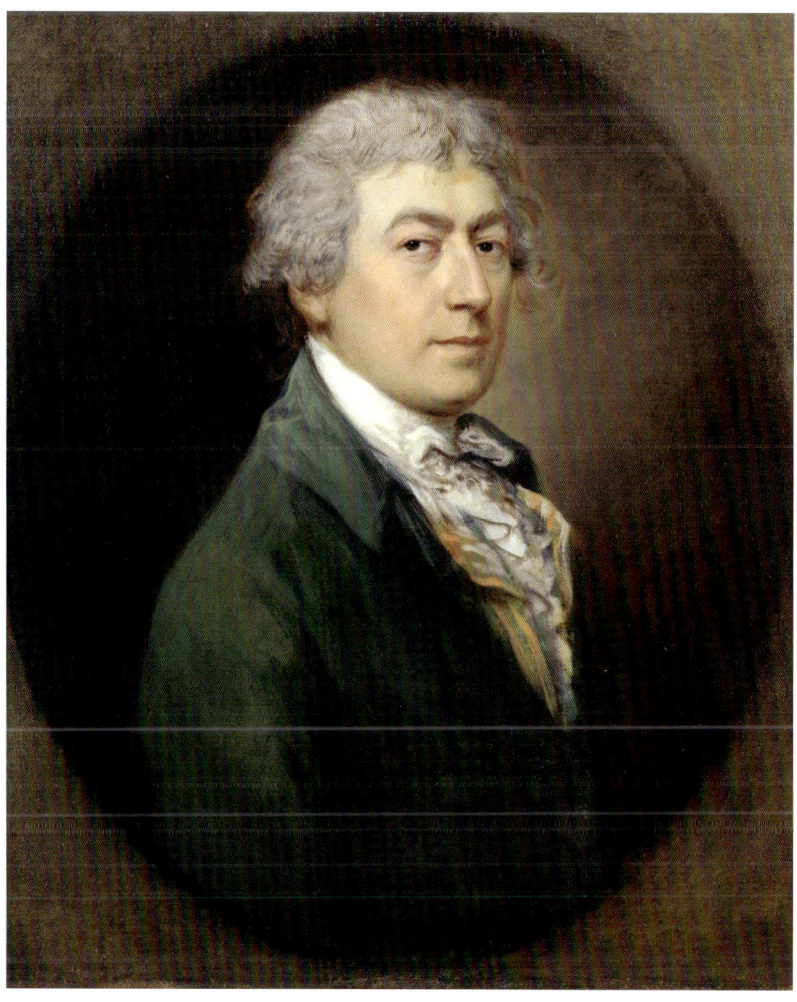

PROVENANCE

Presented by Margaret Gainsborough, the artist's daughter, to the Royal Academy of Arts, London, May 1808.

SELECTED LITERATURE

Fulcher 1856a, 148, 205; Fulcher 1856b, 151–52, 209; Tuer 1882, 2: 138; Armstrong 1898, 121, 195; Chamberlain 1903, 194–96; Armstrong 1904, 161, 266; Fletcher 1904, 211; Boulton 1905, 181, 321; Whitley [1915] 2016, 329, 340; Stokes 1925, 120; Waterhouse 1953, 45; Waterhouse 1958, 69; Ripley 1964, 68; Williamson 1972, 204, 211; Hayes 1975, 15; Lindsay 1981, 191, 196; Cormack 1991, 172, no. 71; Kalinsky 1995, 5; Cole 1997, 375; Asfour and Williamson 1999, 123; Vaughan 2002, 198; Martinez 2009, 139, 140; Hamilton 2017, 358; Belsey 2019, 1: no. 375.

SELECTED EXHIBITION HISTORY

Manchester 1857, no. 310; London 1867, no. 519; Leeds 1868, no. 1043; London 1880, no. 143; London 1885, no. 1; Ipswich 1887, no. 120; Berlin 1908, no. 61; Rome 1911, no. 29; Ipswich 1927, no. 73; Manchester 1934, no. 63; London 1936, no. 19; Lisbon and Madrid 1949, no. 20; London 1953a, no. 54; London 1977, no. 12; London 1980–81, no. 136; Paris 1981, no. 61; London 1985, no. A7; London 1988a, no. 14.1; Sudbury 1988, no. 13; Oxford 1999 (no catalogue); Southampton 2001, no. 25; Enschede 2016 (no catalogue); London and Princeton 2018–19, no. 47.

BERNARD HOWARD,
LATER 12TH DUKE OF NORFOLK

1788

Oil on canvas
88 x 54 in. (223.5 x 137.2 cm)
His Grace, the Duke of Norfolk,
Arundel Castle, Sussex

BERNARD EDWARD HOWARD (1765–1842) was twenty-three and nearly three decades from succeeding as 12th Duke of Norfolk when Gainsborough painted his portrait. His black Van Dyck dress aligns him with the full-length Gainsborough painted in 1784 of Bernard's third cousin Charles Howard (fig. 63), who—after becoming 11th Duke of Norfolk in 1786—had the artist add in symbols of his new titles, including a crown, coat of arms, and Earl Marshal's baton.[263] With six children outside his marriage, the 11th Duke had no legitimate sons with his wife, who began to suffer from bouts of madness shortly after they wed and subsequently lived her life in confinement.[264] The present portrait, likely commissioned by the 11th Duke, thus visualizes Bernard as the legitimate heir to the dukedom. The historical dress connects both paintings to ancestral portraits from the seventeenth century by Van Dyck that are still with the Dukes of Norfolk today.

Bernard Howard may be the last portrait painted by Gainsborough before his death, in August 1788. On May 21 of that year, the *Morning Post* reported that "Mr. Howard, brother to Lady Petre, has lately had his portrait painted by Mr. Gainsborough—it is not yet finished—neither is it, in point of attitude, what entirely pleases the artist."[265] Presumably, the sitter's attitude—facing almost fully frontally while looking wistfully to the right—satisfied the artist before his death a few months later, though Gainsborough's illness was in the same

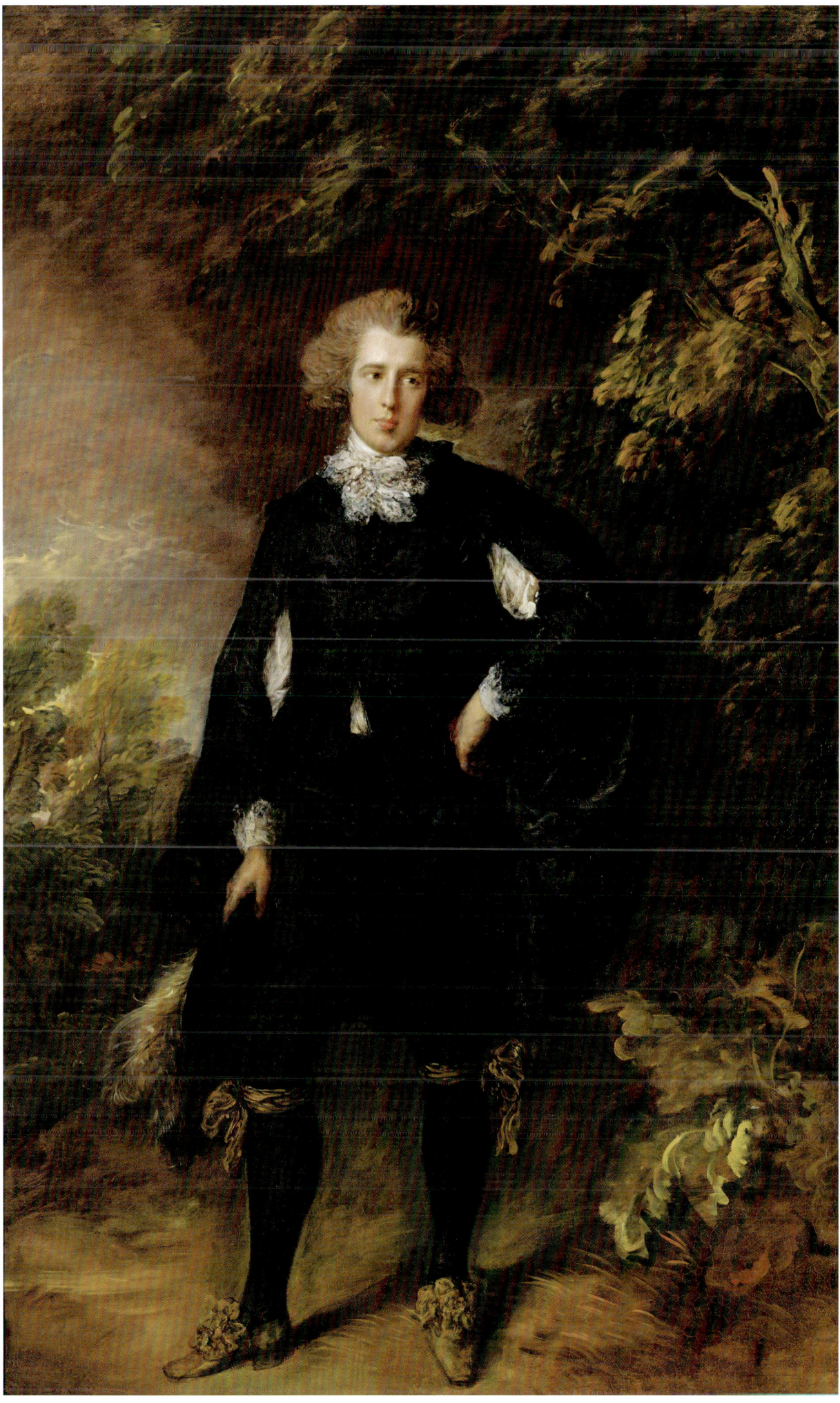

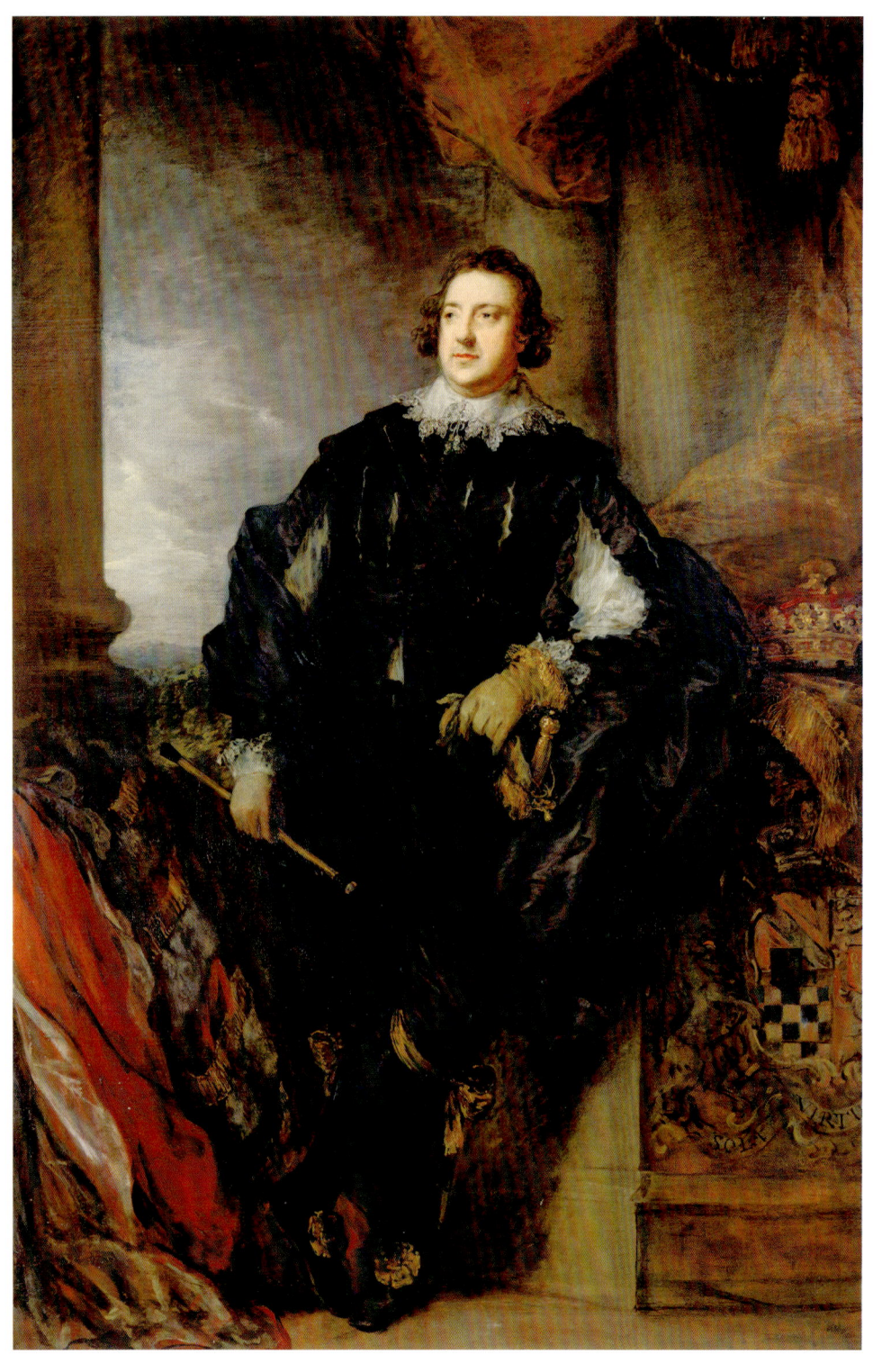

FIG. 63
Thomas Gainsborough
Charles Howard, 11th Duke of Norfolk, 1784–86/87
Oil on canvas
91½ x 60 in. (232.4 x 152.4 cm)
National Portrait Gallery, London; exhibited at Arundel Castle, Sussex (NPG 5294)

month reported as having made him "unable to exercise his pencil."[266] Gainsborough presents Bernard in similar but not identical Van Dyck costume to that of his cousin. He holds a black hat with white feathers in his right hand while his left arm is akimbo, a pose familiar from Van Dyck's prototypes. With apparently natural, semi-powdered hair, the sitter presents himself with fashionable elegance as opposed to authority; Gainsborough eschews the grandeur and pomp of the 11th Duke's portrait, with its billowing fabrics and monumental architecture, instead immersing the youthful heir-apparent in a romantic outdoor setting like that in *Mrs. Sheridan* (cat. 23).

In 1789, the year after Gainsborough painted him, Bernard married Lady Elizabeth Belasyse. Their son would succeed him as 13th Duke of Norfolk.[267] The marriage, however, appears to have been arranged against her wishes (she had hoped to marry the Hon. Richard Bingham) and was short-lived. Unlike the 11th Duke, who was an Anglican (variously nicknamed "the Protestant Duke" and "the Drunken Duke"), Bernard sustained his family's Catholic tradition despite penalties for practicing the religion in England, which included "civil disabilities" such as being barred from sitting in the House of Lords, a right otherwise granted to the nobility and which the 11th Duke exercised.[268] Still, Bernard filed for divorce in 1793, apparently for his wife's benefit, for "as a practising Catholic he could not marry again in any case."[269] Lady Elizabeth married Bingham as soon as the divorce was granted. Bernard worked to support the Catholic Emancipation Act, and in 1829, as 12th Duke of Norfolk, he was finally able to take his seat in the House of Lords, the first Catholic member of the family to do so since 1678.[270]

PROVENANCE

By descent.

SELECTED LITERATURE

Probably *Morning Post*, May 21, 1788; Waagen 1854, 31; Armstrong 1898, 200; Fulcher 1856a, 209; Fulcher 1856b, 213; Armstrong 1904, 275; Whitley [1915] 2016, 338; Stokes 1925, 118; Manners 1926, 79; Waterhouse 1953, 80; Waterhouse 1958, 27, 28, 83, no. 518; Hayes 1975, 229, no. 136; Lindsay 1981, 195; Cherry and Harris 1982, 291, 298–300; Pointon 1993, 23, 24; Rosenthal 1999, 155, 158, 242, 244; Belsey 2019, 2: no. 683.

SELECTED EXHIBITION HISTORY

London 1880, no. 132; London 1885, no. 153.

NOTES

1. H. Belsey (in London and Sudbury 2003, 18) compares the right-hand figure with a fashion plate by Hubert-François Gravelot (with whom Gainsborough also trained) and argues that the figure on the left "is clearly based on the attenuated anatomy of a lay figure."

2. Transcribed by J. Hayes in Ferrara 1998, no. 3: "Peter Darnal Muilman Esq' son of Henry [and his] wife, the daughter of Sʳ Thomas Darnal of Dagnahm Park Essex Charles Crokatt Esq of Luxborough Hall Essex who married Anne Muil[man] sister of the Peter Darnal Muilman whose daughter Emelia married Ascoughe Bourcherett Esq of Willingham Lincolnshire and also the portrait of Mʳ Keables the Artist who painted the figures the Landscape is by Gainsborough." Perkins (2002, 7) notes that Emilia Crokatt married Ayscoughe Boucherett in 1789, giving the label a *terminus post quem.*

3. For biographies, see H. Belsey in London and Sudbury 2003, 18, and H. David in Chu 2017, who clarifies the birth year of Charles Crokatt. Perkins (2002, 8) claimed circumstantial evidence for Muilman being the youngest.

4. Plans were made for Muilman to marry Crokatt's sister, but the marriage never took place. After Crokatt's suicide in 1769, Anna married John Julius Angerstein, whose collection formed the nucleus of the National Gallery in London.

5. Perkins 2002, 13, and H. David in Chu 2017.

6. H. Belsey in London and Sudbury 2003, 18.

7. J. Chu in Chu 2017.

8. H. David (in Chu 2017) quotes correspondence from Peter Manigault to his mother about the Muilmans and Crokatts in 1750 and 1751. Perkins (2002, 13) and Belsey (2019, 2: 621) suggest Crokatt on the left; the latter notes the "hauteur" of the rightmost figure.

9. Perkins (2002, 11) notes that Percy Moore Turner, organizer of the Gainsborough Bicentenary exhibition (Ipswich 1927), was the first to propose Gainsborough's authorship for the whole composition. M. Woodall (in Bath and other cities 1949, 13) and Waterhouse (1958, no. 747) assert that the entire composition is by Gainsborough.

10. "Keable's face has been reworked so that it appears more opaque than the other faces in the X-radiograph; indeed, the paint layer is visibly thicker to the naked eye and there are tiny shrinkage cracks"; Hellen and Gent 2017.

11. Postle 2002, 17. H. Belsey (in Charleston 1999, 91) notes that Andrew Wilton was the first to suggest that Keable's own self-portrait was in the composition. Gainsborough's teacher, Hayman, may have been the last to work on what has been described as "one of the most hybrid works ever painted"; see fig. 44 in this publication.

12. London 1977, no. 13.

13. Belsey (2002, 27), suggests connections between Gainsborough and Keable, including their attendance at St. Martin's Lane Academy in London and interest in music.

14. Postle 2002, 15.

15. On what has changed of the view, see Hayes 1975, 41, 203, no. 12; Potterton 1976, 9–13.

16. Bills 2018, 20.

17. Bensusan-Butt (1992/93, 33) notes that when the portrait of the Carters was exhibited in 1983, it was said by family tradition to have been painted as "a gift to the sitters in return for favours done."

18. London 1963a, 28.

19. Bensusan-Butt (1992/93, 36, 69) discusses the inheritance and suggests that Robert Andrews commissioned the portrait to commemorate the union of his land in 1750.

20. Hayes 1982, 1: 69. Rosenthal (1982, 42) draws attention to the specificity of the farmland.

21. On the picture, see MacLaren 1991, no. 1305, and Smith (1982, 265–67), who discusses a similar Dutch example—Frans de Hulst and Gerard Donck, *Burgomaster Cornelis Damasz. van der Gracht and His Wife* (SMK, Copenhagen), on which see Paulson and Holm in Copenhagen 2009–10, 41.

22. Paulson and Holm in Copenhagen 2009–10, 40, citing Adams 2002.

23. Vaughan 2002, 57. Rosenthal (1999, 293n.33) discusses Andrews's publications on farming, including the paper, "On the Advantages of Mixing Lime with Dung," published in 1785. Rosenthal (1997, 39–40) argues for "plenty of patronal input," for when Gainsborough was left to his "own inclinations, he did not paint enclosures."

24. Bermingham 1986, 30.

25. Solkin (2015, 113) discusses the Game Act of 1671, which assigned the right to hunt to those who owned substantial property and land; in the mid-1740s, a "vociferous public campaign" began to promote the opening up of hunting to a wider group.

26. On their clothing, see Bermingham 1986, 28–29. Contemporary texts offer conflicting perspectives on Robert's hat, which was either highly fashionable at the time or just slightly passé; see Rosenthal 1999, 17.

27. Belsey (2019, 1: 33) discusses other occasions on which dead pheasants appear in portraits. Egerton 1998, 38.

28. On debates around the dating, see Belsey 2019, 1: 414.

29. His first wife and son died in the late 1730s. Bensusan-Butt (1993, 76) suggested a date around 1754 based on research on John Gravenor's second marriage to Ann Colman on February 13, 1738/39, and the birth years of their daughters, together with Gravenor's "emergence to political importance." Prior to Bensusan-Butt's research, the daughters' names were confused in literature, with Ann at times referred to as Dorothea, the name of her own daughter and eventual owner of the picture.

30. Webster 2011, 114.

31. The curatorial file on the painting at the Yale Center for British Art includes scholarship on shortages of grain in Ipswich and John Gravenor's political role in pricing and providing access. See Clarke 1830, 100, 130.

32. E.g., Cormack 1991, 52; Vaughan 2002, 56: "Three of them lurch uncomfortably to the left, as though they had been at the cider too much at lunchtime. Yet despite such awkwardnesses, there is an engaging frankness in all their too believable faces."

33. Cormack (1991, 52) underlines that Gainsborough's conversation pieces cannot be organized in a "convenient stylistic chronology that moves from a seeming gaucheness to greater sophistication between 1747 and 1754."

34. R. Jones in London, Norwich, and Newcastle 1997, 19, 21, 22, 25. See also p. 37 in this publication and with thanks to Jessica David, Conservator at the Yale Center for British Art.

35. Shawe-Taylor 2009, 148.

36. Sloman (2002, 47) writes, "During the visit of 1758–9 the artist seems to have been fully occupied in painting portraits and it was only in 1760, when he was secure in the knowledge of regular work and settled accommodation, that he was able to make the excursions which proved so influential. The Bath visit of 1758–9 is scarcely discernable in his work, but its impact was life-changing—it was this busy few months that convinced him to make a permanent break with East Anglia."

37. Davidson 1968, 42–44. Hayes (1965, 70) remarks, "The *Lady Innes* is pure Van Dyck" and compares it to Van Dyck's *Elizabeth Cecil, Countess of Devonshire* (Petworth). Later, Hayes (1975, 208) dated the portrait to about 1757 and noted that despite its overall stiffness, its "handling, colour and the motif of the hand holding a rose all indicate that Gainsborough was already conscious of Van Dyck." Cherry and Harris (1982, 296) refer to the painting as "his first recasting of Van Dyck" and suggests "it would appear that he was already reaping the benefits of a visit to Wilton, for in both the pose derives from the foreground female figure in the Wilton group."

38. On the rose inviting viewers "to contemplate the passage from youth to age, the transience of beauty," see Rosenthal 1999, 147.

39. *The Public Advertiser*, November 18, 1766, announced the wedding: "Ipswich, Nov. 14. On Tuesday Capt. Innes, of the 2d Regiment of Dragoon Guards, was married to Miss Hodges, only Daughter of Thomas Hodges, Esq; of this Town."

40. She died two months after her father and was buried with him at St. Matthew's, Ipswich, where, eventually, they would be joined by her mother, husband, and daughters, who appear to have remained unmarried: Elizabeth Charlotte died aged ninety-two and Sarah Catherine died at seventy-five; see Haslewood 1884, 257–58.

41. Ribeiro 1995, 54; Belsey 2019, 1: 495.

42. Bridge 1919–20, 85.

43. Ribeiro 1995, 54.

44. Belsey (2019, 1: 495) observes that the proportions are repeated in only one other canvas of the period (ibid. no. 999).

45. Belsey 2019, 1: no. 376.

46. Belsey (2019, 1: 360) suggests honeysuckle was a common symbol of "interdependence between married couples."

47 Waterhouse 1973, 365. Scholars have also emphasized the portrait's connection to Van Dyck's portraiture; see, for example, Hayes 1975, 38.

48 Barrow 1838, 197. Lord Howe was created Earl Howe and Baron of Langar in Nottingham, the latter title to descend to his eldest daughter Sophia and her male heirs.

49 Letter from Gainsborough to James Unwin, October 25, 1763; Hayes 2001, 22.

50 Letter from Gainsborough to James Unwin, March 1, 1764; Hayes 2001, 25.

51 For biographical details, see Bryant 2003, no. 43 (though the date of Howe's succession to the earldom is erroneously given as 1782).

52 Belsey 2019, 1: no. 505.

53 Barrow 1838, 73.

54 A. Ribeiro (in London 1988b, 31–35) discusses details of the subject's attire.

55 On specialization in stringing jewels, see Clifford 2004, 124.

56 V. Pemberton-Pigott in London 1988b, 37–43; Bryant 2003, 190.

57 Barrow 1838, 360.

58 Barrow 1838, 376.

59 Bryant 2003, 192, citing Barrow 1838, 376.

60 On Gainsborough and the Old Masters, see J. Yarker in Belsey 2019, 2: 987–1008.

61 Seven copies after Van Dyck were listed in the 1789 sale catalogue at Gainsborough's studio. Edwards (1808, 139) notes that the sale included fifty-six paintings and one hundred forty-eight drawings in addition to works by "Flemish and other masters" that Gainsborough had collected.

62 *Morning Chronicle*, August 8, 1788: "He seems almost the only painter of this country, who attempts the thin brilliant style of pencilling of Vandyke; and yet, with all this blaze of excellence, with all this accuracy of resemblance, and he gives not merely the map of the face, but the character, the soul of the original, his likenesses are attained by the indecision more than the precision of the outlines."

63 On the Van Dyck portrait, see O. Millar in Barnes 2004, 603, no. IV.221.

64 As noted by Belsey (2019, 2: 1006), no engraving of Van Dyck's double portrait existed in the eighteenth century.

65 Dorothy Richardson described seeing his copy of Van Dyck's Pembroke family portrait in Gainsborough's Bath studio, but not the present painting. See J. Yarker in Belsey 2019, 2: 988.

66 The 3rd Earl's renovations to Cobham Hall—beginning before May of 1767—may have required the art collection to be removed to Berkeley Square; see Cornforth 1983, 508, 510.

67 *Theodosia Hawkins-Magill, Countess of Clanwilliam* (Ulster Museum, Belfast), see Belsey 2019, 1: no. 182. Belsey (2014, 305 [19A]) transcribes a letter from Gainsborough to the 3rd Earl of Darnley at Berkeley Square, presumably dated 1765, referring to "Miss Magill's Picture" having come "safe to hand" and asking the earl to call on him, suggesting that Gainsborough would be reworking it.

68 *John, 4th Earl of Darnley* (National Gallery of Art, Washington); see Belsey (2019, 1: 236), who mistakenly states that the 4th Earl commissioned Gainsborough's earlier portrait of *Theodosia Hawkins-Magill*.

69 Darnley sale 1925.

70 Copies of telegrams in the Frick curatorial files: "Has old varnish ever been removed from Darnley Gainsboro Stop Is there absolutely no Gainsboro blue stop. Surely some blue somewhere stop" (March 28, 1925). The response on March 31, 1925: "You ask if the blue is Gainsborough blue. I think I am correct in saying that it is not, and that even when cleaned it will not come out a Gainsborough blue, but is an exact copy of the Van Dyck. Anyhow, it is a most attractive colour."

71 Copies of telegrams in the Frick curatorial files; March 27, 1925.

72 The memoirs were published with a biographical account; Erskine 1954. See also Laing 1995, no. 8.

73 Laing 1995, 32.

74 Erskine 1954, xi. Hervey wrote that January 9, 1754, was "the first day I ever felt the attack of the gout"; ibid. 163.

75 Belsey 2019, 1: no. 102.

76 A. Wilton (in London 1992–93, 142 no. 40) pointed out the similarity, in reverse, of Hervey's pose with an anchor to Van Dyck's *Algernon Percy*.

77 Allen (1991, 139–40) describes the group portrait as "one of the most hybrid works ever painted. Although begun in Paris in 1750 . . . it was soon abandoned by [Gravelot] after he admitted having problems with it in a letter to Lady Hervey." Gravelot employed an assistant to work on the architectural elements and the Swiss painter Jean-Etienne Liotard to

work on the four figures at left. Lady Hervey requested the unfinished picture to be sent to London in 1751 and Hayman was commissioned to complete the two figures on the right, Augustus Hervey and his mother, Lady Hervey.

78 S. Sloman in London 2009, no. 126.

79 A son, Augustus Henry Hervey, was born to Chudleigh in 1747 but died in infancy; Erskine 1954, 48 and Ostler 2021, 278.

80 E.g., Waterhouse 1958, 21. On Mulgrave's portrait, see Belsey 2019, 2: no. 668.

81 Laing 1995, 32. Walpole's annotated catalogue is in the Lewis Walpole Library at Yale University.

82 Belsey 2019, 1: no. 476. Gainsborough's 1783 portrait of the sitter's nephew, *Captain the Hon. John Augustus, Lord Hervey*, hangs alongside the present portrait today at Ickworth House (Belsey 2019, 1: no. 477).

83 On the duke's portrait, see Belsey 2019, 2: no. 645.

84 The duke's account book records visits to Bath in 1768 in January, from April 28 to May 25, and from November 9 to December 6; Belsey 2019, 2: 601.

85 Belsey 2019, 1: no. 116; 2: no. 648 (and a second version, no. 649).

86 When Mary's father, John, 2nd Duke of Montagu, died in 1749 without a male heir, the title died, though her husband, George Brudenell, Earl of Cardigan, had taken the Montagu name when they married in 1730. Through the efforts of Mary's husband, the Earl of Cardigan, George III re-created the title in 1766 with George and Mary as 1st Duke and Duchess of Montagu. The Montagu ducal title died again in 1790 when the duke died, as they lacked a male heir (their son, John, had died in 1770).

87 Cited in Boulton 1905, 175; Walpole 1974, 297–98. Walpole's opinion of her later changed.

88 Vaughan 2002, 115. Millar 1949, 9: "A portrait of rare psychological insight and the most haunting dignity."

89 Clifford 2004, 117–18.

90 Rosenthal 1999, 147.

91 See Belsey 2019, nos. 675, 738, 757, 359, 732, 676, 224, as well as later examples, such as cat. 17 and Belsey 2019, no. 212.

92 On the collection today at Bowhill House, see Buccleuch and Queensberry 2012, and Buccleuch and Queensberry 2022, though the family's collection is distributed among several residences.

93 Hayes (1975, 214 no. 67) suggests that the painted landscape may be "conceivably an actual landscape bought by the Montagus."

94 Hayes 2001, 58. Gainsborough's letter to Garrick annotated with the date August 22, 1768, continues: "But not as if you thought any thing [*sic*] of mine worth that trouble, only to see his <Grace's> Landskips [*sic*] of Rubens, and the 4 Vandykes whole length in his Graces [*sic*] dressing Room." The four Van Dyck portraits remain in the ducal collection.

95 Thanks to Crispin Powell, archivist for the Duke of Buccleuch, for sharing information from Duke George's private accounts. The entry in the duke's accounts for December 6, 1768, for "the Duchess's Portrait" does not explicitly name Gainsborough, but it was most likely to him. The lower fee for the duchess's portrait (no size specified) suggests that the payment may have been for the bust-length portrait known in two versions (Boughton and Drumlanrig; fig. 46).

96 Wake (1953, 254) describes that in "sundry purchases and subscriptions to charities it was their custom to divide the cost equally between them." The duchess's accounts for the late 1760s have not been located. Thanks to Crispin Powell and Jana Shuster for help with Boughton archival material, and Pamela Hunter for help with research into the duchess's accounts at Hoare's Bank and elsewhere.

97 *Gazetteer and New Daily Advertiser*, December 15, 1780: "About six yesterday morning died suddenly Mr. Ignatius Sancho, grocer, and tea-dealer, of Charles-street, Westminster, a man whose generosity and benevolence were far beyond his humble station. He was honoured with the friendship of the late Rev. Mr. Sterne, and several of the literati of these times." The enormously popular subject of Sancho's biography begins with the text by Joseph Jekyll (1754–1837) published posthumously with Sancho's letters in 1782, edited by Lady Frances Crewe (see Crewe 2013 and Carretta 2004, 1: iii–xvi); see also essays in King et al. 1997 and *The Cambridge Companion to Ignatius Sancho*, forthcoming.

98 Jekyll's biography refers to Sancho as the sisters' "slave." Crewe 2013, 1: vi. In 1758, he married Ann Osborne, a woman of West Indian origin (according to Crewe 2013, xi).

99 Sancho's exact term of employment is unknown; see C. Powell in Aljoe and Huang 2025.

100 Crewe 2013, 1: ix–x.

101 See C. Powell in Aljoe and Huang 2025, who discusses the small coterie of Black figures associated with the Montagu household, including servants Julie Green and another "black boy" who were depicted in now-lost portraits, the former painted by Duchess Mary (wife of the 2nd Duke of Montagu). R. King (in King et al. 1997, 29) notes that Duke John's father had a portrait of his steward, Daniel Eaton, offering a precedent for servants' portraits in the family. On servants and portraiture, see G. Waterfield and A. French in London and Edinburgh 2003–4, 38.

102 Belsey (2019, 2: 739) describes the sitter wearing a "red waistcoat trimmed with gold under a dark green coat"; while these colors align with Montagu livery, no evidence suggests that the coat was any other color than the dark blue that appears today. With thanks to Crispin Powell and Christopher Etheridge for their helpful discussions. See the chapter on servants and dress in Buck 1979, 103–19.

103 Its original appearance may have been comparable to *Portrait of a Man in a Red Suit*, formerly attributed to Allan Ramsay, at Royal Albert Memorial Museum & Art Gallery, Exeter (formerly identified as a portrait of Ignatius Sancho).

104 Jekyll recounts, "Painting was so much within the circle of Ignatius Sancho's judgement and criticism, that [painter John Hamilton] Mortimer came often to consult him"; Crewe 2013, xiii–xiv.

105 Noting that Gainsborough's *Ignatius Sancho* used to hang in the library of William Stevenson, and "is now in the hall of his son [Seth] in Surrey street," Chambers (1829, 2: 1093) describes an inscription on the back of the painting: "This sketch by Mr. Gainsborough, of Bath, was done in one hour and forty minutes, Nov. 29th, 1768." The inscription is no longer visible.

106 On Gainsborough and Dupont painting the skirts of Queen Charlotte's portrait in one night, see Belsey 2019, 1: 166, citing James Northcote (1901, 160–61).

107 Waterhouse (1966, 54, no. 57) cites a receipt for this amount dated April of 1768 for a portrait (30 x 25 inches) sent to Mrs. Fortescue in Dublin. A receipt from Gainsborough to George, 1st Duke of Montagu, corroborated by the duke's personal accounts at Boughton House, shows that the duke paid £42 for his half-length portrait by Gainsborough on May 23, 1768. Thanks to Crispin Powell for his help and for sharing the documents with me.

108 For payments and salaries related to Sancho and the Montagu household, see C. Powell in Aljoe and Huang 2025.

109 E.g., G. Waterfield and A. French in London and Edinburgh 2003–4, 49–50; Madin 2006, 39.

110 Sancho produced and published musical works while still a servant, and the dedications of the surviving pieces of Sancho's music are all to members of the Montagu family. See R. King (in King et al. 1997, 22), who also raises the possibility that the portrait was a gift from the painter to Sancho. On Sancho's surviving four volumes of music and his *Theory of Music*, dedicated to the Princess Royal (of which no copies survive), see J. Girdham in King et al. 1997, 120.

111 C. Powell in Aljoe and Huang 2025: "Household accounts describe his purchase as for, 'an entertainment for the servants' at Montagu House on 24 April."

112 On Sancho and slavery, see, especially, J. Walvin in King et al. 1997, 93–113. His business card featured images of an Indigenous figure and a Black figure harvesting and smoking tobacco (British Museum D,2.3977).

113 On Elizabeth and William Sancho, see C. Powell in Aljoe and Huang 2025.

114 Gainsborough did not mention Sancho's portrait when urging Garrick to visit the Montagu portraits in 1768. A letter from Sancho's daughter Elizabeth to William Stevenson (an artist who studied under Reynolds and a family friend and supporter of the Sanchos) dated February 29, 1820, seems to declare the transfer to Stevenson of Sancho's portrait (facsimile in Willis 1980, 358): "Worthy Sir it is with great pleasure I present my Dear fathers portrait to so great a friend of his Daughter If Sir you will be so good to let me know where to send it shall go Directly I hear from you and if my best Sir will be so good to advance me half a year of the income he so kindly allows me being about to move it will greatly add to my comfort I hope your Dear Lady is well and that you enjoy your health I remain Sir with all due respect most gratefully yours Elizabeth Sancho." Stevenson (and subsequently his son) supported Elizabeth with an annuity until her death in 1837; reportedly the Duke of Buccleuch (husband of Elizabeth, for whose father Sancho worked as valet) defrayed the costs of Elizabeth Sancho's funeral.

115 Citing Dupont's indentures, Whitley ([1915] 2016, 373) describes his apprenticeship commencing on the 12th of January 1772, to learn "The Art or Mystery of a Painter" and, in the minutes of the Council of the Royal Academy, that Dupont was a student in the schools of the Royal Academy, admitted in 1775. He notes that Bate Dudley and Thicknesse report that Dupont was with his uncle from an early age.

116 Belsey 2019, 1: nos. 294, 295 (erroneously identified Sarah as Thomas Gainsborough's eldest sister).

117 Belsey (2019, 1: nos. 286–93) proposes eight painted portraits of Dupont and one pastel, with many copies after them. Sloman 2004, 319, refers to five, additionally proposing *The Blue Boy* as a sixth.

118 As Belsey (2019, 1: 278–79) remarks, "Although the resemblance to Dupont's features is strong, Gainsborough's prime purpose for the painting was probably not portraiture; it seems more likely that he is loosening the association with Van Dyck's prototype by adopting his usual practice and using a living model."

119 Belsey (2019, 2: 706) argues that Gainsborough's *William Bouverie, 1st Earl of Radnor* (1773), derives in reverse from his study of Van Dyck's figure of Bernard Stuart (see cat. 6).

120 Armstrong (1898, 152) confuses the provenance of two portraits of Dupont, one from Thicknesse to Bateman (now Waddesdon Manor), praised by Thicknesse and said to have been painted in an hour's sitting, and the other through George Richmond and Sir Edgar Vincent (the present portrait); subsequent scholars followed Armstrong until Sloman (2004, 320–22) identified the Waddesdon portrait as depicting Gainsborough Dupont (not Lord Bateman as previously identified), thus connecting the Waddesdon portrait with the portrait of Dupont discussed by Thicknesse.

121 Scholars have proposed dates around the late 1760s and early 1770s; e.g., McCurdy in London 2022, 53 ("1770"); Belsey 2019, 1: 279 (ca. 1769); D. Solkin in London and Princeton 2018–19, 177 ("c. 1770–5"); Sloman 2004, 320 ("1770–72").

122 Sloman (2004, 322n.21) discusses Allan Cunningham's anecdote in his biography of Gainsborough (Cunningham 1829–33, 1: 319–47).

123 Christie's (Lane sale 1831, lot 54) referred to the painting as the artist's last work. Whitley ([1915] 2016, 349) suggests that "it is probable" that the painting described by Sophia Lane can be identified with the present painting. D. Solkin in London and Princeton 2018–19, 177: "There seems no reason to doubt the accuracy of Sophia's recollection— Gainsborough must have selected this small, incomplete portrait from the piles of old pictures cluttering up his studio, and elevated it to a position of remarkable prominence at a time when he was aware that he was dying."

124 Sloman 2004, 322.

125 In a letter to William Jackson of January 25, 1777, Gainsborough explains why a parcel for Jackson has been delayed, referring to Dupont as one of two "blockheads," who is "too proud to carry a bundle *under his Arm*, though his betters the Journeymen Taylors always carry their foul shirts so"; Hayes 2001, 133.

126 Armstrong (1898, 153) notes, "A great part of the uncle's will is taken up with elaborate precautions against the possibility of the nephew's making some unreasonable claim for remuneration on account of such assistance as he may have rendered in the studio. A legacy of £600 is contingent on no such claim being made."

127 Roberts 1919, 4.

128 On children's clothing developments in eighteenth-century Britain, see Buck 1979, 205, and Ribeiro 2002, 241. On dressing children in the context of the monarchy and nobility, see Reynolds 2023, 143–65.

129 Fulcher 1856a, 224. Belsey (2019, 1: 458) suggests Fulcher may have heard the anecdote directly from the sitter. Bede (1889, 776) claims the portrait was made in 1773 when the sitter was five.

130 Lydia, later Viscountess Downe; Belsey 2019, 1: 458.

131 Belsey 2019, 1: no. 459.

132 See, for example, Robert John and Rhoda Jane Charleton in *The Charleton Children* (Virginia Museum of Fine Arts, Richmond), which

shows the subjects of different ages and genders in similar attire, the boy in the same dress as the present portrait; Belsey 2019, 1: no. 165.

133 Bede 1889, 776.

134 For Abel's biography, see, especially, Roe 2008 and Holman 2010, 169–252. Thanks to Susan Sloman for pointing me to the latter source.

135 *Morning Herald*, August 25, 1788, reports that Abel exchanged with Gainsborough a viola da gamba for "two valuable landscapes and several beautiful drawings." On Abel's walls covered with drawings by Gainsborough, see Angelo 1904, 1: 146.

136 Belsey (2019, 1: 21) draws attention to a comparison made by Hayes (1975, pls. 125, 126) of Gainsborough's *Willoughby Bertie, 4th Earl of Abingdon* (fig. 51) and the present picture, suggesting that the complementary compositions may have been intended to hang together, perhaps in the subscription concert rooms that Abingdon had supported from 1776. On the half-length of Abel, see Belsey 2019, 1: no. 1. Asleson and Bennett (2001, 94) claimed that the present work was the portrait of Abel sold for nine guineas in January 1788 and later placed above the orchestra in the Hanover Square Concert Room; however, the *Morning Post*'s description of that portrait as "a tolerable portrait of *Abel, by Gainsborough*," does not reconcile with the lavish praise given to the present portrait (see below). See also Belsey 2019, 1: 16–18 (citing Roe 2008, 112, in turn citing Lindsay 1981, 194; Lindsay gives no source). Roe and Lindsay were presumably referring to the account by Whitley ([1915] 2016, 400), who seems to be referring to the half-length of Abel.

137 Angelo 1904, 1: 49. Postle 2002, 50: "While Gainsborough could joke to friends about 'Abel's fat Guts', the portrait reflects his friend's refined sensibility and taste."

138 Roe (2008, 123) discusses Abel's snuff boxes and the possibility of the box in Gainsborough's portrait being the "splendid and curious box" decorated with Chinese figures sold as lot 74 in Abel's posthumous sale.

139 Citing a report by Harold Spivacke of the Library of Congress, 1936, in the Huntington curatorial file, R. Asleson (in Asleson and Bennett 2001, 95) suggests that in rhythm and melody (though not in key) the score resembles *Sonata III* of Abel's *Six Sonatas for Two Violins, or a German-Flute and Violin, with a Thorough Bass for the Harpsichord*, published in 1765.

140 *St. James's Chronicle*, April 26–29, 1777.

141 *Morning Post*, April 25, 1777.

142 *Morning Chronicle*, August 8, 1788.

143 Roberts 1921, 23–24.

144 Roe (2008, 125) discusses Abel's possessions and the sale of December 12–13, 1787, through Greenwood, London.

145 Her anonymous sale, Christie's, May 25, 1819, lot 93.

146 Gainsborough to Rev. Henry Bate Dudley, June 20, 1787; Hayes 2001, 164.

147 In her study on Gainsborough's dogs, D. Perkins (in Sudbury 2006, 5) estimates that about forty of the artist's eight hundred paintings include dogs. Hayes (2001, 102) raises the question of why Gainsborough, who excelled at painting dogs, inquired in a 1772 letter to the Hon. Edward Stratford, "whether Mr. Stratford means to have the Dog painted separate by Monsieur [Gainsborough] Dupont, or again put into Mrs. Stratford's Picture to spoil it."

148 Waterhouse (1958, 38) also emphasizes their inclusion as a "deliberate element in that search for informality, in that attempt to paint the private, rather than the public, face, which is the secret of the charm of many of his best portraits." Chamberlain (1903, 162) notes Gainsborough's interest in paintings of animals and dogs by Frans Snyders, whose work he collected.

149 D. Perkins in Sudbury 2006, 11.

150 Belsey 2019, 2: 946.

151 Whitley [1915] 2016, 400, citing a critic of the 1814 exhibition at the British Institution. D. Perkins (in Sudbury 2006, 26) illustrates a variant of the composition that includes two pups (private collection).

152 On the breed, which is related to Spitzes and Samoyeds and today has been bred to be much smaller than in the eighteenth century, see Hicks 1908. Earlier sources refer to the dogs depicted in the painting as "fox dogs." Belsey (2019, 2: 945) suggests that Abel may have been among the first to introduce the dog to Britain.

153 W. Hazlitt in *The Champion*, July 31, 1814, 247: "The *Fox-dogs, 58,* are admirable. The young one is even better than the old one, and has undeniable hereditary pretensions."

154 Pomeranians also appear in Gainsborough's *Lady Whichcote, Mr and Mrs Hallett, Mrs 'Perdita' Robinson*, and others.

155 Belsey (2019, 1: 945–46) suggests that Abel lent his dog to Gainsborough to include in portraits in the 1770s, adding: "It is tempting to assume that the pup was given to the artist (perhaps the canvas was given in thanks) and when it was fully grown it was used to animate a variety of portraits including those of Mr and Mrs Hallett and 'Perdita' Robinson, both of which date form the 1780s."

156 Fulcher 1856a, 134–35: "Mr. Gainsborough, after he had given Mr. Nollekens the two drawings he had selected, requested him to look at a model of an ass's head which he had just made. 'You should model more with your thumbs,' observed Nollekens; 'thumb it about, till you get it into shape.'—'What,' said Gainsborough, 'in this manner?' having taken up a bit of clay; and looking at a picture of Abel's Pomeranian Dog which hung over the chimney-piece—'this way?' 'Yes,' said Nollekens, 'you'll do a great deal more with your thumbs.' Mr. Gainsborough, by whom I was standing, observed to me, 'You enjoyed the music, my little fellow, and I am sure you long for this model; there, I will give it to you;'—and I am delighted with it still."

157 Waterhouse 1953, 121.

158 Whitley [1915] 2016, 400: "One of the 'liberal gifts' disposed of at the sale after Abel's death was acquired by another musical friend of Gainsborough's, the violoncellist Crosdill, whose portrait he sent to the Academy of 1780. The gift referred to was the painting lent by Crosdill to the Gainsborough exhibition held in 1814 at the British Institution, where it was catalogued as *Fox Dogs*. A critic of the exhibition of 1814, who knew Crosdill, says that the dogs at the time they were painted belonged to Abel, and that the picture was presented to him by Gainsborough in return for lessons on the viola da gamba."

159 On the portraits—which depict Frances's half-sister, Anne; the earl; his wife, Anne Duncombe; and their sons—see Smith 2017, 102–4 and Belsey 2019, 1: nos. 90–92, and 2: nos. 760–63.

160 Family tradition holds that she had been betrothed to the earl's eldest son, Jacob Pleydell-Bouverie, future 2nd Earl of Radnor, but after she was discovered to be having an affair with a Mr. Arabin, the engagement was broken and Jacob married her half-sister, Anne; Radnor 1909, pt. 2, 84. Documents, including correspondence among Frances's guardians, report that she had refused betrothal to Jacob Pleydell-Bouverie and married clandestinely John Bowater in 1775. See A. Ng in Mizrahi and Ng 2026, 43–48.

161 Guillery (2012, 6–7), outlines the debts John amassed for luxuries like furniture, jewelry, perfumes, books, and his art collection, which included paintings by Guido Reni and Adriaen van Ostade.

162 See Smith 2017, 92–93.

163 The position of the present sitter's hands is closer to the half-length portrait of Mrs. Graham (National Gallery of Art, Washington). Cherry and Harris (1982, 304–5) suggested that *Mrs. Graham* derives from Van Dyck's *Countess of Chesterfield*, which was acquired by the 1st Earl of Radnor in 1773 and which Gainsborough would have seen during his stay at Longford Castle. On *Mrs. Graham*, see Belsey 2019, 1: nos. 410–11. For Gainsborough's *Mrs. Graham*'s costume as masquerade wear and as Gainsborough's invention, see Ribeiro 2017, 218–20.

164 On the "curious story" of the portrait's passage from Old Dalby Hall, see Frith 1888, 458–63.

165 Their subsequent daughters Mary and Margaret were born in 1748 and 1751, respectively.

166 On the sitter, see, especially, Sloman 1995/96. A 1744 annuity agreement related to Margaret Burr refers to her living at "Dukes Street near Grosvenor Square," placing her in residence in London and thus suggesting she met Gainsborough there. Sloman (2002, 24) notes that Margaret Burr's name has not been found on lists of ratepayers on that street. The text accompanying the entry in London 1885, no. 80, indicates that Margaret Burr was said to have been of "Scottish extraction, and to have suddenly appeared to the artist while he was painting a landscape in a Suffolk wood, and being very beautiful, to have been, without loss of time, represented in the picture." Fulcher (1856a, 4) writes that she was the sister of a man working for Gainsborough's father in the textile trade.

167 Thicknesse 1788, 8.

168 On Margaret Gainsborough's family, see Sloman 2002, 23–25. Gainsborough's daughter Margaret told Joseph Farington that their mother "was a natural daughter of Henry, Duke of Beaufort, who settled £200 a

yr. upon Her which was paid till the last half year which remains unsettled as she died on the 17th of December last, and it was not due till the 25th"; Farington 1978–98, 4: 1979, 1152. Documents regarding her annuity were published in the appendices to Sloman 1995/96.

169 Sloman 1995/96, 57–58. On Gainsborough's financial situation in Sudbury, see Cormack 1991, 14: "In November 1751 he was negotiating a loan through James Unwin for £400, secured on his wife's annuity of £200 paid through the Duke of Beaufort. He was clearly hard up in Sudbury, and in 1752 he moved to Ipswich, where he also remained short of funds, borrowing money on several further occasions." See also Rosenthal 1999, 16.

170 Hayes 1975, 219. His suggestion ("Tempting to think that it was her fiftieth-birthday portrait") has been repeated by subsequent scholars.

171 See Belsey (2019, 1: nos. 376–79), who also proposes (no. 380) a late painting on board as a fifth independent portrait of her (Christchurch Mansions, Ipswich).

172 Hayes 1975, 219.

173 Kalinsky 1995, 94.

174 Hayes (1975, 219) and subsequent scholars speculate about the difficulties of their marriage, citing letters from Gainsborough that admit to his unfaithfulness and include complaints about his wife.

175 Brown 2001, 78, on Joseph Spence's *Polymetis*, published 1775, a copy of which was in Gainsborough's possession, and Solkin 2000/1. The portrait has been associated with the dual nature of the mythological character Juno as a good but overbearing wife.

176 Hayes 1975, 219.

177 Solkin 2000/1, 75.

178 On the Linley family, see, especially, London 1988a.

179 Ingamells states that the identification of the uniform "seems to hinge on the white patch with a gilt button below his stock"; Ingamells 2008, 132, citing a letter by R. Quarm, in turn citing a Mrs. Blackett Barber at the National Maritime Museum.

180 Pointon 1993, 133.

181 Ingamells 2008, 132, citing an 1858 manuscript by Mr. Denning, no. 361: "Commenced and finished in less than one hour, the authority for this [being] the testimony of his own brother," and noting that Denning "overlapped at Dulwich with Ozias Linley who doubtless told him the story." Fulcher 1856a, 222: "Gainsborough had but one sitting for the portrait of Linley," says Mr. Denning, "and did not paint on the picture an hour. I have authority for this." Murray 1980, 60: "Ms catalogue in the Gallery by S. P. Denning in 1858 records: 'This picture was commenced and finished as it now exists in one sitting, and that sitting less than an hour. The authority for this is the testimony of his own brother.'" By 1903, the legend changed to "forty-eight minutes"; see Gower 1903, 113–114, who also recounts erroneously that "Samuel Linley's end was mysterious; he started on a voyage and never returned." Belsey 2019, 2: 554, on Stephen Poyntz Denning, who was curator at Dulwich from 1821 to 1864.

182 Reynolds 1959, 257–58. L. Stainton in Washington and Los Angeles 1985–86, 60.

183 G. Waterfield in London 1988a, 87, and Ingamells 2008, 132. The *Thunderer* landed at Portsmouth with many of the crew sick; his father brought Samuel to London, where he died in December 1778, three months after his elder brother, Thomas, died in a boating accident.

184 On Christie, see Sutton 1966.

185 *Morning Chronicle*, April 25, 1778.

186 *General Advertiser Morning Intelligencer*, April 27, 1788.

187 Fulcher 1856a, 108.

188 Roberts 1897, 11.

189 Whitley 2016, 135–36.

190 Among the sensationalizing biographies of the sitter are Bleackley 1909 189–244, and Manning 2005. Biographical and family details given in Manning 2005, 27–28, differ from Bleackley 1909, though sources are not given. Manning also notes the text on the sitter in the *Dictionary of National Biography* as being "replete with errors." The birth date of "1748" given in London, Washington, and Boston 2002–3, 126, is incorrect.

191 Bleackley (1909, 195), states that her father sent her to a convent school in Flanders, where she remained until age sixteen, when her father brought her back to London. Her niece Frances, Lady Shelley (1912, 43) instead states that she was sent to a convent school in France.

192 On "Eliot" and "Elliott" see Bleackley 1909, 318, appendix E. Bleackley, 1909, 200 refers to a child born to Grace soon after her marriage but does not offer documentary evidence.

193 Confusingly, Graves (1905, 192), identifies the portraits numbered 114, a whole-length, as "Mrs. Elliott" and 115, a half-length, as "Miss Dalrymple," leading some scholars to propose that the Frick bust portrait of Elliott had been shown at the 1778 Royal Academy exhibition before being shown again in 1782; this does not appear to be correct. The half-length portrait shown as no. 115 has not been identified.

194 Whitley ([1915] 2016, 181) suggested that Elliott may have sat a third time for Gainsborough in 1785 as "Madame St. Alban," a proposal followed by Waterhouse (1953, 37). This was disproved; see Bleackley 1909, 220, and a note dated June 1964 signed by H. Chivian in the curatorial files of the Metropolitan Museum of Art. Belsey (2019, 1: 303) mentions a drawing by Thomas Rowlandson in the Cleveland Museum of Art (1997.84) inscribed "Lady Elliott commonly called Dally the Tall." The depicted sitter, however, bears little resemblance to Gainsborough's depictions of Elliott. A portrait once thought to represent her, previously attributed to Gainsborough, to Gainsborough Dupont, or to an unidentified later artist, is in the Lady Lever Art Gallery, National Museums Liverpool; see Kidson 1999, 77.

195 Cherry and Harris 1982, 302.

196 Ribeiro (1995, 195) suggests black silk necklaces were a revival of Jacobean style that drew attention to the whiteness of skin.

197 Baetjer 2009, 104.

198 Bleackley (1909, 217), suggests the names, which included "Dally the Maypole" and "Dally the Colossus," were also intended to ridicule.

199 E.g., Burke 1976, 216. C. Riding (in London, Washington, and Boston 2002–3, 126) suggests the connection to Lely may be more poignant than Van Dyck and that Gainsborough "sought to evoke the hedonism of the Restoration court, and in particular the mistresses of Charles II." Belsey (2019, 1: 303) stresses the influence of Van Dyck's *Ann Kirk* (Huntington Library, Gardens, and Museum).

200 Cherry and Harris (1982, 296) note that the format used in this and *Queen Charlotte* was employed by Van Dyck.

201 The abandoned dog appears to have been first noted in a report dated July 2, 1931, signed "Pichetto," in the curatorial file of the Metropolitan Museum of Art: "cleaned. A small dog showed up in the right lower corner but was too vague to be preserved. Probably the artist changed mind about putting it in."

202 Hallett 2014, 274.

203 *Morning Chronicle*, April 25, 1778.

204 *General Evening Post*, April 30–May 2, 1778: "A striking and beautiful portrait of an unfortunate lady (Miss D----ple), of whom we may say with Pope, 'If to her share some female errors fall,/ Look on her face, and you'll forget them all.'"

205 *Morning Chronicle*, April 25, 1778: "They were very fit subjects for Mr. Gainsborough's pencil, since he is rather apt to put that sort of complexion upon the countenances of his female portraits, which is laughably described in the School for Scandal as *coming in the morning, and going away at night*, than to blend what is, properly speaking, *nature's own red and white*." The reference to *The School for Scandal* was to Richard Brinsley Sheridan's popular play, a comedy of manners, of the previous year.

206 E.g., Belsey (2019, 1: 303), who also erroneously connects the 1782 review in the *London Courant* ("wanton countenance") to the present portrait rather than to the 1782 bust portrait of Elliott (see cat. 21).

207 On condition, see Baetjer 2009, 102–4.

208 Belsey (2019, 2: 609) includes a transcription of the inscription on her tomb at Bristol Cathedral.

209 Misreading their clothing, Murray (1980, 60) mistook the children for girls.

210 A. Sumner in London 1995, 58.

211 Ingamells (2008, 206) suggested the similarity to Gainsborough's *Mrs. Henry Beaufoy* (Huntington Library, Art Museum, and Botanical Gardens); Belsey 2019, 1: no. 60.

212 Ingamells (2008, 206) commented: "The changes did not enhance the picture. The original graceful figure became a somewhat dysfunctional mother, without her pearls, inconvenienced by her two sons, and looking askance."

213 Ingamells 2008, 206.

214 On Merlin's biography and inventions, see Bauwens 2004; Bryant 2003, no. 47; and A. French in London 1985, 17–46. According to Rimbault (1895, 28), Merlin came to London in 1760 with the Count de Fuentes, who was the Spanish ambassador.

215 On Merlin's inventions, see M. Wright in London 1985, 47–59.

216 On Merlin and music, see E. Palmer in London 1985, 85–96.

217 Burney 1907, 53. Reynolds's portrait of Charles Burney is today in the National Portrait Gallery, London.

218 London 1782, no. 43, as *Portrait of a Gentleman*. According to Whitley ([1915] 2016, 219–20), the *St. James's Chronicle* offered a tepid review ("the subject affords no great scope for genius").

219 *London Courant*, May 1, 1782.

220 L. Stainton in London 1977 (unpaginated), no. 11. Bryant (2003, 211), suggests that as a customer, Gainsborough "may have painted the present portrait for Merlin by way of payment."

221 On Merlin's scales, for which an advertisement survives in the British Museum, see A. French and M. Wright in London 1985, 71.

222 A. French (in London 1985, 23) notes that the "abiding impression of Fanny Burney's *Diary* is that Merlin remained, to a large extent, an outsider."

223 A. French in London 1985, no. A1, 33.

224 Bowes Museum, Barnard Castle, County Durham (2016.1/BM). Belsey 2019, 2: no. 631.

225 On Merlin's will, see London 1985, 14–16, 122; on the museum remaining open until midsummer 1808, 15.

226 L. Stainton in London 1977, no. 11. Waterhouse (1958, 70, no. 312) had expressed uncertainty about the identification of the sitter as Giardini. On Giardini's portrait (Knole House, Kent), see Belsey 2019, 1: no. 395.

227 Baetjer (2009, 102), emphasizes the present portrait as "A very much more seductive and private image" than the full-length.

228 Grace Dalrymple Elliott's niece Frances, Lady Shelley, recounts meeting her aunt once in 1803, whom she described as "the most beautiful woman I had ever beheld"; she was "dressed in the indecent style of the French republican period," with "transparent drapery . . . over a bust of ivory"; Shelley 1912, 1: 42.

229 Noting the rarity of English portraits of identified sitters wearing patches, possibly because of patches' associations with vulgarity, Ribeiro (2011, 194–6) suggests Elliott may wear a patch. Regarding the practice of artificially darkening eyebrows, Manning (2005, 22) notes her hair was "dark blond or light brown, apparently, from a lock of hers preserved on the back of a locket-shaped miniature portrait in a private collection"; "her eyebrows are dark and no doubt enhanced by black frankincense, resin or mastic. . . . Rubbing the eyebrows with burnt cork, burnt cloves, or elderberry juice would also darken them."

230 Lady Shelley (1912, 1: 42) mentions her made-up appearance: "Tears were rolling down her cheeks; this heightened her beauty without defacing the rouge which had been artistically applied. . . . The odour of musk enchanted me."

231 *London Courant*, May 9, 1782.

232 He had exhibited portraits of the king and queen in 1781.

233 *Morning Herald and Daily Advertiser*, December 24, 1781: "The *Dalrymple* has declared herself *pregnant*, and taken care to have it well understood that Lord C----y cannot possibly lay claim to a single feature of the *amorous produce*, be it what it may; solemnly averring upon her *honor*, that his Lordship was totally effaced from her memory before she had the faintest *conception* of the bliss that now awaits her! However difficult it may be to a'certain [sic] it's [sic] *real sire*, one is already named for it, who is said to be extremely flattered by the *novelty of the title*, and has already given orders that the *ceremonies of the straw* be supported with the utmost *magnificence*, and *eclat*!" Bleackley (1909, 219) discusses the July 30, 1782, baptism at St. Marylebone Church, for which the register records: "the daughter of His Royal Highness George, Prince of Wales."

234 Just two weeks before the opening of the exhibition, Gainsborough had withdrawn his portraits of the Duke of Dorset (who objected to his picture being exhibited alongside Gainsborough's full-length of his mistress, Giovanna Baccelli) and of Mary Robinson, who, it was reported in the daily papers, had just accepted £10,000 as hush money from the Prince of Wales in exchange for not publicizing his letters to her. See Perry 2007, 65–66.

235 *Public Advertiser*, May 2, 1782. See Solkin 2000/1, 115–16, and Conway 2001, 40–41.

236 The head of Mrs. Fitzherbert, instead, was noted specifically as having been "delivered unfinished by His Highness's orders"; see cat. 22.

237 For a biography of the sitter, see Wilkins 1905.

238 The Act of Settlement of 1701 and Royal Marriages Act of 1772 restricted the prince's options to marry a Catholic, to marry without the monarch's consent, and to do so when under the age of twenty-five.

239 Belsey (2019, 2: no. 898), suggests that the commission of *Miss Elizabeth Tyler* by her lover, John, Viscount Bateman, "goes some way to explain the intimate pose and the element of *déshabillé*."

240 Monkhouse 1897, 35. Walker 1992, 97 (cited in Belsey 2019, 1: 319), recounts: "It is not known why the portrait remained unfinished. Family tradition is divided and states that the sitter was dissatisfied with the length of her 'resolute chin and aquiline nose.'"

241 Waterhouse 1946, 276; Millar 1969, 35.

242 Millar 1969, 35: recorded in store at Carlton House in 1816 (327, measurements given as 29½ x 24½ in).

243 On "The Linley Cult," see G. Waterfield in London 1988a, 31–38. See also Christensen and Luciano 2013, 238.

244 Samuel Foote's *The Maid of Bath*, 1771.

245 For the portrait of their son Tom (1775–1817), see Belsey 2019, 2: no. 815.

246 Belsey (2019, 2: no. 814) proposes five, including a lost clay head (on which see Thicknesse 1788, 39–40). The three other extant portraits of Elizabeth are *Elizabeth and Thomas Linley*, 1768 (Clark Art Institute, Williamstown); *Mrs. Sheridan*, ca. 1775 (Philadelphia Museum of Art); *The Linley Sisters*, 1772 and 1785 (Dulwich Picture Gallery, London). Christensen and Luciano (2013, 238) propose six, including a lost 1783 full-length portrait and one (possibly two) now-lost clay heads. On the possibility of two clay heads, see Gower 1903, 63.

247 *Morning Herald*, March 30, 1785. Fulcher (1856a, 123–24) identified the present portrait with that shown in 1783. Whitley ([1915] 2016, 230–31) suggested that the 1783 portrait is lost and that the present portrait was commenced in 1785 and shown at Schomberg House in 1785. Christensen and Luciano (2013, 240) suggest that the newspaper (cited but not identified by Whitley [1915] 2016, 291, of spring 1786), referring to the "new portrait of Mrs. Sheridan" precludes the portrait having been already exhibited in 1783; however, Belsey (2019, 2: 758), revising a previous position on the dating (H. Belsey in San Marino 2013, 73), suggests that the reworked 1783 portrait was shown in 1786 as if it were a new painting. Waterhouse (1958, 89) wrote that it is "Probably R.A. 1783 (140), but it may have been begun as early as 1774, and Gainsborough was certainly still working on it in 1785; it remains not quite finished."

248 Belsey (2012, 126) suggested Richardson misidentified the portrait; later (2019, 2: 758) he corrects this proposal and suggests that she either misidentified the lamb as a dog or conflated the description with a portrait of Mrs. "Perdita" Robinson. The reference to a "River & Cascade" brings to mind Gainsborough's *Lady Brisco* (English Heritage, Kenwood House, London), which features a prominent waterfall, as well as a dog at the subject's feet.

249 Letter of January 1786 from Betsy Sheridan to Alicia LeFanu; see W. LeFanu, 1986, 80, cited in Christensen and Luciano 2013, 240n.19.

250 *Morning Herald*, December 30, 1786.

251 *The World*, March 26, 1788.

252 In their analysis of examination results, Christensen and Luciano (2013, 240) describe the shape evident at the lower right corner in the X-radiograph as a "lamb or other small animal nestled at her feet."

253 *Public Advertiser*, May 29, 1783.

254 Belsey 2019, 2: no. 590.

255 Hayes 1975, 225.

256 On the portrait, see Belsey 2019, 1: no. 366.

257 Early portraits in Houghton Hall and the National Portrait Gallery show him with his hand tucked into his waistcoat; Belsey 2019, 1: nos. 369–70. X-radiography reveals that the portrait now in the Courtauld Gallery, the attribution of which has been variously given in whole and in part to Gainsborough Dupont, originally portrayed him with a similar gesture; Belsey 2019, 1: no. 371. Besides the family portrait in the National Gallery, London (Belsey 2019, 1: no. 368), the conversation piece in the Louvre (ibid. no. 367) has been proposed to represent Gainsborough and his wife, among other subjects.

258 He wears nearly identical clothing in portraits of another type known in three versions; Belsey 2019, 1: nos. 372–74.

259 Hayes 2001, 175.

260 Whitley (2016, 339–40) records an announcement made in May 1788: "We state with infinite regret that Mr Gainsborough has been for some weeks past so much indisposed as to be unable to exercise his pencil. His indisposition proceeds from a violent cold caught in Westminster Hall [at the trial of Warren Hastings]; the glands of his neck have been in consequence so much inflamed as to require the aid of Mr John Hunter and Dr Heberden. The friendly attention of the latter is almost without intermission, and from Mr Hunter's skill it is hoped that ten days or a fortnight may restore him to the practice of that science of which he is so distinguished an ornament."

261 A. Griffiths (in London 1978, 40–41) writes that Gainsborough's "style of painting was an engraver's nightmare."

262 Suggesting that the other portrait may have been the Courtauld picture, Belsey (2019, 1: 359) cites (with thanks to Susan Sloman) the letter from Mary Gainsborough to Bartolozzi in Tuer 1882, 2: 138: "She [Mary Gainsborough] is sure that so great an artist as Mr. B[artolozzi] will see what she means respecting the nose, etc., as she thinks this picture more like her father than the other."

263 On Gainsborough's portrait of the 11th Duke of Norfolk, see Belsey 2019, 2: no. 681.

264 On the 11th Duke's wife, Frances Scudamore: "The Scudamores had a strain of hereditary madness which shortly after the wedding made its appearance in the Duchess and she had to be confined as a lunatic at Holme Lacy for the whole of her life. She outlived the duke by five years so it was impossible for him to remarry or to have a legitimate son to succeed him. He consoled himself with a series of mistresses, one of whom eventually became his 'official mistress,' Mary Gibbon. . . . They had six children, two of whom were appointed to the College of Arms as heralds"; Robinson 1995, 172–73.

265 *Morning Post*, May 21, 1788. Above this notice was printed: "The report, which has contracted Mr. Howard to the Hon. Miss Petre [sister of the Howards' sister's husband], is not true." Both notices probably refer to Bernard Howard as the eldest of his brothers, Henry Thomas and Edward Charles. Their sister, Lady Petre, was painted by Gainsborough in March and April of 1788; Belsey 2019, 2: no. 719.

266 Whitley [1915] 2016, 339–40; see note 260 above.

267 On the Norfolk family, see Robinson 1995.

268 Robinson 1995, 171.

269 Ibid., 193–94: "He did not sue for damages and made it clear that he considered all the parties 'free from any severe censure.'"

270 Robinson 1995, 191.

Abel sale 1787
Catalogue of the Capital Collection of Manuscripts and Other Music, an exceeding valuable and fine-toned Viol de Gamba, a Forte-Piano by Buntebart, a Violin, etc. A Number of fine Drawings, and four pictures by Mr. Gainsborough; several gold snuff boxes, and watches, plate, trinkets, fine Dresden China, etc. Of Charles Frederick Abel, Esq. Sale cat. Greenwood, London, December 12–13, 1787.

Adams 2002
Adams, Ann Jensen. "Competing Communities in the 'Great Bog of Europe': Identity and Seventeenth-Century Dutch Landscape Painting." In *Landscape and Power*, edited by W. J. T. Mitchell, 35–71. 2nd ed. Chicago and London, 2002.

Aljoe and Huang 2025
Aljoe, Nicole, and Kristina Huang, eds. *Cambridge Companion to Ignatius Sancho.* Cambridge, 2025.

Allen 1991
Allen, Brian. "The Age of Hogarth 1720–1760." In *The British Portrait, 1660–1960*, by Sir Roy Strong, Richard Charlton-Jones, Kenneth McConkey, Christopher Newall, Martin Postle, Frances Spalding, and John Wilson. Woodbridge, 1991.

Allen 2005
Allen, Denise. "In Focus: Gainsborough's 'Sarah, Lady Innes.'" *The Frick Collection Members' Magazine* 5, no. 3 (Fall 2005): 10.

American Art News 1911
"Frick Collection Enriched." *American Art News* 9, no. 32 (June 1911): 1.

Amsterdam 1936
Twee Eeuwen Engelsche Kunst. Exh. cat. Amsterdam (Stedelijk Museum te Amsterdam), 1936.

Angelo 1904
Angelo, Henry. *The Reminiscences of Henry Angelo, Illustrated and Reproduced from Originals in the Collection of Joseph Greco.* 2 vols. London, 1904.

Armstrong 1898
Armstrong, Walter. *Gainsborough and His Place in English Art.* New York, 1898.

Armstrong 1904
Armstrong, Walter. *Gainsborough and His Place in English Art.* London, 1904.

Art of Beauty 1760
The Art of Beauty, Or, a Companion for the Toilet . . . . London, 1760.

Art Journal 1911
"Two Unrecorded Gainsboroughs." *Art Journal* (1911): 423–24.

Art News 1938
"The Harding Collection: A Document of American Taste." *Art News* 37, no. 11 (December 10, 1938): 14–15.

Art News 1946
"Gainsborough." *Art News* 45, no. 9 (1946): 35.

Asfour and Williamson 1999
Asfour, Amal, and Paul Williamson. *Gainsborough's Vision.* Liverpool, 1999.

Asleson and Bennett 2001
Asleson, Robyn, and Shelley M. Bennett. *British Paintings at The Huntington.* New Haven and London, 2001.

Badea-Päun 2007
Badea-Päun, Gabriel. *The Society Portrait from David to Warhol.* New York, 2007.

Baetjer 1999
Baetjer, Katharine. "British Portraits in the MMA." *Metropolitan Museum of Art Bulletin* 57, no. 1 (Summer 1999): 1, 5–72.

Baetjer 2009
Baetjer, Katharine. *British Paintings in the Metropolitan Museum of Art, 1575–1875.* New York, 2009.

Baker 1933
Baker, C. H. Collins. *British Painting.* Boston, 1933.

Baker 1936
Baker, C. H. Collins. *Catalogue of British Paintings in the Henry E. Huntington Library and Art Gallery.* Chicago, 1936.

Barnes 2004
Barnes, Susan J. *Van Dyck: A Complete Catalogue of Paintings.* New Haven, 2004.

Barrow 1838
Barrow, John. *The Life of Richard, Earl Howe, K. G., Admiral of the Fleet, and General of Marines.* London, 1838.

Bath 1995
"A Nest of Nightingales": The Linley Family and Musical Life in 18th Century Bath. Exh. cat. Bath (Holburne Museum and Crafts Study Centre), 1995.

Bath 2019
Hugh Belsey and Susan Sloman. *Gainsborough and Theatre.* Exh. cat. Bath (Holburne Museum), 2019.

Bath and other cities 1949
Mary Woodall. *An Exhibition of Paintings: Thomas Gainsborough.* Bath (Bath Assembly), Ipswich, Worcester, York, Bolton, and Darlington (venues unknown), 1949.

Bauwens 2004
Bauwens, Pierre. "Jean-Joseph Merlin, Hutois, inventeur génial à Londres." In *Hutois inventeur du roller: Jean-Joseph Merlin & la fabuleuse histoire du patin à roulettes*, 11–25. Ville de Huy, 2004.

Bede 1889
Bede, Cuthbert. "Gainsborough's 'Master Heathcote.'" *The Boy's Own Annual* (1889): 776–77.

Bedford 1954
Paintings by Thomas Gainsborough, RA, 1727–1788. Exh. cat. Castle Close, Bedford (Cecil Higgins Museum), 1954.

Bell 1897
Bell, Mrs. Arthur. *Thomas Gainsborough: A Record of His Life and Works by Mrs. Arthur Bell (N. D'Anvers) with illustrations reproduced for the most part direct from the original paintings.* London, 1897.

Belsey 2002
Belsey, Hugh. *Thomas Gainsborough: A Country Life.* Prestel, 2002.

Belsey 2012
Belsey, Hugh. "Some Artists' Studios Described in 1785." In *Windows on That World: Essays on British Art Presented to Brian Allen*, 113–42. London, 2012.

Belsey 2014
Belsey, Hugh. "New Documents by Thomas Gainsborough." *Burlington Magazine* 156, no. 1334 (2014): 303–6.

Belsey 2019
Belsey, Hugh. *Thomas Gainsborough: The Portraits, Fancy Pictures and Copies after Old Masters.* 2 vols. New Haven and London, 2019.

Bennett 2013
Bennett, Shelley M. *The Art of Wealth: The Huntingtons in the Gilded Age.* San Marino, 2013.

Bensusan-Butt 1992/93
Bensusan-Butt, John. "The Carters and the Andrews." *Gainsborough's House Review* (1992/93): 33–37.

Bensusan-Butt 1993
Bensusan-Butt, John. *Thomas Gainsborough in His Twenties: A Memorandum Based on Contemporary Sources.* 3rd ed. Colchester, 1993.

Berger 1972
Berger, John. *Ways of Seeing.* Harmondsworth, Middlesex, 1972.

Berlin 1908
Ausstellung Älterer Englischer Kunst. Exh. cat. Berlin (Königliche Akademie der Künste), 1908.

Bermingham 1986
Bermingham, Ann. *Landscape and Ideology.* Los Angeles, 1986.

Bermingham 1995
Bermingham, Ann. "The Consumption of Culture: Image, Object, Text." In *The Consumption of Culture, 1600–1800*, edited by Ann Bermingham and John Brewer, 1–12. London, 1995.

Bills 2018
Bills, Mark. "The Gainsborough Family: 'With Something Mysterious in His History.'" In Bills and Jones 2018, 17–25.

Bills and Jones 2018
Bills, Mark, and Rica Jones. *Early Gainsborough: "From the Obscurity of a Country Town."* Sudbury, 2018.

Birmingham and Toronto 1995
Paul Spencer-Longhurst and Janet M. Brooke. *Thomas Gainsborough: The Harvest Wagon.* Exh. cat. Birmingham (Birmingham Museum and Art Gallery) and Toronto (Art Gallery of Ontario), 1995.

Bleackley 1909
Bleackley, Horace. *Ladies Fair and Frail: Sketches of the Demi-Monde During the Eighteenth Century.* London 1909.

Boggs 1971
Boggs, Jean Sutherland. *The National Gallery of Canada.* Toronto, 1971.

Bomford, Roy, and Saunders 1998
Bomford, David, Ashok Roy, and David Saunders. "Gainsborough's 'Dr. Ralph Schomberg.'" *National Gallery Technical Bulletin* 12 (1998): 44–57.

Bordeaux 1962
Gilberte Martin-Méry. *L'Art du Canada.* Exh. cat. Bordeaux (Musées Classés de Bordeaux), 1962.

Borenius 1926
Borenius, Tancred. "The Michelman Collection." *Apollo* 4 (1926): 139–40.

Boston 1928
Exhibition of Paintings loaned by Governor Alvan T. Fuller. Exh. cat. Boston (Boston Art Club), 1928.

Boston 1939
Paintings, Drawings, Prints, from Private Collections in New England. Exh. cat. Boston (Museum of Fine Arts, Boston), 1939.

Boston 1959
Memorial Exhibition of the Collection of the Honorable Alvan T. Fuller. Exh. cat. Boston (Museum of Fine Arts, Boston), 1959.

Boulton 1905
Boulton, William B. *Thomas Gainsborough: His Life, Work, Friends, and Sitters.* Chicago and London, 1905.

Brenneman 2003
Brenneman, David A. "Thomas Gainsborough and the 'Thin Brilliant Style of Pencilling of Vandyke.'" *Huntington Library Quarterly* 66, nos. 1–2 (2003): 80–95.

Brewer 1997
Brewer, John. *The Pleasures of the Imagination: English Culture in the Eighteenth Century.* New York, 1997.

Brewer 2011
Brewer, David A. "Review of Thomas Gainsborough and the Modern Woman, by Benedict Leca, Aileen Ribeiro, and Amber Ludwig." *Eighteenth-Century Studies* 44, no. 4 (Summer 2011): 569–72.

Bridge 1919–20
Bridge, James Howard. *Pictures in the Collection of Henry Clay Frick, at One East Seventieth Street, New York.* New York, 1919–20.

Brock-Arnold 1881
Brock-Arnold, George M. *Gainsborough.* London, 1881.

Brown 1913
Brown, Eric. "The National Gallery of Canada at Ottawa." *Studio* 58 (1913): 15–21.

Brown 2001
Brown, Hilary S. "Gainsborough's Classically Ambivalent Wife." *British Art Journal* 3, no. 1 (Autumn 2001): 78–79.

Brussels 1929
Exposition Rétrospective de Peinture Anglaise (XVIIIe et XIXe siècles). Exh. cat. Brussels (Musée Moderne), 1929.

Brussels 1973
Treasures from Country Houses of the National Trust and the National Trust of Scotland. Exh. cat. Brussels (Palais des Beaux-Arts), 1973.

Bryant 2003
Bryant, Julius. *Kenwood: Paintings in the Iveagh Bequest.* New Haven and London, 2003.

Buccleuch and Queensberry 2012
Buccleuch and Queensberry, Duke of. *Bowhill: The House, Its People, and Its Paintings.* Hawick, 2012.

Buccleuch and Queensberry 2022
Buccleuch and Queensberry, Duke of. *Boughton: The House, Its People, and Its Collections.* Hawick, 2022.

Buck 1979
Buck, Anne. *Dress in Eighteenth-Century England.* London, 1979.

Burke 1976
Burke, Joseph. *English Art, 1714–1800.* Oxford, 1976.

Burney 1907
Burney, Frances. *The Early Diary of Frances Burney, 1768–1778.* Edited by Annie Raine Ellis. 2 vols. London, 1907.

Burney 2001
Burney, Frances. *Journals and Letters.* Edited by Peter Sabor and Lars E. Troide. London, 2001.

Cambridge 1803
Cambridge, Richard Owen. *The Works of Richard Owen Cambridge, esq., Including Several Pieces Never Before Published, with an Account of his Life and Character by his Son, George Owen Cambridge, M. A.* London, 1803.

Cambridge 1930
Exhibition of Eighteenth Century English Painting. Exh. cat. Cambridge, MA (Fogg Art Museum), 1930.

Campbell 1969
Campbell, R. *The London Tradesman.* London, 1747. Repr. New York, 1969.

Carretta 2004
Carretta, Vincent. "(Charles) Ignatius Sancho." *Oxford Dictionary of National Biography.* Article published online September 23, 2004. Accessed June 28, 2023. https://www.oxforddnb.com/view/10.1093/ref:odnb/9780198614128.001.0001/odnb-9780198614128-e-24609

Carter 1926
Carter, A. C. R. "Forthcoming Auctions." *Burlington Magazine for Connoisseurs* 49, no. 283 (October 1926): xxxix–xliii.

Chamberlain 1903
Chamberlain, Arthur B. *Thomas Gainsborough.* London, 1903.

Chambers 1829
Chambers, John. *A General History of the County of Norfolk.* 2 vols. Norwich, 1829.

Charleston 1999
Marie D. McInnis with Angela D. Mack, eds. *In Pursuit of Refinement: Charlestonians Abroad, 1740–1860.* Exh. cat. Charleston (Gibbes Museum of Art), 1999.

Chater 2009
Chater, Kathleen. *Untold Histories: Black People in England and Wales during the Period of British Slave Trade, c. 1660–1807.* Manchester and New York, 2009.

Cherry and Harris 1982
Cherry, Deborah, and Jennifer Harris. "Eighteenth-Century Portraiture and the Seventeenth-Century Past: Gainsborough and Van Dyck." *Art History* 5, no. 3 (September 1982): 287–309.

Christensen and Luciano 2013
Christensen, Carol, and Eleonora Luciano. "The Evolution of Gainsborough's Portrait of Elizabeth Sheridan." *Burlington Magazine* 155, no. 1321 (April 2013): 238–42.

Chu 2016
Chu, John. "Un aller-retour pour Knole: Thomas Gainsborough's Portrait of Louis-Pierre, Marquis de Champcenetz." *National Trust Historic Houses & Collections Annual,* published in association with *Apollo* (2016): 53–59.

Chu 2017
Chu, John, ed. "In Focus: Peter Darnell Muilman, Charles Crokatt and William Keable in a Landscape, ca. 1750, by Thomas Gainsborough." *Tate Research Publication,* 2017. Accessed July 18, 2023. www.tate.org.uk/research/in-focus/muilman-crokatt-ke-able-thomas-gainsborough.

Cincinnati 1931
Exhibition of Paintings and Drawings by Thomas Gainsborough, R.A. Exh. cat. Cincinnati (Cincinnati Art Museum), 1931.

Cincinnati and San Diego 2010–11
Benedict Leca. *Thomas Gainsborough and the Modern Woman.* Exh. cat. Cincinnati (Cincinnati Art Museum) and San Diego (San Diego Museum of Art), 2010–11.

Clarke 1830
Clarke, G. R. *The History and Description of the Town and Borough of Ipswich.* London, 1830.

Clifford 2004
Clifford, Helen. *Silver in London: The Parker and Wakelin Partnership, 1760–1776.* New Haven, 2004.

Cole 1997
Cole, Michael. "Gainsborough's Diversions." *Word & Image* 13, no. 4 (October–December 1997): 366–76.

Comstock 1936
Comstock, Helen. "The Connoisseur in America." *Connoisseur* 97, no. 414 (1936): 97–101.

Comstock 1941
Comstock, Helen. "The Connoisseur in America." *Connoisseur* 108, no. 479 (1941): 28–35.

Conway 2001
Conway, Alison. *Private Interests: Women, Portraiture, and the Visual Culture of the English Novel, 1709–1791*. Toronto, 2001.

Copenhagen 2009–10
Hanne Kolind Poulsen and Henrik Holm. *Nature Strikes Back: Man and Nature in Western Art*. Exh. cat. Copenhagen (Statens Museum for Kunst), 2009–10.

Cormack 1985
Cormack, Malcolm. *A Concise Catalogue of Paintings in the Yale Center for British Art*. New Haven, 1985.

Cormack 1991
Cormack, Malcolm. *The Paintings of Thomas Gainsborough*. Cambridge, 1991.

Cornforth 1983
Cornforth, John. "Cobham Hall, Kent—II." *Country Life* 173 (March 3, 1983): 508–71.

Corri 1983
Corri, Adrienne. "Gainsborough's Early Career: New Documents and Two Portraits." *Burlington Magazine* 125, no. 961 (April 1983): 210–16.

Craven 2009
Craven, Wayne. *Gilded Mansions: Grand Architecture and High Society*. New York, 2009.

Crewe 2013
Crewe, Lady Frances, ed. *Letters of the Late Ignatius Sancho, an African: To Which Are Prefixed, Memoirs of His Life, 1782*. Cambridge, 2013.

Cummins 2010
Cummins, Genevieve E. *How the Watch Was Worn: A Fashion of 500 Years*. Woodbridge, 2010.

Cunningham 1829–33
Cunningham, Allan. *The Lives of the Most Eminent British Painters, Sculptors, and Architects*. 6 vols. London, 1829–33.

Cyr 1987
Cyr, Mary. "Abel's Solos: A Musical Offering to Gainsborough?" *The Musical Times* 128, no. 1732 (1987): 317–21.

Dallas 1938
British Portraits of the Eighteenth Century. Exh. cat. Dallas (Dallas Museum of Fine Arts), 1938.

Daniels 1981
Daniels, Jeffrey. "Gainsborough the European." *Connoisseur* 206 (February 1981): 110–15.

Darnley sale 1925
Property of the Rt. Hon. The Earl of Darnley removed from Cobham Hall, Kent. Sale cat. Christie, Manson & Woods, London, May 1, 1925.

Davidson 1968
Davidson, Bernice. *American, British, Dutch, Flemish, and German*. Vol. 1 of *The Frick Collection: An Illustrated Catalogue*. New York, 1968.

Davis 1972
Davis, Frank. "An Early Gainsborough Revealed." *Country Life* 152 (September 1972): 556.

Davisson 1946
Davisson, Gay Drake. *Bulletin of the California Palace of the Legion of Honor* 4, nos. 3–4 (July and August 1946): 26–31.

Detroit 1963
Masterpieces from Canadian Museums. Exh. cat. Detroit (Detroit Institute of Art), 1963.

Dibdin 1923
Dibdin, E. Rimbault. *Thomas Gainsborough, 1727–1788*. London and New York, 1923.

Dorment 1986
Dorment, Richard. *British Painting in the Philadelphia Museum of Art: From the Seventeenth through the Nineteenth Century*. Philadelphia, 1896.

Dossie 1758
Dossie, Robert. *The Handmaid to the Arts*. London, 1758.

Dublin 1861
Official Catalogue of the Exhibition of Fine Arts, 1861. Exh. cat. Dublin (New Hall), 1861.

Duff Gordon 1932
Duff-Gordon, Lady Lucy. *Discretions & Indiscretions*. London, 1932.

Duveen 1941
Duveen Brothers. *Duveen Pictures in Public Collections of America*. New York, 1941.

Edinburgh 2003
Hugh Belsey. *Gainsborough's Beautiful Mrs. Graham*. Exh. cat. Edinburgh (National Gallery of Scotland), 2003.

Editorial 1944
"Editorial: Gainsborough's Collection of Paintings." *Burlington Magazine* 84, no. 494 (1944): 106–10.

Edwards 1808
Edwards, Edward. *Anecdotes of Painters who have Resided or been Born in England: With Critical Remarks on Their Productions*. London, 1808.

Egerton 1998
Egerton, Judy. *National Gallery Catalogues: The British School*. London, 1998.

Engravings 1874–75
Engravings from the Works of Thomas Gainsborough. Vol. 1. London, 1874–75.

Equiano 2003
Equiano, Olaudah. *The Interesting Narrative and Other Writings*. Edited by Vincent Carretta. London, 2003.

Erskine 1954
Erskine, David. *Augustus Hervey's Journal: Being the Intimate Account of the Life of a Captain in the Royal Navy Ashore and Afloat, 1746–1759*. 2nd edition. London, 1954.

Estrangin 1930
Estrangin, H. Fritsch. "Review: Retrospective Exhibition of British Art in Brussels." *American Magazine of Art* 21, no. 1 (January 1930): 39–41.

Evans 1985
Evans, Nesta. *The East Anglian Linen Industry: Rural Industry and Local Economy, 1500–1850*. Pasold Studies in Textile History, vol. 5. Aldershot, Hants, England and Brookfield, VT, 1985.

Fairfax Murray 1894
Fairfax Murray, Charles. *Catalogue of the Pictures Belonging to His Grace the Duke of Portland, at Welbeck Abbey, and in London*. London, 1894.

Farington 1978–98
Farington, Joseph. *The Diary of Joseph Farington*. Edited by Kenneth Garlick, Angus D. Macintyre, and Kathryn Cave. 16 vols. New Haven, 1978–98.

Farrer 1908
Farrer, Rev. Edmund. *Portraits in Suffolk Houses (West)*. London, 1908.

Ferrara 1998
John Hayes, ed. *Thomas Gainsborough*. Exh. cat. Ferrara (Palazzo dei Diamanti), 1998.

Fielding 1742
Fielding, Henry. *History of the Adventures of Joseph Andrews, and His Friend Mr. Abraham Adams*. Vol. 1. London, 1742.

Fletcher 1904
Fletcher, A. E. *Thomas Gainsborough, RA*. London, 1904.

Foister 1997
Foister, Susan. "Young Gainsborough and the English Taste for Dutch Landscape." In London, Norwich, and Newcastle 1997, 3–11.

Folkestone 1967
18th Century Painting, Covering the Period 1720–1820, including works by Opie, Romney, Constable, Alexander and Turner. Exh. cat. Folkestone (New Metropole Arts Centre), 1967.

Fowles 1976
Fowles, Edward. *Memories of Duveen Brothers*. London, 1976.

Fredericksen 1972
Fredericksen, Burton B. *Catalogue of the Paintings in the J. Paul Getty Museum*. Los Angeles, 1972.

Fredericton 1991
Ian G. Lumsden. *Gainsborough in Canada*. Exh. cat. Fredericton (Beaverbrook Art Gallery), 1991.

Frith 1888
Frith, William Powell. *My Autobiography and Reminiscences*. New York, 1888.

Fry 1934
Fry, Roger. *Reflections on British Painting*. London, 1934.

Fulcher 1856a
Fulcher, George Williams. *Life of Thomas Gainsborough by the Late George Williams Fulcher, edited by His Son*. London, 1856.

Fulcher 1856b
Fulcher, George Williams. *Life of Thomas Gainsborough by the Late George Williams Fulcher, edited by His Son*. 2nd ed. London, 1856.

Gent, Roy, and Morrison 2014
Gent, Alexandra, Ashok Roy, and Rachel Morrison. "Practice Makes Imperfect: Reynolds's Painting Technique." *National Gallery Technical Bulletin* 35 (2014): 12–31.

Gerzina 2022
Gerzina, Gretchen. *Black London: Life Before Emancipation.* New Brunswick, NJ, 1995. Revised ed., *Black England: A Forgotten Georgian History.* London, 2022.

Glanville 1988
Glanville, Helen. "Gainsborough as Artist and Artisan." In London 1988a, 15–33.

Gockel 1999
Gockel, Bettina. *Kunst und Politik der Farbe: Gainsboroughs Potraitmalerie.* Berlin, 1999.

Goldyne 1980
Goldyne, Joseph R. "British Art at San Francisco." *Apollo* 111, no. 217 (March 1980): 112–92.

Goodison 1977
Goodison, J. W. *British School.* Vol. 3 of *Fitzwilliam Museum: Catalogue of Paintings.* Cambridge, 1977.

Govier 2010
Govier, Louise. *Hogarth to Turner: British Painting.* London, 2010.

Gower 1903
Gower, Lord Ronald Sutherland, FSA. *Thomas Gainsborough.* London, 1903.

Graves 1905
Graves, Algernon. *The Royal Academy of Art: A Complete Dictionary of Contributors and their Work from its Foundation in 1769 to 1904.* Vol. 3. London, 1905.

Green 1982
Green, Timothy R. "Thomas Gainsborough 'Pomeranian Bitch and Puppy.'" In *Completing the Picture: Materials and Techniques of Twenty-Six Paintings in the Tate Gallery,* edited by Stephen Hackney, 23–25. London, 1982.

Greig 2013
Greig, Hannah. *The Beau Monde: Fashionable Society in Georgian London.* Oxford, 2013.

Guillery 2012
Guillery, Peter. *Woolwich.* Vol. 48 of *Survey of London.* New Haven and London, 2012.

Gunn 1973
Gunn, Fenja. *The Artificial Face: A History of Cosmetics.* New York, 1973.

Gunnersbury 1776
Gunnersbury, Amelia. *Memoirs of a Demi-Rep of Fashion.* Vol. 1. Dublin, 1776.

Hall 1994
Hall, Michael. "The English Rothschilds as Collectors." In *The Rothschilds: Essays on the History of a European Family,* edited by Georg Heuberger, 265–86. Woodbridge, 1994.

Hallett 2014
Hallett, Mark. *Reynolds: Portraiture in Action.* New Haven and London, 2014.

Hamburg 2018
Christoph Martin Votherr and Katharina Hoins, eds. *Thomas Gainsborough: The Modern Landscape.* Exh. cat. Hamburg (Hamburg Kunstalle), 2018.

Hamburg and other cities 1949–50
British Painting from Hogarth to Turner. Exh. cat. Hamburg (Kunsthalle), Oslo (Kunstnernes Hus), Stockholm (Nationalmuseum), and Copenhagen (Statens Museum for Kunst), 1949–50.

Hamilton 2017
Hamilton, James. *Gainsborough: A Portrait.* London, 2017.

Hartford 1937
A. Everett Austin. *43 Portraits: An Exhibition of the Wadsworth Atheneum.* Exh. cat. Hartford (Wadsworth Atheneum), 1937.

Haslewood 1884
Haslewood, Rev. Francis. *The Monumental Inscriptions, in the Parish of Saint Matthew, Ipswich, Suffolk.* Ipswich, 1884.

Hayes 1965
Hayes, John. "Some Unknown Early Gainsborough Portraits." *Burlington Magazine* 107, no. 743 (February 1965): 62, 64–74.

Hayes 1975
Hayes, John. *Gainsborough: Paintings and Drawings.* London, 1975.

Hayes 1982
Hayes, John. *The Landscape Paintings of Thomas Gainsborough: A Critical Text and Catalogue Raisonné.* Vol. 1. Ithaca, 1982.

Hayes 1983
Hayes, John. "Four Gainsboroughs for the Nation." *National Art-Collections Fund. Review 1983* 109 (1983): 98–100.

Hayes 1992
Hayes, John. *British Paintings of the Sixteenth through Nineteenth Centuries.* Washington, DC, 1992.

Hayes 1993
Hayes, John. "The Theory and Practice of British Eighteenth-Century Portraiture." In *The Portrait in Eighteenth-Century America,* edited by Ellen Gross Miles, 19–32. Newark and London, 1993.

Hayes 2001
Hayes, John, ed. *The Letters of Thomas Gainsborough.* New Haven and London, 2001.

Heilmann 1978
Heilmann, Christoph. "Zu Gainsborough Bildnis der 'Mrs. Thomas Hibbert.'" *Pantheon International Art Journal* 36 (1978): 222–30.

Hellen and Gent 2017
Hellen, Rebecca, and Alexandra Gent. "Painting the Picture. Peter Darnell Muilman, Charles Crokatt and William Keable in a Landscape, ca. 1750, by Thomas Gainsborough." *Tate Research Publication,* 2017. Accessed July 18, 2023. www.tate.org.uk/research/in-focus/muilman-crokatt-keable-thomas-gainsborough/the-painting/painting-the-picture.

Herbert 1990
Herbert, John. *Inside Christie's.* New York, 1990.

Herrmann 1974
Herrmann, Luke. *British Landscape Painting of the Eighteenth Century.* New York, 1974.

Hicks 1908
Hicks, G. M. *The Pomeranian.* Manchester, 1908.

Higonnet 2024
Higonnet, Anne. *Liberty, Equality, Fashion: The Women Who Styled the French Revolution.* New York, 2024.

Hollander 1971
Hollander, Anne. "The Clothed Image: Picture and Performance." *New Literary History* 2, no. 3 (Spring 1971): 477–93.

Holman 2010
Holman, Peter. *Life after Death: The Viola da Gamba in Britain from Purcell to Dolmetsch.* Woodbridge, 2010.

Honegger 2011
Honegger, Andreas. *Die Blumen der Frauen: Blumensymbolik in Gemälden aus 7 Jahrhunderten.* Munich, 2011.

Honour 1989
Honour, Hugh. *The Image of the Black in Western Art.* Vol. 4. Cambridge, MA, and London, 1989.

Houston and other cities 2012–13
Julius Bryant, Susan Jenkins, and Walter Liedtke. *Rembrandt, Van Dyck, Gainsborough: The Treasures of Kenwood House, London.* Exh. cat. Houston (Museum of Fine Arts), Milwaukee (Milwaukee Museum of Art), Seattle (Seattle Art Museum), and Arkansas (Arkansas Arts Center), 2012–13.

Houston, San Francisco, and Nashville 2014–15
David Cholmondeley and Andrew Moore. *Houghton Hall: Portrait of an English Country House.* Exh. cat. Houston (Museum of Fine Arts), San Francisco (Fine Arts Museums of San Francisco), and Nashville (Frist Center for the Visual Arts), 2014–15.

Howard 2010
Howard, Jeremy. *Colnaghi, The History.* London, 2010.

Hubbard 1948
Hubbard, R. H. *Catalogue of Paintings, National Gallery of Canada.* Ottawa, 1948.

Hubbard 1957
Hubbard, R. H., ed. *The National Gallery of Canada, Catalogue of Painting and Sculpture.* Vol. 1. Ottawa and Toronto, 1957.

Ingamells 2004
Ingamells, John. *National Portrait Gallery: Mid-Georgian Portraits, 1760–1790.* London, 2004.

Ingamells 2008
Ingamells, John. *Dulwich Picture Gallery.* London, 2008.

Ipswich 1887
Ipswich Fine Art Club Exhibition, 1887. Exh. cat. Ipswich (Ipswich Fine Art Club), 1887.

Ipswich 1927
Bicentenary Memorial Exhibition of Thomas Gainsborough, R. A.: Illustrating the Various Periods of His Work, also the Work of His Antecedents and Contemporaries and His Influence on the Art of His Own and Later Times. Exh. cat. Ipswich (Ipswich Museum), 1927.

Jenyns 1790
Jenyns, Soame. "The World." In vol. 2 of *The Works of Soame Jenyns*, edited by C. N. Coke, 93. London, 1790.

Johnson 1755
Johnson, Samuel. *A Dictionary of the English Language.* 2 vols. London, 1755.

Jones 1997
Jones, Rica. "Gainsborough's Materials and Methods: A 'Remarkable Ability to Make Paint Sparkle.'" In London, Norwich, and Newcastle 1997, 19–26.

Jones 1999
Jones, Rica. "The Rev. John Chafy Playing a Violincello in a Landscape." In *Paint and Purpose: A Study of Technique in British Art*, edited by Stephen Hackney, Rica Jones, and Joyce Townsend, 48–53. London, 1999.

Jones 2015
Jones, Rica. "Studio Practice and the Training of Painters: A Technical and Contextual Study of the Young Gainsborough." Paper presented at *The Painting Room: The Artist's Studio in Eighteenth-Century Britain*, Gainsborough's House, Sudbury, October 30, 2015.

Jones and Townsend 2016
Jones, Rica, and Joyce H. Townsend. "Drying Crackle in Early and Mid-Eighteenth-Century British Paintings: An Explanation of the Phenomenon of Microcissing." In *5th International Symposium, Painting Techniques: History, Materials, Studio Practice*, edited by Arie Wallert, 174–82. Rijksmuseum, 2016.

Kalinsky 1995
Kalinsky, Nicola. *Gainsborough.* London, 1995.

Kidson 1999
Kidson, Alex. *Earlier British Paintings in the Lady Lever Art Gallery.* Liverpool, 1999.

King et al. 1997
King, Reyahn, Sukhdev Sandhu, James Walvin, and Jane Girdham. *Ignatius Sancho: An African Man of Letters.* London, 1997.

Kirby 1993
Kirby, Jo. "Fading and Colour Change of Prussian Blue: Occurrences and Early Reports." *National Gallery Technical Bulletin* 14 (1993): 62–71.

Kirby and Saunders 2004
Kirby, Jo, and David Saunders. "Fading and Colour Change of Prussian Blue: Methods of Manufacture and the Influence of Extenders." *National Gallery Technical Bulletin* 25 (2004): 73–99.

Kirby, Spring, and Higgitt 2007
Kirby, Jo, Marika Spring, and Catherine Higgitt. "The Technology of Eighteenth- and Nineteenth-Century Red Lake Pigments." *National Gallery Technical Bulletin* 28 (2007): 69–95.

Klein 1995
Klein, Lawrence E. "Politeness for plebes: Consumption and Social Identity in Early Eighteenth-Century England." In *The Consumption of Culture, 1600–1800*, edited by Ann Bermingham and John Brewer, 362–82. London, 1995.

Laing 1995
Laing, Alastair. *In Trust for the Nation. Paintings from National Trust Houses.* London, 1995.

Lane sale 1831
Richard James Lane Collection. Sale cat. Christie's, London, February 26, 1831.

Langford 1989
Langford, Paul. *A Polite and Commercial People: England, 1727–1783.* Oxford and New York, 1989.

La Rochefoucauld 1933
La Rochefoucauld, F. de. *A Frenchman in England, 1784.* Cambridge, 1933.

Laskin and Pantazzi 1987
Laskin, Myron, and Michael Pantazzi. *European and American Painting, Sculpture, and Decorative Arts.* 2 vols. Ottawa, 1987.

Lavezzari 1983–84
Lavezzari, Paola. "Spunti dal Trattato di Leonardo nella cultura artistica del Settecento inglese: la ritrattistica tarda di Gainsborough." *Prospettiva* no. 33/36 (April 1983–January 1984): 313–25.

Leeds 1868
R. N. James and L. Lefèvre. *National Exhibition of Works of Art at Leeds.* Exh. cat. Leeds (venue unknown), 1868.

Leeds 1936
Masterpieces from the Collections of Yorkshire and Durham. Exh. cat. Leeds (City Art Gallery), 1936.

LeFanu 1986
LeFanu, William, ed. *Betsy Sheridan's Journal: Letters from Sheridan's Sister, 1784–1786 and 1788–1790.* Oxford, 1986.

Leslie and Taylor 1865
Leslie, Charles Robert, and Tom Taylor. *Life and Times of Sir Joshua Reynolds, with Notice of Some of His Contemporaries.* 4 vols. London, 1865.

Lindsay 1981
Lindsay, Jack. *Thomas Gainsborough: His Life and Art.* London and New York, 1981.

Lisbon and Madrid 1949
Ellis Waterhouse. *A Century of British Painting.* Exh. cat. Lisbon (Museu de Arte Antiga) and Madrid (Museo Nacional del Prado), 1949.

London 1770
The Second Exhibition of the Royal Academy. Exh. cat. London (Royal Academy of Arts), 1770.

London 1777
The Ninth Exhibition of the Royal Academy. Exh. cat. London (Royal Academy of Arts), 1777.

London 1778
The Tenth Exhibition of the Royal Academy. Exh. cat. London (Royal Academy of Arts), 1778.

London 1782
The Fourteenth Exhibition of the Royal Academy. Exh. cat. London (Royal Academy of Arts), 1782.

London 1783
The Fifteenth Exhibition of the Royal Academy. Exh. cat. London (Royal Academy of Arts), 1783.

London 1814
Catalogue of Pictures by the late William Hogarth, Richard Wilson, Thomas Gainsborough, and J. Zoffany. Exh. cat. London (British Institution), 1814.

London 1817
Exhibition of Old Master Paintings. Exh. cat. London (British Institution), 1817.

London 1832
Catalogue of the Winter Exhibition of the Works of Deceased and Living British Artists. Exh. cat. London (Royal Society of British Artists), 1832.

London 1859
Exhibition of Old Master Paintings. Exh. cat. London (British Institution), 1859.

London 1862
International Exhibition. Exh. cat. London (Exhibition Palace), 1862.

London 1864
Exhibition of Old Master Paintings. Exh. cat. London (British Institution), 1864.

London 1867
Catalogue of the Second Special Exhibition of National Portraits Commencing with the Reign of William and Mary and Ending with the Year MCDDD. Exh. cat. London (South Kensington Museum), 1867.

London 1868
Catalogue of the Third and Concluding Exhibition of National Portraits Commencing with the Fortieth Year of the Reign of George the Third and Ending with the Year MDCCCLXVII. Exh. cat. London (South Kensington Museum), 1868.

London 1873
Exhibition of Works by the Old Masters and by Deceased Masters of the British School, Paintings in Oil and Watercolours, and Sculpture. Exh. cat. London (Royal Academy of Arts), 1873.

London 1875
Winter Exhibition: Exhibition of Works by The Old Masters, and by Deceased Masters of the British School. Exh. cat. London (Royal Academy of Arts), 1875.

London 1876
Winter Exhibition: Exhibition of Works by The Old Masters, and by Deceased Masters of the British School. Exh. cat. London (Royal Academy of Arts), 1876.

London 1880
Winter Exhibition. Exhibition of Works by the Old Masters and by Deceased Masters of the British School. Including a Special Collection of Works by Holbein and His School. Exh. cat. London (Royal Academy of Arts), 1880.

London 1882
Winter Exhibition: Exhibition of Works by the Old Masters and by Deceased Masters of the British School. Exh. cat. London (Royal Academy of Arts), 1882.

London 1885
Exhibition of the Works of Thomas Gainsborough, R.A., with historical notes by F. G. Stephens; and a collection of drawings by the late Richard Doyle. Exh. cat. London (Doherty & Co.), 1885.

London 1886
Winter Exhibition: Exhibition of Works by the Old Masters and by Deceased Masters of the British School. Exh. cat. London (Royal Academy of Arts), 1886.

London 1891
Royal Naval Exhibition. Exh. cat. London (Royal Hospital), 1891.

London 1894a
Summer Exhibition: Fair Women. Exh. cat. London (Grafton Galleries), 1894.

London 1894b
Winter Exhibition: Exhibition of the Works by The Old Masters and by Deceased Masters of the British School. Exh. cat. London (Royal Academy of Arts), 1894.

London 1897
Exhibition of Dramatic & Musical Art 1897. Exh. cat. London (Grafton Galleries), 1897.

London 1902
Eighth Annual Exhibition on behalf of the Artists' General Benevolent Institution at the Galleries of Thomas Agnew & Sons. Exh. cat. London (Thos. Agnew & Sons), 1902.

London 1904
Catalogue of a Collection of Pictures, Decorative Furniture and other Works of Art. Exh. cat. London (Burlington Fine Arts Club), 1904.

London 1906a
Winter Exhibition: Exhibition of Works by the Old Masters and Deceased Masters of the British School. Exh. cat. London (Royal Academy of Arts), 1906.

London 1906b
Spring Exhibition: Illustrating Georgian England. Exh. cat. London (Whitechapel Art Gallery), 1906.

London 1907
Winter Exhibition: Exhibition of Works by The Old Masters and Deceased Masters of the British School including a collection of Watercolours and Chalk Drawings. Exh. cat. London (Royal Academy of Arts), 1907.

London 1908a
Spring Exhibition. Exh. cat. London (Whitechapel Art Gallery), 1908.

London 1908b
Annual Exhibition on behalf of the Artists' General Benevolent Institution. Exh. cat. London (Thos. Agnew & Sons), 1908.

London 1908c
Exhibition of Old Masters. Exh. cat. London (Knoedler Galleries), 1908.

London 1909
A Catalogue of the Pictures, Drawings, Prints & Sculpture in the Exhibition of Fair Women arranged by the International Society of Sculptors, Painters & Gravers. Exh. cat. London (New Gallery), 1909.

London 1909–10
A Catalogue of the Pictures and Drawings in the National loan Exhibition, in aid of National Gallery Funds. Exh. cat. London (Grafton Galleries), 1909–10.

London 1911
Exhibition of English Masters. Exh. cat. London (Knoedler Galleries), 1911.

London 1928
Winter Exhibition: Exhibition of Works by Late Members of the Royal Academy and of the Iveagh Bequest of Works by Old Masters (Kenwood Collection). Exh. cat. London (Royal Academy of Arts), 1928.

London 1929
Catalogue. Exh. cat. London (Thos. Agnew and Sons), 1929.

London 1931
The Four Georges: Loan Exhibition in Aid of the Royal Northern Hospital. Exh. cat. London (25 Park Lane), 1931.

London 1932
Art Treasures Exhibition. Exh. cat. London (Christie, Manson & Woods), 1932.

London 1934
Exhibition of British Art, ca. 1000–1860. Exh. cat. London (Royal Academy of Arts), 1934.

London 1936
Gainsborough Loan Exhibition in aid of the Royal Northern Hospital. Exh. cat. London (45 Park Lane), 1936.

London 1937
A Loan Exhibition Depicting British Country Life Through the Centuries. Exh. cat. London (39 Grosvenor Square), 1937.

London 1947
Some Pictures from the Dulwich Gallery. Exh. cat. London (National Gallery), 1947.

London 1953a
Ellis K. Waterhouse. *Thomas Gainsborough, 1727–1788: An Exhibition of Paintings Arranged by the Arts Council of Great Britain and the Tate Gallery.* Exh. cat. London (Tate Gallery), 1953.

London 1953b
Summer Exhibition: Coronation Year. Exh. cat. London (Leggatt Galleries), 1953.

London 1956–57
Winter Exhibition: British Portraits. Exh. cat. London (Royal Academy of Arts), 1956–57.

London 1963a
Philip Hendy, ed. *Acquisitions 1953–62.* Exh. cat. London (National Gallery), 1963.

London 1963b
Horace Buttery, 1902–1962. Exh. cat. London (Thos. Agnew & Sons), 1963.

London 1967
Christie's Bi-Centenary Exhibition 1766–1966. Exh. cat. London (Christie's), 1967.

London 1977
Lindsay Stainton. *Gainsborough and His Musical Friends.* Exh. cat. London (Kenwood House), 1977.

London 1978
Timothy Clifford, Antony Griffith, and Martin Royalton-Kisch. *Gainsborough and Reynolds in the British Museum: The Drawings of Gainsborough and Reynolds with a Survey of Mezzotints after Their Paintings and a Study of Reynolds' Collection of Old Master Drawings.* Exh. cat. London (British Museum), 1978.

London 1980
English Pictures from Suffolk Collections: A Loan Exhibition in Aid of The Suffolk Historic Churches Trust. Exh. cat. London (Thos. Agnew & Sons), 1980.

London 1980–81
John Hayes. *Gainsborough, 1727–1788.* Exh cat. London (Tate), 1980–81.

London 1982–83
Oliver Millar. *Van Dyck in England.* Exh. cat. London (National Portrait Gallery), 1982–83.

London 1985
John Jacobs and the Greater London Council on Public Relations Branch. *John Joseph Merlin: The Ingenious Mechanick.* Exh. cat. London (Kenwood House), 1985.

London 1987–88
Manners and Morals: Hogarth and British Painting 1700–1760. Exh. cat. London (Tate Gallery), 1987–88.

London 1988a
A Nest of Nightingales, Thomas Gainsborough: "The Linley Sisters." Exh. cat. London (Dulwich Picture Gallery), 1988.

London 1988b
Ann French, ed. *The Earl and Countess Howe by Gainsborough: A Bicentenary Exhibition.* Exh. cat. London (Kenwood House), 1988.

London 1991
The Portrait in British Art. Exh. cat. London (National Portrait Gallery), 1991.

London 1992–93
Andrew Wilton. *The Swagger Portrait: Grand Manner Portraiture in Britain from Van Dyck to Augustus John, 1630–1930.* Exh. cat. London (Tate Gallery), 1992–93.

London 1995
Conserving Old Masters: Paintings Recently Restored at the Dulwich Picture Gallery. Exh. cat. London (Dulwich Picture Gallery), 1995.

London 1999
Martin Kemp. *Paintings from Dulwich Picture Gallery.* Exh. cat. London (Dulwich Picture Gallery), 1999.

London 2009
Karen Hearn, ed. *Van Dyck & Britain.* Exh. cat. London (Tate), 2009.

London 2011
"Masterpiece a Month: September, Mrs. Sheridan." Exh. pamphlet. London (Dulwich Picture Gallery), 2011.

London 2018
Mark Hallett and Sarah Victoria Turner. *The Great Spectacle: 250 Years of the Royal Academy Summer Exhibition*. Exh. cat. London (Royal Academy of Arts), 2018.

London 2022
Christine Riding, Susanna Avery-Quash, Melinda McCurdy, Jacqueline Riding, Imogen Tedbury. *Gainsborough's Blue Boy: The Return of a British Icon*. Exh. cat. London (National Gallery), 2022.

London 2023
Anna Reynolds. *Style and Society: Dressing the Georgians*. Exh. cat. London (The Queen's Gallery), 2023.

London 2024
Dorothy Price et al. *Entangled Pasts: 1768–Now. Art, Colonialism and Change*. Exh. cat. London (Royal Academy of Arts), 2024.

London and Edinburgh 2003–4
Giles Waterfield and Anne French, with Matthew Craske. *Below Stairs: 400 Years of Servants' Portraits*. Exh. cat. London (National Portrait Gallery) and Edinburgh (Scottish National Portrait Gallery), 2003–4.

London and New Haven 2001
Catherine MacLeod and Julia Marciari Alexander. *Painted Ladies: Women at the Court of Charles II*. London (National Portrait Gallery) and New Haven (Yale Center for British Art), 2001.

London, Norwich, and Newcastle 1997
Susan Foister, Rica Jones, and Olivier Meslay. *Young Gainsborough*. Exh. cat. London (National Gallery), Norwich (Castle Museum), and Newcastle (Laing Art Gallery), 1997.

London and Princeton 2018–19
David H. Solkin and Susan Sloman. *Gainsborough's Family Album*. Exh. cat. London (National Portrait Gallery) and Princeton (Princeton University Art Museum), 2018–19.

London and Sudbury 2003
Hugh Belsey. *Gainsborough at Gainsborough's House*. Exh. cat. London (Thos. Agnew & Sons Ltd.) and Sudbury (Gainsborough's House), 2003.

London, Washington, and Boston 2002–3

Michael Rosenthal and Martin Myrone, eds. *Thomas Gainsborough, 1727–1788*. Exh. cat. London (Tate Britain), Washington (National Gallery of Art), and Boston (Museum of Fine Arts), 2002–3.

Los Angeles 1944
The Balch Collection and Old Masters from Los Angeles Collections. Exh. cat. Los Angeles (Los Angeles County Museum), 1944.

Lotut 2018
Lotut, Zoriana. "Blue in Eighteenth-Century England: Pigments and Usages." *Revue de la Société d'études anglo-américaines des XVIIe et XVIIIe siècles* 17–18, no. 75 (2018). Accessed November 5, 2024. journals.openedition.org/1718/1214.

MacLaren 1991
MacLaren, Neil. *National Gallery Catalogues: The Dutch School, 1600–1900*, revised and expanded by Christopher Brown. Vol. 1. London, 1991.

MacLeod 2001
MacLeod, Catherine. "'Good, but not like': Peter Lely, Portrait Practice, and the Creation of a Court Look." In London and New Haven 2001, 50–61.

Madin 2006
Madin, John. "The Lost African: Slavery and Portraiture in The Age of Enlightenment." *Apollo* 164, (August 2006): 34–39.

Madrid 1988–89
Pintura Británica de Hogarth a Turner. Exh. cat. Madrid (Museo del Prado), 1988–89.

Madrid and Bilbao 1999
Giles Waterfield, Francisco Calvo Serraller, and Ian Dejardin. *Obras Maestras de la Dulwich Picture Gallery*. Exh. cat. Madrid (Banco Bilbao Vizcaya) and Bilbao (Museo de Bellas Artes), 1999.

Manchester 1857
Catalogue of the Art Treasures of the United Kingdom: Collected at Manchester in 1857. Exh. cat. Manchester (Museum of Ornamental Art), 1857.

Manchester 1928
Exhibition of Old Masters presented to the Nation by the late Earl of Iveagh. Exh. cat. Manchester (Manchester City Art Gallery), 1928.

Manchester 1934
British Art Exhibition. Exh. cat. Manchester (Manchester City Art Gallery), 1934.

Mandy 2016
Mandy, Kristina. "Gainsborough as a Copyist." *Hamilton Kerr Institute Bulletin*, no. 6 (2016): 7–20.

Manners 1926
Manners, Lady Victoria. "The Later Historical Portraits in the Collection of the Duke of Norfolk, E.M. at Arundel Castle." *Connoisseur* 75, no. 298 (June 1926): 74–79.

Manning 2005
Manning, Jo. *My Lady Scandalous: The Amazing Life and Outrageous Times of Grace Dalrymple Elliott, Royal Courtesan*. New York, 2005.

Mannings 2000
Mannings, David. *Sir Joshua Reynolds: A Complete Catalogue of His Paintings*. 2 vols. New Haven and London, 2000.

Martinez 2009
Martinez, Cristina S. "'Odd Scratches and Marks': Thomas Gainsborough and the Idiosyncrasy of the Brush." In *Originality and Intellectual Property in the French and English Enlightenment*, edited by Reginald McGinnis, 125–52. New York and London, 2009.

McPherson 2000
McPherson, Helen. "Picturing Tragedy: Mrs. Siddons as the Tragic Muse Revisited." *Eighteenth-Century Studies* 33, no. 3 (Spring 2000): 401–43.

Menpes and Greig 1909
Menpes, Mortimer, and James Greig. *Gainsborough*. London, 1909.

Milan 1975
Pittura inglese 1660/1840: Due secoli di cultura, storia e costume in Inghilterra. Exh. cat. Milan (Palazzo Reale), 1975.

Millar 1949
Millar, Oliver. *Thomas Gainsborough*. London, 1949.

Millar 1969
Millar, Oliver. *The Later Georgian Pictures in the Collection of Her Majesty the Queen*. 2 vols. London, 1969.

Minneapolis 1952
Loan Exhibition of Great Portraits. Exh. cat. Minneapolis (Minneapolis Institute of Arts), 1952.

Minneapolis 1972
The J. Paul Getty Collection. Exh. cat. Minneapolis (The Minneapolis Institute of Arts), 1972.

Mizrahi and Ng 2026
Mizrahi, Isaac, and Aimee Ng. *Gainsborough's The Hon. Frances Duncombe*. New York, 2026.

Monkhouse 1897
Monkhouse, Cosmo. "A Northern Art Patron. II—The British Portraits." *Art Journal* (1897): 33–37.

Montezuma 1888
Montezuma. "My Note Book." *Art Amateur* 19, no. 3 (August 1888): 50–51.

Montreal 1942
Art Association of Montreal. *Loan Exhibition of Masterpieces of Painting*. Exh. cat. Montreal (Montreal Museum of Fine Arts), 1942.

Montreal 1967
Terre des Hommes: Exposition Internationale des Beaux-Arts (Man and His World International Fine Arts Exhibition Expo 67). Exh. cat. Montreal (Montreal Museum of Fine Art), 1967.

Morriello 2023
Morriello, Francesco A. *Messengers of Empire: Print and Revolution in the Atlantic World*. Liverpool, 2023.

Mould 2006
Mould, Anthony. "Gainsborough Dupont (1754–97) and Thomas Gainsborough (1727–88) Copying Van Dyck." *British Art Journal* 7, no. 1 (2006): 45–54.

Mourey 1905
Mourey, Gabriel. *Gainsborough: Biographie Critique*. Paris, 1905.

Mourey 1909
Mourey, Gabriel. "Les peintres de la femme au XVII Siècle. Ecole Anglaise." *L'art et les artistes: art ancien, moderne, décoratif* 9 (1909): 77–98.

Mullins 1983
Mullins, Edwin, ed. *The Arts of Britain*. Oxford, 1983.

Munns and Penny 1999
Munns, Jessica, and Penny Richards, eds. *The Clothes that Wear Us: Essays on Dressing and Transgressing in Eighteenth-Century Culture*. Newark, 1999.

Munro 2014
Munro, Jane, ed. *Silent Partners: Artist and Mannequin from Function to Fetish*. New Haven, 2014.

Murray 1980
Murray, Peter. *Dulwich Picture Gallery: A Catalogue*. London, 1980.

Musick 1943
Musick, James B. "Lord John and Lord Bernard Stuart by Thomas Gainsborough After Sir Anthony Van Dyck." *Bulletin of the City Art Museum of St. Louis* 28, nos. 1–2 (May 1943): 7–10.

National Gallery 1962
The National Gallery: January 1960–May 1962. London, 1962.

Nevinson 1964
Nevinson, J. L. "Vandyck Dress." *Connoisseur* 157, no. 833 (November 1964): 166–61.

New Haven 1980
Ellen D'Oench. *The Conversation Piece: Arthur Devis and His Contemporaries*. Exh. cat. New Haven (Yale Center for British Art), 1980.

New Haven and London 1987
Brian Allen. *Francis Hayman*. Exh. cat. New Haven (Yale Center for British Art) and London (Iveagh Bequest, Kenwood), 1987.

New Haven and London 2007–8
John Baskett. *Paul Mellon's Legacy: A Passion for British Art*. Exh. cat. New Haven (Yale Center for British Art) and London (Royal Academy of Arts), 2007–8.

New Haven and San Marino 2001–2
Malcolm Warner and Robyn Asleson. *Great British Paintings from American Collections: Holbein to Hockney*. Exh. cat. New Haven (Yale Center for British Art) and San Marino (Huntington Library & Museum), 2001–2.

New London Toilet 1778
The New London Toilet . . . London, 1778.

New York 1912
Loan Exhibitions of Old Masters. Exh. cat. New York (Knoedler Galleries), 1912.

New York 1914a
Catalogue of the Special Loan Exhibition of Old Masters of the British School being a selection from pictures acquired from Messrs. Duveen Brothers within the Last Three Years. Exh. cat. New York, (Duveen Brothers, 720 Fifth Avenue), 1914.

New York 1914b
Exhibition of Paintings by Thomas Gainsborough, RA and J.M.W. Turner, RA for the Benefit of the Artists' Fund and Artists' Societies. Exh. cat. New York (Knoedler Galleries), 1914.

New York 1931
Exhibition of Important Paintings: Old and Modern Masters in the New York Art Market from The Collection of Leading New York Dealers. Exh. cat. New York (Anderson Galleries), 1931.

New York 1936
Inaugural Exhibitions at the Galleries of James St. L. O'Toole. Exh. cat. New York (O'Toole Galleries), 1936.

New York 1939
George Henry McCall and William R. Valentiner. *Catalogue of European Paintings and Sculpture from 1300–1800*. Exh. cat. New York (New York's World Fair), 1939.

New York 1940
Forty British Portraits. Exh. cat. New York (Duveen Galleries), 1940.

New York 1942
Loan Exhibition of French and English Art Treasures from the XVIII Century. Exh. cat. New York (Parke-Bernet Galleries), 1942.

New York 2016
Stijn Alsteens and Adam Eaker. *Van Dyck: The Anatomy of Portraiture*. Exh. cat. New York (The Frick Collection), 2016.

Northcote 1901
Northcote, James. *Conversations of James Northcote, R. A., with James Ward, on Art and Artists*. London, 1901.

Norwich 1948
Loan Exhibition of the Portraits in the Landscape Park from Norfolk and Suffolk Houses. Exh. cat. Norwich (Norwich Castle Museum), 1948.

Norwich 1961
Music and Painting. Exh. cat. Norwich (Norwich Castle Museum), 1961.

Oakland 1969
Art Treasures in California. Exh. cat. Oakland (Oakland Museum), 1969.

Ostler 2021
Ostler, Catherine. *The Duchess Countess: The Woman Who Scandalised a Nation*. London, 2021.

Parent 1999
Parent, Barbara. "Fashion's Stamp." *Country Life* 193 (February 18, 1999): 90–91.

Paris 1913
Exposition de Tableaux Anciens Provenant de Collections particulières. Exh. cat. Paris (Knoedler & Co.), 1913.

Paris 1938
La peinture anglaise, XVIIIe & XIXe siècles. Exh. cat. Paris (Musée du Louvre), 1938.

Paris 1953
Le Paysage anglais de Gainsborough à Turner. Exh. cat. Paris (Orangerie des Tuileries), 1953.

Paris 1981
John Hayes. *Gainsborough, 1727–1788*. Exh. cat. Paris (Grand Palais), 1981.

Paris and London 2006–7
Citizens and Kings: Portraits in the Age of Revolution, 1760–1830. Exh. cat. Paris (Galeries nationales du Grand Palais) and London (Royal Academy of Arts), 2006–7.

Paulson 1975
Paulson, Ronald. *Emblem and Expression: Meaning in English Art of the Eighteenth Century*. London, 1975.

Perkins 2002
Perkins, Diane. "An Early Gainsborough Masterpiece: Thomas Gainsborough's 'Portrait of Peter Darnell Muilman, Charles Crokatt, and William Keable in a Landscape.'" *British Art in Focus, Patron's Papers* 5 (October 2002): 5–15.

Perry 2007
Perry, Gill. *Spectacular Flirtations: Viewing the Actress in British Art and Theatre, 1768–1820*. New Haven and London, 2007.

Perry, Retford, and Vibert 2013
Perry, Gill, Kate Retford, and Jordan Vibert. *Placing Faces: The Portrait and the English Country House in the Long Eighteenth Century*. Manchester and New York, 2013.

Pittsburgh 1919
Catalogue of a Loan Collection of Paintings from the National Gallery of Canada. Exh. cat. Pittsburgh (Carnegie Institute), 1919.

Pointon 1984
Pointon, Marcia. "Portrait-Painting as a Business Enterprise in London in the 1780s." *Art History* 7, no. 2 (June 1984): 187–205.

Pointon 1993
Pointon, Marcia. *Hanging the Head: Portraiture and Social Formation in Eighteenth-Century England*. New Haven and London, 1993.

Pointon 2009
Pointon, Marcia. *Brilliant Effects: A Cultural History of Gem Stones and Jewellery*. New Haven and London, 2009.

Poole 1998
Poole, Robert. *Time's Alteration: Calendar Reform in Early Modern England*. London, 1998.

Porter 1990
Porter, Roy. *English Society in the 18th Century*. Rev. ed. London, 1990.

Postle 1991
Postle, Martin. "Chapter 3: The Golden Age, 1760–1790." In *The British Portrait 1660–1960*, edited by Martin Postle, 184–241. Woodbridge, 1991.

Postle 2002
Postle, Martin. *Thomas Gainsborough*. London, 2002.

Potterton 1976
Potterton, Homan. *Reynolds and Gainsborough*. London, 1976.

Providence 1945
The Catalogue of Old and New England. An Exhibition of American Painting of Colonial and Early Republican Days, together with English Painting of the same time. Exh. cat. Providence (Museum of Art of the Rhode Island School of Design), 1945.

Radnor 1909
Radnor, Helen Matilda, Countess of, William Barclay Squire, and Jacob, Sixth Earl of Radnor. *Catalogue of the Pictures in the Collection of the Earl of Radnor.* Part II. London, 1909.

Rayner 2018a
Rayner, Kari. "Exploring Gainsborough Dupont's Role in Thomas Gainsborough's Studio through the Portrait of Mrs. Audley." *Hamilton Kerr Institute Bulletin*, no. 7 (2018): 98–110.

Rayner 2018b
Rayner, Kari. "Material Trends and Transformations in Eighteenth-Century British Painting." Paper presented at the *Works-in-Progress Lecture Series*. National Gallery of Art, Washington, DC, September 17, 2018.

Rayner 2019
Rayner, Kari. "Found in Translation: Exploring Dutch Influence on Eighteenth-Century British Landscape Painting." In *Trading Paintings and Painters' Materials 1550–1800, CATS Proceedings, IV, 2018*, edited by Anne Haack Christensen and Angela Jager, 77–87. London, 2019.

Rayner and Greenwald (unpublished)
Rayner, Kari, and Diana Greenwald. "The Artistic Division of Labour and the Changing Materiality of Eighteenth-Century British Paintings on Canvas." (unpublished)

Rempel 1997
Rempel, Lora. "The Matter of Style: Thomas Gainsborough, the Portrait in a Landscape and the Mark of the Modern Painter." PhD diss., City University of New York, 1997.

Retford 2017
Retford, Kate. *Conversation Piece: Making Modern Art in Eighteenth-Century Britain.* New Haven and London, 2017.

Reynolds 1908
Reynolds, Joshua. *Discourses; with biographical introduction by Hannaford Bennett.* London, 1908.

Reynolds 1959
Reynolds, Joshua. *Discourses on Art.* Edited by Robert R. Wark. San Marino, 1959.

Reynolds 1971
Reynolds, Graham. "Holbein to Turner." *Apollo* 93, no. 111 (May 1971): 408–15.

Reynolds 2023
Reynolds, Anna. *Style & Society: Dressing the Georgians.* London, 2023.

Ribeiro 1977
Ribeiro, Aileen. "Some Evidence of the Influence of the Dress of the Seventeenth Century on Costume in Eighteenth-Century Female Portraiture." *Burlington* 119, no. 897 (1977): 834–40.

Ribeiro 1995
Ribeiro, Aileen. *The Art of Dress: Fashion in England and France 1750 to 1820.* New Haven and London, 1995.

Ribeiro 2002
Ribeiro, Aileen. *Dressing in Eighteenth Century Europe, 1715–1789.* New Haven and London, 2002.

Ribeiro 2011
Ribeiro, Aileen. *Facing Beauty: Painted Women and Cosmetic Art.* New Haven and London, 2011.

Ribeiro 2017
Ribeiro, Aileen. *Clothing Art: The Visual Culture of Fashion, 1600–1914.* New Haven and London 2017.

Rimbault 1895
Rimbault, E. F. *Soho and Its Associations, Historical, Literary & Artistic.* Edited by George Clinch. London, 1895.

Ripley 1964
Ripley, Elizabeth. *Gainsborough: A Biography.* Philadelphia and New York, 1964.

Roberts 1897
Roberts, William. *Memorials of Christie's: A Record of Art Sales from 1766 to 1896.* Vol I. London, 1897.

Roberts 1906
Roberts, William. "Mr J. Pierpont Morgan's Pictures: The Early English School, II." *Connoisseur* 16 (November 1906): 135–43.

Roberts 1912
Roberts, William. "Mr. H. C. Frick's Collection of Pictures. *Connoisseur* 34 (1912): 147–55.

Roberts 1914
Roberts, William. "Two Whole Length English Portraits in The Frick Collection." *Art in America* 2, no. 3 (1914): 204–14.

Roberts 1919
Roberts, William. *Gainsborough Dupont by Thomas Gainsborough.* London, 1919.

Roberts 1921
Roberts, William. "English Whole length portraits in America; Gainsborough's Mr. Abel." *Art in America and Elsewhere* 10, no. 1 (1921): 23–26.

Robinson 1995
Robinson, John Martin. *The Dukes of Norfolk: A Quincentennial History.* Oxford, 1995.

Roche 1994
Roche, Daniel. *The Culture of Clothing: Dress and Fashion in the "Ancien Régime."* Cambridge, 1994.

Roe 2008
Roe, Stephen. "The Sale Catalogue of Carl Friedrich Abel (1787)." In *Music and the Book Trade from the Sixteenth to the Twentieth Century*, edited by Robin Myers, Michael Harris, and Giles Mandelbrote, 105–43. London, 2008.

Rome 1911
Sir Isidore Spielmann. *International Fine Arts Exhibition, Rome 1911. Souvenir of the British Section.* Exh. cat. Rome (British Fine Arts Palace), 1911.

Rosenthal 1982
Rosenthal, Michael. *British Landscape Painting.* Oxford, 1982.

Rosenthal 1997
Rosenthal, Michael. "The Rough and the Smooth: Rural Subjects in Later-Eighteenth-Century Art." In *Prospects for the Nation: Recent Essays in British Landscape, 1750–1880*, edited by Michael Rosenthal, Christiana Payne, and Scott Wilcox, 37–59. New Haven and London, 1997.

Rosenthal 1999
Rosenthal, Michael. *The Art of Thomas Gainsborough: "a little business for the eye."* New Haven and London, 1999.

Rotterdam 1955
Engelse landschapschilders van Gainsborough tot Turner. Exh. cat. Rotterdam (Museum Boymans [sic]), 1955.

Rouquet 1755
Rouquet, Jean André. *The Present State of the Arts in England, by M. Rouquet, Member of the Royal Academy of Painting and Sculpture; Who resided Thirty Years in this Kingdom.* London, 1755.

Russell 1926
Russell, Charles Edward, and John Chaloner Smith. *English Mezzotint Portraits and Their States: From the Invention of Mezzotinting until the Early Part of the 19th Century.* London, 1926.

Saltaire 1887
The Royal Yorkshire Jubilee Exhibition. Exh. cat. Saltaire (Exhibition Building), 1887.

San Francisco 1933
Loan Exhibition of British Painting of the Late Eighteenth and Early Nineteenth Centuries. Exh. cat. San Francisco (California Palace of the Legion of Honor), 1933.

San Francisco 1939–40
Seven Centuries of Painting: A loan exhibition of Old and Modern Masters. Exh. cat. San Francisco (California Palace of the Legion of Honor and the M. H. de Young Memorial Museum San Francisco), 1939–40.

San Marino 2013
Hugh Belsey. *Gainsborough's Cottage Doors: An Insight into the Artist's Last Decade.* Exh. cat. San Marino (Huntington Library, Art Collections, and Botanical Gardens), 2013.

Santa Barbara 1951
10th Anniversary Loan Exhibition: Old Master Paintings from California Museums. Exh. cat. Santa Barbara (Santa Barbara Museum of Art), 1951.

Scott and Dalrymple 1911
Scott, Lord Henry, and Sir Hew Hamilton Dalrymple, Baronet. *Catalogue of the Pictures at Dalkeith House.* Edinburgh, 1911.

Secrest 2004
Secrest, Meryle. *Duveen: A Life in Art.* New York, 2004.

Shawe-Taylor 1999
Shawe-Taylor, Desmond. *The Georgians. Eighteenth-Century Portraiture & Society.* London, 1999.

Shawe-Taylor 2009
Shawe-Taylor, Desmond. *The Conversation Piece: Scenes of Fashionable Life*. London, 2009.

Shelley 1912
Shelley, Lady Frances. *The Diary of Frances, Lady Shelley, 1787–1817*, edited by her grandson Richard Edgcumbe. 2 vols. London, 1912.

Simon 2013
Simon, Jacob. "'Three-quarters, kit-cats and half-lengths': British portrait painters and their canvas sizes, 1625–1850." London, 2013. Accessed September 24, 2024. www.npg.org.uk/collections/research/programmes/artists-their-materials-and-suppliers/three-quarters-kit-cats-and-half-lengths-british-portrait-painters-and-their-canvas-sizes-1625-1850/.

Siple 1936
Siple, Ella S. "The Opening of The Frick Collection." *Burlington Magazine for Connoisseurs* 68, no. 395 (1936): 102–3.

Sitwell 1936
Sitwell, Sacheverell. *Conversation Pieces: A Survey of English Domestic Portraits and Their Painters*. London, 1936.

Sloman 1995/96
Sloman, Susan. "Mrs. Margaret Gainsborough, 'A Prince's Daughter.'" *Gainsborough's House Review* (1995/96): 47–58.

Sloman 1996
Sloman, Susan. "Artists' Picture Rooms in Eighteenth-Century Bath." In *Bath History*, edited by Brenda J. Buchanan, 132–43. Bath, 1996.

Sloman 1997
Sloman, Susan. "Sitting to Gainsborough at Bath in 1760." *Burlington Magazine* 139, no. 1130 (May 1997): 325–28.

Sloman 2002
Sloman, Susan. *Gainsborough in Bath*. New Haven and London, 2002.

Sloman 2004
Sloman, Susan. "'A Divine Countenance': Gainsborough's Portrait of his Nephew Rediscovered." *Burlington Magazine* 146, no. 1214 (May 2004): 319–22.

Sloman 2013
Sloman, Susan. "Gainsborough's 'Blue Boy.'" *Burlington Magazine* 155, no. 1321 (April 2013): 231–37.

Sloman 2021
Sloman, Susan. *Gainsborough in London*. London, 2021.

Smith 1828
Smith, John Thomas. *Nollekens and His Times: Comprehending a Life of that Celebrated Sculptor, and Memoirs of Several Contemporary Artists, from the Time of Roubiliac, Hogarth, and Reynolds, to That of Fuseli, Flaxman, and Blake*. 2 vols. London, 1828.

Smith 1982
Smith, David R. "Rembrandt's Early Double Portraits and the Dutch Conversation Piece." *Art Bulletin* 64, no. 2 (June 1982): 259–88.

Smith 2017
Smith, Amelia. *Longford Castle: The Treasures and the Collectors*. London, 2017.

Smollett 2015
Smollet, Tobias. *The Expedition of Humphry Clinker*. London, 1771. Repr. edited by Evan Gottlieb. 2nd Norton Critical Edition. New York, 2015.

Solkin 2000/1
Solkin, David H. "Gainsborough's Classically Virtuous Wife." *British Art Journal* 2, no. 2 (Winter 2000/1): 75–77.

Solkin 2001
Solkin, David H., ed. *Art on the Line: The Royal Academy Exhibitions at Somerset House, 1780–1836*. London, 2001.

Solkin 2015
Solkin, David H. *Art in Britain, 1660–1815*. New Haven, 2015.

Southampton 2001
Edward Chaney and Godfrey Worsdale. *The Stuart Portrait: Status and Legacy*. Exh. cat. Southampton (Southampton City Art Gallery), 2001.

Stevens 1772
Stevens, George Alexander. *Songs, Comic and Satyrical*. Oxford, 1772.

St. Louis 1927
Catalogue of an Exhibition of Selected Paintings Lent by Saint Louisans. Exh. cat. St. Louis (City Art Museum St. Louis), 1927.

St. Louis 1935
"A Loan Exhibition of Old Master Paintings Selected from St. Louis Collections." *Bulletin of the City Art Museum of St. Louis* 20, no. 3 (July 1935), 26.

Stokes 1925
Stokes, Hugh. *Thomas Gainsborough*. London, 1925.

Sudbury 1961
Frank Rees, Esq. *Gainsborough's House*. Exh. cat. Sudbury (Gainsborough's House), 1961.

Sudbury 1988
Hugh Belsey. *Gainsborough's Family*. Exh. cat. Sudbury (Gainsborough's House), 1988.

Sudbury 2006
Diane Perkins. *Gainsborough's Dogs*. Exh. cat. Sudbury (Gainsborough's House), 2006.

Sutton 1966
Sutton, Denys. "The King of Epithets: A Study of James Christie." *Apollo* 84 (November 1966): 364–75.

Sydney, Brisbane, and Adelaide 1998
Malcolm Warner and Julia Marciari Alexander. *This Other Eden: British Paintings from the Paul Mellon Collection at Yale*. Exh. cat. Sydney (Art Gallery of New South Wales), Brisbane (Queensland Art Gallery), and Adelaide (Art Gallery of South Australia), 1998.

Syer 1987
Syer, Geoffrey. "Beethoven and William Gardiner." *The Musical Times* 128, no. 1731 (May 1987): 256–58.

Tatlock et al. 1928
Tatlock, R. R., and Roger Fry, et al. *A Record of the Collections in the Lady Lever Art Gallery*. 3 vols. London, 1928.

Taylor 1951
Taylor, Basil. *Gainsborough (1727–1788)*. London, 1951.

The Hague 2015
Lea van der Vinde. *The Frick Collection: Art Treasures from New York*. Exh. cat. The Hague (Mauritshuis), 2015.

Thicknesse 1770
Thicknesse, Philip. *Sketches and Characters of the Most Eminent and Most Singular Persons Now Living*. Bristol, 1770.

Thicknesse 1788
Thicknesse, Philip. *A Sketch of the Life and Paintings of Thomas Gainsborough, Esq*. London, 1788.

Thicknesse 1789
Thicknesse, Philip. *A Year's Journey Through France, and Part of Spain*. Vol. 2. London, 1789.

Thieme and Becker 1920
Thieme, Ulrich, and Felix Becker. *Allgemeines Lexikon Der Bildenden Kunstler von der Antike Bis Zur Gegenwart*. Vol. 13. Leipzig, 1920.

Thompson 1756
Thompson, Edward. *The Demi-Rep: By Author of the Meretriciad*. London, 1756.

Thompson 1974
Thompson, E. P. "Patrician Society, Plebeian Culture." *Journal of Social History* 7, no. 4 (1974): 382–405.

Tietze 1936
Tietze, Hans. "Die öffentlichen Gemäldesammlungen in Kanada." *Pantheon* 17 (June 1936): 180–85.

Tinker 1938
Tinker, Chauncey Brewster. *Painter and Poet: Studies in the Literary Relations of English Painting*. Cambridge, 1938.

Toronto 1919
Catalogue of a Loan Collection of Paintings from the National Gallery of Canada. Exh. cat. Toronto (Art Museum of Toronto), 1919.

Transactions 1783
Transactions of the Society, Instituted at London, for the Encouragement of Arts, Manufactures, and Commerce 1 (1783): i–viii, 1–331.

Trial of Elizabeth Coleburn 1719
"Elizabeth Coleburn. Theft; pocketpicking. 15th January, 1719." Old Bailey Proceedings Online. Accessed October 22, 2024. https://www.oldbaileyonline.org/record/t17190115-37?text=t17190115-37.

Trial of Henry M'allester and Archibald Girdwood 1775
"Henry M'allester. Archibald Girdwood. Theft; grand larceny (to 1827), Violent Theft; highway robbery, Violent Theft; highway robbery. 12th July 1775." Old Bailey Proceedings Online. Accessed March 1, 2025. https://www.oldbaileyonline.org/record/t17750712-25?text=t17750712-25.

Trial of Thomas Mayo 1750
"Thomas Mayo. Violent Theft; highway robbery. 11th July 1750." Old Bailey Proceedings Online. Accessed October 22, 2024. https://www.oldbaileyonline.org/record/t17500711-62?text=t17500711-62.

Tuer 1882
Tuer, Andrew W. *Bartolozzi and His Works: A Biographical and Descriptive Account of The Life and Career of Francesco Bartolozzi, RA.* Vol. 2. London, 1882.

Tyler 1997/98
Tyler, David. "Out from the Shadows: Robert Gainsborough, the Artist's Eldest Brother." *Gainsborough's House Review* (1997/98): 55–65.

Vanderbilt Bequest 1920
"The William K. Vanderbilt Bequest." *Metropolitan Museum of Art Bulletin* 15, no. 12, pt. 1 (December 1920): 261, 268–71.

Vaughan 2002
Vaughan, William. *Gainsborough.* New York, 2002.

Vickery 2009
Vickery, Amanda. *Behind Closed Doors: At Home in Georgian England.* New Haven, 2009.

Waagen 1854
Waagen, Gustave Friedrich. *Treasures of Art in Great Britain: Being an Account of the Chief Collections of Paintings, Drawings, Sculptures, Illuminated Mss., Etc. Etc.* 3 Vols. London, 1854.

Wake 1953
Wake, John. *The Brudenells of Deane.* London, 1953.

Walker 1992
Walker, Richard. *The Eighteenth and Early Nineteenth Century Miniatures in the Collection of Her Majesty the Queen.* Cambridge and New York, 1992.

Walpole 1974
Walpole, Horace. *Horace Walpole's Correspondence with Henry Seymour Conway, Lady Ailesbury, Lord and Lady Hertford, Mrs. Harris.* Edited by W. S. Lewis et al. New Haven, 1974.

Wark 1974
Wark, Robert R. "A Note on Gainsborough and Van Dyck." *Museum Monographs: Papers on Objects in the Collections of City Art Museum of Saint Louis* 3 (1974): 43–53.

Warsaw 1992
Christopher Brown and Andrzej Ciechanowiecki. *Kolekcja dla króla: obrazy dawnych mistrzów ze zbiorów Dulwich Picture Gallery w Londynie.* Exh. cat. Warsaw (Zamek Królewski w Warszawie), 1992.

Washington 1985–86
Gervase Jackson-Stops, ed. *The Treasure Houses of Britain: Five Hundred Years of Private Patronage and Art Collecting.* Exh. cat. Washington (National Gallery of Art), 1985–86.

Washington and Los Angeles 1985–86
Collection for a King: Old Master Paintings from the Dulwich Picture Gallery. Exh. cat. Washington (National Gallery of Art) and Los Angeles (Los Angeles County Museum of Art), 1985–86.

Waterfield 1981
Waterfield, Giles. "Winning Parisian Hearts: Thomas Gainsborough at the Grand Palais." *Country Life* 169 (April 16, 1981): 1050–52.

Waterhouse 1946
Waterhouse, Ellis. "A Gainsborough Bill for the Prince of Wales." *Burlington Magazine for Connoisseurs* 88, no. 524 (November 1946): 276.

Waterhouse 1953
Waterhouse, Ellis. "Preliminary Check List of Portraits by Thomas Gainsborough." *Volume of the Walpole Society 1948–50* 33 (1953): iii–140.

Waterhouse 1958
Waterhouse, Ellis. *Gainsborough.* London, 1958.

Waterhouse 1962
Waterhouse, Ellis. *Painting in Britain: 1530 to 1790.* 2nd ed. London, 1962.

Waterhouse 1973
Waterhouse, Ellis. "Bath and Gainsborough." *Apollo* 98, no. 141 (November 1973): 360–65.

Waterhouse 1981
Waterhouse, Ellis. *The Dictionary of British 18th Century Painters in Oils and Crayons.* Suffolk, 1981.

Waterhouse 1994
Waterhouse, Ellis. *Painting in Britain: 1530–1790.* 5th ed. New Haven, 1994.

Watson 1969
Watson, Ross. "British Paintings in the National Gallery of Art." *Connoisseur* 172 (September–December 1969.) 55–61.

Webster 2011
Webster, Mary. *Johan Zoffany, 1733–1810.* New Haven and London, 2011.

Wendeborn 1791
Wendeborn, F. A. *A View of England towards the Close of the Eighteenth Century.* Vol. 1. London, 1791.

West Palm Beach 2015
Laurie E. Barnes, ed. *High Tea: Glorious Manifestations East and West.* Exh. cat. West Palm Beach (Norton Museum of Art), 2015.

Whitley [1915] 2016
Whitley, William T. *Thomas Gainsborough.* London, 1915. Repr. London, 2016.

Whitley 1928
Whitley, William T. *Artists and Their Friends in England 1700–1799.* Vol. 2. London and Boston, 1928.

Wilenski 1934
Wilenski, R. H. *Masters of English Painting.* London, 1934.

Wilkins 1905
Wilkins, W. H. *Mrs. Fitzherbert and George IV.* New York, London, and Bombay, 1905.

Williamson 1972
Williamson, Geoffrey. *The Ingenious Mr. Gainsborough: Thomas Gainsborough—A Biographical Study.* New York, 1972.

Williamson and Sassoon 1931
Williamson, G. C., and Philip Sassoon. *English Conversation Pictures of the Eighteenth and Early Nineteenth Centuries.* London, 1931.

Willis 1980
Willis, John Ralph. "New Light on the Life of Ignatius Sancho. Some Unpublished Letters." *Slavery and Abolition* 1, no. 3 (June 2008): 345–58.

Willoughby 1906
Willoughby, Leonard. "The Marquess of Bristol's Collection at Ickworth." *Connoisseur* 14 (April 1906): 203–10.

Wilson 1977
Wilson, Michael. "Gainsborough, Bath and Music." *Apollo* 105, no. 180 (February 1977): 107–10.

Woodall 1949
Woodall, Mary. *Thomas Gainsborough: His Life and Work.* New York, 1949.

Woodall 1963
Woodall, Mary. *The Letters of Thomas Gainsborough.* Bradford, 1963.

Wraight 1974
Wraight, Robert. *The Art Game Again!* London, 1974.

INDEX

Page numbers in italic type indicate illustrations.

IMAGE CREDITS

This catalogue is published on the occasion of
Gainsborough: The Fashion of Portraiture,
an exhibition on view at The Frick Collection from February 11 to May 11, 2026.

The exhibition is made possible with support from an anonymous donor in honor of Ian Wardropper.
Additional funding is provided by Michael and Jane Horvitz, Dr. Arlene P. McKay, The Helen Clay Frick Foundation,
James K. Kloppenburg, David and Kate Bradford, Katie von Strasser – InspiratumColligere, the Dr. Lee MacCormick
Edwards Charitable Foundation, Edward Lee Cave, Mr. and Mrs. Hubert L. Goldschmidt, Jennifer Schnabl,
the Malcolm Hewitt Wiener Foundation, Bradley Isham Collins and Amy Fine Collins, Siri and Bob Marshall, Bailey Foote,
Alexander Mason Hankin, Brittany Beyer Harwin and Zachary Harwin, and Otto Naumann and Heidi D. Shafranek.

This catalogue is funded by Dr. Tai-Heng Cheng.

First published in the United States of America in 2026 by
Rizzoli Electa, a division of
Rizzoli International Publications, Inc.
49 West 27th Street
New York, New York 10001
rizzoliusa.com

Publisher: Charles Miers
Associate Publisher: Margaret Chace
Senior Editor: Philip Reeser
Production Manager: Alyn Evans
Design Coordinator: Tim Biddick
Copy Editor: Claudia Bauer
Managing Editor: Lynn Scrabis

in association with

The Frick Collection
1 East 70th Street
New York, New York 10021
frick.org

Editor in Chief: Michaelyn Mitchell
Assistant Editor: Gemma McElroy

Designer: William Loccisano

A CIP catalogue record for this book is available from the Library of Congress.
Hardcover edition ISBN: 978-0-8478-7623-5
Paperback edition ISBN: 978-0-8478-7675-4
Library of Congress Control Number: 2025941676

2026 2027 2028 2029 / 10 9 8 7 6 5 4 3 2 1
Printed in China

The authorized representative in the EU for product safety and compliance is
Mondadori Libri S.p.A.
Via Gian Battista Vico, 42
20123 Milan
Italy
mondadori.it

Page 2: Detail of *Grace Dalrymple Elliott* (cat. 18)
Page 5: Detail of *Sarah Hodges, Later Lady Innes* (cat. 4)
Page 7: Detail of *John Joseph Merlin* (cat. 20)
Page 8: Detail of *Mrs. Sheridan* (cat. 23)
Page 13: *Mrs. Sarah Siddons*, 1785. Oil canvas, 49⅝ × 39³⁄₁₆ in. (126 × 99.5 cm).
The National Gallery, London (NG683)
Page 19: Detail of *Lords John and Bernard Stuart* (cat. 6)
Page 31: Detail of *The Hon. Frances Duncombe* (cat. 14)
Page 49: Detail of *Peter Darnell Muilman, Charles Crokatt, and William Keable* (cat. 1)
Page 63: Detail of *Margaret Gainsborough* (cat. 15)
Pages 76–77: Detail of *Mr. and Mrs. Andrews* (cat. 2)

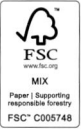

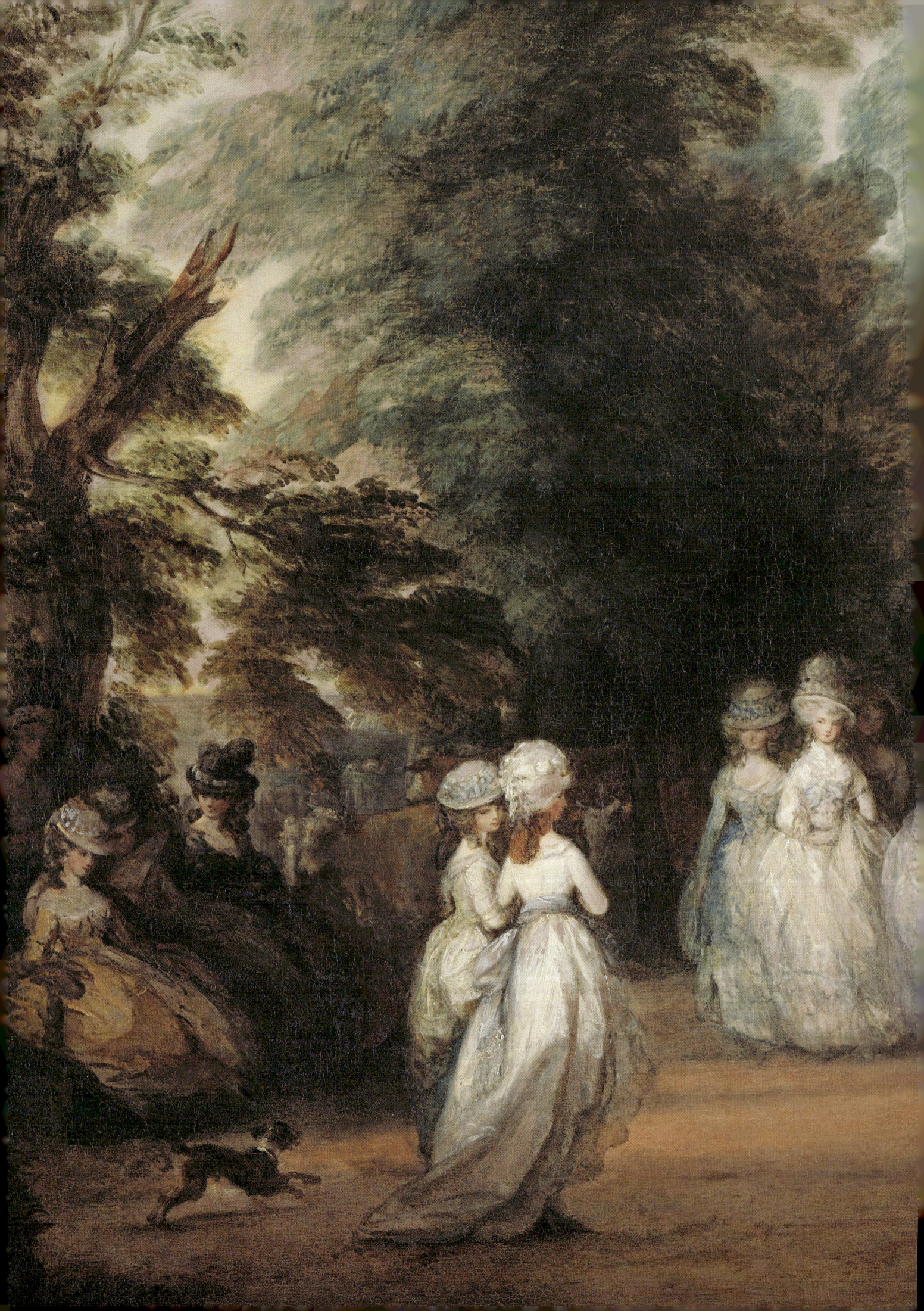